A GOOD COMRADE

To the memory of my parents
Jay Gough (1934 – 1987)
and
Norman Gough (1930 – 2001)

A GOOD COMRADE

János Kádár, Communism and Hungary

ROGER GOUGH

I.B. TAURIS

LONDON · NEW YORK

Published in 2006 by I.B. Tauris & Co Ltd
6 Salem Road, London W2 4BU
175 Fifth Avenue, New York NY 10010
www.ibtauris.com

In the United States of America and in Canada distributed by Palgrave Macmillan
A division of St. Martins Press, 175 Fifth Avenue, New York NY 10010

ISBN 10: 1 84511 058 7
ISBN 13: 978 1 84511 058 1

A full CIP record for this book is available from the British Library
A full CIP record for this book is available from the Library of Congress

Library of Congress Catalog Card Number: available

Printed and bound in Great Britain by TJ International Ltd, Padstow, Cornwall
From camera-ready copy edited and supplied by the author

CONTENTS

LIST OF ILLUSTRATIONS

ACKNOWLEDGEMENTS

Writing a book is often a lonely process, yet by its end an author acquires a vast number of debts. I am very conscious of what I owe to those who have helped, advised and encouraged me over many years. At the same time, none of those who have been so helpful can be held accountable for any errors or omissions on my part; nor – given a figure as controversial as János Kádár – can all or perhaps any of them be expected to endorse my interpretations and evaluations of the man and his career. All this remains my responsibility.

My first, rather quirky thanks must go to a historian writing about an – apparently – unrelated subject. More than twenty-five years ago, I read Alison Hanham's book, *Richard III and his early historians*. Remarking on how Richard's abilities might – had he survived longer – have enabled him to live down the memory of how he came to power, Dr Hanham added, 'A striking modern example of such a recovery of prestige against great odds is furnished by Janos Kador [*sic*] of Hungary.'[1] Without encountering this stray remark, I would not have begun my interest in Kádár and Hungary. I am grateful to those who encouraged my interest at that time, notably the late Béla Szász, with whom I both met and corresponded, and Bill Lomax, with whom I again made contact when I began serious work on a Kádár biography two decades later.

This book has benefited from the willingness of many people – former colleagues and associates of Kádár, historians, foreign observers – to give their time for interviews. In Hungary: László Ballai; Dr Magdolna Baráth; Dr Csaba Békés; János Berecz; Mr and Mrs Zoltán Bognár; the late Éva Bozóky; the late Professor Béla Csikós-Nagy; Piroska Döme; György Fejti; György Földes; János Fekete; József Füleki; László Gyurkó; Gyula Horn; István Horváth; István Huszár; Professor Sándor M. Kiss; György Konrád;

Ernő Lakatos; György Lázár; József Marjai; His Excellency Valeri Musatov, Ambassador of the Russian Federation; Rezső Nyers; Imre Pozsgay; László Rajk; Péter Rényi; Sándor Révész; Mátyás Szűrös; Mátyás Timár; Dr Tibor Zinner. In Great Britain: Sir Bryan Cartledge; Christopher Long; Rt Hon Sir Malcolm Rifkind MP; Peter Unwin. In Germany: Dr Horst Teltschik.

My thanks go to the staff of the archives that I have consulted. At the Hungarian National Archives (MOL), I am particularly grateful to György Majtényi, who (in addition to reading and commenting on one chapter of this book) was a constant source of help and advice; I must also thank Mrs Kovács, István Simon and their colleagues. I encountered similarly helpful attitudes from the staff of the following institutions in Budapest: the Institute of Political History (PIL), especially Piroska Darvasi; the 1956 Institute, especially Mrs Judit Gyenes and András Lenárt; the Open Society Archives, especially Robert Parnica and Botond Barta. I must also thank the staff of the British Library and of the library of the School of Slavonic and East European Studies, University College London.

A visit to the National Archives and Records Administration (NARA), College Park, Maryland, was made very productive through the help of Sally Kuisel, Civilian Records Archivist, and of Ron Sodano of the Nixon Presidential Materials Staff. Douglas Selvage of the State Department's Office of the Historian went far beyond the call of duty in advising me of the location of significant files. Albert Nason of the Jimmy Carter Presidential Library in Atlanta, Georgia, was helpful in advising me of the materials available concerning the return of the Crown of St. Stephen and sending them to me. The US Department of State gave prompt responses to my requests for documents under the Freedom of Information Act, and I owe particular thanks to Margaret Roman, who gave a human face to officialdom and was a tremendous source of help and advice in tracking down documents.

I have also benefited from the work of Hungary's modern historians. Those with whom I had lengthy interviews are listed above. I must also thank Dr János M. Rainer, director of the 1956 Institute, for guidance concerning archival and other sources; Dr Magdolna Baráth, head of research of the Historical Archives of the State Security Services, for sharing with me some important documents on Hungarian-Soviet relations and for answering some further queries; Sándor Révész of *Népszabadság* for sending me his article collating the assessments of Kádár by his long-term associate (and Mr Révész's biographical subject) György Aczél; and Dr Attila Pók of the Hungarian Academy of Sciences for supporting my applications to research in the MOL and PIL, and for sending me his paper on German-Hungarian relations. Professor Miklós Kun recommended me to his television film *Birodalmi helytartók* (imperial governors). I benefited from enjoyable discussions with István Ötvös of the Pázmány Péter Catholic University, who also suggested and set up several interviews for me. The writings of Professor Tibor Huszár, Kádár's Hungarian biographer and author and editor of other important studies of the period (including a collection of Kádár's letters), have put a vast amount of information in the public domain, from which I have benefited.

I am also grateful to Katalin Jalsovksy of the Hungarian National Museum and Zoltán Szántó of MTI for their help in finding the photos used in this book, and to Zoltán Pólya for allowing me to use his striking 1987 picture of Kádár. At the start of my researches in Hungary, I incurred an important debt to András Geszti, who helped to arrange several early interviews. I also benefited from the kind hospitality and encouragement of György and Zsófi Antall.

Outside Hungary, Professor Rudolf Tőkés, author of an outstanding study of Kádár's Hungary, made an unprompted offer to read parts of the manuscript and delivered a marvellous combination of encouragement and critique. George Schöpflin MEP, another authority in the field, also gave very helpful comments on the manuscript. In addition, I had very useful discussions with Bill Lomax and Timothy Garton Ash. Lord Skidelsky gave wise guidance on the biographer's art. Misha Glenny responded promptly and positively to an inquiry about his BBC Radio series 'Pushing Back the Curtain' and his equally helpful colleague Maria Balinska supplied the transcripts and a tape of interviews from the programme.

Sylvia Víg, Zsuzsa Pontifex and Katalin Lászlóffy were all excellent teachers of Hungarian; any remaining shortcomings are very much my own responsibility. I did, nonetheless, continue to rely on interpreters for interviews. Fortunately, I was in excellent hands. Éva Valis undertook most of the interviews; I am deeply grateful for her skill and professionalism. The same can be said of Regina Fülöp, who interpreted at a number of interviews in the later stages of the project, and Béla Vorsos, who did so at one of the earlier meetings. Continuing with linguistic debts, Christina Barnes translated Russian documents with impressive speed.

At I.B.Tauris, my commissioning editors, Dr. Lester Crook and Liz Friend-Smith have been models of helpfulness, good humour and, it must be said, patience. I am also grateful to Dr Mark Pittaway of the Open University, who read the text, for his comments and correction of a number of errors on my part. Thanks are also due to Audrey Daly for her meticulous copy-editing and to Elizabeth Munns for guiding the production stages of the book.

Some people belong to the 'without whom …' category. Annabel Barber, a friend for twenty years – now editor-in-chief of the Blue Guides series, and co-author of an indispensable guide to Budapest – nagged me to stop talking about Kádár and start writing, then helped kick-start the project by arranging interviews, translating articles (at a time when my capacities in Hungarian were rudimentary) and sharing her knowledge of the history and geography of Budapest. She also found me a superb researcher in Rita Galántai. Rita tracked down interview subjects and institutional contacts with skill and indefatigable determination; as time ran out in the later stages of the project she also carried out additional archive research on my behalf. My friends David and Angela Harvey deserve a particular mention: at a time when the prospects of getting the book published were looking bleak, they encouraged me to talk to Professor Peter Hennessy. Peter was remarkably generous with his time and advice, and it was after discussion with him that I contacted I.B.Tauris.

I have imposed on many personal friends. I am very grateful to my two devoted readers. Rob Marshall's comments – winging back across the electronic ether with extraordinary speed – saved me from error or infelicity on many points. Michael Baptista took time from his busy schedule to offer wise and challenging suggestions that have raised my game considerably. Both were great sources of advice and, just as importantly, encouragement. I also had a lot of encouragement from Károly Grúber, who in addition organised further archive and translation work for me when I had finished my visits to Hungary; my thanks to him and to those who worked on my behalf. John Bassett suggested some helpful ways of untangling Kádár's complex role in the Czechoslovak crisis, and set me right on military terminology. Dr Paul Kerr helped me to understand Kádár's medical problems. Órla Morris gave help and guidance on IT matters. Other friends have helped in various ways: thanks to Melanie Baptista, David Cavicke, John Gardner, Regina Grafe, Tim Hames, Alex Irigoin, Simon Lawson, Sarah Livingstone, Peter Lloyd-Sherlock, Jane Orr and Alison Ramage.

Lastly, family. I have dedicated this book to the memory of my parents; they both had more to do with my writing it, and with informing the thinking and values that underlie it, than can easily be summarised. They both knew (at very different stages) of my interest in this subject; neither, however, lived to see it completed. My brother Nick has gamely put up with more Kádár anecdotes over more lunches over more years than either of us will willingly recall. My parents-in-law, Fran and Tony, have offered hospitality – Fran will recall the rules of the Silent Order during our stays with them – and encouragement, while Tony's help and expertise in IT matters has been invaluable, as was his willingness to store backups of all my work. I doubt if he ever expected to be the custodian of an electronic Kádár archive, but so it turned out.

My wife Michelle has helped in many practical ways – including casting a clear and unsentimental eye over a number of chapters when the text had to be cut back – but above all by the patience and good humour with which she has taken so much of the burden of this project. Through our marriage, a house move, and the subsequent arrival of Marlowe the greyhound (who made writing the book much less lonely) and our son William (who made its final stages happier but more protracted), she has gracefully accepted not only the moodiness of a writer but the brooding and lugubrious presence of János Kádár. That ghost is now laid.

INTRODUCTION

In late 1999, several media organisations ran a competition in which Hungarians could vote for their country's greatest figures of the millennium. The winner, unsurprisingly, was Saint Stephen, Hungary's first King and the effective founder of the Hungarian state; in second place was the great nineteenth century reformer István Széchenyi. But in third place, and thus by implication the greatest twentieth century Hungarian – to the astonishment of many and the revulsion of not a few – was János Kádár, the country's long-standing Communist leader and the man who had crushed the 1956 Hungarian revolution. A subsequent opinion poll gave a broadly similar picture.[1]

This was merely the latest – posthumous – twist in a career marked by extraordinary upheavals and changes of fortune. Kádár rose from the deepest poverty, through the dangers of an underground activist of an illegal party, to power. In Stalinist Hungary, he was both persecutor and victim. From prison under the system that he had helped to build, he rose to power once more, becoming one of his country's most durable leaders.

His decision to betray and suppress the 1956 revolution earned him obloquy at home and abroad, exacerbated by the brutality and personal betrayals of the reprisals launched against the revolutionaries. Yet he transformed his position to win respect, even popularity; remarkably, he became one of the Soviet bloc's more acceptable faces – a good comrade indeed – and by the early eighties the West's interlocutor of choice. Then the story changed again: in 1988, he was ousted amid economic failure and recrimination. The last year of his life saw a tormented reckoning with the long-suppressed crimes of 1956 that drew irresistible comparisons with Shakespearean tragedy.

Yet if Kádár's story is one of high personal drama, it also has wider implications. Firstly, because his Hungary was the central testing-ground for reform Communism, the attempt to resolve the failures and excesses of Stalinism without abandoning the core tenets of a Marxist-Leninist state. This effort – above all, through Hungary's distinctive economic model – and its failure played a significant part in the collapse of European Communism.

Secondly, a biography can illuminate not only an individual life but also the forces and events that shaped it. Kádár's career reflects much of the history of the Soviet empire: not only its lurid side, the beatings and executions of the Stalinist era, but also the great crises over Hungary, Czechoslovakia and Poland. It also reveals the bargaining relationships between the Soviet Union and its satellites, the impact of the détente era and the Helsinki agreement and the slow constriction of the economic crisis that gradually overtook the bloc from the mid-seventies onwards. Finally, the Hungary that is now a member of NATO and of the EU cannot be fully understood without reference to Kádár and his era.

Despite this, there is no up to date biography of Kádár in English. William Shawcross' *Crime and Compromise*, published in 1974, had ground-breaking information at the time (notably on Kádár's birth and parentage), but has been overtaken by events and by the mass of material released since the fall of Communism. László Gyurkó's official biography in *János Kádár, Selected Speeches and Interviews*, had a curious genesis. Commissioned by Robert Maxwell, no less, its author had been imprisoned briefly in the aftermath of 1956, but had subsequently made his peace with the regime and was the protégé of Kádár's cultural policy impresario, György Aczél. Gyurkó inevitably laboured under huge political constraints, exacerbated by his subject's lack of enthusiasm for the project.

This book – drawing on research in the national, party and other archives in Hungary, and on interviews with many of Kádár's colleagues and associates – aims to fill that gap. It is unabashedly chronological in approach, not least because this helps avoid the temptation to be over-schematic, capturing instead the transience and messiness of political decision-making, 'the reality of improvisation, trade-offs, confusion, discomfiture and sheer fatigue.'[2] This is especially apt for Kádár who, while not lacking in strategic sense, was a quotidian politician to his fingertips. It nonetheless seeks to present a concise but rounded portrayal of the austere, withdrawn and tenacious man at the centre of world attention fifty years ago, who dominated his country for three decades and who left his mark on Hungary, on Europe and on the history of international Communism.

1

'WE ARE NOT BEGGARS'

The man who became known as János Kádár and who was to lead Hungary was born János Csermanek in Fiume – now Rijeka, Croatia – on 26 May 1912. His mother was half Slovak, and his father's family name was German.

'The most difficult fate is bearable if one is loved'[1] was a lesson that he was to draw from his childhood. Such love was not found easily; he was illegitimate, and for many years did not know his father's identity. His mother was initially preoccupied with the daily struggle for survival, and it was with a foster family that János Csermanek first found a temporary security.

János' mother, Borbála Csermanek (the family name was sometimes spelt Csermanyik or Czermanik) had been born in 1884 in the Slovak village of Ógyalla (now Stará Dala), the daughter of a landless Slovak labourer and a Hungarian mother. It was probably the lack of work opportunities that led her to leave the village around the summer of 1910. It seems that by spring 1911 she was some four hundred kilometres away, working as a chambermaid in a small hotel in the Adriatic spa resort of Abbazia (now Opatija).[2]

Borbála – an 'ill-starred woman', in her son's words – had had only two years of elementary schooling and was to a greater or lesser degree illiterate. Kádár's official biographer László Gyurkó – drawing on conversations with his subject – described her as 'unstable, quick to lose her temper, and quick to become sentimental'. She sought to live by the precepts of her peasant upbringing and Catholic faith, but poverty and the instability of her relationships vitiated her attempts to gain a degree of control over her life. Yet there was another, stronger side to her. She was bold enough to seek work far from her native village, and she was to be ambitious for her son. Those who knew her in later years describe a proud, hard-working woman, a 'real character' who maintained her dignity amid a constant battle against poverty and social stigma.[3]

János Csermanek's father is a much more shadowy figure. There were various stories about his identity, the most colourful of which named the sixty-nine year-old Miklós Konkoly Thege, the local landowner in Ógyalla and pioneering astrophysical researcher.[4] However, there is little reason to doubt that the father was one János Krezinger; this is what the son came to believe, and Krezinger acknowledged it in the years before his death in 1965.

Krezinger came from a peasant family in the small village of Pusztaszemes in western Hungary, south of Lake Balaton. Though the family's name was German — reflecting, like many others in western Hungary, settlements encouraged by the Habsburgs from the end of the seventeenth century — they were Hungarian by language and culture. Twenty-three years old in the summer of 1911, Krezinger was performing his military service as an army batman in Fiume. An anecdote from the end of his life suggests that he was headstrong and perhaps vain; he refused to have a leg amputated even though his blood vessel problems were life threatening.[5]

Abbazia was half an hour's boat ride up the coast from Fiume and a favourite haunt of Hungarian soldiers. No one knows exactly how Krezinger and Borbála met, or just how transient their affair may have been, but by the late summer of 1911 Borbála was pregnant. By one account, Krezinger was willing to marry her but his family considered her 'no better than a beggar'. Since, however, the Krezingers were as landless as the Csermaneks, this seems unlikely, though it is possible that there was some other reason for family opposition. More probably, Krezinger simply beat a rapid retreat from the unwanted consequences of what had seemed like a transient summer affair with a slightly older woman. [6]

Abandoned, Borbála gave birth to a boy in Fiume's Santo Spirito Hospital on 26 May 1912. He was named János József Csermanek. A line was put through the entry in the birth register for his father's name.[7]

János Csermanek was born at the close of an unusually bright period in Hungarian history — though its benefits did not spread significantly to those of Borbála's social class. Turn of the century Hungary had been shaped by a combination of repression and accommodation that was to find echoes in János Csermanek's (or Kádár's) career. The suppression of Hungary's revolution against Habsburg rule in 1848-49 — with the help of Russian troops — was followed by severe reprisals, including the execution of the Prime Minister, Batthyány. Later, however, the Emperor Franz Joseph sought accommodation with the defeated country, and the resulting Compromise of 1867 gave Hungary significant autonomy within the 'dual' Austro-Hungarian Monarchy. The Emperor was crowned King of Hungary — hence the term *k.u.k* (*kaiserlich und königlich* – imperial and royal) given to the era – and, gradually putting the harshness of his early rule behind him, mellowed into a benign if still authoritarian father figure.

Yet if the ambiguous political culture of the *k.u.k.* era found echoes in János Csermanek's later life, his immediate prospects were shaped by its social and economic structures. While industry and transportation surged ahead and Budapest expanded at a rate comparable to many American cities, development in the countryside was far slower and inequalities still greater. The result was a profoundly bifurcated economy and society, of a kind that has since become very familiar in many developing countries, notably in Latin America. Within this, Borbála Csermanek's origins were especially unfavourable. She was from a landless peasant family, and minority nationalities, such as the Slovaks, were among the poorest groups.[8]

She may have gone to the Adriatic to escape rural poverty, but she soon had to return her baby son to it. For the first three months of János' life, she was able to stay in the Santo Spirito hospital; however, once she had to leave, she was unable to find work. It was late in the holiday season, and no one wanted to employ a single mother with a baby. Borbála set off in pursuit of János Krezinger in Pusztaszemes.

The Krezinger family, it seems, refused to receive her. An angry Borbála put the crying baby down in the hedge outside the house and retreated to a distance to see if the family would come out. Still getting no response, she walked with János to Kapoly, a small town of four thousand households almost ten kilometres away. There she reached an agreement with a family named Bálint that she would pay them to foster János while she sought work in Budapest.[9]

Since Kapoly had a railway station, Borbála was able to visit on holidays; however, until the age of six, János was to see relatively little of her. In his earliest memories, Kapoly was 'home'. His foster parents were Imre Bálint, then in his mid-forties, and his much younger wife. However, by 1916 many of the family's men had left the village to play a part in the war effort. The one whom János was to remember, and think of as his foster father, was Imre's older brother and next door neighbour, 'Uncle Sándor'.

'Except for his wife and his mother,' Gyurkó recorded, 'I have not heard him speak of anyone with such warmth and love as he does of Uncle Sándor.' The accuracy of his portrayal of Sándor Bálint as a salt of the earth character, keeping his dignity and self-discipline as he struggled with poverty and nursed an invalid wife, can only be guessed. However, Uncle Sándor clearly took a warm interest in the boy. He was the *kisbíró* (town crier) and would sometimes take János out with him when making announcements; similarly, János accompanied him when he cut down a tree for Christmas.[10] He seems to have been the only man with whom János had a close and positive relationship throughout his childhood.

In the straitened circumstances of the Bálint family, János started to work early – 'as soon as he could walk and talk'– helping out in the house, supporting Uncle Sándor in looking after his sickly wife and accompanying the swineherd. In the years that followed – whether as a worker or as a politician – he was to show an austere self-discipline; his years in Kapoly help to explain this. Imre Bálint's son, also named Imre, remembered him rising at dawn to work with the animals.[11]

Inevitably, there are stories told – in some cases recycled rather frequently – to suggest that his progress towards Marxism had at least some roots in this experience. There are sayings attributed to Uncle Sándor: 'Remember, Jani, that a poor man's child always has to work' ('the first piece of Marxist education I had,' according to the elderly Kádár); and, 'If they feed you, they can hit you.'

The latter related to an alleged incident in which János (then aged about six) was blamed for setting fire to the house of a minor local notable, an inspector. The culprit was the inspector's son, but János was nonetheless blamed: 'because I was the bastard, I got beaten.' However, another version omits the 'class' angle, simply telling of a fire that was set off by the children, of Janos' fear that he would be punished, and of Uncle Sándor's forgiveness of him. This suggests that the story had its origins in an incident that indeed took place, but may have grown in the telling.[12]

In spite of the work and grievances, he would keep fond memories of these early years, of flying kites in the fields and of joining the other children to jump on a peasant cart as it passed. (One farmer, knocking him off with a whip, told him, 'You're such a cheeky kid, you'll be a big man one day.')[13] If, as has been suggested, he idealised Kapoly,[14] it was partly because of its contrast to what followed. In 1918, when he was six, Borbála claimed him back and – despite János' distress, and that of the Bálints[15] – took him to Budapest. She had found work as an assistant caretaker and wanted János to get his schooling amid the greater opportunities of the capital. They arrived there in time for the start of term at the beginning of September.

Coming out of Budapest's Southern Railway Station for the first time, János found the roar of the city and its modern facilities 'wonderful, alien and awe-inspiring', as were the 'enormous crowds of people who were strangers'.[16] His unease in the big city seemed justified when, sitting with his mother on a tram during his first hours there, a little basket containing all his belongings was stolen. His memory of an initial disorientation – which, he said later, continued for some years – was surely genuine. He missed the countryside, keeping a rooster to remind himself of his life there. At school he was mocked for his bumpkin manners; he remembered into old age his class and teacher laughing at his peasant terms.[17]

In addition, 'it took time for mother and son to make friends'. They clashed over religion, for János had started to grow up without his mother's Catholic beliefs. When he did not join her in prayer, she forced him to kneel on corn as a punishment. But the boy showed his stubbornness. 'When she finished her prayers, Borbála Csermanek went to bed. The child did not move from the corner. Neither of them could sleep. Then the mother begged her stubborn son to come to bed. The offended child would not move. He did so only when his mother tearfully coaxed him.'[18] This was the beginning of an intense, sometimes difficult relationship, one of mutual dependence, between János and his *Mutter* – the term which he always used. It was to endure until her death.

The political movement that was to dominate János Csermanek's life swept improbably through Budapest soon after his arrival. In the chaotic aftermath of the war, and of newly independent Hungary's loss of two-thirds of its former territory (later ratified by the 1920 Treaty of Trianon), the leader of the newly formed Communist Party of Hungary, Béla Kun, took power in March 1919. His Hungarian Soviet Republic lasted only until August, when it collapsed amid military defeat and Romanian troops marched into Budapest. Nonetheless, the reaction against Kun's combination of nationalisation, collectivisation of agricultural land, assaults on church schooling and thuggish commandos (the 'Lenin boys') was to shape the politics of the next quarter of a century.

János later claimed recollection of a personal experience that tied him to this political and social upheaval. In the block in Városház Street, in the city centre of Pest, where Borbála was an assistant caretaker, most of the families were upper middle class. For a while, János and the caretaker's son, the two poor children in the building, were invited into the affluent families' homes; then, just as abruptly, he found one day that he was no longer welcome. 'I didn't understand what had happened. Later it came to me: that was when the Soviet Republic fell.' The story sounds too neat, too politically didactic to be entirely plausible; yet he told it from long before he was a public figure. At the very least, he believed it to be true. Perhaps it was; or perhaps he was identifying his fate with that of the Communist movement.[19]

Now the reaction set in. If Kun had practised 'Red Terror', his opponents – increasingly coalescing around the former head of the Imperial Navy, Admiral Miklós Horthy – turned 'White Terror' against leftists, former Red Army soldiers and Jews. (The Jewish antecedents of Kun and a number of his associates would provide a staple of interwar right-wing propaganda.) The throne was declared empty, and on 1 March 1920, Parliament – encouraged by a large military presence – appointed Horthy to the revived medieval post of Regent. He would prove a durable leader. Communists later used the term 'Horthyite-Fascist' as though they were one and the same. This was sloppy agitprop: Admiral Miklós Horthy de Nagybánya was never anything so vulgar as a Fascist. Rather, his was an authoritarian right-wing regime in which power shifted among groups ranging from conservative liberals to those who were indeed closer to Fascism – but in which Horthy kept the last word.

After an initial highly reactionary phase, power concentrated among the more moderate of the Regent's supporters. Count István Bethlen, Prime

Minister for a decade from 1921, constructed a variant of the pre-war *k.u.k*
system: an authoritarian regime with a constitutional façade that left a little
room for criticism and dissent. Though ballots in the towns were secret,
those in the countryside were open, helping to secure control. Bethlen
offered enough to split the Left, tolerating the Social Democrats and (non-
political) trade union activity while keeping the Communists banned.
Economic stability was restored, but without achieving progress in living
standards for the urban working class or the rural poor.

Even if those in power were not wholly backward looking, it was still a
highly stratified society. And Borbála and János Csermanek were towards
the bottom of it. Borbála worked doggedly to ensure not only their
survival, but also that János' education would be better than hers had been;
in addition to being an assistant caretaker, she delivered newspapers and
took in washing. Piroska Döme, who met her twenty years later,
remembered that 'she worked very hard, her hands were disfigured from
it'. János too had to work, before or after school, often getting up at five.
Though money was always very tight, Borbála had strict limits on what was
acceptable. When she discovered that a job helping a blind woman meant
collecting money as she begged in cafés, she quickly pulled János out from
it. 'We are not beggars,' she insisted.[20]

János also earned money by working in the countryside each summer. It
would have been logical for him to go back to Kapoly, and he sometimes
claimed that he did so until he was fourteen.[21] This is almost certainly
inaccurate: local accounts range from his never coming back after 1918 to
(most probably) doing so for a few years. However, he was no longer at
home: 'in Budapest I was called a "country boy" while in the village I was a
"city boy", so that in fact my contemporaries looked upon me as
fundamentally alien both here and there.'[22] While the urchins of Kapoly
bathed naked in a local pool, he wore what they viewed as snooty city
clothes. Only the intervention of older children prevented him from being
beaten up. For whatever reason, his visits to Kapoly petered out and he
worked instead in Pest County and the much more distant Békés County.[23]

His life in the city was also alienating. Living in Városház Street helped
get him into a good primary school, but in such comfortable and
respectable surroundings his poverty and illegitimacy stood out the more:
'this alienated or isolated him; in any case, it made normal human
development difficult.'[24] Then came another step down. Borbála became
pregnant again and János' half-brother Jenő was born in 1920. Nothing is
known about this liaison, but once more Borbála and the father neither
married nor formed a lasting relationship.

Borbála lost her job, and they moved to Hungária Boulevard (close to
the border of the tough Angyalföld area of the 13th District), which meant
a long walk to school. János also had to play his part in bringing Jenő up,
feeding him, changing his nappies and sharing a bed with him. The next
few years saw further moves, switching between the 6th District, near

Pest's main boulevard, Andrássy Street, and part of the 7th, a heavily Jewish area of small workshops; there János lit fires and turned on lights for families on the Sabbath.[25] What remained constant was the financial struggle, lived out in a succession of bare one-room flats.

As a result of this disruptive home life, and through running errands to earn money, the boy started to wander the city, getting to know it and being drawn to its greener areas such as the City Park and Gellért Hill. He recalled his loneliness in an uncharacteristically personal speech on his sixtieth birthday: '... my circumstances were such that in the family where I was brought up it was not customary to celebrate wedding anniversaries, birthdays, or namedays. ... The celebration of birthdays as a family matter is the right thing to do and is also a tradition with our people. I regret that I had no experience of it at the age when one grows up physically and spiritually; I feel this lack, but I can no longer do anything about it.'[26] Even the choice of words – 'the family where I was brought up' – is revealing.

The most obvious lack was that of a father, whose identity remained a mystery; Borbála refused to discuss it. Krezinger had not provided any support immediately after János was born, but according to an unconfirmed story within his family he later sent Borbála money that he earned as the village bell-ringer. An entirely separate report has it that, when János was sixteen, he found an old letter from his father to his mother cutting off payments once more.[27] This discovery – if indeed it took place – can have enlightened him little. He had to wait thirty years to find out more.

His first four years of education at Cukor Street elementary school offered exactly the step up in the world that Borbála wanted for him. In spite of his social unease, János was bright and did quite well; however, his discontent manifested itself in truanting, and 'I missed a hideous amount of lessons.' He would often run away to the nearby covered market. 'If I was angry, I went off for three or five days.' Exasperated with his threat to her hopes for him, Borbála hit him frequently. Once, when it emerged that a particular set of beatings had been based on a misapprehension, she remarked, 'There's no harm done, I'm sure that you did something I don't know about, or you will do.'[28]

János completed his education with four years (between 1922 and 1926) at Wesselényi Street, the local higher elementary school – no small achievement at a time when three-quarters of all children left school at ten or twelve. He was bright enough to do reasonably well in most subjects on moderate effort and some swotting for exams. He continued to support himself by working, in the countryside and by serving as a waiter in a restaurant. Yet he saw no benefit in stretching himself and slipped off for games of football during lessons that bored him.[29] He had plenty of energy and an edge of discontent, but little sense of direction.

One enjoyment came from books: 'they opened up new worlds to me.' Since Borbála could not afford for him to burn paraffin late into the night,

János Csermanek in his class photo, 1922

and was unimpressed by this impractical form of self-improvement ('What do you think you are, a gentleman of leisure?'), he would instead read under a street lamp. Not all his activities were so solitary. A friend joined him up to the youth football team attached to the Vasas (Ironworkers) Sports Club, whose seniors played in the national first division. In the juniors, János was centre half, and dreamed, of course, of being a star. He later remembered playing 'in the ankle deep sand of People's Park. We used to play a good three hours, and the score was usually 15:11.'[30]

In 1926, aged fourteen, János Csermanek left school. His education equipped him to be a skilled worker, and there were growing opportunities in light industry. Nonetheless, it took him a year to find a job; after being turned down as a car mechanic, he started work as an apprentice of Sándor Izsák, chief Hungarian representative of Torpedo Typewriter, in the autumn of 1927. Borbála's hopes had been realised; typewriter mechanics had a high standing even among skilled workers, and there were only a hundred and sixty of them in the country.[31]

The fifteen year-old János Csermanek had clearly been marked by his difficult childhood. The closed, introverted personality that he was to show even in his later years of power owed something to the disgrace of illegitimacy and the instability of his upbringing. However, there was another thread to his mature character, a stubborn sense of his own worth, that he may have inherited from his determined mother or perhaps learned from the example of Uncle Sándor. At this stage, it manifested itself in a rather awkward chippiness.

If football offered him a dream of escaping his limiting world, chess – at which he was unusually good – provided another. He sometimes imagined that he would make his name through it, becoming an international grand master. Instead, chess was to provide an introduction to a wholly different world, one in which János Csermanek was to find his vocation.

2

BECOMING COMRADE KÁDÁR

One Sunday afternoon in 1928 János Csermanek won a junior chess competition organised by the Barbers' Trade Union. His prize was Engels' *Anti-Dühring*, a secondary though not minor work in the Communist canon. The tournament organiser 'told me very seriously that if I didn't understand the book he was giving me, then I should simply read and reread it.' Csermanek would later discover that he was a clandestine Communist.[1]

Over the next eight months, Csermanek followed this advice. His friends were unimpressed – 'they tapped their foreheads to show me that in their opinion there was something wrong with me' – but the book had a gnostic appeal for him, offering a key, a hidden code to 'the secret of life'. Doubtless his world seemed in need of explanation. His later judgement was that he had not understood the book fully, but 'I sensed in this initially incomprehensible argumentation something of what later became the meaning of my life ... this book changed the way I thought. It dawned on me that there were immutable laws and connections in the world which, so far, I had not even suspected!'[2]

If *Anti-Dühring* influenced his thinking, however vaguely, more immediate matters drove him to action. In 1929, the last year of his apprenticeship, he flared up at his employer's condescension. When the Depression set in some months later, he was the first to be shown the door; effectively blacklisted, he would never practise his trade as a typewriter mechanic. He was in and out of jobs; by the summer of 1930 he was shifting carpets in a wholesaler's warehouse. He felt keenly the poverty and humiliations of a life of casual, low-paid labour interrupted by stretches of unemployment. 'It was as if I were being given my wages as a favour, and I could never be sure when I would find myself on the dole however well I worked. This offended me, angered me and hurt my pride.'[3]

Unemployment brought him into contact with the Communists, who often sent agitators into the labour exchanges. On one of these occasions, Csermanek 'suddenly realised that he had stood up and started talking.' He had found his voice, and the party had found its man. He was probably first approached by a friend to join the Communists in autumn 1930, though he subsequently dated the approach a year later.[4]

Meanwhile, on 1 September 1930, he took part in a trade union organised strike and protest march of workers and the unemployed. By his later description, the carpet warehouse was suddenly closed, he chanced upon the demonstrators and, when a fight broke out with some strike-breakers, joined in and was knocked unconscious. 'I came round sitting on a bench in Károly Boulevard. I ached all over, but I had never felt better in my life.' This suggests an instantaneous identification with the mobilised masses. However, much of the day's violence, which concluded with the police firing on demonstrators, was stirred up by Communists to outflank the Social Democrats and union leadership. If Csermanek was already in contact with the party, his involvement may have been less spontaneous than he suggested.[5]

The arrest of more than a hundred Communists following the demonstration may explain his hesitation for a year before joining the party. He felt responsible for Borbála and Jenő: 'I had to think about what would happen to them if I weren't there.' Meanwhile, 'I took part in campaigns' such as gathering signatures for candidates of the Socialist Workers' Bloc, an attempted front for the Communists – easily thwarted by the authorities – in the June 1931 elections.[6] In September he went back to his friend and joined KIMSZ, the youth wing of the Communist Party. He joined a party cell named Sverdlov, after one of the Soviet leaders, and took a party alias, János Barna (brown – possibly in contrast to his fair hair).[7] Involvement on the fringes of the party may have made this seem a natural step. And with long stretches of unemployment deepening his and Borbála's poverty, he may also have felt that he had very little to lose.

He had joined a party at the extreme periphery of Hungarian political life. It was illegal, with perhaps a few hundred active members. There was bitter enmity with the Social Democrats and their trade union allies, whose priority was to protect the modest benefits that they had secured under Bethlen. Though the Depression gave some scope for activism and recruitment, the authorities responded predictably, proclaiming martial law in 1931, arresting party activists and executing two of their leaders.

As a new member of KIMSZ, Csermanek was introduced to the illegal party's subculture: 'the Gold and Silverworkers' Club on Kazinczy Street ... a "Workers' Choir" cultural evening at the National Association of Finance Officers on Akadémia Street. I met a lot of comrades, and learned a number of workers' songs, calling people to join the struggle.' He took part in leafleting and demonstrations, and enjoyed heckling the Social Democrat leader Peyer.[8] Though, as he later insisted, joining a small and illegal party could scarcely be considered careerist, it brought important if intangible benefits: a sense of belonging, and the chance to be accepted on his own merits. As his later associate György Aczél put it, the movement was 'a fellowship in which no one had a problem with his bastardy, where there was no problem about his primitive mother.'[9] His identification with the party as an institution would endure.

In his burst of initial commitment, he wrote an article, 'Unemployed', for the party newspaper, *Kommunista*. It was passionate if poorly written, relying on standard agitprop categories and rhetoric about 'a Fascist dictatorship, murderous martial law and Social Democrat treachery'. There was pride in his religious sense of being one of the revolutionary vanguard: 'The starving army of millions knows where to go now, and the way that I have found will be the way that all the other Hungry Jánoses will find as well.'[10]

By the time that the article appeared, in December, Csermanek was in police custody; he had been arrested on 9 November. He denied being a Communist, and was released for lack of evidence on 10 February, but from then on was under police surveillance.[11] Within days he was back in contact with KIMSZ, and was given new responsibilities. By May 1933, he was a member of the KIMSZ Budapest committee, acquiring a new alias (Róna). The party had already suggested that he go to Moscow to study at the Lenin Institute. He declined; he wanted to remain at home to support Borbála and Jenő. 'Maybe this is a mistake for a revolutionary,' he remarked later, 'maybe not.' The long-term implications of this decision could scarcely have been apparent to him then.[12]

His advance as a promising activist came to a sudden end when he and others were arrested on 21 June. He put up 'a violent struggle', trying to fight on even when handcuffed. Perhaps because of their exasperation, the police officers beat him severely. 'Of course they called it an interrogation, because they asked questions; but the point of it was the beating.'[13]

Under pressure, he cracked. Showing him a mass of material that they had seized, the interrogators claimed that they knew everything and threatened to beat him again. 'I realised that there was no point denying anything, so I confessed without a further beating.' When confronted with his arrested comrades, he realised his mistake: they had maintained their denials. Even before his trial in October, he had retracted his confession; like the other main defendants, he was sentenced to two years' imprisonment.

His lawyer told him that, because of his conduct, KIMSZ had suspended him (in fact, it had expelled him). Failing to stand firm under police pressure was understandable and scarcely unusual, though it would later be used against him in the Stalinist theatre of betrayal and confession.

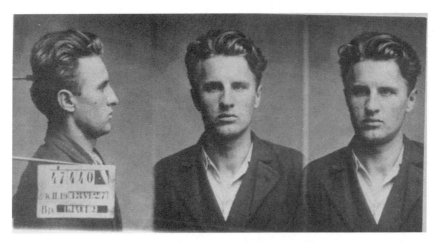

Arrested a second time, June 1933

He was, however, ashamed at having let his comrades down; as he put it later, 'I brought shame on KIMSZ ... and this upset me for the rest of my life. I have never considered myself a traitor, but from a moral point of view I stand guilty.'[14]

He spent 1934 in prison. In June he took part in a hunger strike by Communist prisoners over grievances ranging from food (he suffered a gastric ulcer from this prison term) to access to books. By his own account, he was force-fed and punished for his role in the protest. In November, his lawyer tried to secure his early release, emphasising that 'my client is the only support for his disabled and sick mother.' Borbála was still trying to make her living selling newspapers, but was reliant on charity and her health was suffering. This was what had worried Csermanek about joining an illegal movement, and he suffered pangs of guilt: 'he felt that he had left his mother in the lurch.'[15]

The plea was turned down, but soon afterwards – on 24 January 1935 – he was temporarily released while evidence was gathered for an appeal hearing. He needed a job, and Bernát Kaszab, the Jewish owner of an umbrella factory, employed him on a personal recommendation. Csermanek served as a general office delivery boy and errand runner; he would stay in this unchallenging job for much of the next seven years.[16]

Politically, he was in limbo. From mid-1936, it was doubtful whether there was even a party for him to join: in June the Comintern, exasperated by the Hungarian party's dogmatism and openness to police infiltration, dissolved the organisation. Militants were stood down from their illegal activities, and told to work in the Social Democrats and trade unions under loose guidance from a Prague-based party leadership. This reflected the 'Popular Front' line that the Comintern had established in 1935, in which Communists should work with other anti-Fascist groups, albeit with the aim of long-term hegemony. Csermanek persuaded himself that these 'enormous changes' were the reason that no one contacted him. The harder truth was that the remaining activists did not trust him. He tried to keep up informal links and got involved in trade union activity; however, 'I can't say that it was serious [party] work.'[17]

Meanwhile, the remaining four months of his prison sentence were still outstanding, and, appeals exhausted and prison space found, he and his co-defendants were taken to the Csillag jail in Szeged in February 1937. The records on prisoner Csermanek (8667/1936) noted that 'he maintains his principles … He must be watched at every turn.' As for his attitude to religious services, 'in his life outside [prison] he doesn't bother with religion.'[18]

Csillag held a number of Communists; the dominant figure among them was Mátyás Rákosi, then in his mid-forties and an internationally famous political prisoner. A junior commissar in the Hungarian Soviet Republic, he had been sentenced to eight years' imprisonment in a high-profile political trial in 1924, then given a life term when his release approached. Though he later made much of his initial surprise at Rákosi's unprepossessing appearance, Csermanek was, unsurprisingly, in awe of him. 'A condescending father-son relationship' grew up between them, one that 'affected his entire life'. The one story suggesting anything other than deference on Csermanek's part – laughing at the comical figure that Rákosi cut operating a foot-pumped spinning wheel – indicates a somewhat adolescent cheekiness rather than any equality of relationship.[19]

Rákosi interrogated him about his conduct with the police and heard his confession as to his shortcomings. He also questioned Ervin Rudas, one of Csermanek's co-defendants, and compared their stories. He seems to have concluded that Csermanek was a young man who had made an honest mistake. Whether or not because of Rákosi's imprimatur, Csermanek's three and a half years of political isolation came to an end. Rudas told him that they should meet once they were freed in June, and recommended that they should work together in the Social Democrats in Csermanek's home area, the 6th District.[20]

Csermanek followed Rudas' instructions: 'it was advice, but I took it as an order.' Over the next few years, he would be an effective infiltrator. The tenacity with which he rebuilt his standing in the movement was testimony to how central politics and the party had become to his life. He was one of a group of young Communists who showed up in the 6th District Social Democrat organisation from spring 1937 onwards. They made no secret of their Marxist views, and initially even left-leaning Social Democrats found them difficult to work with. They talked about working class unity, but 'in practice the transplant was difficult … their gaze was directed first and foremost towards the Soviet Union.' Nonetheless, they worked effectively, especially in the youth section – Csermanek helped organise weekly political 'youth seminars' with a pro-Communist slant – which both locally and nationally became a Communist redoubt.[21]

The world of the Social Democrats was that of the petit bourgeoisie and of the more respectable, unionised working class, the latter a world that János Csermanek had briefly approached but from which he had quickly been excluded. Poverty still kept him on the outside; he went often to the Ironworkers' Hall, but had no beer money and was to be found out in the corridors, drinking water and playing chess.[22] He lived with Borbála and Jenő in a windowless one-room flat in Jókai Square and still shared a bed with his half-brother. A couple of years later, he told his girlfriend Piroska Döme that his ambitions were to have a bed of his own and shoes that did not leak in winter.[23]

The 6th District Social Democrats also had a significant middle-class and intelligentsia membership. Csermanek's main Communist contact, György Goldmann, was a sculptor, and he later acted as contact with a party cell in the nearby Jewish hospital. These were social circles in which Csermanek was always uncomfortable. Yet he had a strong drive for self-improvement. Klára Vértes, who worked in the umbrella factory and who in the very different world of a decade later was his secretary, thought him intelligent and keen to learn; she gave him books and tried to teach him smatterings of foreign languages.[24] Working in the Social Democrats, Csermanek encountered strong traditions of workers' education, making use of sympathetic professionals and intellectuals. Alien though he found the intelligentsia, Csermanek may have benefited from these opportunities; some of those who dealt with him in later life certainly thought so.[25]

Nonetheless, his approach to politics was consciously down to earth; he was an effective speaker on bread and butter issues such as the cost of medical insurance, and thought little of the asceticism that he encountered from some Communist activists. 'He thought that if the party were to try to win over the workers only after they had stopped drinking, smoking, playing cards, and cursing, then the party had had it, and so had the working class.'[26] From early on, he was a pragmatic member of a utopian movement.

While Csermanek focused on prosaic political activity – party organisation, youth and trade union work – an era of great causes and intense political and intellectual debate appeared to pass him by. The leadership suggested that he go to fight in Spain, but – unlike many of his contemporaries – he declined, preferring to 'fight Fascism' at home and to support Borbála.[27]

Nor did he play any part in the response to the 'Populist' movement, the most striking political-intellectual development of the time in Hungary, which focused on the wretched conditions in the countryside. Some Communists, notably a student and intellectual group in Debrecen, sought to link up with the March Front, set up in 1937 and representing the left-leaning elements of the Populist movement. Some of these Debrecen Communists – Géza Losonczy, Ferenc Donáth, Lajos Fehér and Gyula

Kállai – would play significant parts, but with dramatically varying fates, in János Csermanek's later life.[28]

For some of them, this form of left-wing politics – less sectarian and more oriented to rural conditions than orthodox Stalinism – would prove an enduring influence. Csermanek's world, however, was very different. When he had to deal with Populism later in his career, it was as a political factor to be taken into account, not as something that had commanded his personal engagement.

He made a pleasant, sympathetic impression on those around him. To Irén Sugár, later György Goldmann's wife, he was a 'slim, kind young man who was always smiling'.[29] His affable if reserved style may have led some of the more austere militants to underestimate both his commitment and his abilities. Pál Demény, leader of a left-wing dissident faction of the Communist movement with strong support in some industrial districts, seems to have viewed him as a rather laddish lightweight. Demény's perception of Csermanek has been summarised by the historian Rudolf Tőkés as 'a low-key introvert, a moderate drinker, a chess player of some promise, and an avid physical fitness enthusiast with a flair for making a lasting impression on his female comrades in the Communist youth movement.'[30] Csermanek was scarcely, in truth, a Lothario of the workers' movement, though his name was linked with that of a party activist, Livia Deák, and he undoubtedly had a serious and lasting relationship with another, Piroska Döme.[31]

Piroska – known then by her first husband's name of Schlesinger – was a month younger than Csermanek, whom she met in the 6th District Social Democrat offices, probably in 1939. Born Piroska Steiner into a liberal middle-class Jewish family, she had reacted against the thuggish anti-Semitism of the Horthy era and joined the party in the early thirties. She had made an intense commitment to the movement, hiking with a rucksack in the summer heat in heavy clothes to train herself for a life of revolutionary asceticism and dropping a boyfriend who had apparently shown insufficient commitment. By the time that she became one of Goldmann's activists in the 6th District, she was married with a small son, though the marriage was 'getting cold'.[32]

She thought János Csermanek 'a very handsome young man, cutting a fine figure.' Though he could only afford one red-brown tweed suit – remembered by a fellow-activist as 'ghastly'[33] – for work, he saved enough to maintain a more dapper appearance outside. Their early meetings were political discussions along with Goldmann, but soon they were taking long walks together in Andrássy Street. 'While we talked about the affairs of the world, love blossomed between us' and they started spending nights in the City Park. At these times 'his disciplined nature unwound'. He teased her, 'Won't your husband knock you about with the bed-board for coming home at dawn?' Since the marriage was effectively over, she felt able to commit herself to the 'strange, wonderful love' that she felt for János

'A flair for making a lasting impression on his female comrades':
with women from the umbrella factory, 1938

Csermanek. On another occasion, 'János ceremoniously told me that the party leadership had permitted our being together. It was like an official wedding.'

The differences in their families and circumstances caused some strains. Piroska had to put up with constant mockery from her parents about János' unappealing red suit. Equally, when they met outside the umbrella factory and walked back to Jókai Square for lunch with Borbála, 'it broke my heart when I saw him struggling to swallow potatoes cooked in salty water.' Borbála remarked that there was little else that he could eat after the damage done by 'that prison'. When Piroska showed up a few days later with a new grinder to purée beans for János, 'his mother almost threw me out, saying that they were no beggars and did not want to accept anything.' Meeting her that evening, Csermanek took his mother's side. 'You've got no sense. You don't understand anything.' Piroska was left feeling guilty about her more privileged upbringing.

Apart from their respective families, they had only one major topic of conversation: 'we didn't only talk about politics, but mostly.' How did János relax when he wasn't saving the world? 'Saving the world *was* his hobby.' They must have been a very intense couple, but there was a difference between them. Politically committed though she was, Piroska's other concerns – in particular, her son – gave her a somewhat different perspective from a lover who was, she noted, bound by the 'fetters' of his cause. The demands made by that cause were about to increase dramatically.

In November 1940 the party recalled Csermanek to its ranks. 'György Goldmann told me that the party was up and working and that if I agreed with party policy and wanted to join, then I was welcome to do so.' As for Csermanek's past infractions, his good work meant that this 'had been taken care of'.[34] The chance to rebuild the organisation had come with the Nazi-Soviet Pact. For many militants this had been a traumatic event; Csermanek, however, showed no doubts. 'The whole of the youth group – in which János [Csermanek], György Goldmann, Piroska Döme and others carried out the work of political instruction – took their stand with the Soviet Union in these confused times.'[35]

With relations thawing between Horthy's Hungary and the Soviet Union – one sign of rapprochement was the swapping of Rákosi for the Hungarian national colours taken by the invading Tsarist armies in 1849 – communication between Moscow and party activists in Hungary became much easier. The Comintern decided in autumn 1940 to re-establish a party organisation: hence Goldmann's approach to Csermanek. A new leadership sent in from the Soviet Union set up a Central Committee in January 1941.

Initially, the party preferred to use activists such as Goldmann with no police record, while Csermanek took on more responsibilities within the 6th District Social Democrats. However, soon after Hitler's invasion of the Soviet Union in June, which Hungary joined a few weeks later, Csermanek was told to wind down his legal political activities and take an active role in the clandestine party organisation. He did so, though the leadership also used him to keep in touch with Communists still active in the Social Democrats.[36]

His return to illegal party work had its price. Around the turn of 1941-42 he helped Piroska move into a new flat. Watching him happily busying himself with the lights and furnishings, she asked, 'Are you moving in too?' 'No,' he answered gloomily, 'the time's not right yet.' It was scarcely in keeping with the rules or security of a clandestine movement for two of its members to live together. 'He was a very realistic person ... there were so many dangers ahead.'[37]

The dangers were growing along with party activity. With the defence of the Soviet Union now the main priority, the Communists sought the widest possible 'patriotic' anti-German coalition, sheltering under the politically capacious banner of commemoration of 1848. Distrust of the Communists limited the effectiveness of these tactics; however, they once more drew the attention of the political police. By now Horthy and his advisers realised that they had probably committed themselves to the losing side and were seeking to keep their distance from the Nazis. From March 1942, a new Prime Minister, Miklós Kállay, a protégé of Bethlen, pursued this policy with determination and initiated contacts with the

Western Allies. However, this risky strategy made the government still less prepared to tolerate renewed Communist activism.

In May and June, the political police rounded up several hundred activists, including most of the leadership. Many, including Goldmann, would perish in prison or in concentration camps. However, before his arrest, Goldmann was able to warn Csermanek to go into hiding.[38]

He did so, erasing the identity of the János Csermanek known to the police. When he showed up unexpectedly at a 6th District colleague's flat in mid-May, 'he had changed so much externally, with a smart suit and an umbrella, that for a moment I didn't recognise him.' For the only time in his life, he grew a moustache; according to his later wife, Mária Tamáska, it was 'a very ugly copper coloured brush'. His days were a mixture of tension and tedium, spent on trams, in pubs or in cinemas, staying out of his flat to avoid arousing suspicion.[39]

His relationship with Piroska came under strain. He warned her to leave Budapest at the time of the arrests. When she returned in September, they met in the Buda hills, walked in the woods and spent the night in a cave, 'which didn't fit in with the so-called conspiratorial rules. It goes to show that we too are human.' This was, she wrote later, 'an encounter, a togetherness that would never recur'. But they saw little of each other afterwards, and separation may have exacerbated tensions in the relationship. Fiery in her commitments, Piroska was frustrated at János' undemonstrative nature: 'he was so subdued, so hard to loosen up.' His thoughts on their compatibility – or otherwise – are unknown.

They met again on a cold day at the start of 1943. As he sat, tired and somewhat depressed, in her flat, she waited: 'Waited for him to reach his hand out to me, pull me towards him, into a warm embrace, to a love that I had missed for so long. [But] he seemed happy to be sitting there … The fact that he wasn't throwing himself at me made me feel slighted as a woman.' Angrily, she made up an excuse that she had to go out, and his attempt to be affectionate – 'but I've got time to be with you now' – came too late. That was the end of the affair. When Piroska was arrested in October 1944, the police showed her Csermanek's photo; she was able to say, quite truthfully, that she had not seen him for more than a year.[40]

Csermanek's main worry at this time was to keep the party alive. Before the onslaught of spring 1942, there had been contact with four to five hundred activists; in its immediate aftermath, it was at most only ten or twelve. This tiny group struggled to rebuild the network. Csermanek may have joined the Central Committee as early as 20 May, while the arrests were still going on; he was certainly a member by the autumn.[41] István Kovács, acting party leader from December 1942, thought well of Csermanek – 'he was extremely modest, a clever man but not then theoretically trained' – and brought him in to the party Secretariat, the core of the organisation.[42] By January 1943, contact had been re-established with seventy or eighty activists. In February, however, this patient reconstruction was torn apart by fresh arrests, Kovács among them.

For a short period this left Csermanek with only one contact, Gábor Péter, a one-time tailor's assistant who had been a party activist for ten years and had been trained by the Soviet political police. However, it soon became clear 'that there were people still remaining and it wasn't just the two of us'. A new leadership group of four – Csermanek, Péter, István Szirmai and Pál Tonhauser – was established; Csermanek became its secretary. In this highly attenuated form he took on, for the first time, the leadership of his party.[43]

He faced a testing dilemma. The Kállay government quietly tolerated the emergence of a reformist, anti-German coalition, embracing moderate conservatives, Social Democrats and the peasant-based Independent Smallholders. The Communists were at risk not only from the police, but also of becoming irrelevant in a fast-changing political situation.

This was underlined in May when Csermanek met with the leading left-wing Social Democrat Árpád Szakasits. The question of who initiated the meeting would later become significant when Csermanek's actions in 1943 came under attack. He insisted that it was Szakasits, though the evidence both of Szakasits' daughter and of the intermediary of the meeting, Sándor Haraszti, was against him.[44] Szakasits urged Csermanek to stop the party's illegal agitation, insisting that Social Democrats and Communists could not otherwise cooperate. Csermanek refused – 'in a Fascist country the party could not renounce its illegal methods'[45] – but he and the other remnants of the Communist leadership were feeling their isolation. They were already considering dissolving the party.

It was, allegedly, Gábor Péter who in February had first suggested an apparent party dissolution. He argued that the 1936 dissolution had enabled activists to operate for several years with little police harassment while a core group maintained a structure unknown even to party members. Csermanek rejected the suggestion, but the idea of this 'double illegality' idea grew on him.[46] Then, on 15 May – not long after Csermanek's meeting with Szakasits – came news from Moscow of the dissolution of the Comintern. This was Popular Front politics of the broadest sort, aiming to break down the distrust of potential partners and to build a wide anti-Nazi coalition.

Csermanek concluded that he could pull off a tactical coup. 'I was being clever, saying that we should take a decision to dissolve the party while in reality doing nothing of the kind. All we would do was swiftly change the party's name and then we would be able to approach the masses openly.'[47] An apparent party dissolution would combine Péter's aim – throwing the police off the trail – with pursuit of a Popular Front strategy.

The decision was taken in early June. By Csermanek's account, the leadership was divided: Péter was in favour, Szirmai cautiously supportive, Tonhauser against. The decision was deferred for a day, and Csermanek consulted with his contact Ferenc Donáth, a March Front-linked activist and agricultural expert. Donáth supported the idea, and at a second meeting, the doubters came round. The party was dissolved and some ten thousand leaflets announcing it were printed and distributed. The name for the replacement organisation – the Peace Party – was agreed a few weeks later, and it was launched in August.[48]

Since there were no records of the meetings, and all those involved later had powerful reasons to play down their responsibility, the truth remains elusive. However, it seems likely that Csermanek was a more active advocate for the decision, and some of his colleagues were more dubious, than his recollection suggested. Other accounts suggest that Szirmai was wary of the proposal and he later recalled Csermanek vigorously winning him round between the two meetings. Likewise, Donáth's account suggested that he had been informed rather than consulted.[49] These discrepancies would also be significant a few years later.

The decision quickly came under fire, both from the Moscow-based Hungarian Communists led by Rákosi and from many domestic militants. Csermanek had shown himself a 'party liquidator'; in a spirit of 'right-wing opportunism', he had dissolved the party's identity into a mushy wider anti-Nazi front. There was the potential for a still more serious charge: that of deliberately sabotaging the party's structures. In a Stalinist party, with its cycles of denunciation and purging, even the most senior figures had items from their past that could be held against them; however, the party dissolution provided a particularly fat item for his dossier.

Such charges were unjustified. If Csermanek had misinterpreted the Comintern dissolution, he had understood the spirit of the decision correctly: a tactical move to win allies, while leaving party goals and structures unchanged. Just as the Comintern continued to exist in practice after its formal dissolution, so '[we] considered the Peace Party to be a Communist party working under another name ... and its organisational principles and methods were in accordance with that.'[50] As for the initiative's immediate effects, the police were not fooled; their pursuit of Communist/ Peace Party activists continued unabated. The new party did make some headway, especially in provincial towns and in villages through 'peace committees'.[51] Progress was, however, very limited until the German occupation of Hungary radically changed the political situation.

Csermanek's decision to dissolve the party was, as he put it later, 'the bane of my life'; Aczél found that it was one of a handful of topics that he refused to discuss.[52] The sense that he had been entrusted with a major party responsibility and had mishandled it clearly troubled him. Later, this was compounded by the way in which the 'liquidation' was used against him. As he put it in 1954, 'Even if I were given three lifetimes, it still wouldn't be enough to allow me to redress the wrong I had done the Party, completely unintentionally.'[53]

Although underground life had helped end Csermanek's relationship with Piroska, it brought him into contact with the woman he would later marry, Mária Tamáska. They had first met some years before – by Mária's recollection, in 1933.[54] There was, she said, 'nothing romantic' about it. 'We came into contact with each other through the movement.' Shared political commitment helped cement a durable marriage; there was also a lot of common ground in background and experience. Like János Csermanek, Mária Tamáska was born in 1912 (on 8 April, almost two months before him). She too had a Slovak mother,[55] and like him had to work from a young age: her father's ill health and low-paid work left him unable to support his family. Like Csermanek, she had eight years' schooling.

She worked as a shop assistant, but it was the youth section of the ironworkers' trade union that brought her – along with her brothers and some friends – into left-wing politics. She studied at trade union school, and in 1937 joined the Communist Party. Interviews given at the end of her life revealed a woman of limited horizons; she saw events almost entirely through the prism of her own experience and that of those around her. However, she was tough, feisty and shrewd, with strong opinions and a caustic turn of phrase.

She married another Communist, Ottó Róna, and in early 1944 Csermanek, who knew Róna well, came to stay with them on the pretence of being a lodger. If, as seems possible, a relationship – or at least a strong attraction – was established between Csermanek and Mária soon after he moved into the flat, it probably followed rather than caused the effective breakdown of her marriage. Certainly, Róna showed no sign of a grudge against Csermanek; he too remarried after the war, and the two couples remained on very friendly social terms.[56] In any case, when Csermanek was arrested a few months later, Mária would commit herself to getting him out of prison with an intensity that went beyond the call of normal comradely duty.

This crisis was an indirect result of the German occupation of Hungary on 19 March. With the Red Army advancing, Hitler was not prepared to tolerate an unreliable ally. Aside from its most evident consequences – Kállay's replacement by a pro-German puppet, and the onset, after several years of resistance by Horthy and Kállay, of the Hungarian Holocaust – the occupation spurred the Peace Party to both political and military initiatives. It was one of a number of parties that formed an anti-German coalition named the Hungarian Front in May, though even then many of the Communists' potential partners remained wary of them, and the Front could not gather mass support.[57]

Parallel with this political initiative, the party prepared partisan operations against the occupation. Csermanek was present at preparatory discussions of the party's Military Committee in early April.[58] Shortly afterwards, he tried to cross the border into Yugoslavia with the intention

of making contact with Tito's experienced partisans.[59] It is likely that the
party also hoped to establish better contacts with Moscow; it had been
trying to do so via its Slovak and Yugoslav counterparts since 1942.[60]

With a new identity – put together by Péter – as an army corporal
named János Lupták and accompanied by a Yugoslav woman courier,
Csermanek reached the Yugoslav border around 19-20 April.[61] There the
plan misfired and they were arrested. Csermanek stuck to his assumed
identity, claiming to be an army deserter. It was a risky strategy, but less
dangerous than the truth. He was brought before a military court. His alias
held up; as 'Lupták', he was sentenced to two and a half years in prison.
His light punishment was perhaps testimony to the military judges' feelings
about the German occupation.[62]

'Lupták' started to serve his sentence in Conti Street prison, working in
the prison office. Rákosi and others would later express incredulity that the
authorities had not realised his identity, implying that Csermanek had been
protected because he was a police agent. There was no evidence for this;
luck and the incompetence of officialdom remain the most plausible
explanations for his survival. Indeed, on 28 July, the senior SS officer Otto
Winckelmann reported to Berlin that Csermanek had been arrested – but
this was a case of mistaken identity after the arrest of another
Communist.[63]

Csermanek smuggled out messages hinting at his whereabouts to Mária
and to his half brother. Jenő Csermanek, who worked in a cobbler's
workshop, was a tall, blond daredevil, 'a totally different character from
[János], an explosive, wild man'.[64] However, the half-brothers had one
important point in common: Jenő too was a Communist. The messages
got to Péter, who organised a plan for 'Lupták' to be released on health
grounds. Mária played a central role, delivering a bribe to a lawyer named
Szöllősy, who was to broker the scheme; she also visited Csermanek in
prison to reassure him that the lawyer did not represent a trap by which he
might give away his real identity. Nonetheless, he remained uneasy at his
case being stirred up. 'Relax,' Szöllősy told him, 'Don't worry about
anything.' 'I was completely relaxed until I met you,' was Csermanek's
rather sour reply.[65] However, a compliant doctor was found and his release
seemed imminent.

Then another political crisis intervened. Horthy, who – after a period of
passivity – had started to reassert himself over the summer, broadcast on
15 October calling on Hungarian troops to cease fighting the Soviets, who
were now in the east of the country. A few days earlier, he had met
representatives of the Hungarian Front and looked for their support.
Reportedly, some of the Regent's followers sought out Csermanek for
negotiations; they did not realise that he was in one of their jails, and the
party prudently did not tell them.[66]

Horthy's manoeuvre was ineptly executed, and the Germans quickly
forced him to rescind his declaration and abdicate, replacing him with

Ferenc Szálasi, long-term leader of the far-right Arrow Cross party. Szálasi inaugurated a new and terrifying regime, its worst measures aimed at the Jews of Budapest. The capital was made ready for a stand against the approaching Soviet troops.

This change of regime had immediate consequences for 'Lupták' in Conti Street prison: a new Arrow Cross governor vetoed his release. His luck was running out, and soon afterwards he narrowly avoided exposure. When the prisoners were assembled for evacuation, he encountered two activists from his 6th District days, Livia Deák and György Goldmann's wife Irén. The latter recalled how 'János stood, just skin and bone, in the prison yard. He indicated with his eyes that I must not recognise him.'[67]

On 12 November, the prisoners set out on a march to Komárom, on the Slovak border. At some point Csermanek discovered how the journey was meant to end: 'we were going to be packed into trucks and taken to Germany,' most probably to Dachau. 'I decided to run away. I would rather have shot myself in the head; there was no way I was going to Germany.' He escaped near Nyergesújfalu, a village by the Danube. As prisoners washed in a courtyard and mingled with guards, he and others saw their chance. 'I thought to myself: this is it! Now or never!' They jumped a fence into an orchard; the demoralised guards, who 'had absolutely had enough of the marching and the bad food', made ineffectual efforts to stop them.[68]

The escaped prisoners wandered for several days, resting in woods, avoiding checkpoints and patrols and breaking up into smaller groups until Csermanek was alone.[69] The story that he walked all the way to Budapest, carrying a log or plank and claiming at checkpoints that he was taking it to the next village,[70] is a romantic embellishment. He reached the town of Dorog and, using some money given him by a fellow prisoner in Conti, took an early morning train to Budapest, where he made his way to a safe house. It had been a round trip since he left Conti of six days, with long walks, little food and little rest. He slept for much of the next two days.[71]

In returning to Budapest, Csermanek was quite literally heading for the sound of gunfire. The Soviet army was approaching the city; by 23 December it was surrounded. Amid a bitter central European winter, the Germans, the Arrow Cross and some Hungarian army units fought almost to the last. 'The battle for Budapest was one of the longest city battles of the Second World War ... equalled in ferocity only by those for Leningrad, Stalingrad and Warsaw.'[72]

Party militants tried to sabotage the German and Arrow Cross defences. The original plan of the Hungarian Front had been to launch an uprising and assist the Soviet assault. A Liberation and National Insurrection Committee was set up. However, in December the plan was betrayed and its leaders executed. László Rajk, General Secretary of the (renamed) Hungarian Communist Party and organiser of the party's military effort was also arrested and survived only because he had a brother in the Arrow

Cross. Csermanek – who later claimed that other militants had been very critical of Rajk's efforts – was put in charge of the military committee for a couple of weeks, probably in early December, and tried to help a partisan group and to get arms to sympathetic workers. These efforts were, however, utterly marginal to the main developments of the siege.[73]

There was, however, one further incident that damaged Csermanek's party standing. During his imprisonment, Conti had taken a direct hit from an American bombing raid, almost blowing his cell apart; unsurprisingly, 'this had a traumatic effect on [Csermanek].'[74] The memory was still with him, and at some point – probably when the siege became more intense shortly after Christmas – he suffered a 'nervous crisis'. He holed up in Ferenc Donáth's safe house in Hungária Boulevard and refused to come out; every time there was a bombing raid he panicked and ran down into the cellar. István Kovács – whose good opinion of Csermanek had already been dented by the party dissolution – tried to censure him for cowardice and evading party work. The issue was only resolved after the end of the siege by the new party leadership, helped by Donáth arguing that Csermanek's earlier experience made his reaction understandable.[75]

The Soviet advance passed through Hungária Boulevard soon after 10 January. The battle continued in Pest for another week, that in Buda until mid-February. Csermanek and his colleagues emerged from their hiding-place to a changing country. Horthy and his system were gone. So were the Arrow Cross. The Red Army occupied the country and, in an interim government that had been set up under Soviet auspices in Debrecen on 22 December, there were three Communist ministers. This was an astonishing change for a party that had been persecuted and politically marginal for a quarter of a century – and with this, Csermanek's prospects too were transformed.

In these new conditions, with a national political career now open to him, he decided to change his name – presumably thinking that the Slavic-sounding Csermanek would be a hindrance. He opted for a name that he had already been using in the underground,[76] that of Kádár: solidly Hungarian, meaning a cooper or barrel-maker.

So, meet *Kádár János elvtárs* – Comrade John Cooper.

3

SALAMI

The end of the war brings about a sharp change of focus in Kádár's story. It is not only that he moved from the political margins and the fears and dangers of the underground to ever higher political office. Nor that, at this point, his history and that of his country start to mesh much more closely. He also moved from quarry to hunter, from a political dissident to one of the builders of a brutal police state. He quickly showed that he had absorbed the strict consequentialism of Marxist-Leninist ethics, and years in an underground party had reinforced a hard-edged view of political struggle.

Zoltán Vas, the advance representative of the Moscow-based Hungarian Communist leadership, arrived with the Soviet Army and a Budapest Central Committee, with Kádár as a member, was created on 19 January. This first meeting was indicative of Kádár's subsequent direction in two respects. Firstly, 'Comrade Kádár addressed the organisational questions', such as getting the party legalised, establishing a proper headquarters and a party membership card. It was in organisation, rather in ideology, economics or agriculture that he would make his mark over the next few years.

Secondly, Kádár identified as 'the most important task' control of the police. In the power vacuum following the defeat of the Arrow Cross, the party aimed – with the advice of the Soviet political police – to get control of the security organs. Some of Kádár's comrades proposed that he should head the Budapest force; Vas thought him very suitable for the role. However, he appears to have refused it, saying that 'you needed a military man there.' He served until April as deputy under the army officer and overt Smallholder (but covert Communist) László Sólyom.[1] This gave him direct oversight of the work of Gábor Péter, his underground associate, who quickly and with some eagerness became head of the political division; over time, Péter built up a political police empire, the ÁVO (*Államvédelmi Osztály* – State Security Department).[2] The party also made sure that there were no competitors in its immediate political ground; Péter arrested Pál Demény, whose organisation might rival the party, within days of the Soviet takeover of Budapest. Demény was not freed until 1957.

Conditions in the shattered city were chaotic, with none of the utilities functioning (except water), food and goods in short supply and prices rising rapidly. In some places competing police forces were in operation. Across the country, the Red Army carried out an orgy of rape, looting and the deportation of 100,000 civilians to Soviet labour camps. Even Communists were shocked; on 9 February Kádár, writing to the Interior Minister to report the development of the Budapest police force, noted that 'the Soviet command caused really big difficulties in our work, especially in the beginning, and they still do.'[3]

In these conditions, he was, as deputy chief of police, a man of some authority. Piroska Döme's parents, who had once found his sartorial style so comical, now paid anxious visits to see if he could find out her whereabouts. Similarly, he made an impression when he arrived in a large black car to pick up Borbála and Jenő from Kapoly, where they had sat out the final months of the war.[4]

János Kádár – as he had become – in 1945

Nonetheless, within the party he was under something of a cloud. Rákosi's deputy, Ernő Gerő, arrived in Budapest on 23 January and swiftly rebuked Kádár for the party dissolution. His behaviour during the siege may also have counted against him, and some of his colleagues – feeling that he had been over-promoted during the war – were keen to put him down.[5] An ugly incident in the post-war settling of accounts earned him another rebuke. On 4 February, two soldiers with a record of brutality in running the labour service battalions in which many Jews perished on the Eastern Front were hanged publicly in Budapest's Oktogon Square. Kádár was deeply involved: he signed off the charge sheet against the men, and was an organiser of the executions. It was to be the occasion for a big Communist demonstration, and Kádár and Péter took the blame for its mismanagement, which included demonstrators being exposed to German heavy artillery still active in Buda.[6]

However, his eclipse did not last long. He had experience, ability and, as a non-Jewish worker, the right profile. With Rákosi's return to Budapest in late February, the party's conventional structures were established. A new twenty-five strong Central Committee (CC) was set up to unify those in Budapest and Debrecen: Kádár was a member. Usually elected by party congresses or special conferences, the CC was a relatively large body (later of over a hundred members), meeting a few times a year. Its resolutions were the formal statements of party decision-making. The CC notionally elected the Political Committee or Politburo (PB), normally with a membership of around ten senior party figures: in effect, the cabinet of the party organisation. When a new PB was set up at the party's 'Whitsun conference' in May, Kádár was one of its eleven members.

There were also usually around five CC Secretaries, mostly PB members, responsible for directing policy in particular areas. Each Secretariat member was served by a CC department, the party's permanent civil service (though a successful career in this apparatus was often a precursor to serving in senior 'elected' positions). From April Kádár doubled up as a CC Secretary and as head of the cadres division. However, he did have one setback: for some weeks in April-May he was also Budapest party secretary, but gave up the post, not entirely willingly, on László Rajk's return from Germany.

The General Secretary chaired meetings of both the PB and Secretariat. Rákosi was elected to this post in February. His dominance, along with that of the other members of the 'quartet' of returning 'Muscovites', would soon bypass many of the formal structures. Rákosi's fame and qualities – he was quick-witted, multilingual and could maintain at least an appearance of affability – ensured his leadership, but he was less secure than he looked; Stalin distrusted him and some of his colleagues (notably Gerő) had much better connections at the highest Soviet levels. Little wonder that Rákosi later liked to be known as 'Comrade Stalin's best Hungarian disciple'; nor that his countrymen, noting his squat, bald ugliness, referred to him instead (in private) as 'Arsehead'.[7]

The other members of the 'quartet' were Gerő, a chilly former NKVD agent turned economic expert, József Révai, cultivated but dogmatic, responsible for cultural and ideological issues, and Mihály Farkas, a former Czechoslovak Communist and Red Army officer who took control of the security organs. Interestingly, it was to the latter – 'a Soviet *condottiere* with all the recklessness, opportunism and perversity of a mercenary'[8], the least appetising member of the unappealing 'quartet' – that Kádár was to become close.

The quartet asserted their leadership from the start. Kádár and Kovács noted with some puzzlement their utter lack of interest in the domestic Communists' experience and outlook. Yet the latter – impressed by their comrades' knowledge of the Soviet Union, and exhilarated by the contrast to their illegal past – seem to have accepted this without demur.[9] Nor were they completely subordinated; a number of their leaders became important second-tier figures, ranking below the 'quartet' but more important than the other 'Muscovites'.

Thus Kovács became a PB member and head of the CC's Organisation Department, while Péter built up the political police. Rajk – relatively young at thirty-six, charismatic and with the prestige of a Spanish Civil War veteran – quickly became the highest-profile domestic Communist. He had returned from a German concentration camp only in late May 1945, but by February 1946 was Minister of the Interior. In this role he would prove brutally effective at breaking the other political parties.

As head of cadres, Kádár supervised membership and appointments. Party membership could bring access to goods and to civil service jobs; and, with the Red Army in the country, it looked a promising side to join. Nor was the party overly fastidious about new recruits, including former members of the Arrow Cross.[10] The Communists' membership soared from perhaps 2,500 at the start of 1945 to 150,000 by May and half a million by October. Kádár's role brought him a wide range of contacts within the growing party. The contrast with Rajk – who had a higher national profile, but was less known within the party – would later be significant.

Hungary in 1945 was making a sharp break from the past, as figures from the previous regimes were arraigned before 'People's Courts' and the radical land reform of March 1945 broke the power of the larger landowners. The Communists, knowing that this mood did not extend to support for adopting the Soviet model, emphasised their moderation. However, their violent methods – in particular, the arrests and tortures practised by the political police – told a different story, and behind them stood the Soviet troops occupying the country.

Nonetheless, a takeover was not imminent. The Western powers had conceded Hungary to the Soviet sphere of influence, and the Allied

Control Commission was dominated by its chairman, the Soviet Marshal (and PB member) Kliment Voroshilov. Stalin seems, however, to have envisaged a more gradual approach in Hungary than in countries bordering the Soviet Union such as Poland, Romania and Bulgaria. Communist control of the security services, coupled with high levels of state (and Soviet) control over the economy, seemed adequate for Stalin's purposes, and the party may have been expected to live with at least aspects of a multi-party system for ten to fifteen years.[11] In addition, Rákosi was confident of electoral success. Defeat in the Budapest municipal elections in October was a traumatic shock, followed by parliamentary elections on 4 November, in which the Smallholders – transcending their rural origins to emerge as a catch-all party of the Centre-Right – won a massive 57 per cent of the vote. The Social Democrats ran second, with 17.4 per cent, the Communists third with 16.9 per cent. This was, however, enough to elect Kádár to Parliament.

Rákosi's misjudgement had undermined the Communists' previously strong position, and drastic action was needed to restore it. Voroshilov insisted that the coalition should continue, and that the Communists should hold the Ministry of the Interior. Control of the police, coupled with Soviet backing and hidden allies within the other parties, enabled the party to reverse the election result over the next eighteen months. As Rákosi put it in 1952: 'Salami, an expensive food, is not eaten all at once, but is cut one slice at a time as it is used ... [Our] step-by-step approach was known as the 'Salami tactic', and thanks to it we were able, day after day, to slice off, to cut up the reactionary forces skulking in the Smallholders' Party.'[12]

The first slice came when, under Communist and Soviet pressure, the Smallholders expelled twenty of their more right-wing parliamentarians from the party. Soon afterwards, some 60,000 civil servants were driven from their jobs in a political purge. Kádár was active among the salami-slicers, presenting the Communist demands in Parliament. He may have been a little blunt for some of his colleagues' tastes, letting slip the political nature of the so-called 'B-list' rather than falling back on the official justification of the need to improve civil service efficiency.[13]

The party's thuggish methods provoked a reaction, and Kádár acted as a troubleshooter in several crises stirred up by its agitation. In March 1946, he was among those sent to Szentes in southern Hungary, where an anti-Communist local police chief had been murdered. To limit the damage, the party expelled a number of its local members; Kádár was critical of the 'anarchist' nature of the murder, though he also lamented the sacrifices that the party had to make 'because of one rotten individual'.[14] Similarly, in July he was sent to Miskolc, where miners, exasperated by shortages and hyperinflation, had lynched alleged black marketeers (this, like a number of other similar incidents, had anti-Semitic overtones) and then turned on the police. The party was vulnerable, having whipped up feeling in a campaign against speculators. A local meeting was rough – a miner reportedly struck Kádár in the face – but the situation was eventually calmed.[15]

While the Smallholders were the Communists' main target, the Social Democrats were officially fellow members of a 'Left-Wing Bloc' established in March 1946. Though their effectiveness was diminished by splits between their predominantly anti-Communist base and more left-wing elements in their leadership, they were nonetheless competitors for working class votes. The capital's big factories were a critical battleground, and this was Kádár's responsibility: from November 1945, he was once more secretary of the Greater Budapest Communist Party (in other words, taking in both the city and the surrounding 'Red Belt').

Kádár's sense of rivalry with the party of which he had once been a member was intense: 'party chauvinism is really strong in Social Democrat circles.'[16] As early as summer 1945, he was grumbling that, when it came to jobs in the state apparatus, 'the SocDems completely thrashed us … and the more right-wing sort, into the bargain.'[17] Reviewing the November 1945 elections, he identified Communist weakness within the trade unions as a key problem: 'we speak to the leading trade union people once or twice all told and they get the political line on the basis of Social Democrat chatter.'[18]

Elections to factory works committees, in which the Communists had built a strong position, were vigorously contested in early 1946. With a further challenge at the start of 1947, Kádár and Antal Apró were given responsibility for the campaigns. Meeting senior Budapest party figures on 2 January, Kádár urged that, 'We must organise our forces much better than we did last year …we must organise ourselves to push out those elements among the Social Democrat candidates who are not favourable to the working class, and put in suitable Communists.' The party pushed for speedy elections in those factories in which it was strongest and, aided by heavy intimidation, secured good results in the first week of voting. The Social Democrats were cowed into suspending the remaining elections for a year.[19]

At the party's Third Congress in September 1946, Kádár was appointed one of Rákosi's two deputies. In part, this reflected the need for a senior domestic Communist in the post. He also brought credentials that the party desperately needed in its leadership. 'He wasn't a Jew, he wasn't an intellectual either, he was unquestionably a worker.'[20] Since the quartet were all Jewish, raising memories of the heavily Jewish leadership of Kun's Republic, it mattered that Kádár was not. His social background meant that, unlike most of his senior colleagues, he could take on the chairmanship of his old football team, Vasas, without seeming out of place. The appointment was also an endorsement of his work so far, and he kept his responsibility for Budapest and for cadres. It is little wonder that he was 'swamped with work'.[21]

Nonetheless, he found time for self-improvement, joining some colleagues for Russian lessons. The language did not come easily, but Kádár persevered over a number of years. Later, when he was in power, it was widely believed that he knew no Russian; in fact, 'This was a bit of an act on his part.' He was not a fluent speaker, but he had a good passive knowledge; he deliberately underplayed his abilities with successive Soviet leaders to give himself thinking time while the interpreter was speaking. [22]

He also sustained his passion for reading. A particular favourite was Jaroslav Hašek's *The Good Soldier Švejk*, which appealed to his well-developed sense of the grotesque.[23] It is easy to see how the figure of Švejk – the ordinary 'little man', who maintains an ambiguous obedience to the ever more crazy orders of his superiors, never revealing his own intentions but somehow coming out on top – might appeal to Kádár.

Physically, he filled out a little in the years after the war, although this was only a correction from his painfully lean condition after the stresses and privations of the underground. He kept in good shape, playing the occasional game of football for a party team. However, like so many of his generation, he was a compulsive smoker, although the effect of this on his health was not to become apparent for many years.

His domestic arrangements had become complicated. He was said to be living with his mother as late as August 1947; she still cooked his supper, though with his long working days she saw little else of him. However, at around this time he set up home with Mária, who had separated from Ottó Róna at the end of the war and divorced in 1948. Borbála nonetheless continued to stunt their relationship: Kádár would not marry so long as his mother lived. He was caught between two strong-willed women; he later told his official biographer, Laszló Gyurkó, with a sly wink that, 'I couldn't ask either of those women to share a flat with the other.' He let slip something of his unease in 'a most unusual answer' when Aczél asked why he was not married. 'Look, I've got a mother who is a very simple woman. I'm not going to subject any woman to the fact that I can't get away from her. I don't expect any woman to have to put up with her whims and coarseness. I'm not going to allow any woman, no matter who, to be bossed around by her just because she's my mother.'[24]

He was popular with his colleagues; several – who by then had little reason to be fond of him – recalled later a peculiar empathy and humanity that marked him out from other party leaders. Jenő Széll, who worked for him in the Budapest party organisation, had 'only good memories of Kádár' and described his warmth, willingness to help and interest in others.[25] To Éva Bozóky, who had married Ferenc Donáth, his colleague from the underground, 'there was something in his whole character that was engaging and attractive.' Kádár and Donáth went shooting together on Sundays – this formerly aristocratic pastime was to become a lifelong enthusiasm – and as Éva made up a picnic basket, Kádár chatted with her and cadged food, pleading that at home he was kept on a dull diet to protect his weak stomach.[26]

This was, of course, very different from the harsh face that he – and many of his colleagues – showed to political opponents. Perhaps more significantly, his loyalties to others had yet to be tested under conditions where political and personal survival was at stake. The understanding of others that can manifest itself in empathy can also be used to manipulate, and there was more ambition in him than was suggested by the persona, so comfortably adopted, of the straightforward, dutiful party worker.

The Communist takeover accelerated. In January 1947, Rajk unearthed a fabricated plot by a conservative group, the Hungarian Brotherhood Community. This was used first to implicate the Smallholder secretary-general, Béla Kovács, who was kidnapped by the Soviets, and a few months later the Prime Minister, Ferenc Nagy, who was forced into exile. With this, the Smallholders effectively disintegrated. In July, the Hungarian government rejected participation in the Marshall Plan, and a month later launched the first Three-Year Plan, increasing state control of the economy.

Yet the takeover was far from complete. That month also saw fresh parliamentary elections. Kádár was still not one of the party's leading public faces, but he was an effective public speaker, natural and informal; as an election campaigner, 'he was a great success.' In any case, he had his role as 'manual worker number one in the Communist shop window'. Party propaganda could portray him as a down to earth figure who knew what transport costs meant to working-class families.[27]

The Communists emerged as the country's biggest party; however, in spite of electoral manipulation and outright fraud, they won only 22 per cent of the vote, while conservative parties polled strikingly well. With the Cold War deepening, Moscow instructed the Hungarian party to implement the full model of a Stalinist one-party state. In late 1947, the pressure was increased on the right-of-centre opposition parties: one of them was closed down, and their leaders fled. Nationalisation accelerated: by March 1948, it embraced all companies with more than a hundred employees, as well as the utilities and banks.

The Communists also demanded that they merge with – in practice, take over – the Social Democrats. The tools were an aggressive recruiting campaign and the use of the allies from the Social Democrat Left to undermine the party's will to fight. As the campaign reached its climax in early 1948, Kádár was active in pushing for the merger in the big factories. In the second week of February, he spoke in the giant Csepel works, insisting that 'we could do more useful work if there were just one party of the Hungarian working class ... their [the Right's] chief representatives must be expelled from the Social Democratic Party.'[28]

A few days later, resistance was broken and the Social Democrat leadership agreed to purge the Right and to enter talks with the

Communists. With this, there was a surge of applications to join the Communists; much of the party leadership worried that the Social Democrats would collapse before the merger was completed. They urged a 'stop' on new members joining the party. Kádár was less worried by this possibility than some of his colleagues, and wanted only a partial 'stop' while recruitment continued in at least some factories. Nonetheless, the leadership opted for a two-week moratorium.[29] Discussing the issue again a few days later, Kádár was keen on a merger 'because the Social Democrats as a party will be ghastly partners in governing the country … we won't be able to work seriously with them in the leadership of the big factories.' As for the Social Democrat Right, 'We must sit down with the Left and say this to them: where there's a leadership list, this is who must be expelled, this is who must be dismissed.'[30]

Kádár played an active role in the mechanics of the takeover, which was completed at a 'unification congress' on 12-13 June. He served on a joint committee for party organisation and led the Communist side in the talks over the unification of the two parties in Budapest. Rezső Nyers, later to be a leading policy-maker in the Kádár era, was then a young Social Democrat and member of the committee. His first impression of Kádár was of an intelligent but unschooled man: 'It was obvious that his style was not that of a member of the intelligentsia, but of an intelligent skilled worker.' He was the dominant figure on the Communist side in the meetings, and inevitably 'the Social Democrats were on the defensive, the Communists were pushing forward.' Nonetheless, he played a strong hand in relatively moderate fashion, and 'he was very tolerant of old Social Democrat members.'[31] This ability to maintain a clear-sighted grasp of the realities of power, while playing down its trappings, was to become a distinctive feature of his political style.

At the congress, Kádár's address made less impact than the more strident declarations of Rákosi and Révai. He focused on practical tasks ahead and said that the members from different parties 'should be knit together as brothers in one family'. It was important, he said, to value individual cadres, and he quoted Stalin to prove the point.[32] He was appointed Deputy General Secretary of the new Hungarian Workers' Party (MDP).

Even as they were completing the destruction of their opponents, the Communists were also turning on one another. At the centre of the conflict was Rajk, whose strong view of his authority and prerogatives as Interior Minister was incompatible with Péter's drive for an independent ÁVO reporting directly to Rákosi. Péter and Farkas – who also had security responsibilities – started to work together against Rajk. Kádár was not a central figure in these battles, but seems to have sided with Péter and Farkas, passing on the ÁVO's complaints about Rajk to the leadership. At a meeting of the Secretariat in December 1947, he raised the conflict

Happy New Year, 1948: Communists including Rákosi (front left), Kádár (to right of woman in hat) and Péter (with moustache, to right of Kádár) greet the year of their takeeover

between Rajk and Péter as an issue of concern. The resulting inquiry served to undermine Rajk's position as Interior Minister. [33]

There is some evidence that Kádár was jealous of Rajk's early prominence and success. Some years later – admittedly under conditions unlikely to encourage objectivity – he wrote that, 'when, on Rajk's return, I was removed by the Party from the post of Budapest Secretary, I felt neglected and injured.'[34] Similarly, when he visited Romania in 1948 along with the writer Tibor Déry, their hosts mentioned Rajk's recent move to the Foreign Ministry and asked who the new Interior Minister was. Déry turned to Kádár for help. Jenő Széll, who witnessed the scene, noted that Kádár laughed as he identified himself as the minister in question, but still had the feeling that 'to the end of his days our János couldn't forgive Déry for that'. He realised that 'in Déry's eyes Rajk was an outstanding personality, whereas he was Kádár the cadre, one of a whole host of officials.'[35]

Kádár was also siding with his established allies. He had worked closely with Péter during and immediately after the war, and had more personal connections with the ÁVO. His half-brother Jenő quickly became an officer; later, after a period working for the Party and then for the Interior Ministry, Mária too moved to the ÁVO, working with the rank of Captain under Mihály Farkas' son Vladimir. Kádár's friendly relations with Farkas extended to their immediate families: Borbála lived close to Vladimir Farkas, often visited him and his family and had help from them during her frequent visits to hospital. By contrast – despite some later legends of an almost brotherly relationship – Kádár does not seem to have been especially close to Rajk, although they were both part of a social circle of former underground Communists whose meetings tailed off in 1947.[36]

In May 1948, however, Kádár and Rajk spent a month together in the Soviet Union – Kádár's first visit to the Marxist-Leninist Rome. Looking across Red Square on 1 May, for the first and only time he glimpsed Stalin.[37] They did not meet any of the highest-ranking leaders; nonetheless, the Soviets were presumably checking them out. Whatever the test, Kádár clearly passed it. He returned home, however, to a shock: Jenő had been killed in a bizarre accident, crushed under a collapsing balcony while raising the Red Flag for the May Day celebrations. Kádár was devastated – 'it's as though my own child had died' – and unsurprisingly, the effect on Borbála was deeper still.[38]

Whatever his personal sorrows, they did not detract from Kádár's energy – or ruthlessness – in the following months. In early June, an incident in the village of Pócspetri, in which a policeman had been accidentally killed during unrest over the recently decreed nationalisation of church schools, gave an opportunity to attack and intimidate the opposition. Kádár, accompanied by Péter, travelled to Pócspetri and reported back to the leadership. With the support of a menacing investigation and the occupation of the village by some two hundred police – 'the whole village population feels guilty and fears for the consequences,' Kádár wrote – the incident was presented as an act of violence provoked by the local priests. One death penalty and various other sentences were handed down, and Kádár arranged for local activists to carry out door to door agitation in favour of nationalisation.[39]

Two months later, on 5 August, Rajk was moved to the Foreign Ministry and Kádár succeeded him as Minister of the Interior. One of his first acts indicated his alliance with Péter and Farkas. In September the ÁVO was renamed the ÁVH (*Államvédelmi Hatóság* – State Security Authority), with greater powers than before. In his early months in office, Kádár was to give the ÁVH strong support, lobbying for increased numbers and better pay, and bringing some other units (for example, the police dealing with economic crime) under its control. He asked for Soviet specialists to help improve its work.[40]

By early 1949, however, there were signs that the tension between Interior and the ÁVH had not gone away with Rajk. When the idea of giving the political police a fully independent structure and budget was raised, Kádár – for whatever reason – deferred it with the argument that 'the comrades are all very busy'.[41] Thus the original source of tension was not removed; meanwhile, there were a number of minor but bad-tempered clashes, and Péter attacked one of Kádár's associates, claiming that he was hostile to the ÁVH.[42]

Kádár ran his department on a tight rein. He set up a Political Council of close advisers to keep him informed and to ensure that his orders were enacted. The powers and responsibilities of the new Interior Minister were vast. In addition to the conventional police and prison systems, Kádár had his ambivalent responsibility for the ÁVH and its 35,000 strong network of informers. He also served on the top secret State Security Committee, overseeing the running of the party and security organs. On 26 October, a still more secretive 'operative directing committee' was set up, comprising Rákosi, Farkas and Kádár. Every three days, Gábor Péter sent this troika a report on the national political situation, based on the reports of informers.

Arriving at the Interior Ministry, Kádár inherited slanted investigations into the Hungarian-American oil company MAORT. In late September, he announced that there had been sabotage at the company, and the process ended with a show trial and the nationalisation of the company without compensation. This was followed by another attack on American economic interests, the Standard Electric trial, following which two Hungarian citizens connected to the company were hanged in May 1950.

However, the two most significant targets were the peasantry and the church. A collectivisation drive had just started and met with fierce resistance; the authorities cast opponents – even the owners of seven-hectare plots – as kulaks, that class of rich peasants whom Stalin had famously pledged to liquidate. Kádár's approach was brutally straightforward: he built up special units of the ÁVH, giving them a distinctive uniform 'to make the kulaks more afraid of the power of our people's democracy.'[43]

Policy aimed to break the churches as independent organisations. Protestant and Catholic alike suffered, but the latter was the tougher proposition, not least because of its uncompromising Primate, Cardinal József Mindszenty, no friend of the postwar republic and still less of the Communists.[44] His powerful campaign against the takeover of church schools raised particular alarm among both local party activists and the leadership. After efforts to persuade the Vatican to remove Mindszenty failed, the Cardinal was arrested on 26 December 1948. Six weeks later, drugged and tortured, he made his confession of treason to the Budapest People's Court and was sentenced to life imprisonment.

Kádár also oversaw the liquidation of other political parties, a process that he and Rajk had foreshadowed during their Moscow talks. A 'Hungarian Independence-Popular Front' was created on 1 February 1949 to absorb the other parties; it won 96 per cent of the vote in fresh elections held on 15 May. In later years, Kádár was to argue that the creation of a monolithic one-party state had been a mistake, but that was probably because he later associated it with the development of Rákosi's personal dictatorship and the use of state terror against senior Communists. He showed no signs of that belief at the time. In the new government appointed in June Kádár remained at Interior.[45]

Meanwhile, his personal life underwent a decisive change. In February 1949, Borbála died. Most of her life had been lived in poverty and obscurity, but Rákosi, Kovács (who gave the address) and other party leaders attended her funeral in Budapest's Kerepesi cemetery. The party newspaper *Szabad Nép* (Free People) assured Kádár that the masses grieved with him. 'The fighting son of the people can never be an orphan.' He was hit hard by the loss of the mother with whom his relationship, while sometimes uneasy, had been so close. In the cemetery, 'this serious, grown man sobbed like a child.'[46]

He was, however, now free to marry Mária. The ceremony, on 19 July 1949, was characteristically austere and practical. 'It was a strange wedding,' Mária recorded, with a certain understatement. 'The day before, we went to the 3rd District magistrate's office and asked them to open up at eight the following morning, because we wanted to get married, but we also had to go to work.' Kádár brought along two witnesses: Kovács and Péter.[47]

This curious secret policeman's wedding says a lot about the forces with which Kádár had become aligned. Some six weeks previously, those forces had claimed another victim. On 30 May, Rajk had been arrested.

4

'YOU'RE THE ENEMY'S MAN'

When, after 1956, Kádár earned a hangman's reputation, the first item on the charge sheet was his role in the show trial and execution of László Rajk. He was not the initiator of this late flowering of the Stalinist show trial model, but he was an active participant. The charges against Rajk were absurd, and, with his inside knowledge of the workings of the ÁVH, Kádár can have had no illusions about how confessions were extracted and the case against Rajk built. At the same time, he had powerful motives for acquiescence: survival perhaps above all, but also a resentment of the more flamboyant Rajk's earlier advancement and the enjoyable sense of being at the heart of affairs. Although this must have required particularly heroic efforts of self-deception, he seems to have persuaded himself that the process was somehow justified – at least until its grisly conclusion.

In 1948, Kádár had appeared to become closer to Rajk and his family. Shortly after the war, Rajk had married another underground Communist activist, Júlia Földi; when their first child, László, was born in January 1949, Kádár became his godfather in a secular name-giving ceremony. By Kádár's account, given some years later, the relationship was not all that it seemed: 'In the spring of 1948, on the instructions of the party leadership – at a time when serious objections were being raised to Rajk's behaviour – I got closer to him, so that perhaps he would listen to me, someone who had known him of old. At the end of 1948 my relations with Rajk became closer still; we went to each other's houses and played chess together.'[1]

Kádár may have been laying a false trail; at the time when he was speaking, Rajk was still officially a traitor. However, if he was telling the truth, there was a manipulative element in his relationship with Rajk, though one that he portrayed as the benign role of an honest broker. However, Kádár was – also by his own account – present at meetings as early as January 1948 at which Farkas (admittedly, without securing general agreement) was describing Rajk as an 'enemy'. Reportedly, Rákosi sent Kádár on his Soviet trip with Rajk some months later 'not for a summer holiday'.[2] Given this, his role was probably less that of an intermediary than of a spy.

Rajk's downfall reflected a confluence of personal rivalries, the dynamics of Stalinist politics in Hungary and the intensifying Cold War. As Interior Minister, he had made enemies of both Péter and Farkas. However, the latter probably also had the longer-term aim of succeeding Rákosi and thus sought to remove those who were the most plausible alternatives – Rajk and, later, Kádár. In addition, Rákosi – who seemed initially to have good relations with Rajk – came to fear the younger man as a potential rival. This reflected not only Rajk's personal qualities, but also his role as chief patron of the 'People's Colleges', aimed at educating poorer students, especially those of peasant origin. Although initially encouraged by the Communists, the People's Colleges' links back to the Populist movement of the thirties aroused suspicion, augmented by Rajk's generation of a potential following.

The deeper underlying force behind the Rajk trial, however, lay in the drive for a total Stalinist dictatorship, ensuring that the new satellites did not become independent centres of power. The intensification of the Cold War gave an opportunity to export and repeat the process that Stalin had carried out in the Soviet Union through the purges of the thirties, creating a supine, traumatised party and society, incapable of resistance. The successful rejection of Soviet control by Tito's Yugoslavia in the summer of 1948 gave Stalinism a new bogeyman and added urgency to the drive for uniformity.[3] Kádár was certainly aware of the process: in his early weeks as Interior Minister, he was briefed by a Soviet intelligence officer on the need to unmask traitors within the party. The Hungarian party's links to Tito added to fears of possible Yugoslav influence within it, but the Rajk trial had parallels in other satellites: Koci Xoxe in Albania, Traicho Kostov in Bulgaria and a series of purges in Czechoslovakia, culminating in the Slánský trial in 1952.[4]

For Rákosi, this meant the opportunity to entrench his personal dictatorship. Just as the Soviet purges had destroyed those with knowledge of the pre-Stalin party, now Communists whose careers had been shaped outside Stalin's Moscow were the main targets. Arrests of party figures with experience of the West and now said to be members of a spy ring – the most senior being Tibor Szőnyi, head of the cadre division – began in mid-May. It may only, however, have been later in the month that Rákosi, reading the signs from Moscow, decided to go higher and make Rajk the focus of his purge. The arrests began to take in people closer to the Foreign Minister.[5]

Kádár later portrayed himself as a by-stander, detached from the arrests, interrogations and beatings that were the groundwork for the trial. Yet he

Enforcers: Kádár replacing Rajk as Interior Minister, 5 August 1948

was complicit in all the key decisions and was present – usually with Farkas – at many interrogations.[6] He gave a graphic account of Szőnyi's questioning – albeit claiming, rather implausibly, that he had wandered into it 'by chance'. 'Gábor Péter, Ernő Szűcs and other ÁVH officers were surrounding Mihály Farkas, who stood at the head of the table, yelling at Szőnyi, who was half dead from fear, things like, "You scummy bastard, spy, don't lie, admit it, was Rajk a spy, or wasn't he?"'[7]

He stuck to the leadership line in other respects. When Aczél protested at the arrest of a friend, and offered to take care of his children, Kádár's response was icy. When they met again soon afterwards, Kádár asked Aczél 'with chilling humour', 'Are you still at liberty?' By July, Aczél was under arrest: Kádár had passed his words on to the leadership. Aczél later believed that 'this didn't signify wickedness, but came from [fear that] somebody might have bugged our conversation, or got me to set him up.'[8]

Kádár was directly involved in Rajk's arrest. He was present at the meeting of the senior party leadership on the morning of 30 May at which the order was given. By at least some accounts, he undertook a particularly unsavoury task: to divert Rajk with a chess party so that he would arrive home that evening at a time convenient for the ÁVH, led by Péter in person, to arrest him.[9]

By this point, a number of the prisoners, including Szőnyi, had been broken by interrogations and beatings, and had signed confessions. Rajk proved to be a rather different proposition. Despite severe beatings, he refused to confess; when confronted with Szőnyi and his statement, he told him, 'Look me in the eye when you say that!'[10] He continued to insist on meeting representatives from the party leadership. On 7 June, Péter agreed that he could – 'just so you can see how fair we are.' Farkas and Kádár were dispatched to the villa where Rajk was held.

They arrived at about 11pm. The meeting was recorded – which was standard procedure – and a transcript survives. Though there are some questions about the transcript – of which more later – it is an important starting-point.

The opening sentences set the tone:

Kádár: Have you got something to tell us?
Rajk: I want to tell you, I'd like to know the position that's been taken because …
Kádár: Have you got something to tell us?
Rajk: I do have something to tell you.
Kádár: We've come here to give you a chance to talk to the party for the last time in your life. I haven't got much time for you. Bear that in mind. And so tell us what you want.[11]

Kádár takes the leading role in the questioning, especially in the earlier parts of the interview. With his use of constant, grinding repetition, he sounds like a stereotypical interrogator:

Kádár: … You know who and what makes up our party leadership.
Rajk: I know.
Kádár: And you really believe that our party leadership will fall for what you've been dishing out here for a week? You believe that?
Rajk: Well, for the time being …
Kádár: You believe it?
Rajk: All I can say is …
Kádár: Tell us. Do you believe that?
Rajk: I believed and still believe in the party.
Kádár: That they'll fall for what you've been dishing out here for a week?
Rajk: I believed and continue to believe in the party. I have nothing to do with these accusations …
Kádár: Hold on. Do you believe the party leadership is taken in by what for a week you've been dishing out here?
Rajk: I'm sorry, but I'm not dishing out anything.
Kádár: Do you or don't you believe it?
Rajk: I have got to believe it, because I am telling the truth.
Kádár: That the party leadership is taken in by what you've been dishing out for a week?
Rajk: They've got to believe it, because I'm telling the truth.

Kádár and Farkas urge Rajk to confess to the charges against him and Kádár sums up the points that he wants Rajk to understand. 'You're not our man, you're the enemy's man. And don't you forget it! ... Second, so you shouldn't have any illusions, our Party leadership is in full agreement about this thing. Am I understood?' In other words, Rajk should abandon any thoughts that the ÁVH had exceeded its authority, or that there might be any relief to look for from Rákosi, or from his former chess partner.

Kádár and Farkas then pick through Rajk's career to show an apparent pattern of sabotage: 'whenever and wherever you showed up, confusion reigned in the party.' At each point Rajk protests that, while each event cited is accurate, the slant put on it is not, and that these reflect honest mistakes rather than treachery. The closed circle of the inquisitors' logic is made apparent:

Rajk: ... And if I'm an enemy agent, I don't want to go through it all, why would the enemy intern me in '41, in the most critical times?
Kádár: Well, that too is an interesting ...
Rajk: And keep me in the internment camp the whole time ...
Kádár: To keep you in reserve.
Rajk: And if I ...
Farkas: We're familiar with the imperialists' methods.
Rajk: I really see that it's such a strong, united front that's shaped up about me having been an imperialist agent ...

Rajk is presented with a Morton's Fork of alternatives: either through weakness he allowed himself to be blackmailed into becoming an enemy agent, or he consciously set out as one right from the start. While blackguarding his record, Kádár and Farkas appeal to his loyalty and sense of guilt: 'Hasn't the party done everything for you? ... Haven't you got enough decency in you when it comes to the party to honestly reveal what you're up to? Haven't you got enough decency?'

Rajk seems susceptible to appeals to Party loyalty, and at times accepting of his fate: 'it's obvious, if such a view has taken shape inside the party leadership, unanimously ... or the other variant, then there's no other alternative for me but the ending of my life.' Nonetheless, the interview ends inconclusively, with Rajk still seeking to explain himself rather than write the required 'confession'. It also ends with a clear threat to his family:

Rajk: ... All I request is just that while this matter is being cleared up and closed as far as I'm concerned, my wife shouldn't come to harm.
Farkas: That depends on how you behave!

The transcript differs significantly from versions of the meeting that circulated in the West after 1956, and which had their origins in Rákosi's later attempts to shift the blame for the Rajk affair onto Kádár. All of the latter refer to a conversation involving only Kádár and Rajk, in which Kádár emphasised that 'no one in the party leadership believed that Rajk was guilty.' He praised Rajk's past record of risking his life for the movement, and asked him to make a false confession for the sake of exposing Tito. 'He would not be executed, merely spirited away' to the Crimea with his family, and given an important position under an assumed identity.[12]

This 'Western' version has been tremendously influential, and allots to Kádár a role of exquisite betrayal and duplicity – especially when added to exaggerated accounts of his earlier relations with Rajk. For the literary-minded, it bears a satisfying resemblance to the dénouement of the émigré Hungarian Arthur Koestler's *Darkness at Noon*, written a decade previously, in which the old Bolshevik Rubashov is persuaded to confess to help the party.[13]

Unlike the transcript, this version omits the presence of Farkas, giving the discussion between Kádár and Rajk a much more personal tone. The transcript also gives no sense of Kádár admitting that the leadership knew Rajk to be innocent – quite the opposite. Critically, at no point in the transcript is any promise given that Rajk's life would be spared. Above all, the tone of the two accounts is radically different. In the 'Western' version, there is an insinuating quality to Kádár's approach, an appeal not only to Rajk's party loyalty but also, by implication, to their friendship. In the transcript, the tone is blunt, brutal and impersonal. But how accurate is the transcript?

The recordings of the Rajk interview – along with a lot of other compromising material – were destroyed after Kádár took power in 1956. However, a copy of the transcript, which in 1956 had been presented to a committee investigating the role of Mihály Farkas, survived to be unearthed in 1991-92. What is unclear is how faithfully the transcript rendered the original interrogation. There were strong rumours that Rákosi and his associates later tampered with evidence relating to the show trials. There is some reason to believe that this is true of the Rajk interrogation: at no point in the transcript did Kádár state that he was acting on behalf of Rákosi, yet two ÁVH officers remembered him doing so. Kádár insisted to the committee that, contrary to the impression given in the transcript, it was Farkas who set the tone of the interrogation and that he played a secondary role. The recollections of one senior Communist who claimed to have heard the tape agree with Kádár's account. For whatever reasons, the committee was willing to believe Kádár and complained that the transcript was mangled.[14]

What can be said with confidence is that Kádár visited Rajk and interrogated him on 7 June in the company of Mihály Farkas. The transcript gives at least some idea of the content of the interrogation. Insofar as the record is accurate, Kádár's manner was cold and bullying, rather than the more friendly and imploring tone presented in some later accounts. It seems that no promise was made that Rajk's life would be spared. Even so, given the friendship that Kádár had cultivated with Rajk and his family, his behaviour still gives a strong whiff of betrayal.

When Rajk still failed to confess, he was taken into a small room and beaten by a gang of ÁVH officers. 'During this Mihály Farkas, Kádár and Péter were in the neighbouring room, they heard everything and every so often sent in Péter to ask Rajk if he was willing to 'talk'. Rajk did not 'talk', for which they beat him more.' In the succeeding days, Rajk underwent more beatings and sleep deprivation, but to little avail: one ÁVH officer admitted that, after a week, 'We were more tired than he was.'[15]

Early 'Western' accounts suggested that Kádár's visit was critical in getting Rajk to confess.[16] It is true that at a CC meeting on 11 June, three days after the interrogation, Kádár indicated – in very general terms – that Rajk had confessed; furthermore, the leadership went public on Rajk's alleged conspiracy and arrest a few days later. However, at this stage Rajk's confession was very partial, and he was still denying conscious wrong-doing.[17] At most, therefore, the Kádár-Farkas visit played a part in wearing Rajk down by depriving him of any hope that sympathetic members of the leadership might get him a fair hearing.

In the aftermath of the interrogation, Kádár remained deeply involved in the plans for the trial. On 8 June, the PB appointed him a member of a 'committee to liquidate the spy network', though this was little more than a formalisation of the work already being done by the inner circle of the leadership. On 11 June and in a final summing-up on 3 September, just two weeks before the trial, he reported to the CC about the 'conspiracy'.

In his initial presentation on 11 June, he seemed to take some relish in the secret information to which he – unlike the majority of his listeners – was privy, explaining that the interests of the party and the working class demanded confidentiality. He also emphasised that 'among the members of the spy network uncovered up to now there is not a single worker or working peasant'; indeed, among the conspirators' crimes was to have held back working-class cadres.[18] Could he have been thinking of the way in which he had been superseded by the more educated Rajk?

From around mid-July, Kádár's role in the trial preparations was reduced sharply; the Soviet political police became directly involved, and their main point of contact in the Hungarian leadership was Rákosi himself. The indiscriminate beatings were stopped, and a more collaborative relationship developed with the prisoners; it was in this changed atmosphere – much more reminiscent of Koestler than the crude bullying of Kádár and Farkas – that Rajk made his full confession. The Soviets also developed a clear 'concept' for the trial, giving the Tito angle – already touched on in some of the charges and interrogations – much greater prominence. Rákosi added the lurid touch that Rajk had plotted with Tito to have the Hungarian leadership assassinated.[19]

Kádár found some aspects of this story hard to swallow. He later made much of his doubts about a claim that Rajk and the Yugoslav Interior Minister Ranković had held a conspiratorial meeting in a hunting-lodge in Hungary. Why, Kádár reasoned, would Rajk have taken such an unnecessary risk when it would have been possible to meet more safely in Yugoslavia? However, an hour and a half's discussion with Rákosi was sufficient to set his mind at rest.[20] It seems that Kádár wanted to be convinced, and that the meeting was a way of taking some of the moral burden off his shoulders.

The People's Court opened its sessions – which were broadcast on radio – on 16 September in the Metal and Engineering Workers' trade union building. Rajk and five other defendants made fluent confessions and indicated their acceptance in advance of whatever sentence the court might pass. The verdict was announced on 24 September, with death sentences for Rajk, Szőnyi, and Szőnyi's young assistant, András Szalai.

On the morning of 15 October, Rajk, Szőnyi and Szalai were hanged in the courtyard of Conti Street prison. Rajk's wife Júlia was watching from one window, Péter, Farkas and Kádár from another. In the days before the executions, Farkas had telephoned Péter repeatedly to demand that he be able to attend ('I want to be there! I want to see!'). And, as he explained after the hangings, 'I brought Kádár along. He should see it – it won't do any harm.'[21] Perhaps Kádár felt under pressure to attend, or agreed to do so out of bravado; in any case, what he saw made a profound impression on him.

Some years later, he described the events. 'Standing between Mihály Farkas and Gábor Péter I saw the executions of Rajk, Szőnyi and Szalai through to the end. Rajk went to his death crying, "Long live Stalin! Long live Rákosi!" Szőnyi without a word, Szalai crying out, "I am innocent. I was tortured." I was shocked by this unbelievable behaviour by men I thought of as convicted spies. Mihály Farkas and Gábor Péter saw this and declared that the "vile creatures" were "provocateurs to their last breaths". This did not reassure me.'[22]

Afterwards, at what appears to have been a post-executions drinks party in the prison offices, with a number of those present buoyantly merry, Kádár spoke to the ÁVH officers who had been with the condemned men. He asked what they had been saying before their executions. One of the officers, Colonel Szűcs, described how in the final moments before he was taken out into the prison yard, Rajk 'embraced and kissed him, and asked him to, "Remember me to the comrades."' Péter hastily interrupted this conversation, sent the officers away and had Cardinal Mindszenty brought from the cells, presumably to provide a distraction from any distress caused by the spectacle of Rajk's execution. Kádár, however, did not take part and left.[23] There are persistent though unconfirmed reports that around this time he was seen vomiting.[24]

Kádár's reaction damaged his standing with Rákosi. In one – probably not reliable – account he went to Rákosi, 'utterly devastated', told him of the last words of Rajk and his colleagues and cast doubt on the idea that they had been traitors. To which Rákosi allegedly replied, 'Kádár, my boy, you've got a lot to learn.'[25] Even if this is overblown, Kádár seems to have taken calls from Rákosi the next day questioning him about his behaviour. 'Why are you in such a bad mood?' the leader asked him. 'Did the executions affect you that much?'[26]

His one expression of doubt excepted, Kádár had until the day of the executions given no sign that he was troubled by Rajk's destruction. Despite his later attempts to play down his role, or to claim that he had protested against the trial, he was deeply implicated. If Mihály Farkas – admittedly a highly tainted source – is to be believed, Kádár himself knew this, at least soon after his release from prison in 1954. 'Comrade Kádár said that in the Rajk affair three people were responsible: Rákosi, Farkas and Kádár.'[27]

Like others involved in the mechanics of the interrogations and the trial, Kádár would have known that any expression of doubt would be politically damaging, perhaps personally dangerous. Whether through fear or ambition, he played his significant part in the tragedy. He may have somehow persuaded himself that the process could be justified: that Rajk's poor judgement made him dangerous to the Party, that he was therefore 'objectively' an enemy, that some sort of morality play was needed to edify the masses ... or whatever. His reaction to the execution suggests a man who had sustained himself with specious justifications of his actions, but whose self-deception could not fully withstand confrontation with the physical reality of what they entailed.

Sometime in the months after Rajk's death, Kádár lectured at a party college. One of the students was a 29-year-old printer called Péter Rényi, later to be a prominent journalist in the Kádár era. Rényi was struck by Kádár's emphasis – in sharp contrast to other senior figures – on the need for a modest, austere style by party officials and by his thin, haggard appearance, giving the air of a man under strain.[28] This may not simply have reflected distress at his role in Rajk's execution. By this time, Kádár had surely worked out that what had happened to so many people under the system that he had helped to build might also happen to him.

It took a little under eighteen months for his fears to be realised.

5

FULL CIRCLE

One August evening in 1950, Kádár was summoned to Rákosi's office. The leader told him that Árpád Szakasits, the Social Democrat leader with whom Kádár had met in 1943 and who was now under arrest, had confessed to being a police agent and a British spy. He had also implicated Kádár and said that he had been acting under police orders in dissolving the party.

Some years later, Kádár wrote to Rákosi, 'Just once in my life I was in a state of panic, and then in a big way. It was that August evening when you told me, quoting Szakasits' confession ... that you believed me to be a police agent and provocateur. After this I wasn't able to get a grip on myself any more.'[1] He later emphasised his trauma at the idea that his colleagues – and Rákosi in particular – did not trust him, and believed that he could have been a police spy. Given his belief system, this rings true; yet much of his reaction was – very understandably – one of straightforward fear. The interview was the beginning of eight months of agonising suspense that ended with Kádár's arrest; this was followed by interrogation, the fear of the gallows, a trial, a life sentence and long periods of solitary confinement.

In his hour of trial, Kádár was to show a mixture of vulnerability, tenacity and ruthlessness. As the net closed about him, he sought to protect himself by incriminating others. His psychological dependence on the party and on Rákosi meant that he could never face up to the full truth: that the leader himself was behind his persecution, and with the full knowledge that the charges against him were baseless. Instead he went though a tortured, protracted examination of his own 'responsibility' for the decision that still troubled him, the 1943 party dissolution. Later, he searched in similarly obsessive fashion for the master manipulator who had turned Rákosi against him. Yet these delusions also strengthened him. Early in his imprisonment, he showed an obstinate determination to string things out until, he hoped, he could convince the party leadership of his innocence. Only later, with these hopes definitively dashed and in the isolation of solitary confinement, did he sink into an enveloping despair.

Kádár's personality had always been reserved, but arrest and imprisonment added a layer of bitterness and mistrust. He felt that, as a loyal party worker, he had been profoundly ill-used. His sufferings at the hands of the ÁVH – though often exaggerated – were real enough; but they did not produce in him the deep shift in perspective experienced by some other senior Communists who fell victim to the system. Unlike Ferenc Donáth and Géza Losonczy, casualties of the same purge, Kádár did not come out of prison a committed reformer. In so far as his views were to change, that came a lot later.

The terror accelerated in the months after Rajk's execution. Spring 1950 saw a purge of former Social Democrats, starting with Szakasits. Arrested after dinner with Rákosi, Szakasits soon found himself in much less convivial conversation with Gábor Péter; in November, he was sentenced to life imprisonment. The purge took in other pro-Communist Social Democrats and the trade unions, while seven leading military officers – including László Sólyom, Kádár's former chief in the Budapest police – were executed on 20 August. As the lesson of the Rajk trial was reinforced, tension among senior party figures grew. Éva Bozóky noticed that her husband's hunting trips with Kádár were now much less frequent. 'People started to be really afraid, acquaintances crossed the street so they wouldn't have to speak to each other; there was a general atmosphere of fear and suspicion ... the air was thicker than usual.'[2]

Yet political leaders were only a small proportion of the casualties of a reign of terror that was to last until 1953. The ÁVH held files on around a million people (one tenth of the population); up to 400,000 people were imprisoned, whether in regular jails or in the hundred or so labour and internment camps around the country. Executions and other deaths in custody ran in the hundreds.[3] The scale of the cruelty partly reflected the brutal transformation that Rákosi and his associates were imposing on the country. The drive for agricultural collectivisation resulted in food shortages, while Gerő's ambition to make Hungary 'a land of iron and steel' added to the squeeze on living standards. Hungary exceeded all the other Soviet satellites in the extraordinarily high investment rates extracted from the economy, and in the proportion of it devoted to heavy industry.[4]

At the higher levels, purges were driven by the institutionalised paranoia of the Stalinist system. From the break with Tito onwards, the hunt was on across the bloc to unmask traitors, with each revelation generating pressure for more. Rákosi, knowing that his standing with Stalin was ambiguous, had every reason to keep finding enemies. Yet there is no sign that this went against the grain for him. Some parties – notably the Poles – dragged their feet over a purge. Rákosi, however, dispatched his victims with chuckling delight; no wonder that many Hungarians came to see a similarity with Shakespeare's Richard the Third.

The first moves against Kádár came from his former allies. Soon after the Rajk trial, Farkas muttered to Péter about another spy network, 'a pseudo-Hungarian narodnik group … led by Kádár.'[5] Stripping out the contorted jargon, the next target would be the Populist-linked communists of the March Front, with Kádár – who in reality had had little to do with them – caught in the same net.

Farkas probably saw Kádár as another rival for the succession to Rákosi. The unresolved conflicts between the Interior Ministry and the ÁVH poisoned Kádár's relations with Péter. As early as January 1949, Kádár had sought to pull rank on Péter, reminding him who was 'the Politburo member and Interior Minister in one person'. At a meeting in November, he complained at Péter's failure to meet a deadline and said that he was not an easy person to work with; the ÁVH head replied 'in a defiant and malicious tone' that Rákosi had no problem working with him, but 'the enemy' did. The end of the year saw formal independence for the ÁVH from the Ministry, but the battles continued in early 1950 with a screening committee – directed by Kádár and Kovács – to purge the ÁVH leadership of allegedly unreliable elements.[6]

While Péter and Farkas had their own reasons for wanting rid of Kádár, the decision to proceed rested with Rákosi. By early 1950, there were signs that he was prepared to do so. He complained to Soviet advisers that 'the Interior Minister Kádár is run down and indecisive. Besides, he [Rákosi] does not fully trust him after the Rajk affair.' He also made particularly ominous references to Kádár's past failings, including the party dissolution.[7] If he were expected to produce another enemy, it would always suit him to show that the home-based, prewar party had been riddled with nationalists and informers. And the most senior surviving home Communist was Kádár.

The infighting and a growing sense of his own insecurity – in particular, the nagging knowledge that he had lost Rákosi's trust, and that this left him very exposed to Péter's attacks – took their toll on Kádár. By May, he was asking to be transferred away from Interior; Rákosi reported that he seemed depressed and overwhelmed by his work. In late June, he was replaced at Interior by Sándor Zöld, another home Communist and a March Front activist.

Kádár's new post – CC Secretary for Party and Mass Organisations – combined his old responsibility for party cadres with that for the various organisations through which the party sought to control social interest groups: trade unions, the party youth movement, women's organisations and others. He might have felt, understandably, that he was still in a senior position, but that he was safer away from his exposed position at Interior. Understandably, but wrongly.

According to the 'concept' sketched out by Rákosi in early 1950, Kádár had turned traitor after his police confession in 1933. His meeting with Szakasits had been part of a conspiracy – incited by western intelligence agencies – to dissolve the party and thereby weaken it as a potential player in postwar Hungary. Kádár had continued his treasonable activities as an associate of Rajk, and had succeeded him as leader of a spy network that comprised the leading personalities of the March Front. These included Kádár's hunting partner Ferenc Donáth, his successor as Interior Minister Sándor Zöld and the Culture Minister and former journalist Géza Losonczy.

Szakasits was arrested on 24 April; his interrogation soon focused on his dealings with Kádár, and a basic confession was extracted. By July, Rákosi was telling the Soviet ambassador that 'there's something wrong in [Kádár's] past'; he was also demanding written statements from Péter, Szirmai and Tonhauser about the party dissolution. In August, with the other purges largely concluded, Rákosi felt free to make the next move and held his ominous interview with Kádár.

Shocked by the charges, Kádár nonetheless denied them and insisted that he had visited Szakasits with the knowledge of other party leaders. When told that the others denied this, he began to suspect a plot to undermine him. In the ensuing weeks, Rákosi summoned him for further questioning, and the pressure increased. 'I was given responsible jobs and meanwhile they were paying my home-help to eavesdrop on my every conversation. When I was out in the street I was being watched, in my bedroom I had someone listening at the keyhole. And it went on like that for nine months.'[8]

At a Secretariat meeting in October, the state of the Interior Ministry – allegedly still riddled with Horthy-era officers and 'enemy elements' – came under attack. This was now Zöld's responsibility, but the criticisms were clearly also aimed at Kádár. He realised that 'my case began to run along exactly the same lines as Rajk's had. ...things came full circle.' A depressed, fatalistic mood settled over him. 'I decided that I wouldn't think about it any more, whatever would be would be, because I felt that if I thought about this business for another half hour I'd blow my brains out or hang myself.'[9]

Others were called in for questioning, including Donáth, who was head of Rákosi's own secretariat. Attention focused increasingly on Sándor Haraszti, a veteran if rather independent-minded Communist with an ideal 'biography'. He had lived in and had contacts with Yugoslavia, which offered promising possibilities of a Titoist angle; his links to the March Front included his daughter's marriage to Géza Losonczy; best of all, he had been an intermediary in Kádár's meeting with Szakasits.

At the end of November, a celebration of the birth of Ferenc Donáth and Éva Bozóky's first child turned into a bizarre last supper for the home Communists. The Kádárs were among the guests. The vivacious and well-read Éva found Mária friendly enough, but not someone with whom she could sustain more than a few minutes' conversation about the evening's cooking. 'She was simply different, a different world.' Unexpectedly, neither the Harasztis nor their daughter, Losonczy's wife, turned up. The supper went ahead, though with some cryptic remarks from Losonczy about imprisonment adding to the sense of unease. Kádár proposed a toast to the baby boy's future: 'May he be a fine revolutionary.' Another of those present, Károly Kiss, remarked, 'Well, you never know, he might turn out to be a counter-revolutionary.' At this off-colour remark, 'people started looking at each other.' Eventually, the party broke up, but Losonczy stayed behind to talk to Donáth. His news was that his father-in-law, Haraszti, had been arrested.[10]

Early in 1951, Rákosi required both Kádár and Donáth to submit written statements about the party dissolution. Their differing recollections may have contributed to an estrangement between them, and in his third memorandum to Rákosi (9 February) Kádár broke ranks. 'I am daily more strongly aware that Donáth's role was significantly greater than I had thought before now.' He described how his hunting partner had constantly urged a change of the party's name and had emphasised work with peasants and bourgeois intellectuals rather than workers. He also recalled that it was Rajk who had brought Donáth into the party.[11]

Kádár's efforts to make Donáth a scapegoat were unsuccessful. Every attempt that he made to refute or deflect the charges against him met with a new allegation. On 11 February, he wrote again to refute further claims that he rather than the Social Democrats had initiated the Szakasits meeting. At that point he was still defending himself vigorously. However, later in the day his nerve cracked, and a second letter – addressed to Rákosi, Gerő, Farkas and Révai – was full of self-abasement; Kádár spoke of his 'cowardly behaviour' in 1933, and described the party dissolution as 'a crude, opportunistic act' reflecting his being 'ideologically untrained and politically backward'.

He still insisted, however, that he had made an honest mistake. 'I never, for one moment, in any way entered into an alliance with the enemy. ... Looking at the dissolution of the party from today's perspective, when I must presume that *against both my knowledge and my will* I became a tool of the enemy, I feel myself unworthy to hold the high-ranking party offices which I have received.'[12] The letter concluded with an offer of resignation from his senior posts and a hope that the whole affair could soon be resolved.

Still Rákosi did not move against Kádár. Instead, four days after the letter, Donáth was arrested. Trying to find out what had happened to him, Éva Bozoky made a series of phone calls, one of them to Kádár. She

FULL CIRCLE
53

found him gloomy and evasive about Donáth's fate, merely remarking cryptically, 'We didn't think of you.' Weary of his 'meaningless whinging', she gave up the conversation. Many years later, her assessment of the man she had once found so sympathetic was that 'Kádár was a working-class guy with good intentions ... But the basic blemish on his whole morality was his utter cowardice.'[13]

Kádár approached the party's second congress (25 February – 2 March) with some apprehension. His speech was highly self-critical, and he told Mária, 'Don't be surprised if they don't elect me on to any of the committees.' Yet the blow did not fall: he was confirmed in his posts. Kádár drew the conclusion that as in 1945, the party had noted his errors, but had given him another chance. He went to Rákosi and thanked him profusely. However, after he had gone, the leader turned to Péter, asking, 'What do you make of that?' and ruminated on Kádár's reluctance to look him in the eye in recent meetings.[14]

Rákosi had decided that the inconsistency of sustaining Kádár in the leadership and then arresting him was a lesser evil than a disruption to the smooth running of the congress. More March Front activists disappeared during the following weeks, and by the end of March Rákosi was informing Moscow that the arrests of Kádár, Zöld and another home Communist, Gyula Kállai, were imminent. However, the plans for a smooth roundup of the 'pseudo-Hungarian group' were about to be shockingly disrupted.

On 18 April, at an apparently routine meeting of the Secretariat, Zöld was ambushed with manipulated figures purportedly demonstrating his failure to carry out an earlier resolution to purge the higher ranks of the Budapest police of officers with a Horthy era past. In a brutal interview the next day, Rákosi pressed him to resign as Interior Minister. Zöld made a self-critical statement at a PB meeting that afternoon, typed out a letter to his colleagues and took a revolver home. The following morning, 20 April, shots were heard from the house. Anticipating his arrest, Zöld had killed his mother, his wife, their two children and himself.

The leadership was stunned and alarmed by what had happened. Even Péter, surveying the carnage in the Zöld family home, 'was not then like the man that the entire country feared.' The quartet sat in emergency session and decided to arrest Kádár and Kállai before they could hear the news.[15]

Utterly unaware of what had happened, Kádár was having lunch with Mária; he often worked late into the night, and sought to compensate by lunching at home as often as possible. The couple's house, in Cserje Street, was in the green and tranquil Rózsadomb (Rose Hill). From there they could look down on the working-class districts of Pest across the river from which they had both come – literally, though not metaphorically, for their lifestyle remained unpretentious. The house was a relatively short drive from party headquarters. There may have been an additional reason why Kádár was at home that lunchtime: Mária, whose bouts of ill-health were to dog their marriage, had come out of hospital a couple of days before.

During the lunch, Kádár took a phone call asking if he was returning to party headquarters. After the call, 'He didn't say a word, except goodbye. Then he went to the office. Or rather, to prison.' At the corner of the fő street, two ÁVH cars blocked his way. Gábor Péter got out of one, and asked Kádár to get in. Asked afterwards if he had known that this meant he was being arrested, Kádár remarked, 'Well, look, if there are cars across the road in front of me, and there's the head of state security, who was known to have taken Rajk into custody ...'[16]

Driven to an ÁVH villa, Kádár remarked that, after all the months of suspense, his arrest had come as a relief. 'In the last few months, people would barely even return my greeting.' Later that day, if Rákosi is to be believed, he visited Kádár and urged him to confess. It was clear, the leader said, that Kádár had been recruited by the police; it was also clear, he added sympathetically, that Kádár was suffering from his bad conscience. If he 'made a clean breast of it', the party could help him. 'I saw that my words had a great effect on him.'[17]

Kádár's associates shared in his fall. His driver was arrested with him and interned for nearly three years. His secretary, Klára Vértes was interrogated about what she had seen and heard while working for Kádár. When she refused to manufacture incriminating stories, she was sent to the Kistarcsa internment camp. Piroska Döme, who had seen little of Kádár in recent years, was questioned, her interrogator making a crude (and predictably unsuccessful) attempt to stir her jealousy by claiming that she had merely been one of a string of Kádár lovers.

Mária was turned out of the Cserje Street house, dismissed from her ÁVH job and expelled from the party. She spent the following months at her brother's, unable to find formal work and occasionally called in for questioning. She was eventually allocated a job in a suburban factory making teddy bears. She resisted heavy hints that she should consider her own prospects and remarry. For the next three years she had no knowledge as to whether her husband was alive or dead; her letters to the ÁVH and to the party leadership went unanswered.[18]

Kádár's relief at his arrest, and his illusory hope that he might clear his name of the accusations against him, cannot have lasted long. Perhaps because of the rather chaotic conditions – Zöld's suicide had forced Rákosi into precipitate action, and many ÁVH interrogators had little idea of what they were supposed to be proving – surprisingly little attention was paid to him during the first week or two of his detention.[19] Nonetheless, he was soon transferred to Budapest's central prison in Fő Street and put under intensive if rather unselective interrogation. In a 22-page statement on 7 May, he broadly maintained his earlier stance, admitting to grave error over the party dissolution but denying that he had been an enemy agent. He took a similar line – admitting weakness but denying treachery – over his 1933 police confession.[20]

This generated paroxysms of rage from Rákosi, Péter and the three-member committee (Farkas, Kovács and Kiss) set up to investigate the case. The statement was, they declared, 'full of lies'. One evening about a week later, Péter and Farkas called on the latter's son Vladimir, an ÁVH officer. The prevarication, Vladimir Farkas was told, had to end: Rákosi wanted Kádár's confession, and he wanted it on his desk the following morning. Farkas must interrogate Kádár, and his father and Péter would listen in to it in the next room.[21]

This nocturnal interrogation gave rise to the persistent myth that Kádár suffered grotesquely brutal tortures at Vladimir Farkas' hands. The stories varied: that his teeth were shattered in beatings; that his fingernails were pulled out; that Farkas urinated into his mouth. The most dramatic allegation was that Kádár was castrated in prison, a claim that seemed to generate particular enthusiasm among American conservatives. Perhaps there was a retrospective symmetry to it: no balls in 1951, no balls in 1956. Yet another variant had Kádár telling a friend, 'When I was in prison I was so badly beaten in the balls that although I can still fuck I am now sterile.'[22] Yet not one of these stories is true.

The most striking contrast between the treatment of Kádár and that of many others arrested at the same time was that he was *not* physically maltreated, at least not before his trial. Whether he was put under psychological pressure – such as threats to Mária – is not known. But on the matter of physical torture, he was quite clear. Asked at the 1954 rehearing of his trial whether or not he had been maltreated, he replied, 'Physically no,' though he indicated that some unspecified threats had been made. He was to repeat this denial in interviews given towards the end of his life.[23]

Where and how did the story arise? Most probably from Kádár himself, and from those around him; different accounts have named the journalist Béla Kelen or even Mária as the source. Vladimir Farkas, defending himself against the allegation of (exceptional) brutality, claimed that it emanated from Kádár's entourage shortly after he came to power in November 1956.[24] The aggressive spinning of a story that cast him in the sympathetic role of a victim of Stalinist torture was intended to counter his domestic and international image as a Soviet stooge.

However, according to Béla Szász, who had been imprisoned during the 'Rajk affair', Kádár told him as early as 1954 how 'he had been tortured by Gábor Péter's henchmen', and there are other reports indicating that he was telling such a story *before* 1956. This seems an uncharacteristic reversal of Kádár's usual reserve, and in later years he was unwilling to discuss the subject.[25] It also contradicts his statements at his rehearing, just before his release. That, however, was a closed court session; once back in political life, Kádár was probably keen to offset any suggestion that he had been relatively easy for the ÁVH to crack.

By accident, Kádár's interrogation by Vladimir Farkas is the one episode in the entire investigation that survives in transcript. The interrogation, especially in its early stages, was dominated by long monologues from Farkas, some of them evidently shouted; Kádár seemed depressed and submissive, with long silences as he tried to determine what to say. Yet the advantage was not all on one side; Farkas was under pressure to get results, and Kádár still had the weapons of silence and evasion, which sometimes reduced his interrogator – by no means a stupid man – to incoherent rage.

The starting-point of the interrogation was the party dissolution. Farkas sought – with some difficulty - to nail down a clear statement about Kádár's motives:

Farkas: ... Tell me what it means. Explain it to me. What does it mean if someone writes a statement saying that they knew enough at the time to be aware that what they were doing was playing into the hands of the Horthy bourgeoisie? What? What does it mean? Tell me!

Kádár: It means renouncing the leading role of the working class.

Farkas: Horse shit. ... You, when you dissolved the party, in plain, dot-to-dot language, were aware, you were politically experienced enough to know full well, that what you were doing was not helping the Hungarian working class but harming them, and that you were playing into the hands of the Horthy bourgeoisie. Is that what you wrote?

Kádár: Yes.

Farkas: So what does it mean? Does it mean that what you did over dissolving the party was just an accident, a result of your cowardice?

Kádár: I didn't do...

Farkas: What does this statement mean? Answer me. No one dictated it to you; you wrote it yourself, you stand by it. So come on, tell me what it means. Come on, tell me.

Kádár: All right, it means that I knew that I was serving enemy interests by dissolving the Party.

Farkas: What do you mean you knew? What is all this? Why are you beating around the bush like this, glossing over things? You wrote down as clear as day that "I knew..." What's going on? You're talking like a peasant brat out of the f...ing gutter. What does it all mean?

Kádár: I didn't know what I was doing.

Farkas: What didn't you know? When?

Kádár: When I disbanded the Party...

Farkas: For crying out loud! But you wrote this with your own hand! Didn't you?

Kádár: Yes.

Farkas: So what does it mean? What does what you wrote mean?[26]

After yet further haggling over terminology, an exasperated Farkas ('My God, it's slow work dealing with you') finally got Kádár to something like the point that he wanted: an admission that his action had been 'conscious party treason'.

There was a further struggle over Farkas' main objective: to establish that Kádár had acted as a police agent. Farkas offered a way out: Kádár's failings might be put down to cowardice rather than premeditated treachery, but time was running out to persuade the leadership that this was the case. '…Why can't we just get to the bottom of things, bring out the whole truth, clear up this thing once and for all, I mean, don't you see that this is your only chance to stop yourself being talked about as the filthiest scum? That's what the comrades will say about you.'

Faced with this threat, Kádár realised that the issue could be delayed no longer. Yet before 'confessing' he still sought to bargain, to ensure that he would not be made a central scapegoat like Rajk:

> *Kádár:* OK. I'd just like to ask one thing, which… I'd just like to say one thing. I take responsibility for what I did because I have to. All I ask is that my responsibility doesn't…
> *Farkas:* What? Cause other people's guilt to be hushed up?
> *Kádár:* To be overlooked. Or hushed up.
> *Farkas:* Don't worry about that. Why does it worry you?
> *Kádár:* … I just have the feeling – I apologise for putting it like this – but I have the feeling you think I did more than I did.
> *Farkas:* No we don't…. Do you want time to think?
> *Kádár:* No.
> *Farkas::* OK, let's hear it.
> *Kádár:* The police recruited me.
> *Farkas:* Why didn't you say so?
> *Kádár:* Because I was a coward.[27]

Kádár's tactic was to give ground when under pressure, but to do so as slowly as possible, a point at a time. Many details of his supposed police activities were sketchy and implausible, and Farkas – probably out of sheer weariness – allowed some ambiguity to slip in on critical points. The interrogator was left unsure of the value of what he had extracted. Gábor Péter was also sceptical, noting how Kádár made his confession 'in a tired, lifeless, disorientated way … his tone was broken, tired in every way, resigned to everything, lacking in conviction.' Mihály Farkas, however, congratulated his son on his success and telephoned Rákosi to tell him of Kádár's confession. This soon proved premature: the following morning, with another interrogator, Márton Károlyi, Kádár retracted the confession.

Péter returned to the prison, and had Kádár brought up from the cells. The two men spoke for half an hour; what was said is not known, but at one point Rákosi was telephoned. Eventually Kádár, 'amid fits of weeping', reversed himself once more and reinstated his confession.[28] Farkas' investigating committee was able to cite it in a report on 19 May. 'Since 1931, since I came into the workers' movement, confronted with the slightest difficulty, I always took the path of a flinching coward, a liquidator's course, the path of compromise and betrayal ...'[29]

If Kádár was near collapse at his meeting with Péter, he rallied afterwards with a new tactic. He confessed – everything, and a lot more. Eating his lunch in his cell, he would give his latest confession to Károlyi, adding more bizarre elements to the story and generating further confusion. This tactic – an amalgam of Scheherezade and Švejk – both played for more time and gave a signal to anyone in the party leadership who cared to notice that the whole affair was a nonsense, and that Kádár knew it to be so. ÁVH officers received these stories with incredulity: 'I was convinced that Kádár was acting as a provocateur in making an all but unbelievable confession.' In a curious document of 9 July, 'János Kádár's confession in his own hand,' he identified as potential enemy agents a whole range of party functionaries who had never been on the ÁVH's investigation list. Not one of these was subsequently arrested, though they were called in for questioning.[30]

However, Kádár's tactics could make little difference to his position. Given time, the ÁVH could doubtless produce as fluent a confession from him as they had from so many others. In a report to the CC on 22 May, Rákosi reported that, 'Clearing this up is difficult and time-consuming work, but we will bring it to a conclusion, just as back then we brought Rajk to a conclusion.'[31] Presumably this would mean a public 'Kádár trial' just as there had been a 'Rajk trial'; and with the same 'conclusion' for the principal defendant.

Yet, speaking to the PB little more than a month later, Rákosi struck a different note. 'The Kádár affair is such a slippery, watered-down fragment of the Rajk business that we can't bring it into the open and make a second Rajk affair of it.'[32] There was to be no public trial, and this change of plan may well have saved Kádár's life.

It was, it seems, a show trial too far even for Rákosi. With social tensions running high, he may not have wished to strain the morale of an already nervous party. Kádár's disappearance had caused disquiet in the organisation; with his working-class background and stint in the party administration, he was widely known and liked (Rajk, by contrast, had enjoyed a higher national profile but had less of a party base). Jenő Széll recalled how 'I was completely astonished about Kádár. This was the first time that I couldn't swallow it [the official line].' István Kovács, though a member of the investigative committee, was similarly disturbed by the case. [33] In addition, Stalin may have had little enthusiasm for a trial that did not chime in with his increasing preoccupation with 'anti-Zionist' themes. Whatever the reasons, the Hungarian PB shelved any decision on the fate of Kádár and the other detainees for several months and declared the affair secret.

A number of defendants were sentenced at secret trials in the autumn, and on 30 November the CC voted to proceed with those still outstanding: Kádár, Donáth, Haraszti and Kállai. A perfunctory trial took place *in camera* at ÁVH headquarters on 18 December. The imprisoned writer György Paloczi-Horváth, called as a prosecution witness, recalled the occasion and Kádár's conduct:

> The others had been tortured just as much as Kádár. But their faces had gained somehow in dignity. Kádár's was frightening. He looked at me with a terrified stare. He knew that I had every reason to dislike him. He knew the methods of the SP [ÁVH] and was prepared for the worst. The others looked at me with encouraging eyes. One smiled. Some people trust human beings. Some do not. …
>
> Kádár's once handsome face had become more distorted. He had not been above it at all. His face had a cowardly, and at the same time, ferocious expression … The other three looked at me with friendly, approving eyes. In Kádár's gaze there was only misunderstanding and wonder.[34]

Paloczi-Horváth's account is dramatic, but may have been distorted by the bitter prism of post-1956 hindsight. That Kádár was both scared and embittered by the time of his trial is plausible; his subsequent conduct in prison testifies to his sense of grievance and injustice. He had sustained himself with the hope that he could demonstrate the absurdity of the charges against him; that hope had now run out. However, the picture of a cowardly Kádár amid serene fellow-defendants can be put down to poetic licence; for example, Haraszti, who had been impressively blasé during interrogation, was a deeply frightened man by the time of the trial.[35]

Kádár recalled that he upheld his confession in court, but kept his expressions of guilt to the minimum. 'As my final plea I stated – my lawyer will testify to this – that I had committed no other crime beyond deciding to dissolve the party, but that I wasn't a party enemy … I just found it psychologically impossible to … repent of my crimes and make a full confession.' His co-defendant Gyula Kállai had a rather different recollection of Kádár breaking down at the trial and promising to do whatever he could to make things right.[36]

The court handed down a death sentence for Haraszti (though this was never carried out), life for Kádár, fifteen years for both Donáth and Kállai. Péter – almost certainly indulging in special pleading – claimed later that he had changed a proposed death sentence on Kádár;[37] more probably, the leadership decided to avoid possible future embarrassment over the secret execution of such a senior figure. Kádár claimed that he was so disillusioned that he had been indifferent to the thought that 'Comrade Rajk's fate awaited me'; however, after the trial he realised that it would have been a terrible thing to die with his comrades believing him to have been a traitor.[38] The latter is certainly true, for in prison he began a campaign to clear his name.

In the months before his trial, Kádár had become convinced that Péter was the manipulator who had brought about his downfall. Once again, it came back to the details of the meeting with Szakasits: Péter insisted that he had known nothing of it, while Kádár claimed that he had arranged it. As he began serving his sentence in Conti Street, the prison in which he had been held in 1944, Kádár 'began the open struggle to expose Gábor Péter.' In February 1952, he wrote to Rákosi to explain how he had been taken in by Péter's manipulations. The letter had an obsessive quality, full of rhetorical questions and sections underlined for emphasis, mingled with moments of rather deranged exhilaration, the lone prisoner cackling in his cell at the truth that all those fools outside had missed but which he alone had discovered.

Kádár analysed in great detail the events leading up to the meeting with Szakasits, ('[this] was part of our conversation that it is <u>impossible</u> that Gábor Péter cannot remember'). In the examination of his case, 'an abnormal factor intervened, completely misleading the party leader and me, and which inevitably took the ÁVH investigation up a blind alley. ... And I know the reason too!' The 'abnormal factor' was Péter. Kádár urged Rákosi to question Péter, who had been led astray by his quarrels with Kádár, and appeal to his party loyalty. 'What matters, is not whether I live or die, <u>but that the truth is discovered</u>.'[39]

Before even reaching Rákosi, the letter went through the hands of Péter and Farkas, who remarked, 'A pity we didn't string the bastard up.'[40] Kádár claimed that his protests led Péter to punish him with harsher conditions, though some of his statements indicated that these pre-dated the letter, and possibly even his trial. In any case, the regime was severe. He was already held in solitary confinement, but now 'apart from the total, horrible isolation, it also meant that for a certain time they deprived me of drinking water. They wouldn't let me read or write, at night they would not let me sleep, and ... for days I wasn't allowed out to the toilet.'[41]

In his intense isolation, he gave ever-stronger signals of depression. His guards enjoyed inflicting petty humiliations on him, and in ÁVH folklore he was derisively remembered as 'János the Shit ... the most miserable prisoner we had.' He wrote to Rákosi at the time of his release, 'If I could choose my fate, I would always rather spend twelve years as a Communist in the jail of a capitalist country than spend twelve months in the jail of my own people's republic. Unfortunately, I had reason to compare them – the two are not the same, they defy comparison.'[42]

Then, at the start of 1953, came an apparent promise of change. On 3 January, Péter, Károlyi and other senior ÁVH figures were arrested in preparation for a 'Zionist' show trial that would keep Rákosi up with Stalin's increasingly anti-Semitic preoccupations. Shortly afterwards, Farkas and another senior figure in the security apparatus, László Piros, came to question Kádár. Their main concern was Péter, but Kádár's conditions were also discussed, and Farkas indicated that something would be done to alleviate them.[43]

For a while, Kádár gave way to the euphoria of vindication. If Péter had been brought down, his own case would surely be reviewed and the charges against him shown to be baseless. In the meantime, his prison conditions should improve. 'I sat and waited patiently.' And nothing happened. In May, he wrote to Piros, again appealing for his conditions to be improved. There was no reply. It was now, when his hopes had been raised and then dashed, that despair and anger against the party leadership overtook him. He was closer than ever to a complete breakdown. In protest, 'around 10 August … I smashed up everything that was in my cell.'[44]

Yet an event had already place of which he was initially unaware, an event of far greater significance than Péter's arrest. On 5 March, Stalin had died. For Kádár, as for millions of other prisoners across the Soviet bloc, the dictator's death would open the way to freedom.

6

THE APPARAT'S PIN-UP

Rákosi's fall from political grace began with meetings with the new Soviet leadership in the Kremlin on 13-16 June 1953. Stalin's successors, though riven by conflicting views and ambitions, were agreed on dismantling the most dangerous parts of his legacy. At the same time, they were terrified that the system might collapse around them, a fear given substance by severe unrest, markedly political in tone, which convulsed Czechoslovakia and East Germany. Rákosi's policies made Hungary a potential further flashpoint.

The result was a major policy change and the breakup of the quartet. Farkas and Révai were dropped from the PB, while Gerő moved to the Interior Ministry, losing his control of the economy. Most important, Rákosi had to give up the premiership – which he had assumed in 1952 – to Imre Nagy, to whom Moscow gave a clear mandate for change. As the minister responsible for the 1945 land reform, Nagy had more personal credit than any other senior Communist politician; he was not Jewish, a matter which preoccupied the Kremlin intensely[1]; and he had spent nearly fifteen years in Moscow, which suggested reliability. Yet the Soviet leadership did not have the full measure of him.

Fifty-seven years old in 1953, Nagy had been through many typical rites of passage of a party activist: conversion to Communism as a Russian prisoner in the First World War, arrest and surveillance under Horthy and a long spell in Moscow. He was knowledgeable on agricultural issues, and prepared to be unorthodox. Both in Moscow in 1930, and again in Hungary in the late forties, he was an advocate of land redistribution rather than rapid forced collectivisation. Plump, genial and avuncular, his provincial accent was a reminder of his roots in rural Somogy County.

Characteristically, days before the outbreak of the 1956 revolution he could be found at a country wine festival.

This was not – could not be – the whole story. In the Moscow of the purges, he had a shadowy existence as the NKVD's agent 'Volodya', apparently informing on other émigrés – though he was also briefly arrested.[2] And, while he rebelled twice over agricultural policy, twice also he accepted party discipline and recanted. After Nagy's second recantation, Rákosi took him back into government – implementing some of the policies which he had opposed – and even into the PB, where he sat through the horrors of the early fifties. There was a conflict within Nagy – between Communist loyalty and other ideals, whether of humanitarianism or of Hungarian national pride – that the Soviet leaders surely underestimated.

On 4 July, Nagy presented to Parliament a 'New Course' for the country: a shift in the economy towards consumer goods, freedom for peasants to leave collective farms, greater religious tolerance and a new respect for legality. Among the latter measures were the scrapping of the 'kulak lists' used to terrorise the wealthier peasants, and the closure of internment camps. Rákosi, however, remained the party's General Secretary, and soon made clear how little he accepted his demotion. 'A kulak is a kulak, with or without a list,' he told a party audience, to vigorous applause.[3] The resulting three-year power struggle would split the party.

This battle shaped both the circumstances of Kádár's release from prison, and the political world to which he returned. In the shifting sands of post-Stalinist politics, the leading figures – both in Budapest and in Moscow – struggled to find a secure footing, one that could somehow reconcile the pressures for change with stable party rule and with the views of much of the apparatus. In this period, Kádár made some revealing choices. He also demonstrated, for the first time, his distinctive and enduring political outlook and style.

Economic reform was the main priority of the Nagy government, but the new atmosphere made possible a review of Rákosi's abuses of power. Progress was painfully slow; the only effect that Kádár noticed in the second half of 1953 was a modest improvement in his prison conditions.[4] He attributed this to his furniture-breaking demonstration rather than to any wider developments, and it did little to draw him out of his depression. However, his fellow-prisoner Gyula Kállai secured a reopening of his case in late 1953; Rákosi was predictably unenthusiastic, but Gerő, now Interior Minister, knew that the Soviet leadership favoured some reviews, and with support from Nagy pressed ahead. By February the implications for other defendants, including Kádár, were recognised,[5] and on 24 March the PB authorised a full reexamination of the case.

With the launch of the review on 5 April, Kádár and his fellow-prisoners – now transferred to the ÁVH prison in Fő Street – experienced better conditions, working with members of a special Investigating Committee in well-lit rooms. However, some of them, Kádár included, feared that the exercise was a trap. He later made one of his droll stories out of Donáth's obstinate refusal to change his confession – 'whenever he had revoked a confession his fate had taken a turn for the worse'[6] – but his own attitude was not very different.

The charge that Kádár and his co-defendants were foreign agents was soon shown to be groundless. There was more dispute over incidents such as Kádár's police confession and the party dissolution; on this hung his ability to rejoin the party and resume a political career. It may have been a judgement by the leadership that it was safer to have Kádár inside the political machine that led the state prosecutor, Kálmán Czakó, to rule that these issues were essentially closed. In early July, Gerő summoned Mária from the toy factory to tell her that her husband's case was being reviewed. When she was called to Fő Street a few days later, Kádár, 'skeletal-thin', was brought to see her. He told her that he was likely to be released soon.[7]

However, he still had to deal with the past. On 20 July, clearly at his interrogators' request, he wrote an account of the Rajk affair. The toxicity of the issue for the leadership, and especially for Rákosi, prevented a full reappraisal, and Kádár went beyond any official line when he began, 'The Rajk case was not based on reality. It was based on provocation by imperialist spy networks, put into effect by Gábor Péter. László Rajk was a Communist.' However, in making Péter the scapegoat, he was playing safe: the former ÁVH chief had been sentenced to life imprisonment the previous January.

He also blamed the victim. Rajk was 'ideologically untutored … there were signs that chauvinist and Fascist theories had had an influence on his thinking.' He issued 'pernicious' orders, was arrogant and didactic, and 'anyone who was aware of these characteristics and wanted to take advantage of them could get anywhere they liked.'[8] In suggesting how easily someone could have been misled into believing that Rajk was a traitor, Kádár was providing an escape route not only for himself, but also for Rákosi.

The following day, on the eve of the rehearing of his trial, Kádár wrote to Rákosi. After all that had happened, he felt – or at least thought it advantageous to give this impression – that he was the one with explaining to do. He had not retracted his false confession at his trial because 'you'd take it for the actions of a sworn enemy, or at best a base, cowardly, shabby attempt to save my life. And I'd rather be hanged three times than have that happen.' He sought to excuse his own despair in prison, and claimed that, at least until his hopes were raised at the start of 1953, he had understood the leadership's motives in locking him up. 'In your places, I too would have dealt with all similar cases in the same way.'[9] It was all too clearly the letter of someone who wanted to be back at court.

The rehearing before the Supreme Court took place in Fő Street on 22 July.[10] Kádár took the stand first. After a review of the 1951 trial, the questioning took in the now familiar stations of his career. Kádár's responses were carefully measured, emphasising the psychological strain that he was under at the time of his arrest. 'It wasn't the trial itself and the court verdict that upset me, it was what the Party leaders seemed to think of me. That was why my arrest broke my spirit.' He expressed suitable remorse for his past failings, but insisted that 'I was not motivated by a desire to cause harm.' Asked if he had anything to add before the verdict was given, he said only, 'I await a fair verdict with trust in the court and with confidence.' That confidence was justified. He was legally and politically rehabilitated, and – along with the other defendants – set for immediate release.

A 'ravaged' Kádár leaves prison, July 1954

Then a threatened flood of the Danube caused a last-minute delay. Mária, expecting her husband home, put in a worried call to the ÁVH. Eventually, late at night, an officer drove Kádár to Mária's one room flat next to a pig farm in the suburbs. 'I said, I've just phoned Comrade Vladimir Farkas to find out what had happened to you. My husband said … – but no, that's unprintable.'[11]

The Kádár who spent the days after his release trailing round clothes and shoe shops with Mária was a traumatised and disorientated man. An extraordinarily expressive photograph was taken at the time of his release. His hair, which had already been receding, had now thinned dramatically; his face was lined and pinched; his posture defensively stiff and hunched. Those who saw him around this time spoke of a 'ravaged' man, whose very smile was bitter. Éva Bozóky, also recently released, was struck by the change. She found him 'quite primitive', telling her stories of trivial tricks pulled on his prison guards. 'I was sure I'd still give him breakfast if he was hungry, but I wouldn't know what to talk to him about.'[12]

His political drive had not lessened. His first question to Lájos Kelemen, the party official responsible for rehabilitated political prisoners, was, 'How is Comrade Rákosi?'[13] A few days later, he was called in to meet the leader. Rákosi enquired after Kádár's health, and asked why he had not written to him; he expressed indignation that Kádár's earlier letters had been kept back from him. 'And what would you like to do now, Comrade Kádár?' Kádár made a show of suggesting that he might return to being a worker, and Rákosi made a great display of how unthinkable this was. 'And then, I said, I had been a party worker, too.' Rákosi duly offered him the choice of two district secretary roles; Kádár accepted that for Budapest's 13th District, the Angyalföld, in which he had spent part of his childhood. This was a relatively junior post, but Rákosi indicated that in time he would be reinstated to something around his previous level of seniority.[14]

Kádár and Mária spent much of August quietly in a party holiday home by Lake Balaton, interrupted only by a visit from István Kovács; Kádár's self-confidence was boosted by his ability to beat Kovács comprehensively at chess. Soon after their return to Budapest, they moved to a three room flat in the 12th District. It was a big improvement on Mária's flat, which in any case had been in her name. 'I don't want to be my wife's tenant,' Kádár insisted.[15]

During Kádár's imprisonment, Mária had undergone major stomach surgery, and post-operative care had been inadequate.[16] She remained thin and frail, and in November was sent to a sanatorium to recover. Then, and during other periods of absence, she wrote constantly to her husband. He, somewhat less constantly but at rather greater length, wrote back to her.

Though the letters deal with personal, quotidian matters, such as furnishing their flat and the ups and downs of Mária's family, they are revealing of their personalities. Her letters are spiky, irritable, full of slightly old-fashioned slang and affectionate diminutives ('my little János', 'my little boy' and so on). His letters begin, more staidly, 'Dear Mária'; the language is less quirky, more 'official'; they give factual accounts – sometimes even numbered lists – of what has happened to him. Though occasionally leavened by a low-key irony, they have a certain reserve; in one, he describes the death of a friend after a painful illness, yet a sense of how he felt about this is understood rather than stated.

This reserve could cause difficulties. As Mária pointed out, 'we must tell each other more deeply about our problems, however small they may seem. Somehow we've lived in such a way that – out of pure discretion, or because we perhaps thought that the other person (you or me) could not understand – we never let the other know about our problems. I don't think that was good.' She added hopefully, 'I'm very glad that we have – both of us – improved a lot in this respect.'[17]

With Kádár busy and preoccupied, Mária fretted that he would not have time to write to her: 'Don't fail to reply ... You won't be horrible, will you?' In fact, he was a fairly diligent correspondent, sometimes writing late at night after a hectic day. Mária fussed about whether he was looking after himself, often with good cause; on one occasion, Kádár reported that, since he had not gone out to dinner with friends that week, 'I've already had three nights of cold dinners at home, or on Sunday, scrambled eggs.' Mária's sister-in-law Irén was deputed to keep an eye on his needs.[18]

The prosaic letters bespeak a calm contentment, the more deeply appreciated, perhaps, after recent traumas. Occasionally something more comes through. 'You know too how much I miss you,' Kádár wrote when they had been apart for just a couple of days. 'Without you my life cannot be complete, and I'm not thinking about hot or cold meals, but saying generally that I'm already sick of this so-called "independent" life.' And on another occasion: 'I really miss you. You see, we don't get bored with each other.'[19]

If there was one disappointment in their relationship – and this may have added to Kádár's melancholy – it was the realisation that they would be unable to have children. As Mária later mournfully expressed it, 'I'm afraid that I'm the one to blame.' Her health was fragile, and she was forty-two by the time that Kádár came out of prison. By then it may well have been too late. Kádár, Mária remembered, 'was very fond of children, and loved being in their company, when he had the time ... [He] would dearly have liked children, but he never reproached me for the fact that we had none.'[20]

In September, Kádár took up his post as 13th District Secretary. The star by which he set his course – utter loyalty to Rákosi – was apparent when he met the newly released Béla Szász in Kútvölgyi hospital, which both were attending for physical rehabilitation. Kádár, 'huddled in his hospital gown', eagerly told Szász about his arrest – for which he blamed Péter – and about his release – for which he gave the credit to 'Comrade Rákosi', about whom he spoke 'with deep gratitude'. A bemused Szász reflected,

"Was János Kádár the only man in Hungary ignorant of the fact that 'Comrade Stalin's best Hungarian disciple' had been the Budapest director, the puppet-master, of not only the Rajk affair but of all the important show-trials? ... Why was Kádár play-acting for my sake?' Szász concluded that Kádár was working his passage back into the party's inner circles – at whatever price. The 'play-acting' carried over into private discussions. When a friend from the underground, the actor Tamás Major attacked Rákosi's treatment of intellectuals, Kádár defended him, saying that in the later forties he and others had looked up to him like a father. 'Yes,' said Major, 'and sometimes you want to kick your own father in the balls.'[21]

Mid-October saw a standoff between Nagy and Rákosi, with an apparent victory for the Prime Minister. Rákosi departed for an extended visit to the Soviet Union, purportedly for his health. Kádár wrote to him on 11 November, casting himself in the (unsolicited) role of supportive adviser. While paying lip service to the 'New Course', he suggested that its implementation was undermining the leadership's authority. 'People have got to understand that it should not be the government directing the party central leadership, but the other way round.' In other words, Rákosi, not Nagy, should be in charge. The letter also showed Kádár's sense of grievance against the Farkases: he proposed that the father should be investigated and the son dismissed for past abuses.[22]

Why did Kádár support Rákosi rather than Nagy? Ambition and opportunism provide a partial but not full explanation; if anything, it was Nagy who seemed to have the upper hand (and thereby won some surprising allies, such as Mihály Farkas). Kádár's commitment to Rákosi was partly institutional; at various points in his career, he was to show distrust, even horror, at any weakening of the party's leadership structure. Perhaps more important was a psychological dependence that went back to their imprisonment in Csillag. '[Kádár] was impressed that, as he put it, Rákosi was the real revolutionary type, and he could not break free of him. ... the person who knew how to act, and how to strike with all his force when it was needed, was Rákosi, and this revolutionary quality impressed Kádár enormously.' Fear mingled with admiration: to back Rákosi against Nagy was an asymmetric bet, for Rákosi's revenge on his opponents, should he triumph, would surely be more terrible. With his prison experiences fresh in his mind, Kádár was still deeply frightened. According to György Aczél, even in 1955 Kádár was nervous about their conversations being bugged.[23]

By contrast, a Kádár-Nagy meeting in December 1954 was organised by mutual friends and supporters 'with a great deal of pain and sorrow' because of both men's prickly insistence on matters of protocol – neither wished to be seen to take the initiative. Nagy opened up about the opposition he faced from within the party, but Kádár did not respond and thereafter restricted any contact to purely official channels. Nagy, however, still saw him as a potential ally.[24]

Rákosi returned from the Soviet Union in early December. He had news: the Soviet leadership was turning against experiments. Prime Minister Georgi Malenkov, proponent of reform and Nagy's patron, was under pressure (he resigned in February 1955), while power shifted to the head of the party apparatus, Nikita Khrushchev. At another Kremlin meeting in January 1955, it was Nagy who was berated for his policy failings: divisions within the party, increasingly outspoken writers, falls in industrial investment and mass departures of peasants from collective farms. He was instructed to correct his errors, but by the end of the month had suffered a mild heart attack. On 14 April, Nagy was dismissed from the premiership, and a triumphant Rákosi awarded the post to a 32-year-old protégé, András Hegedüs.

Kádár, it seemed, had backed the right horse. Yet at this point, his stance changed, and he started to sound a more independent – and, as time went on, even critical – note.

The proximate cause is not hard to find. On 14 May, Rákosi told him that he would become party secretary for Pest County, the area surrounding (but not including) Budapest. This was a promotion, and gave Kádár the right to attend CC meetings, though not to vote. However, he interpreted it – correctly – as an attempt to sideline him. He may also have known that at the beginning of March Nagy had, by contrast, proposed him for PB membership. He wrote indignantly to Rákosi and the PB, expressing his discontent with the Pest County role. '… I need to know the Politburo's opinion of me: am I needed as a party worker, yes or no? If yes, then I ask that this affair of mine be resolved in a suitable way.' However, Rákosi was immovable, and Kádár went to Pest County. [25]

There were other reasons for Kádár to reassess his stolid loyalism. Nagy's policies, and the stories that began to seep out with the release of political prisoners, had a profound impact within the party, especially among journalists and intellectuals. An internal opposition started to emerge in late 1954; Nagy's subsequent dismissal and his refusal to exercise self-criticism made him a rallying-point. Some critics, such as Donáth and Losonczy, had been victims of the terror. Others, such as the journalists Miklós Vásárhelyi and Miklós Gimes, were exorcising bad consciences at having been Rákosi's cheerleaders. Doubts about Rákosi were also growing among Kádár's natural constituency in the middle-ranking party functionaries. Some – such as Imre Mező, the Budapest party secretary and a friend of Kádár – were sympathetic to Nagy; others sought a compromise position.

Kádár had initially missed this shift in opinion. His public statements as 13th District Secretary were uninspiring. Shortly after his release, a sympathetic editor, Henrik Vass, had commissioned an article but had been disappointed with the draft. 'It did not contain anything that differed from the general thinking of the time.' Kádár took offence at Vass's proposed amendments, and the incident left their relations permanently uneasy. Similarly, his support for Rákosi led to a major row with Aczél, himself a purge victim, after which the two men did not speak for months. Both incidents may, however, have awakened him to the realisation that he risked dissipating a major political asset: the moral capital of a man who had suffered under Stalinism.[26]

In spite of Kádár's hesitations, people kept coming to him. 'At that time old acquaintances often sought me out, but people also came who'd never met me before. These people were in despair, and held the leadership responsible for the overblown industrialisation.'[27] While Rákosi had failed to bind him in, the change of mood within sections of the party was becoming ever clearer. With this, he started to shift his public position – and, quite probably, began to rewrite his own mental history, and to reassess the significance of his imprisonment.

He was also beginning to recover from the physical and psychological damage done by his incarceration. As early as January 1955, Sándor Kopácsi noted that, 'Despite his suffering in prison, [Kádár] radiated strength.'[28] By the second half of the year, he was taking a more confident and distinctive – if still circumspect and calculated – stance. It helped that Rákosi's restoration was less complete than had first appeared. Easing superpower relations worked against a renewed mania for 'vigilance'. Visiting Belgrade in May, Khrushchev renounced the anti-Tito campaign. Since Rajk had been executed as a Titoist, demands grew for his case to be reopened; the most explosive time bomb under Rákosi was starting to tick loudly.

A second meeting between Kádár and Nagy was much more successful than the first. Nagy felt that while he and Kádár did not agree on all issues, 'on fundamental questions they took the same view.' Later in the year, Nagy started circulating to selected party figures essays in which he both defended his record and set out increasingly radical thoughts, notably regarding Hungary's national independence. Kádár was one of the first to see the drafts. Other oppositionists also asked his opinion: the writer and dramatist Gyula Háy consulted Kádár about his play, *The Justice of Gáspár Varró*, a critical examination of collectivisation – 'he made good suggestions about it' – and about his satire on party bureaucrats, *Why don't I like Comrade Kucsera?*[29]

Both the appeal and the limitations of Kádár's new stance were clear from a talk that he gave to students – among them Imre Pozsgay, who was to play a significant role in the later Kádár era – at the Lenin Institute in Budapest in late 1955. Kádár seemed open-minded and spoke in an appealingly natural, jargon-free style; he asked the students to help him in cleaning up the party's 'serious mistakes'. Yet there were still taboos. One of the students asked what should be done about Rákosi and the other senior leaders. 'At that moment he clammed up and returned to the official party phraseology.' Even so, the meeting left a very positive impression on Pozsgay.[30]

Similarly, he was cautiously supportive of the 'writers' memorandum' protesting at official censorship, but took great care not to commit himself publicly. 'Kádár very much approved of the idea ... [but said that] there was no need for party members to sign – so this eliminated the functionaries, which included him – but rather those who were involved in that area.'[31] When the memorandum – signed by sixty writers on 18 October – produced a fierce counterblast from the leadership, he was quick to advocate that the signatures be withdrawn. 'Kádár explained that the clever boxer, fighting a stronger opponent, did not strive to exchange blows, but rather must divert his opponent's blows and so tire him out.' However, when his exasperated former admirer Jenő Széll insisted that the signatures would stay, Kádár accepted it 'and gave a couple of bits of smart advice.'[32]

In fact, most of the writers – under intense pressure – did cave in. Those who did not suffered intimidation and sanctions, though not the arrests that would have been routine a few years before. The memorandum gave Rákosi a pretext for another blow to his opponents. In November, he secured Nagy's expulsion from the party.

However, in early 1956, Moscow once more destabilised Rákosi's uneasy ascendancy with Khrushchev's powerful if selective denunciation of Stalin's crimes at the Soviet Party's Twentieth Congress on 25 February. Rákosi gamely insisted that the 'Secret' Speech had no implications for Hungary, since the country had already been a pioneer in correcting abuses. Kádár saw this as profoundly unrealistic; it may have been at this point that he started to lose faith in Rákosi.[33] With one speech at the CC meeting of 12-13 March, he staked out his own position and achieved a dramatic change in his political standing.

He acknowledged that 'right-wing deviationism' – Rákosi's favourite target – was undesirable, but opposed making Nagy and his associates scapegoats; he recalled a teacher who had asked at a party meeting, 'Where were the other members of the Central Committee, when Imre Nagy was doing all this for the last eighteen months?' The party, he warned, was contradicting itself and failing to give a lead. 'Our party can't allow itself the luxury that, in June 1953, it said once that these were mistakes, and after that we said so and so, and then something else, and then something else again. We don't have that luxury, comrades.'

He served notice that the days of blind obedience to Rákosi were over. He had never, he said, slept so well as in the days when he had simply to divine the wishes of Rákosi and the 'quartet' and then carry them out. 'That was a blessed condition to be in, comrades,' but 'blind belief and blind faith are not healthy features of party life.' He urged again that Mihály Farkas – who had fallen with Nagy and was now in Soviet exile – be called to account. It was wrong, Kádár said, that Farkas was still a member of the CC, wrong that he had to shake his bloodstained hands. 'I have to say, comrades, after what has happened, that there are corpses that lie between Mihály Farkas and me, the corpses of innocent condemned Communists.'[34]

By the end, according to Rákosi, Kádár was in an emotional state, 'beside himself and shouting'.[35] The attack on Farkas combined personal score-settling, displacement of some of his own guilt and the search for another scapegoat to supplement Péter. But to many of the listening committee members, Kádár had made himself a spokesman for those who had lost faith in Rákosi but distrusted the radicalism of Nagy and his supporters. His prison sufferings gave him the aura of the party's better conscience. And now he had said – pungently and with tremendous effect – what many were already thinking. For perhaps the first time, he was seen as a possible party leader.

Kádár was not seeking to supplant Rákosi immediately, but rather to force his way back into the PB and to be the driving force of a new policy. Rákosi – who, he believed, still commanded prestige among the party's simpler souls – would continue as a figurehead. When Jenő Széll told him that he had the power to destroy Rákosi over the Rajk affair, and that Rákosi was already tottering, Kádár replied, 'Yes, that's exactly the problem, because the proles cling to Rákosi. To the proles, Rákosi's a saint … What we've all got to do, who are still on the pitch, is to play football as though Rákosi were unchanged as team captain.'[36]

However shrewd Kádár's manoeuvering within the party, this showed an alarming blind spot about wider Hungarian opinion. For the dictator was on the run. At a meeting in the 13th District on 23 March, a young schoolteacher, György Litván, told him to his face that he had lost public confidence. Four days later, speaking in the provincial town of Eger, Rákosi admitted that 'the Rajk trial was based on provocation.' He tried to blame Péter, but within six weeks he had to accept at least some responsibility. A performance of Shakespeare's *Richard the Third* drew strong audience responses to anything that could be taken to refer to Rákosi. Even efforts to control the situation backfired. A discussion group, the Petőfi Circle, had been set up under the auspices of the party youth wing, in an attempt to keep debate within official bounds. Instead, it hosted ever bigger and more radical debates, attended by hundreds and then thousands.

Rákosi fought back, and Kádár was among his targets. The CC had set up a committee, chaired by Kovács, to investigate Farkas' role, and this provided the arena for the Rákosi-Kádár struggle. In a memorandum submitted to the committee on 3 April, Kádár offered a qualified defence of Rákosi: he had been deceived by Farkas and Péter, and 'every sensible person knows that there is a difference between responsibility and responsibility' Rákosi, however, had no interest in such lukewarm support. On 18 April, he told the Soviet Ambassador, Yuri Andropov, that the committee's investigation had discovered the tape recording of Rajk's interrogation, adding with some relish that this would undercut Kádár's role as an opposition hero.[37]

Reportedly, Rákosi played the tape at a meeting to discredit Kádár – only to be himself discredited when a replay of the tape, or the playing of an uncut version, revealed Kádár's previously omitted opening words: 'I come on behalf of Comrade Rákosi.'[38] Whether or not this dramatic confrontation took place, at least some members of the leadership heard the tape played, and Rákosi clearly tried to exaggerate Kádár's role and to excise his own. Kádár was apparently warned about Rákosi's manoeuvre, probably by the sympathetic Budapest police chief, Sándor Kopácsi, and was able to head it off.[39]

Kádár defended himself before the committee on 23 April, insisting that he had believed in Rajk's guilt, but that Farkas had taken the lead role in the interrogation.[40] The PB, meeting three days later, came to an ambiguous resolution: if Kádár made a self-critical statement before the CC, he could be admitted as a full member of the Committee and of the Secretariat 'and perhaps as a member of the Politburo'. This reflected deadlock at the top. Gerő and Kovács wanted to broaden the leadership's base, and feared that the CC would otherwise force Kádár on them. Rákosi, however, warned that, if elected, Kádár – 'a strong personality and a good organiser' – would overshadow his younger colleagues and emerge as Second Secretary. [41]

Initially, Rákosi and his supporters' briefing of Andropov against Kádár had some effect; on 6 May, Andropov told Rákosi that Moscow shared his unease about the prospective return to the Politburo of Révai (who was also taking a more critical stance) 'and especially Kádár'.[42] A few weeks later, however, Kádár calmed Moscow's concerns when he met a visiting Soviet CC Secretary, Mikhail Suslov, who concluded that he was not anti-Soviet and that his elevation to the PB was acceptable. He continued to play a careful hand: he did not attend Imre Nagy's birthday celebrations on 6 June, on the basis that they were 'a demonstration counter to party unity', but he sent Nagy a letter of congratulation.[43]

Rákosi seized back the initiative when a growing political crisis in Poland erupted with the bloody suppression of workers' demonstrations in Poznán on 27 June. Amid a more defensive mood, Rákosi guided through the CC a resolution all but closing down the Petőfi Circle; unconfirmed rumours spoke of him drawing up a list of four hundred people to be arrested. But then, on 10 July, the Rajk affair at last caught up with him. Péter told Kovács that it was not Farkas, but Rákosi, who had been behind the Rajk case. What – or who – prompted Péter's statement is unclear, but he had provided the smoking gun. In Andropov's understated phrase, 'If this becomes known at the next CC meeting, Comrade Rákosi will be in serious difficulties.'[44]

Khrushchev's associate Anastas Mikoyan was dispatched to try to sustain Rákosi, but rapidly concluded that the leader's position was beyond salvage.[45] At a shell-shocked meeting of the inner circle on 13 July, neither Hegedüs nor Gerő would accept the proffered leadership. Rákosi remarked that, if the issue went to the CC, 'Comrade Kádár's nomination could not be avoided,' while Gerő even suggested that 'in current circumstances' this might be a good thing. Hegedüs, however, remained fiercely opposed to Kádár.[46]

Thus, Kádár was clearly *papabile*. Mikoyan visited him the next day to sound out his views and to question him about his past record. Kádár was outspoken about Rákosi and Gerő's failure to sustain the reforming momentum of the March CC, and said that, whatever Nagy's shortcomings, it had been a mistake to expel him. He raised a laugh from his visitor by teasing him about past Soviet misjudgements: 'Many people here say that the Soviet comrades are always interfering in Hungarian affairs, and it always turns out badly. Why not interfere in this situation now, it might just turn out well.'[47] Mikoyan, however, did not 'interfere'; the decision seems largely to have been left to the Hungarians. The leadership recovered its nerve, and opted for an all too well-known quantity: Ernő Gerő.

Rákosi resigned at the start of the CC meeting of 18-20 July. A few days later – after a rather uneasy farewell dinner, at which he sat next to one of his victims (Kádár) and opposite another (the former Social Democrat György Marosán) – he was flown to the Soviet Union. Budaörs military airfield was his last farewell to the country that he had abused and terrorised for a decade.[48] Gerő was elected First Secretary with no outright opposition; Kádár and Marosán joined the PB; Mihály Farkas was expelled from the party.

Kádár's address to the CC included a self-critical account of the Rajk affair; nonetheless, he was appointed Second Secretary. It was just two years since he had left prison. Without a strong steer from the leadership, he might have gone further still. As one of the leaders, Béla Vég, put it, 'The hearts and minds of the CC were for electing Kádár. Everyone knew that Gerő wasn't the solution.'[49]

If, as de Tocqueville famously suggested, the most dangerous time for a bad government is when it tries to improve, the Hungarian Communist leadership had cause to worry in the late summer and autumn of 1956. Despite proclaiming a 'clean slate', Gerő was an unconvincing reformer, while concessions were made at a grudging, half-hearted pace that reflected the leadership's divisions and which ensured that it stayed several steps behind public opinion. Fear of the authorities had all but evaporated, the economy was sliding and the changes made only whetted the appetite for more.

Kádár favoured more and faster concessions than did the majority of the PB, urging a conciliatory line on the readmission of Nagy to the party and a restoration of membership for writers who had been expelled for supporting him. Some of his colleagues, he charged, were already watering down the policies agreed in July. Whatever the initial motives for the moderate reformism that he had adopted in 1955, it had now become a settled conviction. He urged further changes to the ÁVH and an effort to broaden the regime's base, building 'alliances' that would maintain party control while co-opting some social groups and prominent individuals. He wanted a more flexible system, but one whose essential pillars would remain unchanged. This would be the lasting core of what would become 'Kádárism'.[50]

At its root was a highly paternalistic view of politics, rather like that of an eighteenth century aristocratic British politician to opinion 'out of doors'. 'They [ordinary workers and peasants] have a basic, fundamental requirement,' he had told the CC in March. 'Clear and intelligent leadership in the economic development sphere, and in the political sphere as well.' He took a similarly limited view of the role of the intelligentsia: approached on one occasion to approve a film script, he 'spoke very ironically about writers, saying that writers thought that they brought about change just as the rooster thought that he brought about the dawn.'[51] Events would shortly force him to revise this view.

Gerő and Kádár had a modest success in coming to terms with Nagy. Meeting him on 1 September, they swapped – presumably for effect – their expected roles: Gerő was low-key and conciliatory, Kádár more aggressive.[52] Nagy would not undertake the full self-criticism that the leadership wanted, but on 4 October he wrote asking to be readmitted to the party; nine days later, this was granted. However, this merely deferred the question of his future role.

Meanwhile, the stately rhythms of party life continued. In early September, Gerő left the country for his regular month-long holiday in the Soviet Union; Kádár also spent much of the month out of the country, first in Moscow, then attending the Congress of the Chinese Communist Party. He sent letters back to Mária, enthusiastically relating the new world of travel, sightseeing and novelties such as Chinese food that was now, in early middle age, opening up to him.[53] A Gerő-Tito meeting in the Crimea, engineered by the Soviets, yielded two major initiatives for October: the ceremonial reburial of László Rajk and his fellow victims and the visit of a top-level Hungarian delegation to Yugoslavia.

The reburial took place on the richly symbolic date of 6 October, the anniversary of the 1849 execution of thirteen Hungarian generals who had supported the anti-Habsburg revolutionary regime. If Rajk had brought ruin to Rákosi from the grave, his interment in Budapest's Kerepesi cemetery did the same to Gerő. Amid drizzle and strong winds, and with a 'nightmarish tension' between the representatives of the regime and those of the victims, tens of thousands filed past the coffins.[54] Gerő and Kádár found reason to be in Moscow, but a devastating blow had been dealt to the party's moral authority.

In spite of the growing tensions, on 12 October the most senior leaders – including Gerő, Kádár and Hegedüs – set off for Yugoslavia. Back in the summer the Yugoslavs had preferred Kádár, Rákosi's victim, to Gerő as party leader: Tito now made a point of treating him as a particularly honoured guest. The substantial business of the Hungarian-Yugoslav talks was done by 16 October. Yet, as though reluctant to confront the realities at home, the leaders continued a series of protocol visits for another week; Khrushchev later called it 'an extended swimming holiday on the Adriatic'. Kádár visited Rijeka, the city that he knew to be his birthplace, but of which he had no memories. His interpreter, Zelmanović, remembered him gazing long and impassively out to sea.[55]

It was a bad time for journeys, sentimental or otherwise. In Hungary, independent student groups, more radical than the essentially loyalist Petőfi Circle, were mushrooming. Poland provided a further spark, with the election on 21 October of a new First Secretary, Władysław Gomułka, seen as a reformer and a nationalist. Khrushchev tried to stop it by browbeating the Poles – but then gave way. The implications could scarcely have been clearer. On the night of 22 October, a mass meeting at the Technical University of Budapest put forward the most sweeping programme yet, calling for free elections, a free press and the withdrawal of Soviet troops. With the radio refusing to broadcast their programme, they called a march for the following day in solidarity with the Poles and to press their demands. Another march, from the University of Budapest, was to meet them at the statue of General Bem, a Pole who had fought for Hungarian freedom in 1849.

What followed – the 'thirteen days that shook the Kremlin' – was to be the central episode in Kádár's career. In those days, under conditions of unrelenting pressure, he – along with many others – would face questions of defining, almost existential sharpness: Who are you? What do you believe? Which side are you on? The crisis would bring him to power, but in circumstances that would leave him, in the words of one Hungarian commentator, carrying 'the mark of Cain'.[56]

7

OUR GLORIOUS UPRISING

Tuesday, 23 October

Gerő, Kádár and their colleagues arrived at Budapest's western railway station at around 9:00 a.m. They went immediately to an emergency meeting at party headquarters in Akadémia Street, at which they agreed that the student demonstration should be banned.[1] At around the same time, Nagy met friends and advisers at Losonczy's home. Anticipating – correctly – that the leadership might call for Nagy's help, they agreed that he should return to the premiership only if there were major changes in the party leadership. One was that Kádár should become First Secretary.[2]

Neither meeting bore a realistic relationship to the events that were gathering pace in the streets. Leaders of the Petőfi Circle, alarmed by what they had helped to initiate, suggested that Kádár, as the leadership's most acceptable face, should address the students in Bem Square. However, he gave them no encouragement, remarking that it was impossible to know how the demonstration would turn out, and was equally dismissive of attempts by the Budapest party secretary, Imre Mező, to get him involved.[3]

Others tried to break through the leadership's incomprehension, among them journalists from *Szabad Nép*. Their pleas for concessions encountered a blank insistence that, if the demonstration went ahead, troops would open fire. Révai was particularly strident, shouting repeatedly, 'We would fire! We would fire!' Kádár was quiet for much of the meeting, but when he appealed to 'the interests of the party', the journalist Pál Lőcsei hit back with a reference to the discrediting of that argument by the Rajk affair – and to Kádár's role in it. 'Kádár, troubled, replied that things were not as simple as his interrogator believed.'[4]

The Interior Ministry's ban on demonstrations was announced over the radio at 12:53 p.m. By then, Kádár, like a number of the other party leaders, had left the headquarters to rally support, taking in the state radio station, Radio Kossuth – where he encountered more hostility to the PB's stance – and the headquarters of SZOT, the official trade union body. In his absence, the Budapest police chief, Sándor Kopácsi, told the leadership that his officers lacked the means (and probably the will) to enforce the ban.[5] At 2:23 p.m., with the students already gathering defiantly, it was formally rescinded.

Even as the marches started – one on either side of the Danube – at around 3 p.m., industrial workers joined the students; at the end of the working day, these numbers grew rapidly. Tens of thousands gathered in Bem Square, and the crowds grew still more as they surged back over the Margit Bridge to Pest. More radical, often anti-Russian slogans were heard; more and more national flags were carried with the red star and Soviet insignia cut out; some two hundred thousand demonstrators congregated in Lajos Kossuth Square outside Parliament, with others setting off for the radio building. Kádár, called back from SZOT for an emergency PB meeting, had to struggle his way through the crowds; he was not back in party headquarters, just a few hundred yards from Kossuth Square, until 7:00 p.m.[6]

With demonstrators' chants for his resignation audible from outside, Gerő ran the PB through the speech that he had prepared for broadcast at 8:00 p.m. Remarkably, the party leaders thought it suitable. Gerő's abrasive style and his condemnation of 'a demonstration of nationalist character' overshadowed his vague hints of concessions, and helped turn a demonstration into a revolution.[7]

Events now spiralled out of the leadership's control. In the City Park, a vast statue of Stalin was toppled; meanwhile shooting broke out at the radio station, resulting in the first deaths among the insurgents. Army units were sent in but went over to the demonstrators' side; within a few hours the building was stormed, as were the offices of *Szabad Nép*. At around 9:00 p.m. Nagy arrived at Parliament, having yielded reluctantly to pleas to address the crowd from a balcony. He was characteristically ill at ease in speaking without a clear mandate from the party; his opening word, 'Comrades,' was met with boos and shouts of protest. Nagy speedily corrected his greeting to, 'Fellow citizens.'[8] After a brief and uninspiring speech, he left for Akadémia Street.

Nagy joined a leadership meeting huddled in Gerő's office while the First Secretary spoke on the phone to the Soviet leadership. At the end of the call, Gerő announced that some of the Soviet troops stationed in the country had been called in to Budapest. His colleagues – including Nagy, who was slumped, tired and bemused, in an armchair – greeted the news in silence. Some then muttered their assent.[9]

Strikingly, Kádár barely features in accounts of the first couple of days of the revolution. Like most other leading figures, including Nagy, he seems to have been numbed by the scale of what had happened. At this point – and again Nagy's view was not very different – he took as axiomatic that a direct challenge to 'the people's power' was taking place, and that this required a military response. Yet he lacked the enthusiasm of some of his colleagues for a vigorously coercive line.

A rancorous meeting of the CC – such members as could be assembled – lasted from around midnight until dawn. Gerő sought political cover for the repression of the revolution, proposing Nagy as Prime Minister. There were calls for Gerő's resignation, and Nagy tried to insist on his replacement by Kádár. But Kádár supported Gerő, urging Nagy to 'rise above personal debates' in the party's hour of crisis and claiming, rather implausibly, to lack the experience for the job. At the start of the crisis, he had shown himself unwilling to venture outside orthodox party roles and procedures; now he may have calculated that to take the top job amid such chaotic conditions, with uncertain CC support and without Soviet approval, would be acceptance of a poisoned chalice.[10]

Nagy gave way, and his supporters' plan for a quick overthrow of the existing leadership failed. It is at least arguable that a Nagy-Kádár leadership might have been able to regain the initiative and the party's control of events, as Gomułka did in Poland. But the Hungarian party did not take that path. Though some of his supporters were offered senior posts, Nagy took on the premiership with Hegedüs as his deputy and Gerő still in place. A Military Committee, with a Stalinist-leaning majority, was established to co-ordinate the fight against the insurgents. The CC also voted to proclaim a curfew and martial law.

Wednesday, 24 October

Kádár, like the other senior leaders, had no time to sleep during the night of 23-24 October. That set the pattern for the next few days: no sleep, a constant flow of meetings, no chance to leave party headquarters. Mária, always able to bring the prosaic into the most dramatic historical moments, recalled that during these days, 'from time to time I had a phone call asking me to send clean underwear.'[11]

The first Soviet tanks arrived in the city at around 2:00 a.m. At 8:45 a.m. – half an hour after the official announcement of Nagy's appointment – state radio, now broadcasting from Parliament, announced martial law. Soviet forces soon commanded the main centres in the city, and there was no sign of the previous day's crowds. The leaders in Akadémia Street were no longer besieged.

However, the Soviet intervention (Operation Wave) employed around six thousand troops — enough only for a show of strength. Wave had also assumed support from the Hungarian Army, which was proving unreliable. This eviscerated another source of support: the leadership wanted to mobilise party militants, but did not dare distribute weapons for fear that the army would instead hand them to the rebels. Thus, the authorities' real control was limited, and small but very effective gangs of fighters were formed, especially in Corvin Passage and other narrow streets nearby in the heart of Pest. Meanwhile, insurgents' calls for a general strike met with a rapid response, and the first factory workers' councils were set up.

Nonetheless, Wave produced an illusion of success, one that lasted for perhaps a day. Mikoyan and Suslov, soft and hard cops who arrived from Moscow at party headquarters in the early afternoon, cross-questioned the Hungarian leaders and concluded that Gerő in particular had grossly exaggerated the opposition's strength. By some accounts, they were from the first fiercely critical of Gerő's blundering; whether or not they had yet decided to replace him, he was not heard on the radio again.[12]

Instead, at 8:45 p.m. it was Kádár who spoke on the radio. He had already been taking a more active role, sending out a message to County party secretaries that 'the liquidation of the attempted putsch is progressing rapidly' and asking them to drum up support.[13] His radio address was along similar lines. Although conceding that the demonstrators had valid grievances, he spoke 'with burning anger' of the 'counter-revolutionary, reactionary elements' who had launched armed attacks. They must 'capitulate or be crushed', not least by the Soviet 'allies and brothers'. He nonetheless indicated that, the next day, once the fighting had stopped, the leadership would make a fresh start.[14] After this less than inspiring performance, though one which reflected the belief in Akadémia Street that the crisis was all but over, he joined a PB meeting attended by Mikoyan and Suslov.

Thursday, 25 October

With an appeal to return to work, the authorities effectively lifted the curfew. The misjudgement soon became apparent. There was a surge of people onto the streets, and a fresh student demonstration demanding Gerő's resignation. Encountering Soviet tanks, some demonstrators spoke to the soldiers in Russian, and persuaded them to accompany them to Parliament. By 11:00 a.m., while Mikoyan, Suslov and the Hungarian leadership gathered in Gerő's office, Kossuth Square was packed with thousands of demonstrators, some of them sitting on Soviet tanks draped with Hungarian flags.

At around 11:15 a.m., shooting broke out in the square – perhaps started by newly-arriving Soviet tanks, perhaps by border control units stationed on the roofs of government buildings.[15] In the confusion some Soviet tanks fired in the direction of party headquarters. Plaster fell from the ceiling of Gerő's office as a tank round hit the windows, 'creating panic among the leading Hungarian party functionaries.' After a brief adjournment to a cellar, the shaken leaders returned upstairs.[16] They could not yet know that a hundred people, mostly civilians, had died in the shooting. However, Gerő's position – which was probably in question even before the massacre – was now untenable. Whether on the urging of Mikoyan and Suslov, or of the other Hungarian leaders, he had to stand aside for Kádár. The change was announced on the radio shortly after 12:30 p.m.[17]

Three hours later, Kádár made another radio broadcast. He repeated many of his arguments of the previous evening: the demonstrators had worthy motives, but were hijacked by 'enemies of the people [and] counter-revolutionary forces'. Nonetheless, he promised an (unspecified) deepening of democracy 'in our party, state and social life' and that, once order was restored, the government would negotiate outstanding issues with the Soviet Union 'in the spirit of complete equality'.[18] Speaking just before him, Nagy had gone further, referring to the withdrawal of Soviet troops from the country.

Nagy's announcement reflected the sombre and shaken mood of the leadership. Accounts of the flying of black flags and bloodstained banners brought home the damage that the killings in Kossuth Square had done to the party's standing. Its grip on provincial towns was slipping, with demonstrations taking place and revolutionary committees being established. Acknowledging their weakened position, the party leaders, including even Gerő, recognised that some further concession was required, even if some of them might have hoped to claw it back later.[19]

In an evening dominated by the visits of delegations urging their views on the government, Kádár tried to hold the party together. He called in Donáth and Losonczy, allies of Nagy but critical of his accommodation with Gerő, who were refusing an offer of senior posts. They had taken some heart from Kádár's appointment, and he urged them to reconsider: they could, he insisted, argue their case within the CC. He was not wholly successful, but at least gave them the impression that there was still something to discuss.[20]

Friday, 26 October

The tortuous struggle to find a united party position was resumed at an early morning meeting of the PB, which gave Donáth his chance to press for a purely political solution. The PB appears to have accepted this; its meeting ran directly into the next gathering of the CC, at which Kádár – who seemed rather uncertain in his new role – cautiously put forward a new formulation.[21] He emphasised that 'sectarian mistakes' were the main cause of the crisis, and that 'we must not try to solve this question by military measures.' A government of national unity and concessions to working class demands – including recognition of the burgeoning workers' councils – were the way out. Foreshadowing his most famous later political concept, he emphasised that 'we want to bring together all forces that believe in the people's democratic system and the construction of socialism, indeed in some cases those who don't struggle against it.'

In speaking of the need to 'isolate the counter-revolutionaries from their mass base', Kádár was still some distance from radicals such as Donáth and Losonczy. Nonetheless, he was striking a different note from the party's authoritarians. While not totally excluding the use of force, he was deeply uneasy at its political cost. The behaviour of the trade unions gave him particular pause: that morning SZOT's newspaper, *Népszava*, had called for a political resolution. As he explained later to Mikoyan and Suslov, 'Unfortunately ... the masses are beyond our control. The party's prestige has sunk dramatically, particularly because of past mistakes.'[22] He wanted to widen the leadership's appeal by bringing some non-party personalities into the government – much the line that he had been pushing in calmer, pre-revolutionary days.

If Kádár hoped to unite the CC, he was quickly disappointed. Losonczy and Donáth pressed their most radical case and met with fierce, sometimes abusive, hostility from the hard men of the Military Committee and their allies. The most visceral response came from István Kovács: 'Comrades, this decision is treason against the party and the working class. Let them [the insurgents] destroy us, but I will not vote for them ...' Seeing the trend of the meeting, Kádár quickly backtracked. 'We, the Central Committee, have to say that we can go so far. This far and no further.' Nagy protested at the dominance of the authoritarians, but was outnumbered.[23]

The final resolution was an incoherent compromise. Though offering some concessions, including approving the workers' councils, the party insisted that order must be restored before reforms could be undertaken – under its leadership. An Extraordinary Committee of seven, set up to coordinate the reassertion of control included both Nagy and Kádár, but was tilted towards the advocates of a tougher line.

If relations within the Hungarian leadership were becoming frayed, so were those with Mikoyan and Suslov, who were furious at Nagy's mention of the withdrawal of Soviet troops – 'a crucial issue in relations between our countries.' Although Nagy and Kádár promised to water down the pledge, the envoys' suspicions of the Prime Minister were growing; they wrote critically to Moscow of his 'vacillations' and 'opportunistic personality'.[24] They were right to be concerned; influenced by his talks with opposition writers and students, many of them his former supporters, Nagy was leaning further towards conciliation.

The envoys' attitude to Kádár was different. They noted approvingly how he told them 'calmly and in detail' about the CC meeting. Even if he did not align himself with the authoritarians, he was committed to sustaining the party and its institutions – something that they felt could no longer be taken for granted with Nagy and his circle. When Nagy spoke of disbanding part of the ÁVH, 'Kádár shook his head as a sign of disagreement.'[25]

That night, after an inaugural meeting of the Extraordinary Committee at 10 p.m., Kádár was able to lie down in an office and catch his first significant amount of sleep since the start of the crisis.[26]

Saturday, 27 October

Following their victory of the previous day, the advocates of a military solution were in full cry. Meetings of the Extraordinary Committee and PB drew up plans for arming party militants, taking back control of the media and establishing summary courts. The main – clearly inadequate – political sweetener to accompany this was a new cabinet that included two Smallholder leaders as well as the distinguished Marxist philosopher György Lukács, who had been sidelined under Rákosi.

Antal Apró, chairman of the Military Committee, was the main spokesman for measures to 'restore order'. However, when he claimed that the situation in the countryside was improving, Kádár and Hegedüs made clear that they did not believe him. Going with the predominant bias towards military options, Kádár asked Mikoyan and Suslov whether 'in connection with the unsettled situation in the countryside ... can we increase the number of Soviet troops?'[27]

Yet the PB meeting would prove the high water mark for such thinking. Nagy, clearly under enormous pressure, suffered a fainting fit and mild heart attack in his office;[28] afterwards, however, he revived in force and conviction. A meeting with some of his old associates and with two workers' representatives from the 13th District seems to have settled his mind: a movement with such popular support must not be met with force. His presentation at a meeting of the Extraordinary Committee that evening was sufficiently powerful – fortified with a threat of resignation – to carry the day for a wholly political solution to the crisis.

After his earlier wavering, Kádár supported Nagy.[29] He may have felt that the party could not face the crisis without the Prime Minister's relative popularity; in any case, he had throughout been uneasy at relying on force alone. Soviet support was needed for the new line, and Mikoyan and Suslov 'agreed to have a heart to heart talk with Kádár and Nagy this evening in an unofficial capacity.'[30] At around midnight, the talks were interrupted by news that another pillar of party rule was crumbling. The leadership of SZOT was negotiating and formulating a joint position with the leaders of the student revolutionaries.

Sunday, 28 October

Kádár left the meeting to speak to the SZOT leaders. He knew them well – the head of SZOT, Sándor Gáspár, was an associate from pre-war days – but their message still came as a shock. As he put it later that morning, the incident showed 'how our political line has completely split in two ... A separate declaration [by SZOT] would mean separating the working class from the party.' After five hours of negotiations, he persuaded them to rescind the declaration, but the incident can only have added to his concerns over working class alienation and the effect of Soviet intervention on the party's legitimacy.[31] Now the party's main institutional link to the working class, usually a reliable transmission channel of the leadership line, was starting to take on a life of its own.

Mikoyan and Suslov accepted Nagy and Kádár's proposals. They emphasised that there must be no further concessions, and that a streamlined party leadership must seize back the initiative – but by political, not military means. The latter option had, in any case, suffered another reverse. Members of the Military Committee had plotted a dawn assault on the insurgents around Corvin Passage. They succeeded in sidestepping Nagy's orders to abort the operation, but the attack – in which the rebels destroyed a number of tanks – was a fiasco.

Kádár presented the new line to a morning PB meeting. 'We have to find a way to get the people who took part in the fighting to lay down their arms without regarding them [all] as counter-revolutionaries.' There was still some agonising over terminology: what had happened could not be called a revolution, 'because that means ... that we are counter-revolutionaries.' Instead, it was dubbed a 'national democratic movement'. As for Soviet troops, Kádár argued neatly that the Hungarian government could certainly ask for their withdrawal. 'Whether they withdraw them or not is at the sole discretion of the Soviet Union.' For the party to operate effectively amid the fast-moving events, the PB and CC would cede their functions to a new Presidium (which Kádár was later elected to chair), essentially a continuation of the Extraordinary Committee. The PB and later the CC approved the new direction.[32]

This produced a dramatic shift of power within Akadémia Street. Nagy's supporters swarmed in to help draft a radio speech that he was to give that afternoon. Kádár greeted two of the most radical journalists, Miklós Gimes and Pál Lőcsei, with a sardonic, 'Well, are you supporting us now?'[33] Nagy demanded further leadership changes, and in particular the exclusion of Hegedüs – whom he blamed for much of the Military Committee's antics – from the Presidium. Kádár, ever conscious of party unity, offered a somewhat backhanded defence: Hegedüs was 'a young man' who was 'absolutely honourable in his intentions, dynamic, and hard-working ... [even if] his working methods comprise a lot of the old [ways].' Nagy nonetheless got his way, and later insisted that Gerő, Hegedüs and other representatives of the *ancien régime* must leave for the Soviet Union immediately. By that night they were gone.[34]

Ceasefire orders were announced during the afternoon. Nagy's radio broadcast embraced the revolution and blamed the 'old and criminal policy' of previous leaderships for the crisis. However, the speech still assumed a single-party system and promised only that there would be negotiations about the long-term presence of Soviet troops.

Monday, 29 October
Nagy symbolised his liberation from party orthodoxy by moving out of Akadémia Street and into the Prime Minister's offices in Parliament. The

Parliament would be the political centre of the next few days, one in which Kádár and other leading figures would spend the bulk of their time. Yet the move was also a symbol of the party's disintegration, which made it questionable as to whether the previous day's declaration represented firm political ground on which Nagy, Kádár and others could take a stand.

Though Nagy's broadcast had changed the atmosphere, workers were still on strike and the insurgent groups remained suspicious of appeals to lay down their arms. Both groups wanted guarantees that there would be no return to the previous system. This meant an end to the party's monopoly of power, and the full withdrawal of Soviet troops from Hungarian territory; Nagy had failed to mention the first, and had been deliberately ambiguous regarding the second. The armed insurgents, coordinating their position with the increasing influential Colonel Pál Maléter, commander of the Kilián barracks near Corvin Passage, insisted that these demands be met.

Kádár took his first journey of more than a few hundred yards since the 23rd, visiting the Budapest party headquarters in Republic Square to confer with the Secretary, his long-standing friend Imre Mező. Though a moderate, Mező had also been a member of the Military Committee; he was determined to keep the party infrastructure functioning and had sought to arm a workers' militia. He was disappointed by the vacuum at the party centre and complained afterwards that, 'Comrade Kádár brought us no directives.'[35] It was probably during this expedition that Kádár saw Mária, who was staying with a group of anxious apparatchiks' wives, for about half an hour. It was their only meeting throughout the crisis. 'We all had a good laugh because he had never been a soldier and cut quite a comic figure in the combat helmet he was wearing.'[36]

That Kádár was still more attached than Nagy to salvaging what he could of the party-state was clear when he and some other party leaders – the Prime Minister not among them – met Mikoyan and Suslov that evening. The Hungarians recounted disquieting events, such as the seizure of the printing and editorial buildings of *Szabad Nép* by a group of fighters led by an ambitious and enigmatic ex-political prisoner, József Dudás. The Soviet envoys told them that this was a consequence of undermining the ÁVH, 'the most steady fighters.' Kádár and his colleagues took the point: 'They have begun initiatives to preserve these cadres and aim to use them in protecting order.' [37]

That night also saw news of an Israeli attack on Egypt. The Suez crisis – as it would become – would distract a great deal of Western energy and attention from Hungary in the coming days.

Tuesday, 30 October

If Kádár was thinking in terms of maintaining the party's structures on the Monday night, by the following day he and the Presidium had embraced a much more radical step: the end of the one-party system. Its main proponent was ex-President Zoltán Tildy, a Smallholder and one of the non-Communist ministers in the new government. Kádár, however, did not oppose it or even hesitate. He accepted Tildy's argument that without a multi-party system the revolution could take Hungary sharply to the right. If Soviet military involvement was ruled out – and 'with every Soviet unit that was deployed, we would become stronger in a military sense but correspondingly weaker politically'[38] – then the main priority was to defend as much of the Communist position as possible.

Kádár seems to have envisaged – as did Nagy – a return to the left-leaning but relatively open politics of 1945-48, 'in which we will have a sustainable, or rather significant, influence in the government.' He had not become a believer in multi-party democracy, though some of Nagy's radical supporters surely had; rather, this was a realistic adjustment to the new situation. After all, in 1945 the Communists had expected to operate within some sort of multi-party system for up to fifteen years.

That afternoon, Nagy announced the demise of the one-party system over the renamed Radio Free Kossuth; he now spoke openly of Hungary's 'revolution'. He also announced the establishment of a seven-member inner cabinet, with only three Communist members: Losonczy, Kádár and himself. Speaking in support, Kádár said that the party could now shed the burden of bad leadership and called on those with firm convictions to stay. 'The ranks of our party will shake. But I have no fear that pure, decent-minded, sincere Communists will abandon their beliefs. Those who leave will be those who joined us for their own ends, for their careers or for other purposes.'[39]

Struggling to sustain the government's authority – Dudás' 'Hungarian National Revolutionary Committee' appeared to have ambitions to establish an alternative government, while autonomous bodies had sprung up in the provinces – Nagy, Kádár and other leaders were continually negotiating with delegations. During a meeting with Ferenc Bújáki, a Communist and a representative of the new National Council in Szolnok, Kádár scrawled a message for him to take back to the 'fellow workers of Szolnok'. It promised a party 'delivered from the ashes of the past', and ended: 'Hungarian socialism will triumph in the service of a just ideal – and by the proper methods. With comradely greetings, János Kádár.' He passed the paper to the Prime Minister, who looked it over. 'And Nagy wrote his name next to that of Kádár.'[40]

Kádár and the Interior Minister, Ferenc Münnich, also negotiated for three hours with representatives of the armed groups around Corvin Passage, agreeing an organisation through which the fighters would contribute to the reestablishment of order. Kádár had particularly intense discussions with a group from Tűzoltó Street, one of whose leaders, Per Olaf Csongovai, recalled that 'with Imre Nagy the atmosphere was very tense, but with Kádár we discussed things very directly.' To persuade him of their *bona fides*, half of the fighters produced their party membership cards. One of them, Pista (István) Angyal, urged him to go to Tűzoltó Street 'to see with his own eyes that this was not a gathering of counter-revolutionaries, but of real revolutionaries.' The meeting made a big impression on Kádár. It may have given a misleading (and, for him, excessively comforting) picture: the Tűzoltó Street fighters, with their intelligentsia links and reform Communist sympathies, were atypical.[41]

Later that day, Kádár received shattering news. Fighting had broken out around the party's Budapest headquarters in Republic Square. The building was stormed and a number of its defenders, many of them ÁVH officers, brutally killed. Though angry crowds had lynched some ÁVH men in previous days, this was on a larger and more ominous scale. Mező was gunned down as he surrendered the building; he would die in hospital two days later. Kádár asked Mária to visit him. The dying man said, 'Tell Kádár to look after himself.'[42]

Wednesday, 31 October
Under pressure from the streets, the government had to ask the Soviets for more concessions. Nagy, Kádár and Tildy held yet further talks with Mikoyan and Suslov before their return to Moscow, seeking their acceptance of multi-party elections and the full withdrawal of Soviet troops; they may also have raised Hungary's abrogation of the Warsaw Pact. [43] They tried to offer reassurance: all the leading parties likely to contest the elections would pledge to maintain a broadly socialist economic order, and Hungary would not be used as an anti-Soviet base.

Mikoyan and Suslov proved accommodating, while *Pravda* published a striking Soviet government statement admitting errors in the past handling of the 'people's democracies' and expressing a willingness to negotiate over the withdrawal of Soviet troops from Hungary. After Kádár saw Mikoyan and Suslov to a waiting armoured vehicle, he asked the Prime Minister, 'Imre, have we done it?' 'We've done it, János.'[44] That afternoon, Nagy addressed a crowd from the balcony of the Parliament. He spoke of national independence and sovereignty; it was a world away from his stumbling address of a week earlier.

Kádár, meanwhile, was at a party meeting – to discuss the dissolution of the MDP and the creation of a successor organisation. The day before, he and others had rejected the Presidium member Zoltán Szántó's argument that the revival of the Social Democrats, effectively nullifying the 1948 merger, coupled with the MDP's general discredit, meant that it would have to be dissolved. Now it was clear that, if the leadership did not establish a new party, then others – particularly intelligentsia figures – would. In Kádár's later words, 'It seemed that two or three Communist parties were in the making at the same time.'[45] And so, for the second time in his career, he dissolved the party. Some one hundred and fifty activists attended the founding meeting of the new Hungarian Socialist Workers' Party (MSZMP) and elected a seven-member Temporary Executive

Committee. Kádár was now at the conservative end of a spectrum that included figures such as Donáth, Losonczy and Kopácsi.

The meeting was tense; many Communists were frightened by the shooting of Mező, and some spoke of the party going underground once again. Kádár tore up an attendance list giving the names and addresses of the attendees. He rejected a suggestion that, since he and Nagy were starting to suffer from over-exposure, a lower profile figure such as Losonczy should announce the party's formation: 'this was not just any old event, this was the formation of the new party, and as First Secretary he had to announce it.' He would be very publicly identified with the new party and its programme.[46]

That afternoon, there were reports from eastern Hungary of Soviet tanks coming into the country. Meeting the Polish Ambassador Adam Willman that evening, Kádár and Nagy were uneasy. Why were the troops there? Were they simply securing a route for a quick withdrawal? They hoped that the assurances they had offered Mikoyan and Suslov would enable them to walk the tightrope between popular demands and the limits of Soviet tolerance. 'The main effort of Kádár and Nagy is to halt a further move to the right'; in this, they cast a nervous eye towards the newly released Cardinal Mindszenty. They also feared that, so long as Soviet troops were in the country, their efforts could be undercut.[47]

Kádár probably did not have the time – or the physical and mental energy – to form an ordered and systematic view of developments. 'We were living not a day, but an hour, at a time, dead tired, dispirited, and without precise information. All we had to rely on was instinct and experience.'[48] Some thought that he viewed developments such as a multi-party system as a disaster. However, speaking to the reform Communist Szilárd Ujhelyi, he was determinedly reassuring. He envisaged the party sustaining the left wing of a broadly left of centre political consensus, fighting for measures such as keeping medium-sized companies within state ownership. 'Don't worry that the party's identity will fade away,' he consoled Ujhelyi.[49]

That night, following his pattern of the last few days, Kádár slept at the Ministry of the Interior. At around eleven, he took a call from Jenő Széll, who was now assisting Nagy, reporting that railway workers had seen large numbers of Soviet troops and armoured vehicles heading for Budapest. 'All right,' said Kádár, and rang off.

Thursday, 1 November
If Kádár's initial response to Széll's report had been calm and laconic, he was in a very different mood when they met in Parliament the next morning. 'He was white as a sheet, his lips were trembling and he fell into some sort of hysterical fit. He started shouting at me that just because three counter-revolutionary railway workers had got it into their heads to do some scare-mongering, I'd gone and believed them.'[50] Presumably, he

had spent much of the night worrying about information that he desperately wanted to disbelieve. It was becoming ever harder, however, to run away from the evidence; at 7:30 a.m., Soviet troops had seized control of Ferihegy, Budapest's main airport, and they would continue taking over airfields and advancing their troops throughout the day.

The inner cabinet agreed to draft an accelerated declaration of neutrality and withdrawal from the Warsaw Pact. Meanwhile, Andropov was summoned and an explanation demanded. Kádár's terse later account eloquently captures the Ambassador's stonewalling and the rising tension on the Hungarian side. '… Soviet troops had crossed the border in transport vehicles…. [The cabinet] summoned Andropov. Andropov said that these are railroad workers. Hungarians at the border sent back telegrams saying that these definitely are not railroad workers. Then they reported that Soviet tanks are moving into Szolnok. This was at noon. The government has been thrown into a nervous state. They summoned Andropov. He responded: the withdrawal of wounded soldiers.'[51]

While waiting for a draft of his broadcast announcing the formation of the MSZMP, Kádár talked with the government spokesman Miklós Vásárhelyi about the new party's prospects. In contrast to his panic when talking to Széll earlier, Kádár was now in a good mood, 'definitely hopeful, ready for the struggle, speculating on what needed to be done now and how we needed to take things further.' He spoke optimistically of drawing on the best traditions of the Left, though 'maybe he was convincing himself as well as me.' Vásárhelyi had a favourable view of Kádár – 'a calm, sober, considered, realistic man' – and their discussion reinforced this.[52]

Kádár's speech was a collective effort; he set out the main points that he wanted to put across, and asked his fellow prisoner of the early fifties, Sándor Haraszti, and the *Szabad Nép* editor Márton Horváth to prepare a draft. Nagy, Donáth, Losonczy and Gimes all took part in revising it; Kádár then took it down to the Radio Free Kossuth studios in Parliament and pre-recorded the speech for broadcast that night. One of the editors, Béla Burján, was struck by its radical tone. He asked, 'Tell me, don't you think that the Ruskies will start shooting because of that?' Kádár 'was very quiet and lost in thought, and said, "I hope not." Then he went out.'[53]

Kádár's first interview with a Western journalist, Bruno Tedeschi of *Il Giornale d'Italia*, was similarly radical. He represented, he told Tedeschi, a 'new type' of Communism that had emerged from the revolution itself. 'It is not inspired by the USSR, nor by other types of Communism … it is Hungarian National Communism.' It would 'have the national interests of Hungary at heart and not those of international Communism.' He spoke warmly of Tito and indicated a willingness to accept Western economic aid.[54]

What had come over Kádár? Given his various reversals of the previous ten days, it is temptingly simple to see no more than his moving with the

centre of political gravity. Certainly, much of his response had been a bow
to the apparently inevitable, especially since the Soviet leadership itself
seemed to accept it as such. Yet the breadth and depth of the revolution,
and the participation of many Communists in it, was also making its
impression on him, one that he would find hard to shake off.

By early afternoon, with reports of troop movements flowing in and
Andropov still stalling, the inner cabinet was moving towards a declaration
of neutrality. Kádár urged a further conversation with Andropov, and a
decision was deferred for two hours.[55] Andropov was summoned at 5:00
p.m. Nagy, speaking rather nervously, recalled the events of the morning
and demanded an explanation of the Soviet troop movements. Other
cabinet members, including Kádár, supported him. Andropov's claims that
the movements had no military significance were refuted by the chief of
the Hungarian General Staff. Nagy then proposed that Hungary declare its
neutrality and appeal to the UN for protection.[56]

The inner cabinet members declared their support. György Heltai, who
as Deputy Foreign Minister was present at the meeting, described Kádár's
startling affirmation. 'He said that he knew full well that the declaration of
neutrality meant the end of Communism for Hungary, and that meant the
end of his life, because he had dedicated his whole life to the Communist
Party. ... But if the Soviets attempted to intervene in Hungary with the
further use of arms, it would be the Soviets themselves who brought
counter-revolution to Hungary, and he would take to the streets with a
pistol against Russian tanks and give his life for his country.'[57]

This dramatic incident has often been recounted; but did Kádár really
say this? Heltai, the only source for the story, first described it only a
month after the event. However, Andropov's telegram to Moscow, written
that evening, paints a very different picture. 'Erdei and Losonczy strongly
supported this reply by Nagy. Tildy's response was affirmative but more
reserved, while Kádár's reaction was reluctant.'[58] Heltai's account also
makes the Soviets' later trust in Kádár perplexing. It may be that he
misinterpreted what Kádár said, putting an extra gloss on his evident inner
conflict over very stark alternatives. In addition to his worries over the
domestic consequences of renewed Soviet intervention, Kádár feared that
it could trigger Western action, an international conflict fought out on
Hungarian soil. Neutrality, however unappealing, offered an escape route.

After Andropov had gone, the inner cabinet, including Kádár,
reaffirmed its vote for neutrality. At 7:50 p.m., Nagy announced the move
in a radio broadcast; he explained it by reference to Hungary's long-
standing desire for independence, making no mention of an imminent
Soviet threat. Soon after the speech, the workers' councils agreed a return
to work for the following Monday, 5 November.

At about 10:00 p.m., Radio Free Kossuth broadcast Kádár's pre-
recorded speech. He began with a stinging denunciation of how the MDP
had been 'corrupted by the blind and criminal policies of Stalinism's

Hungarian representatives, Rákosi and his clique, into an instrument of tyranny and national slavery.' This had frittered away the moral capital of the party's years of honest struggle, but was now over. 'Our people's glorious uprising has lifted the yoke of the Rákosi regime from our people and our country. It has achieved freedom for our people and independence for our country, without which there can be no socialism.' He took pride in the involvement of Communists in the uprising, singling out 'the young people of the Petőfi Circle'.

He also issued a warning, expressing the fears of many Communists. 'The people's uprising has reached a crossroads. Either the Hungarian democratic parties have enough strength to stabilise what we have achieved, or we will be confronted with open counter-revolution.' Nor was this the only risk: 'There is also the grave and frightening danger that foreign armed intervention may lead our country to share the tragic fate of Korea.' To avoid this, a stable government, peace and a return to work were necessary. The new MSZMP, 'which once and for all breaks away from the crimes of the past,' would stand for national independence and defence of nationalisation and land reform. It would be socialism developed 'not in slavish imitation of foreign examples, but in ways that match the economic and historical characteristics of our country.'

It was his conclusion that was perhaps most striking:

'Our people have proved with their blood that they support unflinchingly the government's demand for the complete withdrawal of Soviet troops.
We don't want to be dependent any more.
We don't want our country to become a battlefield.
I'm speaking to every honest patriot. Let us unite for the victory of Hungarian independence and Hungarian freedom.'[59]

Shortly before the speech was broadcast, at about 9:30 p.m., Kádár, Nagy and Losonczy met the Chinese Ambassador to explain the declaration of neutrality. During the meeting, Kádár had to leave: he was going, he said, to the Soviet Embassy to discuss the apparent failure to withdraw their troops. His announcement caused no surprise: such discussions had become routine.[60]

Hours passed, and Kádár did not return. By the following morning, it was clear that he had gone missing. His anxious colleagues pieced together an account of what had happened after he had left the meeting, but they still had no idea where he was. What they could not know was that by this time he was in Moscow.

8

WHIRLWIND

Sunday, 28 October – Thursday, 1 November: Moscow
Hungary kept Nikita Khrushchev awake in the early hours of 31 October. 'It was like a nail in my head.'[1] For several days, an uneasy and divided Soviet Presidium had been debating the crisis. An inconclusive meeting on 28 October had shied away from further military intervention, and two days later, the Presidium seemed prepared to accept the fait accompli in Hungary: hence the encouraging statement in *Pravda*.

Yet by the following morning – after Khrushchev's sleepless agonising – the policy was completely reversed. Now Khrushchev told his colleagues: 'We should take the initiative in restoring order in Hungary.'[2] In contrast to Operation Wave, this would be an all-out assault with overwhelming force. It was code-named Operation Whirlwind.

Khrushchev's sole argument was that the abandonment of Hungary would give an unacceptable signal of weakness to the West. Yet other factors must have been at work: the Chinese arguments for intervention; the Red Army's visceral hostility to withdrawal; above all, Khrushchev's fear of being swept away by those who blamed him and his denunciation of Stalin for the 'loss' of Hungary. This internal Soviet debate over how far the clock was to be turned back – with Khrushchev on one side and the former Foreign Minister Vyacheslav Molotov on the other – would have critical implications for a reoccupied Hungary, and for Kádár.

During its 31 October meeting, the Presidium also debated the membership of a new, pro-Soviet 'revolutionary government'. From the first, Kádár was seen as an obvious member. He was the incumbent First Secretary, an important source of continuity and legitimacy in the eyes of party members. He was also regarded as fundamentally sound – in sharp contrast to Nagy – and had made a good impression on Mikoyan and Suslov. Khrushchev's assessment on 30 October was that 'Kádár is behaving well.'[3]

However, the Soviets saw Ferenc Münnich, then Interior Minister in Nagy's cabinet, as a potential strongman: he would serve as Prime Minister, Minister of Defence and Minister of the Interior, with Kádár as Deputy Prime Minister.[4] Münnich was a reassuringly known quantity, a veteran of Kun's Soviet Republic and of the Spanish Civil War, a 'Muscovite' and international Communist operative who had recently served for two years as Hungarian Ambassador in Moscow. He was not an extreme Stalinist – he had reportedly fallen out with Rákosi – but he was a firm authoritarian.[5] Kádár was still relatively unknown in Moscow and, Gomułka notwithstanding, the idea of a leader who had seen the inside of a Communist prison was still a disturbing novelty.

Rákosi, Gerő and Hegedüs were consulted; predictably, they were all in favour of Münnich. His age and indistinct political profile suggested that he was unlikely to serve for long; the exiled leaders may well have hoped that he would serve as a staging-post towards a restoration of Rákosi's associates, if not of Rákosi himself. There were plans for the return to politics of the Moscow-based Hungarians, and at least part of the Soviet leadership endorsed them.[6]

Meanwhile, the reliable comrades, including Kádár, had to be spirited out of Budapest. Mikoyan and others, including the candidate Presidium member Leonid Brezhnev, oversaw the Moscow end of the operation. In Budapest, responsibility lay with Andropov.[7]

Thursday, 1 November: Budapest
During the evening, Andropov rang Münnich – who must have known of Moscow's plans – and asked him to bring Kádár to the Embassy. After Kádár left the meeting with the Chinese ambassador, he and Münnich took a government car to the Soviet Embassy. The building was in darkness, and there was no answer when they rang the bell. They waited. A few minutes later, another car drew up and two Russians got out. After some discussion, the two Hungarians sent their driver away, saying that the Russians would bring them home. Then they got into the Russian car; Kádár was, by one account, uneasy and reluctant.[8]

They were taken to the Soviet base at Tököl on Csepel Island, south of Budapest. It is likely that Andropov met them there.[9] He and Kádár had met in private only once before, when they had discussed the Hungarian political situation in early September. That had not been an obvious meeting of minds. In spite of his low-key, donnish manner and undoubted intelligence, Andropov took a politically unreconstructed line – a sharp contrast to Kádár's then conciliatory stance.[10] Now they would have to work together: the beginning, as it turned out, of a long political association.

Andropov presumably told Kádár that the Soviet leaders wanted to talk to him. It is clear from his later comments in Moscow that Kádár did *not* know for sure that the Soviets were set on military intervention. However, the troop movements, followed by this mysterious summons, must have given him pause. And so he was still apprehensive when he and Münnich were flown in the early hours to Mukachevo in the Ukraine. Brezhnev met them there; they were then flown on in separate planes to Moscow.[11]

Friday, 2 November: Budapest

Nagy set up an urgent inquiry into Kádár and Münnich's disappearance. Establishing the outline of what had happened, he concluded that Kádár had been kidnapped and in an ill-tempered meeting with Andropov demanded to know his two ministers' whereabouts. Andropov denied all knowledge and involvement in their disappearance.[12]

Mária was brought to Parliament; she said, quite truthfully, that she had no idea where her husband was. When told what had happened outside the Soviet Embassy, she became hysterical, recalling Kádár's 1951 arrest and disappearance. 'If János turns up,' she added, 'the only thing I'll let him do is gardening.' She was later seen wandering the building in floods of tears.[13] The government hushed up Kádár's disappearance, keeping him in a further reshuffled cabinet that was announced the following day. But by that time, a number of others who had been informed of Soviet intentions – including Marosán, Apró and Károly Kiss – had found their way to Tököl.

Preparations were made for a return to work on Monday, but reports of Soviet troop movements continued. The revolutionary councils tried to organise defences against an assault, while Nagy urged the UN Security Council to recognise Hungary's neutrality. However, with Western unity shattered over Suez, attention was diverted. Meanwhile, Soviet troops were gathering in assembly points in major towns and cities.[14] In Szolnok, Marshal Konev, commander-in-chief of the Warsaw Pact armed forces and the operational head of Whirlwind, established his headquarters.

Friday, 2 November: Moscow

Kádár was met at the airport by an interpreter, Nikolai Dzhuba. His first task was to take the bedraggled Hungarian shopping and kit him out for an appearance before the Presidium. Shirts and underclothes were found without difficulty, but Kádár baulked at some Italian shoes. 'What would the comrades say back home if I showed up in flashy shoes?'[15] Then to the Kremlin.

Khrushchev and Malenkov had set off on visits to the 'fraternal parties', ensuring support for the invasion, and thus were absent from Kádár's presentation. Nonetheless, the faces confronting him included hardened survivors of the Stalin era such as Molotov, Kaganovich and Bulganin, as well as the more familiar Mikoyan, Suslov and Brezhnev. The other

Hungarians present were Münnich and István Bata, a low-grade Stalinist who had served as Minister of Defence. Kádár was asked to give his assessment of the situation – without knowing the Presidium's view. If the record by the Soviet notetaker, Vladimir Malin, is comprehensive, he was heard out in silence: 'he was being scrutinised.'[16]

Kádár emphasised the good intentions of the demonstrators and even – reflecting the influence of his discussion with the Tűzoltó Street group – of the armed fighters: 'no one wanted counter-revolution.' The leadership's initial misjudgement had 'turned [the people] against us.' However, he also emphasised the dangers: counter-revolutionaries were forming among the armed groups, the other parties in the coalition were untrustworthy and 'Nagy's policy has counter-rev. aspects to it.' The apparent return of Soviet troops had exacerbated these dangers. 'Hour by hour the situation is moving rightward.' On the declaration of neutrality, he emphasised – rather nervously, perhaps – that he had insisted on further negotiations with Andropov before a decision was reached. On the renaming of the party he was more robust, arguing that the MDP's authority had been shattered by the Rajk affair. In any case: 'Yesterday I voted for these two decisions of the government.'

Thus far, Kádár had avoided answering the key question: to intervene, or not to intervene? Right at the end of his presentation, he came to a view. 'The use of military force will be destructive and lead to bloodshed. What will happen then? The morale of the Communists will be reduced to zero.' In other words, the lesser evil was for the Hungarian Communists to fight their political corner without Soviet military intervention. 'The counter-rev. forces are not meagre. But this is a matter of struggle. If order is restored by force, the authority of the socialist countries will be eroded.'

The other presentations were much briefer and very different in tone. Münnich was pessimistic about the effect of withdrawing Soviet troops, while Bata made a crass call for 'a military dictatorship'. His advice was not asked again.

With that, the meeting was over.[17]

Friday, 2 November – Saturday, 3 November: Brioni
Khrushchev and Malenkov's toughest assignment was to get Tito's acceptance of intervention. However, the all-night talks proved easier than expected: Tito, now alarmed at the Hungarian government's growing radicalism, was supportive.

Khrushchev indicated that Münnich might become Prime Minister. The Yugoslavs disagreed, urging a Kádár-led government that would condemn Rákosi's abuses and seek a wide base of support. Khrushchev and Malenkov seemed unenthusiastic. 'He [Khrushchev] was clearly not anxious to accept Kádár, who was not his choice. The Russians again praised Münnich.' Against this, the Yugoslav ambassador to Moscow, Veljko Mićunović, put a telling argument: when Münnich was an ambassador in Moscow, Kádár was Rákosi's prisoner. 'For every Hungarian this would be decisive in Kádár's favour.' Khrushchev took the point, and later remarked that Kádár was 'a good guy'.

The Soviets also asked the Yugoslavs 'to do something about Nagy' – to persuade him both to accept the Soviet intervention and to resign the premiership. The Yugoslavs agreed, although the Soviets would not say when their intervention would take place. This comradely agreement, reached amid the bonhomie of the small hours, would lead to a great deal of bad blood. [18]

Khrushchev, it seems, was swayed by the Yugoslav case for Kádár. His thinking can only be conjectured, but reconciliation with Tito, along with the denunciation of Stalin, was very much *his* policy. Something approaching a Rákosi restoration in Hungary would be a rebuff to Tito and a vindication of Molotov and his fellow diehards. But a new Hungarian government that had Tito's blessing, that could make a success of restoring party control while distancing itself, Khrushchev-like, from the Stalinist past: that would be a very different proposition.

Saturday, 3 November: Moscow
Kádár, it seems, was still told little of what was happening. The events of the previous days must have suggested that a Soviet military intervention was at least highly possible. He may have wondered how, if that were the case, his broadcast of 1 November would sound to the Soviet leadership. In his confused apologia many years later he let slip something of his fear: 'My most important aim then was that I should get to Szolnok in safety. By whatever means.'[19]

Now these anxieties boiled over. When Khrushchev returned to Moscow, Molotov – who, admittedly, had his motives for exaggerating – told him that Kádár still considered himself part of the Nagy leadership. That day 'he [Kádár] began to express anxiety and tried to return to Budapest.'[20] This was, perhaps, less an expression of a serious wish than an attempt to force a resolution to the crisis that Kádár now felt was impending.

Saturday, 3 November: Budapest
The Nagy government's optimism rose when talks with a Soviet military delegation about troop withdrawals got under way. When they were adjourned, it was agreed that they would resume that night at Tököl.

At 8 p.m., the recently released Cardinal Mindszenty made a radio broadcast; later cast by the post-intervention government as a reactionary call to arms, it in fact sketched out a Christian Democratic programme.[21] The current in Hungarian opinion that had been pushed to the margins ten years earlier and which had lacked an institutional base at the start of the revolution had found a voice.

The Soviets had now sealed off the western border. Divisional commanders were given their orders, and units would be at full combat readiness at midnight. Operation Whirlwind was just hours away. Yet the 'revolutionary government' that they were purportedly supporting still lacked a leader.

Saturday, 3 November: Moscow
Towards evening Khrushchev and Malenkov returned to Moscow and an immediate Presidium meeting to discuss the Hungarian leadership. The situation had become critical: Marshal Zhukov warned that Whirlwind could not be delayed.[22] Molotov, fiercely opposed to Kádár's candidacy, 'used an insulting expression' about him and described his attempt to return to Budapest. Khrushchev had to admit that Molotov had a point: 'how can one propose a person who sees himself as a member of the leadership against which we are preparing to strike?' He proposed that Kádár and Münnich be called in. Kádár's moment of decision was upon him.

> We immediately told them frankly that the counter-revolution had begun in Hungary, and that we had to use troops against it. … I was watching Kádár intently. He was listening silently. Then came his turn to speak: 'Yes,' he agreed. 'You are right, in order to stabilise the situation, we need your assistance now.'[23]

If Khrushchev's account is precise, Kádár made his decision before he knew two vital pieces of information: that he would be in an unusually powerful position as both First Secretary and Prime Minister, and that the new regime would distance itself from Rákosi. As during the revolution, he simply bowed to the inevitable. Fear and ambition probably played a part too: acceptance meant that he would have at least some leadership position, and he can have had few illusions as to the likely long-term consequences of refusal. Yet to view siding with Moscow as a betrayal is to use a moral calculus quite alien to Kádár. He was most unlikely to opt for martyrdom based on defiance of the Soviet Union. He may have doubted the wisdom of military action; he certainly could not – at this time, at least – ignore how widespread the support was for the revolution; but there was nothing in his thinking that made Soviet intervention wrong *in itself*.

However, Khrushchev's account may be a very abbreviated description of the long meeting of the Soviet Presidium and Hungarian leaders that began at 8.45 p.m. In that case, Kádár agreed to a much more developed proposition. We have two records of the meeting: one the notes taken by the (Russian-speaking) Hungarian Foreign Minister Imre Horváth, who had just abandoned the Nagy government, the other by Malin. The latter, however, omits the first part of the meeting (a speech by Khrushchev) and has more attendees (some of them secondary figures in the Soviet leadership). It seems plausible that there were, in effect, two meetings running into each other. In the first, comprising the Soviet inner circle plus the Hungarians, the new Hungarian government was decided. In the second, wider meeting (which was the stage at which Malin joined), Kádár was given the floor.

Khrushchev's opening speech – which may, therefore, have been designed to win Kádár over and which reflected his discussions with Tito – was both a denunciation of Rákosi and an admission of Soviet error. While the former leaders were 'honest, loyal Communists', they had made errors: 'R[ákosi] is rough, G[erő] is ham-fisted.' Also: 'Mikoyan and I made a mistake when we proposed Gerő instead of Kádár. We were taken in by Gerő.' He agreed with Kádár that 'a part of the insurgents are not enemies', but counter-revolution was taking over. While Khrushchev insisted that, 'We hold to the declaration [of 31 October]', nonetheless 'This is impossible with I[mre] N[agy].' Therefore, intervention was required: 'We cannot be outsider observers.'[24]

If Kádár had not already given his assent, he must have done so now. The discussion then turned to the composition of the government. Kádár was named as Prime Minister. In normal times the Party Secretary post was the real seat of power, the Prime Minister a policy executor. However, the revolution had shifted power towards the government, and there it was likely to remain in the near term. As it was, Münnich – Deputy Prime Minister in charge of all armed and security forces – was still in a very strong position.

Horváth's notes list the names of Kádár, Münnich and the other members of the new government in two columns. Then, in a third column, he lists a number of Hungarian Stalinists (of whom the most eminent was István Kovács) who had fled Budapest at the end of October and were under Soviet protection in Mukachevo. Beneath this, in Russian, are the words, 'They want to isolate Kádár.'

The probable basis for this cryptic reference was a struggle over the composition of the government. Rákosi later complained that plans for many of the Stalinist refugees to play a leading role in the new government had to be abandoned at the last minute because of Kádár's objections.[25] Since the reference to the planned isolation of Kádár is in Russian, this presumably reflects a Soviet speaker – probably Khrushchev – justifying the Stalinists' exclusion. Kádár was successful: none of the exiles was included in the government that was announced the following morning.

There was a second battle over the text of the new government's initial declaration. A draft worked up by Gerő and Hegedüs (with Rákosi's involvement) seems to have fed in to a Soviet version that Khrushchev and Mikoyan threw out during the Presidium meeting. This may have reflected Kádár's objections; by one account, he was confronted with the draft and objected immediately because it included no denunciation of the old leadership. He claimed later that the explicit breach with the past had been an absolute sticking point for him. A new Soviet draft was drawn up by Mikoyan, Suslov and Foreign Minister Shepilov and then translated into Hungarian.[26]

These two points of contention gave rise to a myth later propagated by Kádár's supporters that he undertook the leadership because of an explicit Soviet threat that the task would otherwise be given to a Rákosi-led group. There is no evidence for this; however, had Kádár not prevailed over both the declaration and the composition of the government, the centre of political gravity in post-intervention Hungary would have been significantly different – and his own position much more tenuous. He won his battles; he may have realised that, with time ticking away towards the intervention, he had a degree of leverage over the Soviet leadership.

Kádár was then, it seems, presented to the wider Presidium, Mikoyan announcing, 'At the head of the govt. is Kádár.' In his speech, Kádár was quite blunt about Soviet errors: 'The Soviet comrades always helped, but there was one mistake: only 3-4 Hungarian cdes. enjoyed the full trust of the Soviet cdes.: Rákosi, Gerő, Farkas … This is the source of many mistakes.' Turning to the immediate crisis, he referred to the killing of Communists and the failure of Nagy's government to prevent it. 'What must be done? Surrendering a socialist country to counter-rev. is impossible. I agree with you. The correct course of action is to form a rev. government.'

Nonetheless, he put a striking emphasis on the public support for the revolution. 'I'd like to dwell on one point: the whole nation is taking part in the movement.' He mentioned the significance of Soviet troops ultimately being withdrawn from Hungary, and of tackling affronts to Hungarian national feelings. He concluded: 'This government must not be puppet-like, there must be a base for its activities and support among workers. There must be an answer to the question of what sort of relationship we must have with the USSR.'[27]

Kádár's speech and the repulsion of the boarders from the Hungarian *ancien regime* reflected the implicit alliance between Khrushchev, Tito and himself that had come together over the previous twenty-four hours. However, the realism of his policy line was questionable. Not only was Molotov far from reconciled to his defeat. Kádár's strategy was predicated on Hungarian opinion accepting the reimposition of party and Soviet rule, even if under less onerous conditions than before. It required a country inflamed by a patriotic uprising and revolutionary transformation to opt for pragmatic half measures. Everything that he had seen over the previous fortnight should have told him that this was not possible. Yet Kádár, so often the most realistic of men, chose to believe it. At this point, it seems he was unable to contemplate just how stark the alternatives really were. He had now shifted his ground once; in the coming weeks he would have to make much more radical adjustments.

Saturday, 3 November, evening: Uzhgorod
Radio Uzhgorod, just on the Ukrainian side of the border, could broadcast
to eastern Hungary. Its chairman gave László Sándor, its Hungarian
broadcaster, two declarations to read out immediately. The recordings
were repeated through the night: western monitoring first picked them up
after 5 a.m. They were a statement by Münnich announcing the formation
of the 'Revolutionary Worker-Peasant Government', and Kádár's fought-
over declaration. He and Münnich had strengthened the Soviet draft a
little: a critical reference to 'the Rákosi-Gerő clique' caused disquiet in
Moscow. Kádár praised the original uprising, but said that the Nagy
government had failed to control the situation and 'the counter-
revolutionaries are becoming ever more impudent.' His fifteen-point
programme pledged national sovereignty, a reduction in bureaucracy, an
increase in living standards through 'a change in the method of economic
management' and an agricultural policy sympathetic to the individual
peasant. Once Soviet forces had 'smash[ed] the sinister forces of counter-
revolution and reaction', there would be negotiations for them to leave the
country. 'Workers, Hungarian brothers! Truth is on our side. We will
win.'[28]

Saturday, 3 November, 10 p.m.: Tököl
Pál Maléter, now Minister of Defence, led the Hungarian delegation to the
Soviet headquarters for the continuing troop withdrawal negotiations.
Between 10 p.m. and midnight, Ivan Serov, head of the KGB, and some of
his officers burst into the room and arrested the Hungarian delegation.
Hungary's defence capacities had been effectively decapitated.

Sunday, 4 November, 4.15 a.m.: Budapest
The code word 'Grom' (Thunder) was sent to Soviet divisional
commanders to launch Operation Whirlwind. From outside Budapest, the
three main divisions of the Special Corps set off for different parts of the
city. One of them, the 2nd motor rifle division, was ordered to seize key
central sites such as Parliament, the Defence Ministry and party
headquarters. In its advance guard was a KGB snatch squad to arrest Nagy
and other members of his government.[29]

Nagy had been warned of an impending Soviet attack a couple of hours
before. He refused to announce on the radio that an attack was taking
place, or to give orders to fire. He had still sought explanations from
Andropov – who had still strung him along. Now Hungarian troops in the
outskirts of the city were quickly overwhelmed, and the Soviet units
headed for the centre.

As reports were rung in to Parliament, Nagy was confronted with the
stark fact of the attack. He still did not give an order to fight, but sought to
rally domestic and foreign opinion through the radio. Broadcasting from
Parliament at 5:20 a.m., with gunfire audible in the background, Nagy

denounced the intervention as a plan to overthrow the lawful government. 'Our troops are fighting. The government is at its post. This is my message to the people of the country and to the public opinion of the world.'[30] Insofar as there was any clear strategy behind the broadcast, it was an attempt to internationalise the problem, to bring the pressure of world opinion to bear. In the eyes of the Soviets, and of their supporters, that was an unforgivable step for a Communist to take.

Soviet advance units broke through into the city centre; Nagy was warned that tanks were approaching Parliament. One of the senior politicians still there, Zoltán Szántó, told Nagy that he had been called during the night by the Yugoslav ambassador to warn of an imminent Soviet attack and to offer asylum in the Embassy. This was the Yugoslavs delivering on their promise to 'do something about Nagy'. But the plan had misfired; to smooth the invasion, Szántó should have delivered his message before Nagy made his broadcast. Instead, the result was to thwart Soviet plans. Between 6 a.m. and 8 a.m., Nagy, Szántó, Donáth, Losonczy and nearly forty other relatives and associates took refuge in the Embassy. The KGB operatives narrowly missed their man.[31]

By around 8 a.m., Soviet troops had secured the Danube bridges and major government buildings. At 7.57 a.m., Kádár's once-favourite writer Gyula Háy broadcast an appeal from the Hungarian Writers' Union to their counterparts around the world: 'Help Hungary ... Help, help, help!' But no help was coming. The Soviet leadership and military had a free hand.

At 8:07 a.m., Radio Free Kossuth went off the air.

Sunday, 4 November – Wednesday, 7 November: Szolnok
Kádár flew first to Mukachevo. There he met Kovács, who demanded to go back to Budapest and undertake 'work' there. Kádár remained firm, and had Kovács dispatched to Moscow to organise Soviet food and medical aid to Hungary. Then he went on to Szolnok, summoning the local radio staff to a meeting in the early afternoon.[32]

While fighting continued around Corvin Passage and other centres of the armed insurgents, and the Soviet military established its grip both in Budapest and across the country, the members of the 'revolutionary worker-peasant government' gathered around Kádár in Szolnok. Marosán, nominated as Minister of State, arrived there on 5 November. He met Kádár in the company of Marshal Konev and a liaison officer, Vladimir Baikov, who would shadow Kádár in the coming months. 'This man was more than an interpreter.' Kádár 'seemed pale and tired, only his eyes sparkled.' He told Marosán that this would probably be the most testing time of their lives; over meals in the next twenty-four hours, he was often sombre and withdrawn.[33]

Kádár may not have known how divided the Soviet Presidium was over policy in Hungary. In three bad-tempered sessions on November 4-6 the

Soviet leaders debated Kádár's approach, in particular his criticisms of Rákosi and his maintaining the party's new name, the MSZMP – effectively justifying the decision of early November to dissolve the Rákosi era MDP. 'What's going on is the creation of a new Yugoslavia,' Molotov complained. However, Khrushchev and his allies outvoted him; as Marshal Zhukov put it, 'We must decisively support Comrade Kádár.'[34]

In the chilly early morning of 7 November, a convoy of Soviet tanks and armoured vehicles brought Kádár and a number of his ministers to Budapest.[35] With some fighting still going on, the route had to be chosen carefully, but they eventually reached Parliament. Kádár went inside. There, waiting for him – if the irrepressible raconteur György Aczél is to be believed – was a furious Mária. 'You should have left this shit to Rákosi's lot,' she snapped. 'It shouldn't be you doing this.'[36]

9

THE MAGGOTS OF COUNTER-REVOLUTION

Returning to Budapest, Kádár seemed a man transformed. Sándor Feri, a lawyer who worked with him in these early days, recalled, 'I found Kádár's appearance and voice more than surprising, they were shocking. I had never seen such a change of personality. Before this he had called me Feri in a friendly way, and now ... he behaved with the condescension of a ruler to one of his subordinates. It was such a change from the former image of Kádár as uncertain and open to debate.'[1] Ernő Lakatos, who worked closely with Kádár, confirmed this decisiveness; from the start, Kádár had the last word 'on everything'.[2] Yet, determined though he seemed, Kádár would have to make rapid changes to the views and strategy with which he arrived on 7 November. What followed was perhaps the darkest chapter in his career.

The situation that he confronted was desperate. The remnants of armed resistance continued for several days, and there was a renewed general strike. Industrial and mining production had collapsed, and as winter approached the country had a coal shortage. While the army, police and civilian bureaucracy were barely functioning – and in parts hostile – much local power was still in the hands of revolutionary and workers' councils. Internationally, the new government was condemned by most of the non-Communist world; the 'Hungarian question' was now firmly, if belatedly, on the UN's agenda.

For several weeks Kádár and his colleagues dared not venture out of Parliament. They slept on heavy padded doors that were detached and laid on the floors; those of their wives who were there (including Mária, who served as a general office assistant) slept on sofas. Visiting Kádár on 8

November, Andropov noted his isolation: 'right in the middle of the working day …the huge Parliament building was completely deserted; there was no one there apart from six ministers and our troops.' Kádár formed an emotional bond with some of those with whom he worked under these claustrophobic conditions, notably Baikov, who along with two other Soviet officers accompanied him everywhere.[3]

Kádár's priority was to re-establish the party's authority. His first cabinet meeting on 7 November reinstated the former state administration and stripped the revolutionary councils of their powers. Armed force – chiefly Soviet troops at this point – and coercion were central from the start. While much was made of the abolition of ÁVH at the first cabinet meeting, rather less was said about the same meeting's decision to create a special forces militia that would support the party in 'restoring order'.

Nonetheless, Kádár sought a relatively wide base of support. Early cabinet decrees offered some popular measures, including wage rises and appeals to national sentiments through changes to the country's flag, army uniforms and holidays. He struck a conciliatory note in a radio address on 11 November and recognised the need for 'people of the most varied party viewpoints and outlooks' to take part in the government.[4]

Some of Kádár's concessions may well have been tactical, but they reflected the thinking with which he had set out from Moscow. Broad-based support would also reduce his dependence on adherents of the old regime. In the first meeting of the MSZMP's small (twenty-three strong) temporary CC on 11 November, he won support for banning more than two dozen Stalinists from leading roles in public life.

The CC meeting showed how deeply the revolution had shaken the confidence of the Communist leaders, some of whom were more radical than Kádár. Aczél complained about the repressive measures that were being taken, and some members were still sympathetic to the neutrality proclaimed ten days before. There was wide agreement that Hungarian-Soviet relations had to be put on a new footing, and Kádár was mandated to ask for a meeting of Communist countries to discuss this. Many members also took a conciliatory stance towards Nagy.[5] All this struck the Soviet leaders as profoundly unrealistic, and their anxieties mounted as the country was not brought back under control. On 10 November, Suslov was sent back to Budapest along with another CC Secretary, Averki Aristov; Malenkov followed on 15 November. They were to stay secretly in Budapest, based in the Soviet Embassy, for a month.

The new team of Soviet emissaries had to intervene in a row between Kádár and Serov over the KGB's sweeping and indiscriminate arrests. Kádár told Serov, 'the government declaration promised that those who give up their weapons and stop their resistance would not be punished. The Hungarian government should not take revenge and be cruel to these individuals.'[6] Worse, the detainees were held in prisons in Soviet Ukraine, and rumours spread that they were being taken to Siberia. Serov doggedly defended his policy but eventually – after Malenkov's arrival – the deportations ceased and some deportees were returned.

The situation continued to deteriorate. The pressures on Kádár were visible: the party official Ágnes Ságvári remembered 'how haggard and deadly pale he was' when he addressed a meeting of Budapest activists.[7] On 12 November, the Writers' Union and other intelligentsia representatives denounced the continuing Soviet occupation. Two days later, district workers' councils united to form the Greater Budapest Central Workers' Council (KMT). An underground opposition newspaper, edited by the former *Szabad Nép* journalist Miklós Gimes, was published on 15 November. A general strike, the denial of domestic legitimacy from an increasingly united internal opposition and the denial of international legitimacy at the UN threatened the re-establishment of party dominance. The opposition also demanded the return to politics of Nagy, whose presence in the Yugoslav embassy was the most visible challenge to Kádár's authority.

Unlike some of his colleagues, Kádár had been determined from the start to remove the former Prime Minister as a political factor. He was angered by the failure of the plan for Nagy to resign and ease the acceptance of his own government. He made frequent, vitriolic reference to Nagy's last broadcast, winning applause when, during a speech to party activists, he addressed the issue of Nagy's popularity: 'What kind of popularity is it, if it's from going on the radio and saying, "Soviet troops are attacking and we are defending ourselves"? – that's a popularity that Communists can do without.'[8] He resented the Nagy group's refusal to rally to him as a bulwark against Rákosi. The longer resistance went on, the more his exasperation grew, and he saw the group in the Yugoslav embassy as the directing force behind the opposition to him.

Kádár nonetheless wished to avoid a confrontation with the Yugoslavs. Speaking to Andropov on 8 November, he suggested that, if Nagy resigned as Prime Minister and pledged along with his colleagues not to attack the new government, then they could leave the country for Yugoslavia. He reiterated that position, albeit in toughly worded terms, in his first talks with the Yugoslav Ambassador Dalibor Soldatić later that day. The Soviet leadership, however, soon set Kádár right, with a telegram from Deputy Foreign Minister Andrei Gromyko warning that Nagy's case was 'an issue of high principle' and that he must not go to Yugoslavia.[9]

The Soviet idea of a 'compromise' came in a letter from Khrushchev to Tito on 10 November: Nagy and his colleagues should be sent to Romania, where they would be granted political asylum. The Yugoslavs were unenthusiastic; they could not be seen to renege on a granting of political asylum, and the outside world would be unconvinced by Romania as a haven for the oppressed.

The Yugoslavs tried frantically to persuade Nagy and his followers to come to terms, but with little success. However, on 16 November Soldatić told Kádár that the group was prepared to admit errors on a number of important issues – though this may have been an optimistic gloss on the ambassador's part. Yugoslavia would therefore end its grant of asylum, so long as it received a written undertaking – a purely private one, of course – from the Hungarian government that no legal measures would be taken against Nagy and his associates. Kádár, while hedging a little on the granting of a safe conduct, responded with apparent enthusiasm.[10]

The next day, however, Kádár reversed his position, insisting that the group must simply be handed over. This tougher stance reflected a meeting the previous evening with Malenkov's group, who appear to have told Kádár of their plan to kidnap the Nagy group, demand a statement of support from them, and deport them to Romania.[11] This cannot have been a great shock to him, and two nights of tough negotiations with the KMT had underlined the need to resolve the government's crisis of authority. The envoys reported: 'We told our plans to Kádár, who was in full agreement.'[12]

Subsequent negotiations took on a wearying and repetitive quality, with the Yugoslavs continuing to demand a written safe conduct; their main concern, as Kádár noted, was to ensure that 'any possible odium should fall not on the Yugoslav government, but on us.' They finally reached agreement after midnight on 21-22 November, Kádár remarking wearily that 'the Yugoslavs have good lawyers who enjoy drafting.'[13] He and Münnich both signed letters of safe conduct.

In the early evening of 22 November, Nagy, his associates and their families left the Yugoslav Embassy on a coach sent by the Ministry of the Interior. It was soon boarded by Soviet soldiers and taken to a military school now used by the KGB. There the men in the group were seen individually by Münnich, who demanded a statement of support for the government; they all refused. The next day they were flown to Romania, officially as (closely supervised) guests.[14] Four days later, Kádár announced that the government had assisted the group's 'genuine wishes' to leave the country. 'We have promised that, concerning their serious past actions – which they have subsequently acknowledged – we will not take criminal proceedings against them. And we will stick to this.'[15]

The government was now striking out against its opponents. A meeting on 21 November to set up a national workers' council organisation was blocked by Soviet troops, and a government decree sought to limit the councils to factory-level activities. Kádár's rhetoric was hardening too; he warned workers' council representatives that, 'We will not stop the arrests. … If the murderers leave off their banditry, stop frightening the miners and workers, then the arrests will cease.'[16]

He also showed his rougher side to the editorial team of the party newspaper *Népszabadság* (People's Freedom, the new name given during the revolution to *Szabad Nép* – as with the party itself, the paper kept its new name). The editors had wanted to respond to a Soviet attack on a speech by Tito, but Kádár blocked it. When he saw an attempt to revise the article, he summoned the editorial team to a 'very tough' late night meeting, opening it with the words, 'You're out of your minds.' When the journalists went on protest strike, he was outraged. 'This is anarchy,' he shouted at Lajos Fehér, the paper's editor-in-chief and a member of the Executive Committee (the temporary successor to the PB). 'We cannot establish order like this.' On 24 November, he forced through Fehér's removal from *Népszabadság* and other measures to bring the press into line. Three weeks later, when the editorial team repented, he was unwilling to forgive them: 'Kádár considered these people traitors.' It took the Executive Committee to limit his desire for further punishment.[17]

The Hungarian leadership had to undergo a humiliating peer review. The Romanian leader, Gheorghe Gheorghiu-Dej, in Budapest to oversee Nagy's deportation, told the CC to get its house in order: 'You must strike! The working class and the party must strike with full force! If the strength of the working class is not felt now, if all those who organised the events are not called to account, then there will be no guarantee that the reaction will not rise again.'[18] Czechoslovak and East German representatives had both already been in town dispensing similar advice and warning against excessive criticism of the past, while Kádár 'had to lower my eyes before the Chinese comrades, because they asked, where is the dictatorship in your country?'[19] Khrushchev's assessment was that 'things weren't going very well in Hungary ... we couldn't let it go on any longer ... My own hopes rested with Münnich. I thought that I could deal with him better than with Kádár.'[20]

Kádár was, however, learning quickly. On 26 November, Malenkov's group reported that they had found him agreeable to their proposal that some captured insurgents be executed to break the spirit of opposition.[21] A few days earlier, they had reported to Moscow their 'good impression' of their protégé: 'As can be seen from his actions and behaviour in recent days, he has begun to understand much better the need to implement a tougher line in the struggle against reaction ...Regarding his personality, he is somewhat soft; and so in a number of cases we have seen that some vacillating people from his close circle influence him. However, we must say that on the issues of principle, which we had to decide together with him, and about which we know that other influences affected him, Comrade Kádár was able to orient himself very quickly in the situation.'[22]

He was, however, a slower learner in reinterpreting the October events. His preferred description was that it was initially 'an uprising, not a revolution, and they acted from a lot of justified grievances, but right from the outset the counter-revolution was there.' However, 'after the ceasefire on 30 October, it was open counter-revolution.'[23] He had reason to insist that the events had not *started* as 'open counter-revolution'; if they had, he had been guilty of vacillation or worse in the face of the enemy. A harsher interpretation would also narrow his base and vindicate those who hankered after a Rákosi-ite restoration.

This thinking informed the first draft of a resolution to go to the CC in early December. However, when Kádár discussed it with Malenkov's group during the evening of 1 December, the emissaries – urged on from Moscow by Khrushchev – told him that 'we must evaluate events in Hungary more clearly and distinctly as counter-revolution.'[24] At the CC the next day, he gave a four-factor explanation: Rákosi's errors; the damaging decision of 'Comrades Imre Nagy and Losonczy' (as they still were) to take their critique of Rákosi out of the party and into the streets; reactionary forces within Hungary; and 'the prime motive force, international imperialism'. And: 'The fundamental character of the whole thing: counter-revolution.' This came as a shock to a number of his colleagues, but after a two-day debate Kádár got his way with only two votes against. He made a few non-essential concessions, and the resolution adopted on 5 December was somewhat confused, containing elements of the earlier approach. Nonetheless, a Rubicon had been crossed.[25]

Contrary to his initial inclinations, Kádár was becoming reliant on forces from the Rákosi era. The Interior Ministry special forces – the notoriously brutal *pufajkások* ('quilted jackets') – were comprised of ex-ÁVH officers, dismissed functionaries and others with a grievance against the revolution. Similarly, in early December, a 'Political Investigation Department' was set up within the Ministry; a review aimed at excluding those involved in past abuses rapidly became a token exercise, and ex-ÁVH officers flocked in. The leadership abandoned a strongly anti-Stalinist political line, fearing that it was discouraging potential recruits to the party. Kádár's attempt to find a political position equidistant between Rákosi and Nagy had failed. With Nagy's followers – along with the bulk of the population – in outright opposition, there was only one grouping to which to turn for support, and which was more than happy to act against the government's opponents.

There were two hundred arrests on 5 December, with the capture of Miklós Gimes perhaps the biggest source of government satisfaction. More measures followed. Security forces fired on demonstrators in provincial cities; the KMT and other territorial workers' councils were abolished; internment camps were reopened; martial law was declared and summary courts established, with the first execution on 15 December. Early in the New Year, strikes were made punishable by death, and factories – including the working class stronghold of Csepel – were occupied by troops. With that, resistance was all but broken.

The next stage was a meeting in Budapest on 1-3 January 1957 of leaders from the Soviet, Hungarian, Czechoslovak, Romanian and Bulgarian parties. The more reformist elements – the Poles and the Yugoslavs – were excluded. Kádár – doubtless after extensive discussions with his Soviet details – urged that it be called 'to debate common steps to be taken in connection with the "Imre Nagy group."'[26] Notes of the meeting indicate discussion of 'the responsibility and accountability of Imre Nagy and others in the Hungarian events, and their legal consequences'.[27] Public confirmation followed when the Hungarian party communiqué spoke of 'the treachery of the Imre Nagy government', while both in public speeches and in a meeting with China's Zhou Enlai Kádár took to speaking of Nagy as a traitor.[28]

Kádár had once again reversed his position in a matter of weeks. He may not have had a single decision point, but rather a process of reaction to a still fluid situation. In his daily dealings with the Soviets, the fear and anger produced by the Polish and Hungarian crises would have been very clear. Khrushchev himself now seemed to backtrack from his assault on Stalin, and from the precarious rapprochement with Tito's Yugoslavia, cast once more as the centre of ideological contamination. The heresy hunt was on, and there was no greater heretic than Nagy. As early as December, Soviet officials were gathering material for an expected Nagy trial, and Romania's Gheorghiu-Dej was confident that 'we will transfer him to the Hungarian comrades, and … he will be hanged for the crimes that he has committed.'[29]

There was also internal political logic to a Nagy trial. Kádár could destroy his main rival and show himself a leader both to the Soviets and to a nervous and vengeful party apparatus. There is no reason to believe that this went against his instincts; the hardening of his attitude when confronted by resistance in November and December fused with the emergence of political conditions that favoured a trial. The move against Nagy matched the increasing arrests and executions and the establishment of the machinery of repression and reprisals. In the spring, 'People's Courts' were established, with procedures weighted against the defendant and with a judge supported by two lay assessors ('people's judges'), often individuals who had suffered during the revolution. Reluctant judges were purged. Many party members were out for revenge, and the leadership, from Kádár down, was determined to frighten Hungarian society into quiescence.

Kádár, meanwhile, had to watch Rákosi and his allies within Hungary. At an Executive Committee meeting in February, he was reminded that many party members were asking awkward questions about his dissolution of the former party in November.[30] He used the CC meeting on 26 February to steer through resolutions condemning Nagy in the harshest terms yet, but also determining that the exiles must remain out of the country for the time being – in the case of Rákosi and Gerő, for at least five years.[31] The exception was Révai, who was allowed to return and to publish in *Népszabadság* an article characteristically entitled, 'Ideological purity.' It is not clear whether Kádár saw him as a potential ally, capable of bringing the problematic intelligentsia to heel, or a useful scarecrow who would frighten more moderate elements into huddling around the existing leadership. If the latter, then Kádár's calculation was vindicated by the hostile reaction to Révai's article.[32]

The Rákosi issue came to a head when Kádár visited Moscow in late March. He later described how Voroshilov brandished a letter from Rákosi – to which Kádár allegedly responded by telling the Soviets that they could back Rákosi if they liked, but he and his colleagues would have nothing to do with it.[33] In fact, the Presidium had already concluded that 'there is no one other than Kádár – we must back him',[34] but decided to show him the Rákosi letter, presumably to keep him under pressure. He was then given some reassurance, and told his Executive Committee that the Soviet leaders considered the exiles 'political corpses, who can never return to power.'[35] A few months later, Rákosi was forced to leave Moscow for the Black Sea. Though Khrushchev still 'treated János Kádár with strong reservations',[36] the ever-clearer signs of quiescence in Hungary undermined the critics.

The Nagy trial was not a quid pro quo for Rákosi's exclusion, but preparations accelerated after the Moscow talks. Kállai had travelled to Romania in late January in an unsuccessful attempt to divide the Nagy group. Prospects for a trial were discussed at Executive Committee meetings in February, and Kállai told the Soviet official Boris Ponomarev that he and Kádár were in favour, but that some CC members were hesitant.[37] On 2 April, Kádár told the Executive Committee that the Nagy issue had been discussed in Moscow. 'We raised it,' he insisted – which may have been true, but merely described the latest in the joint discussions that had been going on since December. '… To my mind, we must say to the Hungarian people, to the Hungarian people's enemies and to the world that it is not possible to organise counter-revolution in a socialist system with impunity. I'm in favour of getting to work and reaching a decision in the foreseeable future – you don't wait eight to ten months, or a year, to draw the sting.'[38]

On 1 May, a mass rally in Heroes' Square drew about a hundred thousand people, a success beyond the leadership's expectations. For Kádár, its significance was emotional as well as political. He kept a large photograph of the rally in his office, and would eagerly show it to foreign visitors, explaining its significance. It was then, he often said, that he realised that the 'consolidation' would succeed.[39] After the intense pressures of the previous months – the fear of failure, and the knowledge of what much of his country and the world thought of him – he must have felt a powerful sense of vindication.

This acquiescence was not based simply on fear. Though party membership, at two hundred thousand, was less than a quarter of the pre-revolutionary level, it was climbing steadily; these members and their families were committed beneficiaries of the system. Economic recovery brought a short-term boost to living standards for the non-party mass of the population. The countryside remained calm, tranquillised by the abolition of forced deliveries of agricultural products and tolerance of private farming.

Yet the success of consolidation produced a narrowing, not a broadening of thinking. Nowhere was this clearer than in economic policy. The December CC resolution had promised to redefine the role of planning and to boost living standards.[40] With these aims in mind, the government set up the so-called Varga committee, a network of expert groups under the aegis of Professor István Varga, an internationally known economist. Among the advisers was Jenő Rácz, a former Finance Minister and, like Varga, a Smallholder. 'It was a very interesting sign that Kádár was willing to employ such people.'[41]

Kádár was open to change and prepared – at least to a certain extent – to give the specialists a freer rein; it was part of his critique of the Rákosi era that their advice had been ignored.[42] Yet he was no economic theorist. Throughout his leadership, he would be exercised by the wasteful nature of the system, but often had little more than anecdotal solutions. 'Here we had Comrade Ho Chi Minh, who doesn't dare leave half a cup of coffee because that would be a waste. If we could have just a fraction of that economising ...'[43] His touchstone was a pragmatic assessment of what was needed to raise living standards.

By June 1957, the Varga committee had produced its proposals, urging a shift from a pure command economy to greater reliance on prices, taxes and interest rates as policy tools. However, the tide was now against comprehensive reform, which was tarred with the dread brushes of revisionism and the Yugoslav way, and in favour of modest changes to policy. In any case, the leadership feared the short-term impact of reform on living standards, while economic recovery removed the sense of an urgent need for change. They were content to cherry-pick a few policies from the reform debate – notably a partial price reform and a charge to companies for use of capital assets – and otherwise stick to a modified, somewhat more rational form of central planning.[44]

The same gradual quietus awaited other proposals to modify the structures of the party-state. Although the government had been determined to crush the workers' councils' political role, it initially envisaged their participating in the running of companies as part of the economic reform. However, once the old mechanisms of control – the official trade unions, local and factory committees – were reconstructed, they sought to eliminate this unwanted rival. At first, Kádár leant against this: 'possibly thirty Communist workers became angry with [the councils], but seven hundred women textile workers did not. ... This is not the way to solve the question.' However, the leadership lost interest and in November 1957 the councils were abolished.[45]

Similarly, Kádár was initially interested in a notionally multi-party system. Reconstituted Smallholder and National Peasant parties would represent rural interests within a Communist-dominated 'front', and a modest surplus of candidates to seats would give voters an element of choice.[46] However, between December and February, these plans – modelled on the Polish system – were abandoned. Kádár found the parties' price for collaboration too high and was nervous of political mobilisation in hitherto quiescent rural areas. Reading a memorandum from the Peasant Party, 'Kádár's first question was: who would guarantee that this would not lead to counter-revolution in the villages?'[47]

Even so, he was already marking out differences from the Rákosi era, denoted in the rhetoric of 'the two-front struggle'. The concept was not original; Poland's Gomułka often characterised his politics in these terms, and it could be traced back to some of Lenin's writings. But for three decades Kádár would make the phrase his own. Rare indeed were the political circumstances for which it could not be lovingly produced and applied. 'Sectarians' or 'dogmatists' to his left, Nagy-like 'revisionists' to his right – and, in the solid centre, pursuing the true Leninist path, Comrade Kádár himself.

The main practical difference between the new leadership and its predecessor was in its attitude to public support. Kádár abandoned the mobilising political approach of the Rákosi era, dropping the '*Szabad Nép* half hour' – compulsory discussion of the party daily in the workplace each morning – in 1957. And while acceptance rather than enthusiasm was expected from the non-party population, the leadership also recognised the need to offer something in return for this quiescence. Hence the anxious attention to living standards.

Kádár's team – in particular, István Szirmai, now heading the Prime Minister's Information Office – also sought new, more sophisticated methods to shape and control public opinion. They aimed at greater diversity in newspaper and magazine styles, and more day-to-day independence for editors – but always with the backstop of editors' 'responsibility' for what they published. As Kádár put it, 'We can't take on ourselves responsibility for the entire press. Of course, I'm not championing freedom of the press here, but the party's guidance must prevail in another way.'[48]

The new line was evident at the special party congress on 27-29 June that sealed Kádár's 'consolidation'. His speeches included harsh and ominous references to the Nagy group, while a doctrinaire intervention by Révai gave him the chance to dissociate himself: 'the fallen leadership … fell in such a manner and under such circumstances that it can never again return to the leadership of the party.'[49] The eleven-member PB and five-member Secretariat elected by the Congress, barely changed from their 'temporary' forerunners, were noticeably younger and less 'Muscovite' than their pre-revolutionary predecessors. Three PB members – Kádár, Marosán and Kállai – had been in Rákosi's prisons, and the centre of gravity was Kádárist pragmatism.

It was, however, events in Moscow that most strengthened Kádár's position. In a marathon CC session on 22-28 June, Khrushchev saw off Molotov and his other opponents, dispatched to oblivion as the 'anti-party group'. This braked the possibility of a full Stalinist restoration. With some satisfaction, Kádár was able to tell his new CC that it was good that the Soviet leadership had 'so decisively defended the main political line established at the Twentieth Congress.'[50]

Even though he needed it, Kádár remained wary of the state security apparatus. Within days of the Soviet intervention, he was complaining that some of the worst ÁVH elements were gathering around the Interior Ministry.[51] He later claimed that some State Security officers were trying to investigate him; one reportedly told a journalist who was being interrogated, 'rest assured, the Kádár business isn't finished yet.'[52] A number of those held by State Security confirm this impression; when the scholar and People's College leader László Kardos showed his surprise at seeing Rákosi's portrait on the wall, his interrogator said, 'What do you think – that we'd put up a picture of János the Shit?'[53]

Thus, when a report on the potential scope of the security organs' record-keeping came before the PB, Kádár dismissed it scathingly. He was critical of the industrial-scale record-keeping of the Rákosi era, dismissed a proposal for the security organs to keep files on party members, and as for their suggested emergency powers, 'this is the kind of point that should never in any way be put into a proposal.' The report had also recommended keeping files on 'leading figures of international reaction'. 'What do we want? Are we going to occupy America? We don't need this and we shouldn't do it.' The PB agreed with him to revise the report, though State Security proved recalcitrant in acting on it.[54]

Unease about State Security notwithstanding, the arrests, trials and executions (approaching a hundred by early summer) continued. According to Ferenc Nezvál, then Minister of Justice, 'Kádár personally drove the settling of accounts with the counter-revolutionaries ... he would have liked to close down this counter-revolutionary business as quickly as possible.' Nonetheless, 'Kádár made enormous efforts that we should undertake everything that we wanted to do legally.'[55] This was an idiosyncratic definition of legality, but it sheds important light on the leadership's self-image. PB members often emphasised among themselves the need to avoid repeating Rákosi's crimes, to act on the basis of evidence and for State Security not to use physical coercion.[56] In practice, however, court systems were designed to secure convictions, evidence was slanted by political considerations and physical maltreatment was frequent for all but well-known prisoners held in the capital.

Kádár's terror was much more selective than Rákosi's. As he put it, 'If the counter-revolution sticks its nose out of its maggot-hole, [the security forces] should not only shake their fists at them, but strike them down right away. But they should not flaunt their power against the people: they must always remember that this power must be used not against the people but against the enemies of the people.'[57] An Interior Ministry report completed in May identified the target groups of the reprisals: leaders and members of armed groups; members of revolutionary and workers councils, and of the resistance groups that emerged after 4 November; leaders of the political parties that had (re)-emerged during the revolution; and the usual class enemies. (To this should be added a further target group, the critical and 'reform Communist' intelligentsia). The report claimed that 'ordinary workers deceived and influenced by the counter-revolutionaries' would not be targeted.[58]

Nonetheless, there was self-deceit here too. Kádár sometimes complained about excessive arrests, and talked as though the reprisals simply meant dealing, as quickly as possible, with a hard core of class enemies: 'the courts should line them up in a row, sentence them to death and hang them.'[59] But since the revolution's social base diverged dramatically from that of the regime's demonology, the reality was very different: the arrests continued, and young working class men who had taken part in the fighting made up a majority of those sentenced to death and executed.

The 'enemies' inevitably included Nagy and his associates, who had been officially arrested and brought back to Budapest in mid-April for interrogation and the preparation of their trial. In August the Interior Minister Béla Biszku conferred with Andropov (now head of the CC department for relations with governing Communist parties), proposing a secret trial of the group in late September, with death sentences for Nagy and six other defendants (one in absentia).[60]

The Soviet leaders, however, had the trial postponed; Nagy's execution would vitiate a tentative rapprochement with Tito, which they hoped would be sealed at a world conference of Communist parties in November.[61] However, the Yugoslavs refused to accept Soviet primacy or to sign a stridently anti-revisionist charter for the Communist movement. Thus on 16 December the Hungarian PB met in closed session with one item – 'penal policy' – on the agenda, in preparation for a CC meeting five days later.[62] Kádár presented the proposal for a trial to the latter meeting: 'if we abandon the struggle now, it would confuse our supporters ... If there were to be an amnesty now, it would cover the most guilty people and that would weaken the people's democracy.' The resolution was passed unanimously;[63] Kádár kept a record of it in his safe until his death. Earlier that day, Géza Losonczy, one of Kádár's fellow-victims in 1951 but now marked for the death penalty, had died in prison in circumstances that remain mysterious.

The trial began on 5 February 1958 in a military courtroom in political police headquarters. The next day, there was another postponement, again at Soviet behest;[64] Khrushchev now feared that Nagy's execution would disrupt a planned superpower summit. Kádár marched his CC troops back down the hill on 14 February, but made clear that this was only a deferral. 'What can we do? One, we delay. Two, we finish it, but influence the proceedings so that the sentences passed don't increase international tensions. However, this option would be very bad.' In other words, he was determined on Nagy's execution.[65]

In contrast to the Soviet eagerness for a trial in early 1957, Khrushchev was, it seems, weighing the international political costs of Nagy's execution. As Kádár reported to the PB in December, 'Comrade Khrushchev said it's right that we want to bring this matter to a close. But he asked: how will we bring it to a close? ... Prison, a reprimand or what?' There is some other anecdotal evidence that the Soviet leader was prepared to consider a lighter penalty.[66]

For Kádár, however, the calculation was much simpler. The Nagy trial was a corollary of the other reprisals: as Kádár put it to the December CC, 'the struggle should be taken to the end on the basis of its own logic.'[67] While the February CC meeting had accepted the proposed delay, the mood had been one of frustration over unfinished business.[68] There was also the self-serving argument – the more seductive because it had a grain of truth in it – that, so long as Nagy's fate was unresolved, there could be no possibility of an amnesty, of an end to the reprisals and to Hungary's pariah status with much of the world. For Kádár himself, there was a simpler, more personal motive: so long as Nagy lived, unrepentant, he represented an alternative and a refutation of all that Kádár had done since 4 November 1956.[69]

Kádár would later say that 'everything hinged on one sentence' – that Nagy's fate was sealed by his refusal to resign.[70] However, by spring 1958 it is unlikely that anything that Nagy could have said or done would have saved him. In any case, he was immovable. He was suffering psychologically from the sheer misery of his situation, and physically from his chronic heart problems;[71] however, after years of doubts and hesitations, he had found a meaning in his October, and he was not going to give it up.

With Soviet-Yugoslav relations returning to shrill polemics, and the East-West summit failing to materialise, Kádár was again given the green light for the trial. In the interim, the most uncompromising defendant, József Szilágyi, was separately (and secretly) tried; he was hanged on 24 April. Meeting in closed session on 27 May, the PB ruled that 'the trial of the Imre Nagy group must be allowed to proceed freely'; Kádár scratched out Nagy's name, replacing it with 'X'.[72]

An informal meeting of the same body on 2 June probably settled the sentences. For Nagy and Maléter, the death penalty came almost ex officio. Other cases were more blurred. Gimes may have been doomed by Kádár's personal animus towards the man who had played a leading role in the opposition after the Soviet intervention, and by the useful political message sent out by including a Jewish writer among those hanged.[73]

'I shall not appeal for clemency': Imre Nagy before the People's Court, 15 June 1958

Donáth, one of those marked for execution on Biszku's August 1957 list, received the lesser sentence of twelve years' imprisonment. Was this, as some rumours had it, Kádár's decision? It is possible; he had kept Donáth's name out of at least one high-profile denunciation and would later show a wish to draw him back into politics.[74] Kopácsi, another marginal case (he was sentenced to life imprisonment), may have been saved by his working-class background and links within the party.

The CC signed off on the trial (in general terms) on 6 June and proceedings began again in Fő Street three days later. The prearranged sentences were handed down late on the afternoon of 15 June. With polite dignity, Nagy told the 'esteemed People's Court Division' that they had got things badly wrong. He would have to bear his fate, but entrusted his reputation to the Hungarian people and to the international working class. 'I believe that I am the victim of a serious error, a judicial error. I shall not ask for clemency.'[75] Shortly after 5 a.m. the next day, in conditions of the strictest secrecy, Nagy, Maléter and Gimes were hanged in the courtyard of the Budapest National Prison, and their bodies buried nearby.

Amid the international outrage that erupted when the executions were announced, Kádár's already low reputation sank even further; yet the prism of the Cold War ensured that much of the blame was directed towards Moscow. The CIA Director Allen Dulles was convinced 'that the signal for the executions had almost certainly come from Moscow ... He thought it likely that in the sequel Kádár would drop out of the political picture quite soon.'[76] The myth that the Soviets forced the executions on a reluctant

Hungarian leader would grow over the years, and there are signs that Kádár and his associates fostered this from the start. The experienced Associated Press correspondent, Endre Marton, was one of those taken in: 'all my sources, *including one who was personally very close to Kádár*, told me how desperate Kádár had been when Nagy was abducted, and when he was executed eighteen months later.'[77]

The campaign of reprisals continued. Day to day responsibility lay with Biszku as Minister of the Interior, along with the Minister of Justice and the Public Prosecutor. Behind them, however, stood Marosán (CC Secretary for Administrative Affairs) and ultimately the PB. The party leadership set out the philosophy of the reprisals and tracked the numbers of arrests, imprisonments and executions; information was also provided to Kádár personally.[78] Throughout 1957, the leadership was urging the process on. At a PB meeting in December, Kádár again lamented the failure to act quickly and 'annihilate' the enemies of the system: 'it would have been a lot better to sentence five to six hundred people to death, and then we'd have had to bang up thirty thousand fewer people in prison.' And, so long as he felt that he was under international pressure, he would not consider an amnesty.[79]

In the three years after the revolution, thirty-five thousand people faced some sort of investigation; of these, between twenty-two and twenty-six thousand cases ended in a sentence. Around thirteen thousand passed through the internment camps, and tens of thousands were dismissed from their jobs. Two hundred and twenty-nine people were executed for their role in the uprising; the latest estimates suggest a total figure, including executions that were an indirect effect of the reprisals (for example, the more severe punishment of common crimes under martial law), of three hundred and forty-one.[80]

By the standards of the twentieth century's most industrially organised horrors, these are relatively modest numbers. On a human, individual scale, they remain a story of brutality and anguish. István Angyal, the Tűzoltó Street insurgent who had wanted to show Kádár what good Communists his fighters were, was executed on 1 December 1958. He wrote from prison: 'We felt that the party should put itself at the helm of the revolution.'[81] Péter Mansfeld had been fifteen years old when he helped the fighters in Széna Square; after his arrest in 1958 as the leader of a gang of rebellious young men, he was condemned to death and executed on 21 March 1959, eleven days after his eighteenth birthday. Mansfeld was not the only teenage victim. Later that year, a group of young working class fighters were hanged, eleven of them on the same day. The writer György Konrád, then a social worker, visited their traumatised community. 'As I arrived there, I heard sobbing from all sides ... Their petition for clemency may not even have reached Kádár. I would think, though, it was in his power to find out about it.'[82] In fact, Kádár rarely involved himself in individual cases, unless they were of great political sensitivity. He did, however, set out the overall aims and methods of the process, monitored it and spurred it on; in that lies his responsibility.

He would later show signs of a bad conscience about Nagy's fate, but never about that of the faceless hundreds who were also hanged. The history of 1956 was rewritten, not only by his official historians, but also in his own mind. Some leading writers visited him in 1959, and put in a word for their imprisoned colleague Tibor Déry. Kádár said that he would look into it, but added, 'Now I'm going to tell you something.' There followed an angry outburst about the Communist victims of 1956, in particular Imre Mező: 'There was a Jewish boy in the party, with whom I was especially close …'[83] Despite their emotive significance in party propaganda, there had in fact been relatively few such killings; they had nonetheless struck genuine fear into Communists, even reformers such as Losonczy. The visceral significance of this justification was reflected in Kádár's (inaccurate) comment to Gorbachev almost thirty years later: 'when the number of death sentences matched the number of innocent victims of the counter-revolution, I asked the comrades to bring it to an end.'[84]

From late 1958, the leadership was looking to bring the process of mass reprisals to a close; however, although 1959 saw fewer prison sentences handed down, there were still many executions, and the last hangings of revolutionaries took place as late as August 1961.[85] The process had continued long after opposition had been crushed, but that too sent a message: we don't do this because we have to, we do this because we can. Social quiescence was confirmed by the parliamentary elections of November 1958, in which the single list presented by the Patriotic People's Front (PPF) secured more than ninety-nine per cent of the vote.

Kádár had successfully, if brutally secured his leadership and re-established the party-state. Yet this stability still left many questions unanswered. Would the ideological anomaly of predominantly private farming be allowed to continue? Given the recreation of old structures, how much room for manoeuvre – in areas ranging from ideology to reliance on heavy industry – was left? With dissenting writers silenced, how tight would be the harness of party control over cultural and intellectual life? 'Consolidation' so far had been based on a combination of severe if selective repression, a partial withdrawal of the system from private life and a mild rise in living standards – but would the balance between these elements change? Could the regime change its reputation and reduce its isolation from the non-Communist world? In resolving these questions, 'Kádárism' – a Hungarian variant on the efforts, seen across the Soviet bloc, to build a post-Stalinist, post-1956 order – would start to come into definition.

10

FOUNDATIONS

With the June 1957 conference, the party's institutions were restored to their normal functioning, represented in Kádár's case by his chairing weekly meetings of the PB and fortnightly meetings of the Secretariat. He was the leading, even dominant, figure in both. Nonetheless, '[he] did not have harmonious relations with the political team that he set out with': too many could see themselves in one or both of his posts. Kiss and – to a lesser extent – Apró represented links to the Rákosi era. Kállai, Kádár's fellow defendant in 1951, fancied himself as the regime's thinker and resented Kádár's pre-eminence. Münnich had been a powerful figure in the early, security-oriented months of the regime, though he had subsided somewhat thereafter.[1]

However, younger PB members such as Jenő Fock and Béla Biszku were loyal, and the former Social Democrat and Rákosi victim György Marosán 'always stood with Kádár at the critical moments'. An abrasive, even thuggish figure with a taste for exhibitionism – he would open his shirt before an audience, saying (incorrectly) that he had invited the Soviets in, and that anyone who did not like it could shoot him – Marosán worked tirelessly to rally the party.[2] Though his class-conscious instincts were sharply to the Left, Marosán supported Kádár both as a bulwark against Rákosi and as a fellow worker.

Unsurprisingly, Kádár had an informal group of associates outside the PB. He would work through the night on his speeches with Szirmai, who in 1959 became CC Secretary for Agitation and Propaganda. József Sándor, head of the Central Committee's Party and Mass Organisations department, was 'a sort of *éminence grise* of the new regime'. At a PB meeting in 1958, Kállai complained bitterly that Kádár was taking decisions with Sándor and the actor Tamás Major over games of *ulti* (a popular card game of which he was very fond). The parties ceased soon afterwards.[3]

The post-Stalinist ideal of 'collective leadership' rendered anomalous Kádár's 'double function' – as Prime Minister and First Secretary – and resulted in jockeying for position throughout 1957, with Kiss reportedly engaged in frantic self-promotion. Kádár remained First Secretary – now, in 'normal' conditions, the centre of power once more – but gave up the premiership to Münnich in January 1958. Kádár 'did not take Ferenc Münnich very seriously', and his intimates carped about Münnich's drinking, womanising and slack approach to work. However, his age and lack of evident ambition made him the ideal successor to the premiership.[4]

Kádár's position was buttressed by his rising standing with the Soviet leadership as the man who had pacified Hungary. This was crystallised during Khrushchev's eight-day visit in April 1958. The Hungarians laid on an impressively choreographed show, with Khrushchev, who fancied himself as a crowd-pleaser, glad-handing enthusiastic miners and peasants. Although Kádár nervously turned down Khrushchev's offer for Soviet troops to leave Hungary[5] – he may well have seen them as a more neutral containing force than the domestic security services – the Soviet leader ended his visit full of enthusiasm. 'Until now I barely knew Comrade Kádár … now we have spent eight days together and I am convinced that he is the sort of comrade that the Hungarian working class can happily rely on.'[6] The visit confirmed Khrushchev's judgement that he had backed the right horse and began a strong alliance, even a friendship, between the two leaders.

A direct relationship with the Soviet leader was all the more important for Kádár since the scale of Soviet involvement in Hungarian affairs meant that they had multiple sources of information. Even in private conversations, Kádár always used terms that could be appropriate for a 'third person' taking part. 'Even from the closest inner circle, everything leaked out – to Moscow and to the neighbouring countries too… Everyone had alliances abroad.'[7] Kádár seems also to have assumed that his office was bugged.[8] He sometimes expressed quite bluntly his opinions of Soviet mistakes, but he was careful to ensure that his ultimate loyalty was not open to doubt.

Kádár lost one of his early Soviet contacts in 1958 when Baikov was suddenly recalled. He made anxious enquiries as to why this had happened, wrote a testimonial on Baikov's behalf and raised the issue on a visit to Moscow.[9] His links with the steadily rising Andropov proved more durable. A Soviet observer captured their curious relationship: 'One could sense in the atmosphere a profound personal liking and at the same time a sharp tension and even embarrassment. There was too much between the two men,' most of it related to 1956.[10] On visits to Moscow over the next quarter of a century, Kádár regularly held informal discussions with Andropov, seeing them as an important source of support at the highest

Soviet levels.[11] As General Secretary in the eighties, Andropov was to show Kádár signs of special favour – personally choosing the presents when Kádár and Mária visited the Soviet Union[12] – though, given his cool inscrutability, it is probably an exaggeration to speak of friendship rather than of a strong political understanding.

Grossly unequal though they were, Soviet relations with Hungary – and with the other satellites – had become more complex after 1956. Instead of the proconsular role of ambassadors such as Andropov, 'consultations' and 'advice' at every level – up to the meetings of First Secretaries – became the favoured method of intervention.[13] In addition, the Soviet leadership was wary of provoking another political crisis within the satellites, and especially in Hungary. This introduced an element of mutual dependence into the relationship, giving scope for bargaining, especially on economic issues.

Though the political demands on Kádár were relentless, he also had more personal matters to attend to. On 31 October 1958 – after, she said, many sleepless nights – Mária wrote him an angry letter. 'I turn to you as a comrade,' she wrote, and it was as a comrade that she seemed to feel slighted. Her career had suffered; she had shared her husband's disgrace in 1951, but had never had full rehabilitation. Kádár, keen to avoid the appearance of special favours, had been no help. Behind this lay frustrations and grievances going back to their early years together. Then, as now, she felt neglected. 'There were times when I asked myself, "why the hell did this man sanctify and legalise our relationship? A dog wouldn't put up with his indifference."'

Now her interests were being given no weight. 'Your excessive party-mindedness and self-regard amount to nothing in human terms.' If her situation was not resolved, she suggested that they move to a small flat where she would keep house. She also threatened to take her case to the PB. 'For years I have been well behaved and stayed quiet about this, because you are my husband. I beg you, how long can this go on? And why am I still just a shadow? … We can argue, we can yell at each other about this thing, but there mustn't be any sermons – that's out of place and doesn't solve anything.' She was not quite sure how to end her letter. 'Maybe like this: I'm asking for some sort of human answer.'[14]

Clearly, it was Kádár's behaviour that was at issue as much as any specific grievance. He may well have been difficult to live with, and not only because of the burden of work. Though some women who worked with him liked his kindness and courtesy, his expectations of them were deeply conservative. Ágnes Ságvári noted his 'peculiar reserve' with women, and his aversion to those who were individualistic and dressed stylishly. Borbála, his own cantankerous madonna, had clearly done much to shape his attitudes. 'He deeply honoured his mother, and mothers bringing up their children alone had a special place in his thinking.'[15] Mária was certainly not the kind of stylish woman who made him uneasy, and like Borbála she was a forceful personality who was nonetheless devoted to him. However, at this time he had taken her too much for granted.

How Kádár responded to the letter is not clear. Mária remained in her job at the Information Office of the Prime Minister (though she was later made its deputy head). Kádár may have made an effort to be a little more attentive. In any case, her next letter to him, written a couple of months later, returns to the former mixture of affectionate diminutives, details of her medical treatment and fussing over whether he was looking after himself. The storm, it seems, had passed.

1958 had already brought Kádár another shock. On a visit to Somogy County, local officials told him that he had a half-brother living nearby who was a party member. This was János Kertész (he had magyarised his name), one of János Krezinger's three sons from his marriage a little over a year after he had made his escape from Borbála. Kertész had also visited party headquarters in Budapest and asked after Kádár. Whatever little information Kádár had gleaned about his father was enough for him to take Kertész's claim very seriously. Writing to him on 31 March – as 'Dear Comrade Kertész' – he stated, 'Quite honestly, I too believe that we are related.' After they met in early May, their letters began, 'Dear Brother.'[16]

*Mária Kádár – stepping out ahead of her husband for once –
at a Budapest flower show in June 1960*

János Krezinger, still living in Pusztaszemes, wanted – somewhat nervously – to meet his son. Kádár did not hurry to do so; it was not until he visited the area again in February 1961 that he met his father along with his half-brothers. He afterwards told Mária that 'it hadn't been easy'; they had talked about Krezinger's health and local farming. The old man said, 'my boys, let's raise our glasses to the family being together.' However, they did not meet again; when Krezinger died in 1965, Kádár sent representatives to the funeral with a wreath, but did not attend. He kept friendly but distant contact with his Krezinger relatives.[17]

Similarly, he took in Kapoly and the Balints' house – 'Here I am,' he said, 'I've come home' – during his visit, but did not return. Kapoly would occasionally surface in talks with interviewers or foreign visitors, but had no other hold on him. He told his biographer, 'I have no time to deal with my past.'[18] By this point, there were perhaps a number of aspects of that past that he preferred not to dwell on. Better by far to deal with the demanding present.

The biggest demands and dilemmas concerned agriculture. Rákosi's aggressive but ineffectual collectivisation programmes had been mostly reversed during 1956 and in particular in its aftermath, as the authorities were preoccupied with reasserting control elsewhere. By the end of 1958, collective farm membership stood at less than half the 1953 level and the farms amounted to little more than a tenth of the country's arable land.[19] Nagy's revolutionary government had swept away another pillar of Soviet-style agriculture – compulsory delivery of products by the collective farms – and Kádár had confirmed their abolition. The relationship between the authorities and the farms was – at least in theory – less that of central planning than of a regulated market, with prices, taxes and credits replacing plan directives as the main tools of policy.

Kádár appointed Lajos Fehér – 'practically the MSZMP's last Imre Nagy-ist Mohican'[20] – as head of the CC's Agriculture Department. This was a sign that he was prepared to draw on domestic traditions of pro-peasant agricultural reform, represented by the March Front and by Nagy, rather than merely replicating the Soviet dogma of collectivisation and the primacy of industry. Fehér had the National Peasant Party agricultural expert (and Nagy government minister) Ferenc Erdei released from prison and set to work on policy formation.[21] The resulting *Agrarian Theses* of July 1957 argued for heavy investments to develop a modern, large-scale agriculture, and a voluntary, long-term approach to collectivisation.[22] Critics of this heterodox policy – whose figurehead was the Agriculture Minister, Imre Dögei – urged the traditional approach of rapid collectivisation driven by coercion and punitive taxation.

Kádár's attitudes were mixed. He was unwilling to jeopardise peace in the countryside and food supplies for the cities, and thus ruled out a return to compulsory deliveries. 'We've got to say this very clearly to the party activists,' he told the PB in December 1957, 'get out of your head the idea that every year we're going to debate purchasing versus deliveries.' Yet he had no natural sympathy for diverting resources towards the richer peasants, and his jibes showed his unease with Fehér's gaggle of agrarian experts. They had deviated, he said, from the party's main policy line and 'perhaps a little from Marxism-Leninism too.' They were always thinking of the peasantry, 'and somewhere in twentieth place the working class comes into their minds.'[23]

Fehér was soon in retreat. A truly pro-peasant stance was quickly undermined by a ten per cent cut in agricultural purchasing prices, and the prospect, however long-term, of collectivisation made farmers unwilling to invest.[24] The most decisive factor, however, was political and 'international'. Khrushchev, seeking to outstrip the West and answer the ideological challenge posed by Mao, encouraged collectivisation drives and accelerated industrial investments across the Soviet bloc. Hungary had to throw its previously cautious three-year economic plan to the winds, with investments leaping 28 per cent in 1958 and 34 per cent in 1959.[25]

Regarding agriculture, Kádár told the CC that the 'justified critics' of Hungary's policy included 'the international working class'. That class had its unique way of making its concerns known. On his visit to Hungary in April 1958, Khrushchev reportedly pressured Kádár to restart agricultural collectivisation. 'János Kádár said, "It's a big issue, but I'll think about it."' Khrushchev's reply: 'Well, now, what a decent fellow you are, because when I took this up with Gomułka, he wouldn't even think about it, you couldn't talk to him about it.'[26]

The April 1958 CC ruled that a plan for 'socialist transformation' of agriculture should be drawn up in the autumn.[27] The passive domestic response to Nagy's execution and the return to Hungary of a number of Rákosi's associates increased the leadership's self-confidence, but this did not make the underlying decision any easier. Fehér's gradualism was clearly rejected, but the political and economic costs of Dögei's coercive approach were unacceptable. Kádár wanted to achieve collectivisation without the disastrous falls in agricultural output seen in Soviet and other experience. Such a policy would be expensive; nonetheless, it was the option that he took.

The PB was still deeply split on the issue in the autumn. Kiss briefed the Soviet Ambassador on the party's divisions, making clear that his sympathies rested with Dögei.[28] Kádár determined that the issue must be resolved at the CC; unusually, that body – a 'dignified' rather than efficient part of the system, a sounding board at best – would see vigorous and genuine debate. Its decision would be final: 'this is an issue on which we must get things in order and afterwards everyone has to stick to it.'[29]

At the CC meeting on 5-7 December[30], Kádár insisted that the issue must not be seen in terms of class war: '[People ask] why do the peasants live better here than the workers? To my mind it's not right to bring the question up, at least not like that.' Instead, it was a question of Hungary playing its part in socialist development: 'Everyone's ahead of us. Even the Albanians are far ahead of us.' Rejecting both Fehér's and Dögei's positions, he said that Hungary should for the present take 'steps' forward to collectivisation, even if in future it might perhaps 'leap'.

He then sternly denounced both Fehér and Dögei and made it clear that he would not tolerate continuing factionalism. 'And I'm telling you, comrades, that we'll clear this up today, or tomorrow, or whenever – if we have to debate it for ten days. And if anyone deviates from it – I tell you, comrades, I wouldn't recognise my best friend any more ...' Fehér made a contrite statement of self-criticism, but Dögei mulishly refused to do so. Kádár had handed out 'comradely' criticism, and Fehér had closed the matter by accepting it. Dögei had not, and this was something that Kádár would not forget.

The CC resolution approved a collectivisation drive, to be achieved without recourse to force, and to be coupled with *increased* agricultural production.[31] This, however dubious its economics, was the two-front struggle in operation. For Fehér's supporters this was at least an indication that agriculture would not be wholly subordinated. As Rezső Nyers, then head of SZÖVOSZ (the co-operative farms association) put it: 'Of course it was an economic absurdity – politically, however, we had to support it, and I did support it.'[32]

With just a few months left of the agricultural off-season, the campaign began immediately in the villages of western Hungary, its first wave lasting until March 1959. Although a modest tax was put on private farmers, the main methods of persuasion were house to house 'agitation' by workers and party members sent into the villages, and threats to those who would not join, often regarding their children's education. Physical force was officially proscribed; it was used much less than under Rákosi, but was far from unknown.[33] There were carrots as well as sticks: ground rent payments for land brought into the collective, pensions and other social benefits. The 'kulaks' were allowed to join the farms and, after a two-year probationary period, could be elected to leadership positions. 'They too are people, let them take up the struggle,' Kádár told the CC.[34] There was also a pragmatic recognition that there would be less friction with richer and poorer peasants joining separate co-operatives.[35]

The campaign benefited from a sense of helplessness arising from 1956: the West would not intervene, and Communist power was there to stay. 'There was a funny thing going round,' Kádár told the CC. 'An ironic song by those [anti-Communist] peasants: "We waited for the Brits until we dropped,/ We had no choice but to join the co-op."'[36] In the early months of 1959, the land area covered by co-operative farms more than doubled, and membership rose from 140,000 to over half a million.[37] However, women and the elderly often joined the co-operatives to protect family rights to modest private plots, while working-age men sought jobs elsewhere. Cynicism and apathy were noticeable. The three-year plan, even after revisions, had inadequate provision for investments in tractors, machinery, fertilisers and, most critically, large-scale shelter for animals. As the year went on, there was ominous evidence of large-scale slaughtering of sows. [38]

One pragmatic response – billed as a temporary measure – was to allow peasants to sustain animals on their private plots with fodder provided by the collective. Another was the toleration of sharecropping and other unorthodox payment methods to improve work incentives. Many of these schemes – which were illegal – went back to the chaotic atmosphere after 1956, when two-fifths of collective farms were in breach of their statutes.[39] Now, with farm leaders desperate to maintain output, these practices spread, and the leadership turned a blind eye.

Meanwhile, Dögei's team at the Agriculture Ministry sought to use 'administrative measures' – such as denial of work permits – to keep workers on the collective farms, and Dögei kept up his sniping at the leadership line.[40] Furthermore, the Soviet embassy was rumoured to be plotting with the party's more Stalinist elements. Kádár's relations with the new ambassador, Terenti Stikov, were already uneasy, and in mid-summer Stikov was getting information from Kiss that collectivisation was not going as well as it seemed. [41] Meeting Kádár on 15 August, Stikov remarked that 'enemy elements' would surely be active in the run-up to the party's Seventh Congress at the end of November, especially in opposition to collectivisation. Kádár replied, 'No, that can't happen. There is no basis for it in the country now.' But Stikov remained unconvinced.[42]

Kádár had to set a clear line on agriculture, and he now moved decisively. At the CC meeting on 22 October, he made clear that, while pressing ahead with collectivisation, the party would take a pragmatic approach to the effective operation of the farms already in existence. Many farms were 'in practice arable co-operatives', with animal husbandry operated from private plots; these animals must have fodder from the collective, 'otherwise they'll have no fattened cattle, no porkers, nothing.'[43] The resolution approved dissemination of new ways to stimulate production. At the meeting, Dögei admitted errors, and repeated this in a letter three weeks later; the CC, meeting on 20 November just before the Congress, judged his repentance insincere.

When the CC met on 5 December, the closing day of the low-key Congress, Kádár announced personnel changes that included Fehér's nomination as a CC Secretary, 'with the idea that he should manage agricultural affairs.' In January Dögei was dismissed as Agriculture Minister, and he was later expelled from the CC. Though Kádár was careful to show that Dögei had practised 'rightist' as well as 'leftist' deviation, he emphasised that he was representative of discontented 'sectarians'; 'they have not learned from 1956. ... This sort can be found not only among ordinary people, but among middle-ranking functionaries too – and here you see the example of one at the highest level.'[44]

Dögei's downfall had symbolic importance. For some time, Kádár had been balancing contradictory political forces. On the one side, his restoration of the party-state had strengthened both the institutions and ideology that looked back to the Rákosi era. On the other, his distrust of the security apparatus, the lessons of 1956 and Hungary's low international standing argued for a more conciliatory policy. For the first time since its earliest days, the Kádár leadership had drawn a clear line halting its general drift towards the old-style Stalinist model.

There were also immediate practical consequences. Newspapers began reporting (approvingly) on the farms' unorthodox practices, and subsequent PB and CC resolutions reinforced this conclusion.[45] Fehér often insisted on the transitional nature of these policies, and Kádár was still more determined to play down suggestions of ideological concession. If it was a question of getting rid of the traditional Soviet 'work unit' system of remuneration, he told the PB, then he was against it; 'developing' the system was, however, a different matter.[46] Yet his actions showed where his priorities lay. He had not simply kept Fehér in place, but promoted him. And he appointed Pál Losonczi, leader of the Red Star co-operative in Barcs – an innovator in introducing incentive schemes – to replace Dögei as Minister of Agriculture. Meanwhile, he could point to some orthodox measures of success. The collectivisation push of 1959-60 saw the land area of co-operative farms more than double, while that of private farms fell by more than half.

Kádár was still having problems with Stikov. He had dropped various heavy hints to the ambassador, recalling the Soviet leaders' judgement that 'you know the situation at home better [than us], you must decide these issues as you think best.'[47] However, the message did not get home. In late spring 1960, Stikov reportedly invited Kádár and other PB members to dinner and criticised Hungary's (relatively) moderate approach to collectivisation and industrial development. Kádár was furious – 'the glass was shaking in his hand' – and, telling Stikov 'beware of forcing your or the Soviet Communist Party's opinion on us', stormed out. Soon afterwards Stikov was replaced as ambassador.[48] There is no documentary confirmation that Kádár secured Stikov's recall, but he left Hungary after only a year in post.

Two months before the Seventh Congress, on 25 September, another powerful symbol of Kádár's 'consolidation' was achieved with the formal reconstitution of the Writers' Union. It had been dissolved during the post-revolutionary repression, and many writers were arrested. The harshest treatment, with long prison sentences, was reserved for Communists – such as Tibor Déry and Gyula Hay – who had sided with the revolution. Their colleagues responded by going on literary strike.

They could, nonetheless, be put under pressure. Gyula Illyés and László Németh, two of the luminaries of the Populist movement, met Kádár to urge lenient treatment of Déry. They were left in no doubt that, if they wanted to help their imprisoned colleagues, they should organise their fellow writers to sign a petition protesting against the UN's continuing investigation of the 'Hungarian question'. More than two hundred signatures were secured.[49] However, the writers, like the peasants, were offered inducements as well as threats. Németh, who had been sidelined in the Rákosi era, was given the top literary award, the Kossuth Prize; meetings were held to try to find common ground; a new, good-quality literary monthly, *Kortárs* (Contemporary), was launched in late 1957.

The regime never seriously pursued the option of bringing forward its own new literary elite. Most of the writers who rallied to its standard early on were all too clearly inferior talents whose rigidity did not chime with Kádár's preferred political line. The experience of the Rákosi-Révai era had also shown that a vanguard of ideologically committed writers could become dangerous to the regime if they lost their faith.[50]

Instead, the Kádár leadership sought a de-politicised literature. They could be more flexible towards the writers precisely because they took them less seriously than had their predecessors. Their style – above all, that of the clever and cynical Szirmai – was consumerist and journalistic, looking towards a mass society in which literature's political role would be sharply diminished. As Kádár told the PB in 1960, 'Firstly [in significance] the daily paper, the radio, the theatre, secondly the literary journal. I don't deal with whatever they print there.' He made the same point two years later: 'In general, we don't pay court to the writers. The situation has moved on, and life has its own rules.'[51] In the meantime, however, writers and artists (especially those well known outside Hungary, such as Zoltán Kodály) could add a certain lustre to the regime, both domestically and internationally.

'In the depths of his soul, Kádár was quite angry with the writers … because they had not sided with him [in 1956].'[52] His underlying attitude to intellectuals in general was wary, reflecting a resentful class-consciousness. As a young man, he had felt that the party intellectuals looked down on the working class – and on him.[53] He later managed to convince writers such as Illyés and Németh of his goodwill, but found dealing with them a strain. 'He was always more relaxed when these meetings were over.'[54] His preferred stance as the man of bluff common sense was reflected in his dismissive comments on the debate in the twenties over Lukács' (then) heretical 'Blum theses'. 'Indeed,' Kádár wrote impatiently, 'this was an issue on the agenda for years – but where? Among twenty to thirty leading Communists! The masses never knew anything about it.'[55]

Yet it would be wrong to cast him as a self-satisfied Philistine and Know-Nothing. His natural intelligence impressed many with much greater formal education. He continued to read widely if unselectively: the same consciousness of his limited schooling that made him uneasy with intellectuals also gave him a hunger to catch up. The later PB member István Huszár was struck that Kádár read *Nagyvilág* (The Wider World), a monthly digest of writing from around the world. 'I don't think there were five other people in the Central Committee who read *Nagyvilág*, but Kádár read it regularly.'[56]

He also recognised the writers' and intellectuals' importance and leaned against some of his own instincts. He once told the CC that he would – if he had to choose – opt for a medium-quality socialist culture rather than a high-quality 'enemy' culture, 'and I'd tell Kodály that, in spite of his scorn – I'm not afraid of that.'[57] However, when Kodály wrote to him complaining about the damage done by narrow-minded cultural bureaucrats to music teaching, Kádár wrote a lengthy and considered reply. He acknowledge the justice of some (though not all) of Kodály's complaints and recalled the composer's presence at his school in Wesselényi Street. 'Even with my child's understanding, I still grasped a little of the great and splendid thing that you and Mr Borus, the music teacher you were supporting, managed to achieve with the school's renowned choir.'

However, he regretted 'your conservative and – forgive me for my frankness – occasionally reactionary political views.' He was not, Kádár insisted, trying to convert Kodály, but 'you ought to show greater responsibility in your social and political appearances ... so as not to take back anything from the people of what you have given them in such profusion in the field of culture.'[58] The letter – 'one man's reasoning', as Kádár put it – with its mixture of praise and apparent bluntness, seems to have had its desired effect; Kodály wrote a warm though far from servile reply, and in later years was willing to lend his prestige to some public events.

Nonetheless, Kádár needed someone who could sustain interaction with the intellectuals with more enthusiasm. He found that person in György Aczél. Born Henrik Appel into a very poor Jewish family in Angyalföld in 1917, Aczél (he first used the name at drama school) had been a builder, would-be actor, underground Communist and post-war apparatchik. After his arrest in connection with the Rajk trial he spent five years in prison. A junior and moderate member of the party leadership after November 1956, he had accommodated himself to the 'consolidation', and in spring 1957 became deputy Minister of Culture.

His true influence would soon exceed this modest official post. He and Kádár had known each other since the thirties, and he would come to be a very close adviser, almost – if not quite – a friend. They were in many respects a study in contrasts. Unlike Kádár, Aczél was engaging and compulsively sociable – and vain. His literary knowledge was undoubtedly superior to Kádár's, and unlike him he aspired to the world of the intellectuals. As a cultural policy manipulator, he had the serious aim of winning over, by a mixture of pressure (including use of his contacts within the political police)[59], flattery and charm, the country's elite to the Kádár leadership's cause. As a literary groupie, he was also delighted with the fringe benefit of leading writers sitting at his dinner table and dedicating books to him.

In mid-1958, Aczél drafted two important policy statements[60]. A characteristic novelty was that leading writers were consulted about them both – albeit in distinctly manipulative fashion – drawing them into a posture of collaborating with the system.[61] The first, on the Populist writers, faulted them at almost every ideological turn, but left open the possibility of accommodation by confirming their place in the nation's literary pantheon. The second, on literary policy in general, laid the basis for one of the defining concepts, not to say clichés, of the Kádár era: the 'three t's.' This was the division of literary work between that which would be officially supported (*támogatott*), that which would be tolerated (*tűrt*) and that which would be banned (*tiltott*). The middle concept created the most interesting grey areas, leaving scope for work that – so long as it was not deemed anti-Communist – did not have to fit into the straitjacket of socialist realism. At the same time, the very elasticity of the concepts left scope not only for censorship, but also for self-censorship.

Aczél's approach was open to dispute. Kádár was initially unimpressed by the three t's: 'Whose idea is this bullshit?'[62] Many of the pro-regime writers and cultural bureaucrats took a more doctrinaire line, and policy was often inconsistent. Thus, the reconstituted Writers' Union – while an improvement on the regime's previous creature, the Literary Council – was launched with a leadership redolent of the Rákosi era past and a speech to match by the CC Culture Secretary Kállai. Nonetheless, over the turn of 1959-60, Németh and, more cautiously, Illyés, started to come to terms with the regime. They could soon feel that they too had gained something: their best-known colleagues, Déry and Háy, were among those released in a partial amnesty in April 1960. The authorities were already pressing these writers for a similar accommodation.

The justification for Aczél's strategy was that, given its relatively short dominance in Hungary, socialism had achieved 'hegemony' but not 'monopoly' in the cultural sphere; accommodating other, broadly 'progressive' viewpoints was an acceptable transitional measure. More than a decade later, Kádár sought similar reasons to justify to Brezhnev his dealings with groups such as the Populists: 'If we've got a 70 year old writer, a bourgeois writer, who's not a Marxist, not a Communist, he can nonetheless be a very honourable, useful person. I can't imagine the same under Soviet conditions, because this 70 year old, the revolution's been there for fifty years of his life, and if he starts to write in bourgeois fashion then he's already an enemy of the revolution.' [63]

This is similar to the argument for the 'transitional' unorthodox measures that were applied in agriculture, raising the question of how far Kádár and other policymakers truly believed that such policies were temporary expedients. There is some evidence that at this time Kádár believed – or persuaded himself – that a new, socialist intelligentsia would gradually emerge.[64] Yet he was not a man to trouble himself too greatly over distant horizons; his acid test was a policy's contribution to solidifying 'people's power', and Aczél's manipulative accommodation with the intellectuals passed it.

The partial amnesty of April 1960, coupled with a decree abolishing internment camps, was intended as a further signal of the changing direction of policy. There had been a partial amnesty a year before, but this one included politically significant individual pardons for Déry, Háy and Donáth. (Mihály and Vladimir Farkas, who had been tried and jailed in 1957 as a small nod of recognition towards the abuses of the Rákosi era, were also pardoned.)

The amnesty was aimed at international as well as domestic opinion. As Biszku put it: 'This step strengthens our and our friends' international position.'[65] As Khrushchev moved, however erratically, towards accommodation with the West, and sought also to gain influence in the emerging post-colonial 'Third World', the continuing probing of the 'Hungarian question' at the UN (and the refusal to formally accept the credentials of the Hungarian government's representatives) was an embarrassment. There was now a clear Soviet interest in easing repression in Hungary. For Hungary itself, diplomatic ostracism exacted a price, not least severe limits to western economic links that could help to increase living standards.

That ostracism was brought home to Kádár when he accompanied Khrushchev to the UN's autumn session. The ten-day journey there on the passenger liner *Baltika* represented a further bonding with Khrushchev, marked by frequent drinking sessions, at which Kádár – usually very restrained – rose to the occasion and showed himself 'no mean imbiber'. He also doggedly showed up for lunch – 'for the sake of the nation,' he told Mária afterwards – when most guests earned Khrushchev's scorn for their inability to cope with the violent tossing of the *Baltika* amid Atlantic storms.[66]

Storms of a different nature awaited him in New York. Demonstrators dogged him on his journey from the Hungarian legation to the UN. He addressed the General Assembly on 3 October; as he went to the podium, around half the delegates walked out. His speech was defiant, restating the official line on 1956 and demanding that the UN remove the 'Hungarian question' from its agenda. He concluded, 'I have been personally attacked a lot in this place. So allow me a personal comment too. ... A person can blunder and get things wrong, but I believe that I served a just cause and I am proud that, at a grave historical hour, together with my loyal colleagues, I took the stand for the working class and the much-suffering Hungarian people. I was there where I had to be, and I did what I had to do.' Despite this vigorous self-defence, the UN experience had some effect on his thinking. He probably realised that his previous strategy of combining partial concessions with the patient expectation that the 'Hungarian question' would be dropped was not yielding results.[67]

The winter of 1960-61 saw the third and final stage of the collectivisation drive, focusing on the centre and east of the country. At its conclusion, co-operative farms covered three-quarters of the country's arable land, and state farms most of the rest. In February 1961, the CC declared with a flourish that the programme had been completed: 'after industry, socialist production relations have also become dominant in agriculture.'[68]

The price of this was high, even without taking into account the psychological pressure and distress – in some cases leading even to suicide – experienced by peasants during these years. Production stagnated, and by some measures fell. Between 1958 and 1961, the agricultural workforce fell about a fifth, and more followed in the years immediately afterwards. Co-operative membership was ageing; in spite of unsustainably heavy subsidies, incomes were low; and in 1960 and 1961 Hungary had to import grain from the Soviet Union and Canada.[69]

Kádár nonetheless saw collectivisation as a triumph, often speaking of it as the second foundation stone of his regime. Nor, viewed in his own terms, was he wrong. He had succeeded where Rákosi had failed, and had resolved the major outstanding issue of 'socialist construction'. By doing so, he had reinforced his credit both with the party domestically and with the Soviet Union. While collectivisation had resulted in significant economic damage, the effects of which would be felt for years, the catastrophic falls in production seen in many other such transformations had been avoided.

While the formal structure of Soviet-style collective farms had been established, underneath was a distinctive Hungarian reality of unorthodox working and remuneration methods. Their emergence reflected the tenacity of peasant efforts to survive and improve themselves, while 1956 and the authorities' caution in its immediate aftermath had allowed them to become more entrenched. Agrarian reform traditions and the expertise embedded in bodies such as the Hungarian Academy of Sciences assisted their spread. Nonetheless, Kádár – however reluctantly, incrementally, responding to events – allowed it to happen.

The conclusion of collectivisation left room for the leadership – should it so wish – to relax its grip a little, and there were good domestic and international reasons for Kádár to do so. Parts of the party and of the security apparatus had different ideas. In June 1960, Interior Ministry officials brought to the PB proposals for further 'struggle' against a familiar cast of enemies. The meeting (from which Kádár was absent) adopted the resolution, but a number of speakers – Szirmai, Kállai, Fock – were clearly dubious about Interior's assessment of the situation.

The same PB resolution gave the security forces authority to move against religious groups identified as dangerous. Starting in November

1960, more than four hundred priests and lay activists were rounded up, and many prison sentences were handed down in trials running through to spring 1961. The arrests focused on secret ordinations of priests by those opposed to the hierarchy's tentative moves towards accommodation with the authorities, and on members of the dissolved youth-oriented Catholic movement, the Regnum Marianum.[70]

This was less an old-style anti-religious campaign than a late phase of 'consolidation', in this case that of the church. Neither Kádár nor church leaders wanted a full confrontation. Kádár was however determined to restrict religious activity to controlled official channels, and the authorities were gratified when, in March 1961 the Bench of Bishops felt constrained to condemn the defendants' unauthorised activities. Significantly, in an effort to contain both the domestic and international repercussions of the affair, the sentences were given minimal publicity.

By the summer of 1961, the leadership had been moving in a more conciliatory direction for some eighteen months. Even the modest steps that it had taken had produced unease. As one CC member put it, many party members 'are prone to think the current leadership liberal, a bit right-wing, others say strongly right-wing.'[71] There was also hostility within the security apparatus: in August and September a number of army officers were arrested for trying to organise a protest against the appointment of a new commander. The men had a shared background in the post-1956 militia and considered themselves the true guardians of the system. They resented being bypassed by loyalists to the Kádár leadership, whose policies they considered 'pinko Social Democracy'.[72]

Kádár was moved to strengthen his grip on the situation. On 13 September, citing the need for a streamlined leadership purportedly demonstrated by the August crisis over Berlin, he took back the premiership from Münnich. Power was now concentrated in his hands – and his friend Nikita Khrushchev was about to give him an opportunity to make use of it.

11

KHRUSHCHEV'S APPRENTICE

The Twenty-second Congress of the Soviet Communist Party sat in Moscow from 17 to 31 October 1961. Khrushchev continued to set ever more ambitious goals – now it was to achieve a full Communist society 'in the main' within twenty years. Two other developments were of greater immediate significance than this utopianism. One was Khrushchev's concept of the 'all-people's state': since class enemies had now been destroyed, the state could no longer be characterised by the dictatorship of the proletariat, and instead – en route, ultimately, to withering away – could represent the whole society. Secondly, Khrushchev struck out at his domestic and international critics by renewing his assault on Stalinism. The dictator's crimes were again denounced, his body removed from Lenin's mausoleum and his followers in the 'anti-party group' expelled from the party.

Overall, the congress 'opened up remarkable though illusory vistas of a reform Communism ... it gave the 1960s a hopeful quality that the area never enjoyed again under Communist rule.'[1] The most profound effects were felt in Czechoslovakia – where it began a process of change that the leadership would ultimately be unable to control – and in Hungary. For Kádár, the new line justified policies that he was already beginning to pursue. While keeping the process of de-Stalinisation under tight control, he could give substance to the two-front struggle, attacking 'dogmatism' as well as 'revisionism'. The 'all-people's state' was an ideological justification for reining back the political police, especially now that collectivisation was completed. Most practically, and most immediately, the expulsion of the 'anti-party group' gave a model of how the past could be used to settle accounts with his opponents.

He wasted little time after his return to Hungary, proposing to the PB on 14 November that a three-member committee should examine Hungary's own Stalinist era. He put the proposal, however, in cautious, laconic terms. 'If the Soviet comrades say that there's such a historical duty concerning this, then maybe we too have such a duty? We must establish how many people were done away with, how many proceedings were brought, how many lives it cost.' It would be an internal investigation, restricted to reviewing court proceedings against Communists and former Social Democrats and ignoring the abuses suffered by ordinary citizens.[2]

Kádár de-Stalinised by Stalinist means.[3] Speaking to the CC on 17 November, he cooked up a witches' brew of conspiracy, bringing together the 'subjective remnants of the personality cult era' such as Dögei and the discontented military officers who, Kádár claimed, had plotted a coup and the murder of the leadership. He used these activities to justify the coming investigation. '... there is a general task, and that is the ideological struggle against the other remnants of the personality cult ... Such as arrogance, insolence, conservatism in thinking, fear of anything new, one-sided thinking and hunger for power.'[4] At this point he opposed suggestions that Rákosi should be expelled from the party. It was Rákosi's followers in the party and (especially) security apparatus who were his main target.

Though selective in his historical approach, Kádár was thoroughly serious about using the message of the Twenty-second Congress to signal a more relaxed political direction in Hungary. He set this out in a speech a few weeks later to the National Conference of the Patriotic People's Front, using perhaps the most famous phrase to be associated with him: 'those who are not against us are with us.'

The phrase had originated with the émigré writer Tibor Méray – an admirer of Imre Nagy – and in using it, Kádár was adopting a criticism as a badge of pride. 'Western publicists say – because they're needling us, and that's not so bad, in our book they're unpaid fellow workers, paid by the imperialists *(laughter)* to keep looking for the Communists' mistakes. Well, now they say, this Kádár lot are really sly, they want to hoodwink everybody. Because in the old days Rákosi's lot used to say: whoever is not with us is against us. This Kádár lot, they now say: whoever is not against us is with us. *(Laughter).* These are the 'mistakes' that western publicists are now talking about. We can be completely relaxed about acknowledging this. Indeed, we look at it like this: whoever is not against the Hungarian People's Republic is with it; whoever is not against the MSZMP is with it; and whoever is not against the People's Front is with it.'

He set out another theme that he would often repeat. A socialist society was being built, not for the sake of ideology, but 'because it ensures a better life for the people, and that the country and the nation flourish.'[5] This well-publicised speech gave a particularly strong signal. For twenty years – arguably longer – Hungarians had experienced a succession of calls to arms for great causes, and had lived through the resulting heroics, follies and crimes. Now they had the novelty of a leader who promised – subject to certain conditions – to leave them alone.

The committee to investigate the 'cult of the personality' was led by Biszku, a guarantee that the process would not get out of hand. Nonetheless, the committee did gradually widen its remit, taking some account of injustices suffered by the non-party population and examining the issue of individual responsibility. It quickly became clear that Rákosi's role would have to be addressed. A draft report also implicated Gerő and Kovács, and a closed PB of 15 May decided that the committee 'should establish the personal responsibility of Comrade Károly Kiss.' He had headed the KEB, the party's disciplinary body, in 1951-52, and was blamed for Rákosi's admission to the new party in March 1957. For Kádár, this was the opportunity to rid himself of a would-be rival; if major names were to be named, there was every reason for Kiss to be one of them.

A PB resolution on 19 June ruled that those most implicated would be barred from working in various key areas: this would accomplish Kádár's aim of clearing out the ex-ÁVH officers working in the political police. He also had a clear ideological objective, blaming the 'sectarian' doctrines of the Rákosi era for what had happened but making sure that no wider-ranging political conclusions were drawn.[6]

The report was handed out at the expanded CC session of 14-16 August. Though it mentioned and quantified the abuses against ordinary Hungarians, it was chiefly devoted to a handful of high-profile cases (including both Rajk and Kádár) affecting a few hundred people in total. Rákosi, Gerő, Kovács and more than a dozen others were to be expelled from the party and Kiss from the PB, while the judicial and security organs were to be purged of the major perpetrators.[7]

Some speakers in the debate argued that Rákosi should be put on trial; others urged greater openness to prevent such abuses recurring. Marosán wanted to play down ideological conclusions, giving pride of place instead to the former leadership's moral failings. Kádár had no interest in a Rákosi trial, and, as for openness, CC members had to hand in their copies of the report before leaving the meeting. Meanwhile, 'I don't agree with Comrade Marosán's proposal' – 'sectarian' doctrine should be identified as the primary cause of the crimes.

Identifying the ÁVH as 'the clique's number one weapon', he neatly addressed the awkward fact that so many of the guilty ÁVH officers had served his own regime, turning it to his advantage: '...it also shows the strength of this resolution that here we are talking about people who were truly serious colleagues in struggle, who helped us in interior and justice work in the merciless fight against the enemies of our Hungarian People's Republic after 1956.' In a second, later intervention, he tore into Kiss, who had tried vainly to defend himself. The resolution was voted through, and Kiss removed from the PB.[8]

Kádár got his purge of the political police: of almost a hundred people removed from their posts, seventy-seven were from the Interior Ministry.[9] The force was restructured and its subordination to the party confirmed. Most of the cashiered officers were found middle to high level positions elsewhere, particularly in tourism and the cultural world (one became a theatre director, another one of Aczél's protégés in publishing with a reputation for promoting 'risky' works). Perhaps the emblematic figure was Sándor Rajnai, an ÁVH veteran of the early fifties and deputy head of the political police after 1956, who had led the team 'investigating' Nagy. When forced (shortly before the August resolution) to leave State Security, he became a diplomat and intelligence officer. His distinguished career culminated with his apt appointment as Ambassador to Andropov's Soviet Union.

Kádár had strong personal reasons to approach the 1962 investigation cautiously, and knew that uncontrolled denunciation of the past could undermine the party's legitimacy; early on, he warned the CC of the dangers that the investigation would 'do the enemy's work'. The final result went further than he had originally envisaged, but he had secured the departure of Kiss and of the former ÁVH officers, while Rákosi's expulsion suggested a decisive break with the past to both domestic and international opinion. However limited and manipulated, Kádár's de-Stalinisation had sent out the signal that he had intended.

Shortly after the CC meeting, Kádár faced an unexpected political crisis: György Marosán went on strike. The reasons for the crisis were almost entirely personal. Though he had been Kádár's deputy since 1959, Marosán was – in his colleagues' unkind but accurate formulation – well suited to the 'open struggle' after 1956, less so to the 'complex and more nuanced questions' of subsequent years.[10] He was a touchy and difficult colleague. 'With one person like that, you've got a problem,' Aczél remarked. 'Two, and you've got a party split.' Weary of his grandstanding, Kádár began to cut him out of decisions. [11]

Marosán's resentment against Kádár's immediate entourage was growing, and in August a series of incidents brought him to boiling point. He objected to new rules for the party congress due to take place in November. Then, at the closed PB of 11 August, Kádár accused Marosán – along with Kiss – of leaking, and claimed that his deputy had accused him of 'acting like Rákosi'. Marosán was shattered by the accusations, still more by Kádár's refusal to discuss and resolve them with him. Then came Kádár's dismissal of his proposed amendment of the 'personality cult' resolution, followed by a refusal to allow him to speak to local party meetings on the decision.[12]

On 1 September, before stopping work, Marosán submitted one of the more bizarre examples of the resignation letter genre. Writing to Kádár, he complained about the 'toadies and plotters' surrounding him and claimed that 'quite a few people are saying that there's a Kádár clique.' He recalled their close work together, but now 'You don't trust me! ... I've felt this for a long time, but now I know it.' He concluded: 'Take care of yourself, your life and your work, for the party and for the country! Whatever has happened, I will always think of you with affection.'[13] He enclosed an eighty-one-page missive to the CC, in which he recounted his injuries and portrayed Kádár as bullying, anti-Semitic and corrupted by power.

Kádár rejected Marosán's claims, describing them as 'a hysterical outburst originating in Comrade Marosán's morbid suspicions'.[14] He urged him to return to work while the PB discussed the issue. Over the next few weeks, possible resolutions were discussed; however, Kádár was not prepared to make any substantive concessions and gradually – perhaps as he was assured of support from his colleagues – hardened his position. Marosán eventually offered to take a sabbatical 'if that would help the party', but Kádár – who had originally floated the idea – was now implacable: the affair was referred to the CC, meeting on 11-12 October.[15]

This became a grand denunciation of Marosán's errors, rudeness to colleagues, self-absorption and persecution mania. The kindest suggestion was that the poor comrade was not quite right after his sufferings in Rákosi's jails. 'He does recognise one mistake of his,' Kádár remarked. 'He should have done this three years ago.' Denouncing Marosán for his 'baseless and anti-party document', the CC dismissed him from his posts and sent him into retirement. There he produced five volumes of memoirs.

The affair was an embarrassment for Kádár. Nonetheless, the dismissals of Marosán and Kiss, coupled with the subsiding influence of the elderly Münnich, reinforced his personal dominance. It was an important part of his self-image that – in contrast to Rákosi – he dutifully followed party rules. However, amid all the wild statements, there was some truth in Marosán's accusations: it was Kádár's voice and leadership that counted, and those around him were his allies and, increasingly, his protégés. As the later PB member István Huszár noted, while Kádár 'not only allowed debate, he encouraged it', he nonetheless 'reserved the right to make decisions.' Overall, it was 'a nicely-presented, rather civilised operation of personal power.'[16]

'People kept a distance of three paces from him; there was respect, but also fear.'[17] This reflected his colleagues' awareness that they were dependent on his goodwill, but his reserved, impassive style – he used the formal mode of address with almost all of them – was also intimidating. 'He was not an easy-going person in company'; there were 'courtiers' around him – even some 'court jesters' – 'not a natural atmosphere at all.'[18] Marosán claimed that many people were 'scared to go to him' because 'Comrade Kádár has become rude and cynical; he has begun to play with people.'[19] This was an exaggeration – Kádár was normally courteous – but there was a sharp, sardonic edge to his comments, and he had no hesitation about conveying his displeasure.

The Marosán affair increased Kádár's isolation. Stung by the 'clique' accusations, he reduced his already limited socialising with some political colleagues and cronies.[20] The exception was Aczél, whose wife was Mária's doctor; the two couples often met socially, and Aczél's influence continued to grow.

The 'popularity' of a politician is an often-elusive concept, the more so when there is no direct prospect of removing him or her from office. Nonetheless, anecdotal evidence, the reports fed back to bodies such as Radio Free Europe and the later, benign place of the sixties in Hungarian folk memory all indicate that Kádár's standing was steadily rising.

His style helped; in the public eye, he was modest and understated, and – in sharp contrast to Rákosi – there was no 'personality cult'. 'He is popular because he can speak the people's language' was one 1961 assessment.[21] His set-piece speeches, especially at congresses, were the despair of intellectuals, but in less formal circumstances he could be very effective. 'Time and again referring to the breach with the past, Kádár chatted, remonstrated, ridiculed and told anecdotes. Judging by his genuine hold on the convention, this 51-year-old former metal worker knew exactly how to appeal to his audience.'[22] To observers of Communist politicians, such as Khrushchev's adviser Fedor Burlatsky, he was a novelty. 'His [speaking] manner was free, unconstrained, extraordinarily democratic and friendly, without a trace of ambition or conceit … His style contrasted sharply even with that of Khrushchev himself, not to mention Tito, Gomułka and other Eastern European figures.'[23]

Stories spread of his frugality and puritanism. Kádár did live austerely, certainly by comparison with the possibilities open to him. In spring 1957, he and Mária had moved back to the Cserje Street house. It was in one of Budapest's most pleasant districts, but of moderate size and inexpensively furnished. When the couple's belongings were auctioned in the early nineties, the main impression was of plainness and, some felt, lack of taste. One of Kádár's neighbours noted the simplicity of his way of life – and his keeping of chickens, an apparent throwback to his rural childhood.

Certain privileges came with the top job. He disliked flying, and had the use of an official train with carriages built in the 1910s and 1920s with royalty and heads of state in mind. There were the various party resorts, though the rooms he stayed in at them were scarcely palatial. He received gifts from foreign leaders, including watches – he accumulated thirty-five – antique hunting rifles and a mother-of-pearl chess table. He also owned a signed Picasso lithograph. Yet his attitude to gifts often smacked of carelessness rather than enjoyment; many were found in the cellar, still unwrapped.[24]

Even when Kádár indulged his love of hunting, he enforced rigid codes of conduct. Left to their own devices, many local party officials hogged the best shooting positions, bullied the staff and left with their car boots stuffed full of dead birds. Kádár insisted on drawing lots for positions, and each huntsman took home two birds, leaving the rest for the collective farm. 'Whatever else you might say about Kádár, if you look at his personal life, including this hunting business, he was very "proper".'[25] In later years, however, he would be accused of being less 'proper' in tolerating corrupt and incompetent colleagues, especially at local level. [26]

He had a steady routine. Shortly before 10 a.m. his car would leave home – a security officer calling his staff to say, 'the comrade is on his way' – for the 'White House', the modern headquarters to which the party leadership had moved in the early sixties. It was a relatively late start, but he frequently took work home and worked through much of the night. Much of his schedule was driven by meetings; although after 1961 PB meetings dwindled to one a fortnight, in the early sixties he had the additional demands of the premiership. Otherwise, he usually started with an hour's paperwork, including the work of the 'complaints office'. Hungarian citizens – including old stalwarts of the movement now fallen on hard times, but also ordinary citizens – petitioned him over problems such as housing, pensions and passport applications. Their efficient resolution was said to be a further source of his popularity.[27]

He generally received visitors in late morning or early afternoon. He took lunch at his desk, followed by a break from work; at various times he dropped in to the offices of CC staff members for informal discussions, keeping himself aware of both issues and personalities. He resumed his paperwork at 4 p.m., working through until 8 p.m. He was disciplined and methodical, and he expected the same of his staff. 'It was not agreeable to have to ask for an extension of a deadline.' If he was a demanding boss, he was also meticulous in remembering the birthdays, name days and important family events of his staff; he made these the occasions for small celebrations.[28]

Still relatively young and physically fit, he kept up a driven pace, working not only through nights but weekends as well. The young apparatchik János Berecz thought that for the much of the sixties and seventies Kádár was 'truly happy … I personally witnessed his love of life and his ability to take action.' By contrast Fedor Burlatsky picked up from his public speaking '…a kind of tiredness, or perhaps bitterness or aloofness … Was this the result of what he had gone through in prison, or of his rather unusual accession to power at a difficult period in Hungarian history?'[29]

The apparent contradiction is superficial – and not only because of the very divergent impressions that a person can give on different occasions. Kádár's conduct during these years suggests strong self-belief and a confidence in what he was doing. It would be a sentimental misreading to suggest that through his policies he was working off guilt over 1956, or over Imre Nagy, whose remains had been moved secretly to an unmarked suburban grave in 1961. However, his growing sense of success certainly made it easier to justify what he had done. Both prison and 1956 had left their mark on him, but he may have felt that he had come through those tests and had been vindicated. There was an edge of contempt in his attitude towards those to whom he had once been close – such as Piroska Döme or Ferenc Donáth – but who had, in his view, given up on the struggle.[30] He, by contrast, had endured, and in that lay his right to rule.

In his speeches at the MSZMP's Eighth Congress (20-24 November 1962), Kádár put great emphasis on his 'policy of alliances'. Since 'we have completed the laying down of the foundations of a socialist society', class antagonisms were easing dramatically – exactly the logic of Khrushchev's 'all-people's state'. 'All this enables us to strengthen and widen the alliance of the labouring classes and develop it into a socialist national unity.'[31] 'Remnants' of the former system and of pre-socialist thinking should be combated by ideological rather than coercive means.

This loose theorising, seasoned with some quotations from Lenin, begged many questions but served to justify decisions already taken for pragmatic reasons. The theory could also justify further moves to co-opt allies, including the continuing cautious accommodation with the writers. Here Kádár's comments were shot through with ambiguities. He was 'against deciding debates on style by regulations or administrative measures … [But] socialism is the ideology of the masses, and he who appeals to the masses must find the way to the thoughts and feelings of the working millions.' He recognised that 'there are still groups of diverse ideological outlook today. Besides art and literature of socialist realism, every other well-disposed artistic activity will be granted scope.' However, this 'does not mean acquiescence or ideological compromise by the party.'[32]

This left room – albeit rather grudgingly – for the Populists. Even in 1961, Illyés had been having a difficult time; when he forwarded an offensive letter that he had received from Kállai, Kádár brusquely refused to get involved: 'I am too busy with other things to be able to undertake work as your postman and clerk.'[33] Nonetheless, with publication of more works in 1962, Illyés got greater official recognition. Among the previously jailed ex-Communist writers, Déry published his first new work in autumn 1962. The following year he was allowed to travel to Vienna, where his loyal performance at a press conference fulfilled the leadership's expectations. However, Háy proved less tractable, and he was bundled out of the country in 1964.

Of more immediate need to the regime than the writers – given the country's economic and social needs – was the technically skilled intelligentsia. Kádár used his congress speech to announce the abandonment of discrimination in university entry against middle-class children, even if this 'did not meet with the approval of certain comrades.'[34] He also emphasised the leadership's willingness to bring forward non-party members to responsible posts. In practice, the party card remained essential for many leading positions and very helpful for many others; nonetheless, there was an increasing desire to make use of the skills of a much larger part of the population, especially in more technical, 'non-political' posts. In any case, the party itself was increasingly open to the intelligentsia, and by the late sixties its composition would be markedly more white-collar than that of most of its Soviet bloc counterparts.[35]

Building alliances also justified the reduction of petty and counter-productive rules, including those governing travel to the West. Significant restrictions remained, and the concession was double-edged: the need to apply for a passport gave an incentive for good behaviour. Nonetheless, in 1963, 120,000 Hungarians travelled to the West, more than four times the number five years earlier.[36] Similarly, in January 1964, the authorities ceased jamming broadcasts of various Western radio stations. The Hungarian chargé d'affaires in Washington, János Radványi, told his American interlocutors that 'Premier Kadar had decided to cease jamming of [Radio Free Europe] to bring some humour into the life of Hungarians.'[37]

Such measures also, of course, helped a much-needed improvement of Hungary's standing with the West. The summer 1961 standoff over Berlin had alarmed the Hungarian leadership, who feared an economic embargo. As Kádár pointed out, 30 per cent of the country's foreign trade was with the West, and a quarter of this was with West Germany – 'that is what the German issue means to us,' he told the CC.[38] The feared embargo did not materialise, but the appointment of János Péter as Foreign Minister in the September 1961 reshuffle was a sign of Kádár's thinking. As a Protestant bishop – albeit one of the regime's tame ones – Péter had an unusual profile for the Foreign Minister of a Communist country. However, he had excellent Western contacts, and that was the reason for his appointment.[39]

The key remained the US, and little progress could be made until the 'Hungarian question' at the UN was resolved. From the very beginning, at least some Americans had not given up on Kádár. A day after his return to Budapest in a Soviet tank, Allen Dulles was speculating that 'he may yet turn out to be a Hungarian Gomułka.'[40] Kádár had done little in the immediate aftermath to justify such hopes, but significant gestures on his part might find a positive response.

In March 1962, János Radványi, the newly appointed chargé d'affaires in Washington, visited the First Secretary. Kádár impressed Radványi with his confidence and determination, his 'sharp and incisive' style; he also made very clear that the problems in Hungary's relations with the US had to be resolved. The sticking point was the American demand for an amnesty of those imprisoned for their role in 1956. Kádár was adamant that he would not be seen to yield to pressure; he repeated his formula that the more overtly concessions were demanded, the less likely they were to be made.[41] Radványi's discussions in Washington soon convinced him that an amnesty was both a necessary and a sufficient condition for the dropping of the 'Hungarian question'.[42]

During the autumn, the two governments advanced through an informal understanding on the linkage between the two issues. On 7 November, Kádár won approval for an amnesty from Khrushchev, and hinted at further releases in his opening speech at the Eighth Congress, adding that, 'with the necessary goodwill,' Hungary and the US could resolve their differences. Soon afterwards, U Thant, the UN Secretary-General, was invited to visit Hungary the following summer. [43]

Kádár announced the amnesty in Parliament on 21 March 1963. Though no figures were given, some four thousand people were released, including well-known individuals such as the political thinker István Bibó and the remaining Nagy trial defendants. The amnesty did not only cover '56-ers, and there were some exceptions in its small print – several hundred people, many of them armed fighters, remained imprisoned. One '56-er was released in May 1974, and he may not have been the last.[44] In addition, though some of the released prisoners – particularly the better known, and that after the passage of time – achieved a degree of rehabilitation, many suffered continuing discrimination, which often extended to their children. Such vindictiveness tended to fade with the years, but by then for many the damage had been done.[45]

Nonetheless, the amnesty drew a very public line under 1956, and thus had an important psychological impact within Hungary. It also achieved its desired international effect; the credentials of the Hungarian representatives at the UN were approved shortly afterwards, and U Thant's visit in July was a success for the regime. Urging President Johnson in April 1964 to look at a full normalisation of relations, National Security Adviser McGeorge Bundy commented, 'Hungary has perhaps gone farther than any other satellite in de-Stalinising the Communist system and the movement in that direction continues.'[46]

If the amnesty drew together domestic and international issues, so did the state's relationship with the churches, especially the Catholic church. The early energies of the Kádár leadership had been devoted to restoring the control that had been disrupted during 1956: forcing out opponents, rebuilding the pro-regime 'peace priest' movement within the Catholic church and enhancing state control over appointments. Meanwhile, Mindszenty, who had taken refuge in the US Legation, continued to issue anathemas on all collaboration with the regime.

Nonetheless, there had also been small conciliatory gestures: some easing of restrictions on religious publications, a small amount of Catholic broadcasting, and the like. A CC resolution in July 1958 made a characteristic Kádárist distinction between anti-state activity ('clerical reaction') and religious belief as such. The latter was still to be fought, but through an ideological battle which 'must not insult the religious sentiments of believers nor restrict their freedom of worship.'[47] This encouraged a battle-weary Bench of Bishops to urge the faithful to support the government in the November 1958 elections.

Kádár had grown up with a deeply Catholic mother. Mária was also rumoured to have held on to her Catholic faith, though she later denied it.[48] He seems to have been rather indifferent to religion, unlike the fiercely hostile Khrushchev. The Hungarian chess champion János Portisch, a devout Catholic, felt that the First Secretary was always respectful of his beliefs.[49] Nonetheless, Kádár's views were strictly orthodox. 'The liquidation of the religious worldview and the spread of the scientific worldview require systematic struggle,' he told the PB. '... [it needs] another two generations.'[50] In the meantime, recognising religion as a continuing reality, he was keen to recruit believers, where possible, as allies.

The main challenge was to end the Vatican's hostility and thereby leave Mindszenty isolated. Hungarian representatives met informally with Cardinal Casaroli, the Vatican's 'foreign minister', in May 1962. In December Kádár attended a meeting in Moscow that brought together the Soviets and a number of Communist leaders with large Catholic populations; shortly afterwards he discussed the possibility of talks with the Vatican with the Soviet ambassador.[51] He had a domestic interest in an accord, and John XXIII's repeated calls for peaceful reconciliation of Cold War conflicts meant that it suited Khrushchev's foreign policy objectives as well.[52] Hungary was also well-placed for such an agreement, with its leadership more set on political opening than in Czechoslovakia, but with the church much more under control than in Poland.

The official talks began in May 1963. The agreement signed on 15 September 1964 – after four rounds of negotiations, carefully monitored by the PB – represented a compromise. Bishops, for example, would be nominated by the Vatican but with the agreement of the state, while a form of words was found to make an oath of loyalty to the state palatable to the bishops. The two sides also agreed to continue negotiations on unresolved issues. The Mindszenty issue was shelved. The Cardinal was by now a thorough nuisance to the Vatican and to the American government. However, Kádár had concluded early on that having him immured in the American Legation was a very convenient solution and had set tough conditions for his being allowed to go. For his part, Mindszenty knew that to leave the Legation (and Hungary) would remove him from any influence over his church's future. He stayed put.

The agreement had important benefits for the church, notably the filling of sees kept vacant by the state and the resumption of regular contact between Hungarian bishops and the Vatican. Nonetheless, Rome had a weak hand to play, and Kádár was the bigger beneficiary. He had secured another diplomatic success, improving the regime's standing at home and abroad. At the same time, the church was firmly under control, while religious publication and especially education were kept as marginal activities. The Vatican was unable to prevent continuing pressures on religious believers, ranging from state propaganda to the risk of discrimination at work or regarding the education of their children.

Growing economic worries only reinforced Kádár's desire for international recognition. The root of the problem was structural: as a small country with minimal raw materials, Hungary was especially ill suited to the heavy industrial base built by Rákosi and Gerő. There were also ominous signs of inefficiency, misdirection of resources (with stocks of unsold goods piling up) and loss of competitiveness.[53] The lurch away from the modest initial three-year plan of 1958-60 and the drain of agricultural collectivisation exacerbated the problems.

In response, there were sharp investment cuts in 1961, which affected agriculture particularly badly, further setting back its recovery. Investment soon bounced back (usually in the least economically justified areas), while the leadership did not dare to rein back consumption. The balance of payments took the strain: a report to the PB in mid-1963 noted that debt to capitalist countries had more than doubled since 1959. The report pointed out that full normalisation of relations with countries such as the US and West Germany could improve access to long-term investment credits, reducing dependence on short-term loans. Kádár welcomed the emphasis on improved German relations.[54]

Kádár and Münnich wrote to Khrushchev in May 1961, asking for Soviet help through grain supplies, increased raw material deliveries (at subsidised prices) and extensions of credit. However, Hungarian negotiators continually found their Soviet counterparts willing to meet only part of their requests. In mid-1962 Khrushchev warned, 'the Soviet Union won't be a sugar daddy any more!' When Kádár visited Moscow a year later, Soviet technocrats raised the issue of relative Hungarian prosperity; as with the other satellites, the Soviets were subsidising living standards higher than their own. Reportedly 'Kádár replied that Hungary had already had a counter-revolution once, the Soviet Union had not.' Whether or not he actually said it, this was the basis of his negotiating stance.[55]

The main domestic initiative – in which Kádár, as Prime Minister and a member of the government's Economic Committee, was deeply involved – was a wave of company mergers in 1962-64. The intention was to create larger, more efficient units, which could deal directly with Ministries, stripping out a layer of bureaucracy. The government also introduced a capital charge in January 1964, with the aim of encouraging companies to use their assets more efficiently. In practice, consolidation would fail to deliver the promised improvements and would leave the problematic legacy of monopoly organisations with formidable bargaining power vis-à-vis the authorities.[56]

Part of the rationale for the mergers was Khrushchev's attempt to achieve an 'international socialist division of labour' within Comecon, the hitherto dormant economic grouping of Soviet bloc countries. Kádár had long noted the irony that the capitalists seemed to be much better at concentrating production while the supposedly co-operative socialist bloc showed an addiction to autarchy.[57] However, the Romanians saw the scheme as thwarting their industrialisation ambitions; they first resisted it, then spectacularly torpedoed it in July 1963.[58]

All these initiatives attempted to make the Hungarian economy more efficient without the fundamental reform that had been proposed in 1957. The September 1962 meeting of the Economic Committee (with Kádár present) that agreed the merger policy also ruled that 'modification or alteration of the system of planning is not timely.' However, 'this issue must be examined at a later date.'[59] Two months later, after the Congress, the former Social Democrat Rezső Nyers was made the new CC Secretary for Economic Affairs. It is unlikely that Kádár had specific policy changes in mind with the appointment, but Nyers had already shown his competence and expertise as head of SZÖVOSZ and then as Minister of Finance. At the end of 1963, he began gathering a group of economic advisers into an informal 'brains trust' to discuss ways out of what was increasingly recognised as a systemic problem.[60]

The signs of crisis were multiplying. Economic growth rates were falling far below the targets of the second five-year plan (1961-65) even as the trade balance deteriorated. In September 1963, Kádár was called urgently to Moscow; Khrushchev told him that, after a wretched grain harvest, the Soviet Union could not meet Hungary's needs.[61] The problems, however, had to do with more than grain, and in February 1964 Nyers published an article indicating that fundamental reform was back on the agenda.

The Kádár-Khrushchev friendship – shared by their wives, Mária and Nina Petrovna – continued throughout the early sixties. After Khrushchev had rung to congratulate him on his birthday in 1961, Kádár wrote, 'I can't and I don't want to flatter, but without any pretty words you must know and feel what my attitude is towards you personally.'[62] The difference of age (eighteen years) as well as of power between them made Khrushchev rather paternalistic: he once remarked that the son he had lost during the war was just a few years younger than Kádár.[63]

Each seems to have enjoyed teasing the other. After Khrushchev's celebrated shoe-banging display at the UN, Kádár produced sniggers among Soviet officials when he remarked, 'Comrade Khrushchev, remember shortly after banging your shoe you went up to the rostrum to make a point of order? Well, at that point, Comrade Sik, our Foreign Minister, turned to me and said, "Do you think he had time to put his shoe on, or did he go barefoot?"'[64] Kádár was mortified when, on a Khrushchev visit to Hungary, some particularly stringy duck was served at an official lunch. Returning home, Khrushchev triumphantly sent him some enormous duck eggs from the Ukraine.[65]

However, their politics were not identical. Kádár was more cautious and less ideological than Khrushchev. His concept of politics was more limited, less mobilising; even if he sought through his policy of alliances to draw on a wider base of support, his instincts left much more scope for the private world of the apolitical 'little man' than did Khrushchev's. He avoided

With Khrushchev in the Soviet Union, 1961

Khrushchev's hubristic promises and compulsive activism; he later admitted to Brezhnev that Khrushchev had bombarded him with schemes, and that he had politely thanked his mentor and then ignored them.[66]

Nonetheless, their interests and beliefs converged. Since 1956, each had been boosted by the other's success. Both saw themselves as breaking away from the Stalinist past; Kádár later insisted to Brezhnev that Khrushchev's Secret Speech was the foundation of his regime.[67] And the personal relationship remained. On his visit to Budapest in April 1964, Khrushchev awarded Kádár the medals of Hero of the Soviet Union and – more prestigiously – the Order of Lenin. Kádár concluded his speech of acceptance with the words, 'it's a very good feeling for me to accept this award from Comrade Nikita Sergeyevich Khrushchev, whom I honour as a fatherly friend and an elder brother – and I always will.'[68]

Six months later, Kádár was in Poland. At lunchtime on 15 October, he took a call from Brezhnev, who told him that the Soviet CC had dismissed Khrushchev from his posts. Brezhnev had replaced him as First Secretary, Alexei Kosygin as Prime Minister. Brezhnev sought to reassure Kádár of his personal goodwill, and emphasised that this would mean no change in policy or relations. Kádár was dumbfounded.[69]

When Khrushchev's departure 'in view of his advanced age and deterioration of his health' was officially announced that night, it produced widespread alarm in Hungary. 'For more than a week,' an internal report to the PB recorded later, 'party members ... were under a pressure from public opinion rarely seen before now.'[70] There were fears that the new Soviet leadership would confront the West and restore harsher discipline within the Bloc. Meanwhile, some 'sectarians' within the party were said to be pleased. A nervous leadership put the security services on alert.[71]

Kádár's schedule kept him in Poland for a couple more days. He sought to steady nerves in the PB by informing them via Biszku of his conversation with Brezhnev: 'the important thing is that the line continues.'[72] He returned to Budapest's Western Station on the morning of 18 October. After a formulaic account of his talks with Gomułka, he paused and said, 'A lot of things have happened this week. There was news that pleased us, and there was also news that surprised us. I want to speak about this openly and frankly.' He then related the official account of Khrushchev's departure. 'For my part, I believe that Comrade Khrushchev had really great accomplishments in the struggle against the Stalinist cult of the personality and for the maintenance of peace. He worked for peace.' He added that the Hungarians who had greeted Khrushchev on his visits 'have nothing to regret. However, what is essential and vital for us is that the political viewpoint of the Hungarian Socialist Workers' Party and the Hungarian People's Republic … has not changed one jot and will not change in the future.' *(Big applause)*[73] He hit exactly the right note. There were reports of anonymous letters arriving at the radio station warning that it would be stormed – as in 1956 – if he were dismissed.[74] Even if the stories were exaggerated or inspired, the fact that they were believable was eloquent testimony to how far he had come in a few years.

A picture of lone heroism on Kádár's part needs some qualification. By one account, he had been able prior to his return to Budapest to secure independent confirmation that his position was secure[75] – though that might have persuaded another man to play safe. Nor was he the only satellite leader to indicate his discontent.[76] None, however, accomplished quite such a striking public gesture; by boosting his domestic support, he pursued the shrewder as well as the bolder course. And in a career not always characterised by loyalty to friends, associates and benefactors, he had on this occasion been able to discharge a personal debt. It was one of his finer hours.

This was not the end of the matter. Biszku was sent to Moscow to gather more information and convey the Hungarian leadership's worries. Kádár met the Soviet ambassador, Georgi Denisov, three times in ten days and spoke on the phone to a rather uneasy Brezhnev, who invited him to Moscow. The CC agreed on 23 October to send a confidential letter to the Soviet leadership setting out its view. Although he had accepted the Soviet explanation of why Khrushchev had to go, Kádár remained deeply uneasy about Moscow's incomprehension of the effect on Hungarian public opinion. He was also worried about the failure to mention any of Khrushchev's 'merits' in public statements. This might indicate a reversal of policy, and gave encouragement to 'sectarians' within Hungary.

The letter was dispatched, but soon afterwards – especially in the run-up to Kádár's visit to Moscow for the 7 November celebrations – he became more nervous. He noted that many of those being brought forward by the new Soviet leaders had been hostile to him in the past. He was also uneasy at the prospect of an orgy of bullish speechmaking by high-level delegations, including the Chinese, as if 'the main obstacle to unity' had now been removed: 'no good will come of it.'[77] He asked the Soviet leadership not to invite their guests to make speeches and, for whatever reason, this was accepted. It was reported that in Moscow, although Zhou Enlai was icy towards him, the Soviets were demonstratively friendly, and in his private talks it was agreed that the matter was now closed. However, he was not fully reassured.[78] His confidential interpreter Károly Erdélyi sought out Denisov at the end of the month to claim that his boss had been bounced and misled into his aggressive stance by colleagues such as Biszku and Gáspár.[79]

Yet if Kádár had to work on his relationship with Brezhnev, he did not entirely forget his old patron, now consigned to obscurity. He took a crate of Khrushchev's favourite Hungarian apples with him during his November visit. The Hungarian embassy was instructed to deliver them, but ran into stony-faced Soviet insistence that no one knew where the former leader lived. Kádár lost his temper and insisted that the Soviet CC be approached. A second consignment was sent, and Khrushchev got his apples. Some years later Kádár ensured that some medicines for which Nina Petrovna had asked were delivered by the Hungarian embassy.[80] He nonetheless felt the need to be careful; when Khrushchev wrote to express his sorrow at the death of Ferenc Münnich in late 1967, Kádár sent his reply via Brezhnev with an anxious covering note. However, when the Soviet authorities refused to deliver the letter to Khrushchev, the Hungarian embassy did so.[81]

When Khrushchev died in September 1971, Kádár sent a telegram of commiseration 'on behalf of my comrades, my wife and myself'. In her reply – addressed to 'Dear Comrade János Kádár, Dear Mária' – Nina Petrovna wrote: 'I and my children always held you [both] to be the best of people and of friends, and so we think of you now despite everything that has happened. To his last day, Nikita Sergeyevich had the same attitude towards you.'[82]

12

GOULASH

'Socialism,' Kádár told the Eighth Congress, 'will establish its final and complete superiority over capitalism by establishing a higher productivity of labour and a greater abundance of goods.' It was Khrushchev who, with characteristic ebullience, had described this approach as 'goulash politics'.[1] However, by the time that he used the phrase – on his last visit to Budapest in April 1964 – the question of how the goulash would be paid for was becoming ever more pressing. With this, the Varga committee's concepts that had been shelved in 1957 came back on the agenda.

Hungary was not alone in its problems: much of the bloc had been affected by a severe economic slowdown in 1962. The years of rapid industrialisation and 'extensive' growth – based on an expanded capital base and labour previously employed in agriculture – were over. Now, to use the fashionable concept, there was a need for 'intensive' growth, driven by improved productivity. The existing system – dubbed by the Hungarian economist János Kornai 'the shortage economy' – was failing to allocate goods efficiently or satisfy demands. Some goods were in shortage, while unsold stocks of others built up. Company managers were aware of potential shortages but faced few price or financial constraints. Driven above all to fulfil their plan targets, they hid their potential from the planners to ensure that they were set easy targets, over-expanded their capacity and hoarded raw materials and cheap, inefficient labour.[2]

For decades, some socialist economists had argued that state ownership could be combined with the price mechanism to produce an efficient planned economy; now these concepts took on practical significance. In examining them, Kádár's Hungary was doing no more than were many other Communist countries, including the Soviet Union, although many would soon run into problems and opposition.

The most urgent economic issue was the growth of short-term foreign debt, and the resolution debated by the CC on 8-10 December 1964 focused mainly on austerity measures. Nonetheless, it contained a few sentences requiring 'a comprehensive, critical analysis of the present economic mechanism ... and a modification of it appropriate to the situation.'[3] A number of CC members were clearly uneasy at this. In his contribution, Kádár said almost nothing about it – but that was enough. As Nyers said afterwards, 'if Kádár had voiced so much as a glimmer of doubt' about the proposal, it would have been abandoned. 'He knew that some way out had to be found.'[4]

In the meantime, the austerity measures – price rises and increases in labour norms - were deeply unpopular. Speaking to Parliament in February, Kádár seemed rattled and irritable, insisting that economic policy was good. 'It's the implementation that is bad,' he snapped. 'Where? Everywhere – at the bottom, at the middle and at the top! Even at the ministerial level it's bad!'[5]

Kádár mentioned the proposed economic reforms over supper with Brezhnev after a hunting trip in February. Brezhnev was amiably non-committal, promising to return to the issue in the future. As an attempt to dispel tensions, the trip was a success; hunting was a common enthusiasm of the two leaders, and 'there was a very good, friendly atmosphere.'[6] Nonetheless, it took a year – during which Kádár met Brezhnev seven times – for relations to recover from their awkward start.[7] On a personal level, they got on quite well. Brezhnev liked to be liked, and Kádár seems to have soon learned to read his mixture of affability, sentimentality and bursts of bullying rage. There was, however, one persistent source of unease. 'As a man and as a politician, Kádár was [of] a higher level than Brezhnev, and Brezhnev sometimes understood it.' Though Kádár was always careful to defer to Brezhnev, the Soviet leader found the complexities of his thinking rather baffling, and Andropov sometimes had to explain Kádár to him.[8]

The advent of the new Soviet leadership deferred Kádár's decision to resign as Prime Minister. There had been reports earlier in 1964 that he was thinking of resigning, but in late October he told ambassador Denisov that 'after the Moscow events ... [it] was now a political question.'[9] He remained in office until the following June; then, citing the need to concentrate on his party functions, he stood down in favour of Gyula Kállai.

Nyers moved fast to develop proposals about the 'economic mechanism', drawing 135 specialists, many of them veterans of the Varga committee, into a network of policy groups. As in agriculture, the political leadership had considerable intellectual reserves on which to draw, should it so wish. Even in the retrograde phase of 1957-59, Kádár had – just –

avoided smothering the development of the academic economics discipline.[10] Bodies such as the Statistical Office under its reformist head, György Péter, were a further source of expertise.

By autumn 1965, the main reform proposals had been drafted. The centrepiece was the abolition of company-level planning, a more radical option than the simplification adopted in the Soviet and East German reforms. Companies would be steered towards fulfilling the five-year plan not by quantitative directives but by 'regulators' such as taxes, prices and credits. More detailed decisions about production and sales would be left to companies, and better wage incentives would encourage a focus on efficiency and profitability. Since prices would have to give much better signals than in the past, a new system of producer prices was also required.

Kádár was fully aware of the group's work, but played little if any direct role in policy evolution. Now, however – with the proposals due to come before the PB and CC – his stance was vital: 'everything depended on him. … two thirds of [the PB] relied on Kádár's opinion for their viewpoint.' [11] His attitudes were complex: even his view of the economic specialists mingled respect and distrust. He was no ideological reformer; indeed, some felt that his core instincts were 'fairly conservative'.[12] However, Mátyás Timár, then Minister of Finance, found him an intelligent man 'who had a definite sixth sense for economic issues. There were many things that he felt more than he knew.'[13]

It did not need a sixth sense to appreciate that urgent action was needed, and there was a clear lesson in the failure of the half-measures adopted after 1957. Kádár may also have been influenced by the opinions of others: not only by Nyers, but also by PB members such as Fehér and Fock, and by the long-standing head of the CC Economics Department, István Friss, who now underwent a dramatic conversion from central planning. He also received letters from the economist József Bognár warning that the existing economic situation was unsustainable.[14]

Kádár worried that the system's wastefulness could not be sustained in a world of peaceful economic competition. 'My feeling is that defeat awaits us if we can't change our ways.'[15] He noted how the French and Italian unions could demand shorter hours, 'but we're still stuck with a 48 hour working week. Why? Because the [work] intensity is low!' By contrast, agriculture, for all its problems, impressed him – as it did many others – as an example of how a more flexible, price-based system might work. [16]

Thus, by the autumn of 1965 at the latest, Kádár 'did not need convincing of the need for reform. He sat down at the discussion table visibly convinced of this.'[17] Nonetheless, he brought to the table a number of political and ideological constraints and these too helped to shape the reform. Above all, he emphasised that, whatever the changes in instruments, there must be 'political and economic policy continuity. …János Kádár set great store by the continuity thing.' [18] Convinced that the policy zigzags of 1953-56 had contributed to the collapse of the party's authority, he would always – then and later – insist that, whatever changes were executed, the party's policy was above all 'principled' and 'consistent'.[19]

Nor was this solely a matter of political judgement. He believed firmly in a planned economy, even if its methods needed changing. 'Where are the tools with which we can influence things?' he demanded at one of the more anxious points during the reform discussions.[20] On one of the major tools he had little cause for concern, since the committees had, from the start and without deep debate, opted for a conservative line, keeping central control over large-scale investments.[21]

Political as well as financial control was important to him. He baulked at the suggestion that, with companies becoming more independent, party committees would have less reason to intervene. Not surprisingly after the experience of 1956, he was hostile to the 'Yugoslav terminology' of worker self-management that was heard in the industrial democracy committee chaired by the former Prime Minister András Hegedüs. He sided firmly with the SZOT leader Sándor Gáspár in believing that worker representation should be through the official trade unions.[22]

Kádár was also – rightly – nervous of the reform's potentially disruptive political consequences. While some prices had to rise and surplus workers should be dismissed, 'in my view we've got to do it in a way that doesn't reduce living standards.' He believed that 'someone who gives to society [by better work] should earn more', but could not accept large differentials between workers based solely on the modernity of the plant in which they worked. He favoured steeper taxation of the highest incomes and a commitment to reduced working hours. 'If people ask what the full construction of socialism amounts to, we can't just answer that there's a foreign exchange shortage … it's very important from the point of view of the working class and politically.'[23]

Nonetheless, at the CC meeting on 18-20 November, Kádár gave a clear and decisive presentation. By speaking immediately after Nyers and emphasising repeatedly how much he agreed with him, he left no doubt as to where he stood. The decision, he said, ranked in importance with the reassertion of power after 1956 and agricultural collectivisation. The reform was based on 'Marxist economic science'; while it involved 'greater attention to the law of value … this is in no way similar to a market economy in a capitalist sense.' While pledging that certain prices would remain controlled, he was dismissive of the prospects for a Communist society in which goods would be free, and quite amusing on the shock that a world of rational pricing and payment by results would bring. 'They'll say, hell, what was all that at the Eighth Congress? This wasn't what we were thinking about, when there was all that about the full construction of a socialist society …' He promised that there would be social measures aimed at maintaining working-class support, but was firm on the overall principle of the reform.

From the debate it was clear that there were doubters, particularly among the nervous working-class members of the CC. 'It wasn't me that won them over,' Nyers said subsequently. 'It was Kádár.' Furthermore, no one was prepared to oppose openly such a clear lead from the top. As the debate drew towards a close, the reformers expressed their gratitude to their protector. György Péter claimed that, while Kádár 'emphasised many times that he is not a specialist, not an economist ... there are quite a few among the economists who could go to school to Comrade Kádár and get acquainted with some basic economic concepts.' The resolution was – of course – approved unanimously. The decisive step would be a new regime of producer prices, to come into effect on 1 January 1968. [24]

The CC meeting also approved further price rises, affecting meat and dairy products. The unpopularity of this gave some ammunition for Kádár's critics. In the early months of 1966 – and to a lesser extent later in the year – there was a whispering campaign against him, with persistent rumours that he might quit. He was said to be too 'idealistic', that he had been too close to Khrushchev and that a 'firm hand' was now needed to restore discipline in society. It was suggested that he might give way – perhaps to Kállai – at the party's Ninth Congress in November.[25] There is no evidence of a serious plot against him, but this was the most testing time for some years.

The price increases of December 1965 were followed by a number of arrests for 'political' crimes, and in the years 1964-66 more than six thousand people were sentenced for political reasons.[26] The political police now operated within the Ministry of the Interior's Third Main Directorate. Its third section – known as III/III – was concerned with 'internal reaction' and thus was most directly involved in surveillance and action against possible opponents of the system. Although there had been major personnel changes, particularly in the higher ranks, in and after 1962, the political policemen still followed old habits and looked for enemies, not least among those released in the amnesty.[27]

Kádár retained a clear-eyed appreciation of the uses of 'administrative measures' – his staff were forbidden to open the III/III reports that went direct to his desk[28] – and was certainly prepared to choke off any overt dissent in the uneasy atmosphere following Khrushchev's ouster and the price increases. Nonetheless, he did not want Interior's self-justifying 'vigilance' to undermine his political strategy through counter-productive zeal; he once remarked pointedly that telling a political joke was not an offence.[29] It was also a matter of defining the enemy; III/III officers were more inclined to pursue traditional 'clerical' and 'revisionist' enemies than critics on the left, though a number of the latter were arrested in 1965-66. In the latter part of 1966, with the economy rebounding, the arrests eased off.

A similar pattern – a period of tension and of temporary tightening – characterised policy towards the intellectual elites. 1965 saw sanctions against the young Populist writer Sándor Csoóri after criticisms from the Soviet Embassy, and the dismissal of András Hegedüs – Rákosi's youthful Prime Minister turned humanistic left sociologist – as editor of the magazine *Valóság* (Truth). These were, however, little more than isolated incidents, and Hegedüs' own field, sociology, provided an example of gradually expanding possibilities.

Major figures in the cultural and intellectual world were still handled carefully. Illyés courted disfavour by publicly raising the taboo issue of the Hungarian minorities, in particular in Transylvania. Kádár was vulnerable on this issue; early on, seeking support from the leaders of Romania and Czechoslovakia, he had washed his hands of it. In both countries – especially in Romania, in which the leadership combined a more independent foreign policy with strident nationalism at home – the condition of the Hungarian minority was deteriorating sharply. Official anger with Illyés was restrained by the belief that he might shortly win a Nobel Prize, and Aczél made sure that plans for a campaign against him were shelved.

At the other end of the spectrum, György Lukács – too famous to be denounced, but too unorthodox for the party's comfort – continued to present a dilemma. Some saw Lukács' eightieth birthday (April 1965) as an occasion to attack his philosophy. However, Aczél oversaw a more conciliatory approach, and two years later helped ensure Lukács' (re)-admission to the party.[30] Kádár stood back from day to day dealings with the intelligentsia, but seemed content to back Aczél's judgement.

The more nervous mood following the price increases spilled over into a PB meeting in early May 1966 intended to prepare for a more detailed CC discussion of the reform programme. Some members expressed disquiet over the reform, Biszku suggesting that it be applied on a trial basis in some factories. Most strikingly, Kádár appeared to be losing his nerve.

He first gave vent to his distrust of the experts taking over the process: '... it's as if twelve months ago we called in 108 economists, like getting the vets to take a look as to how they could cure the horse. ... After twenty years of the working class and the party leading ... some now get this feeling that the economists are taking over the country's leadership.' There was still time to think before the CC meeting, and he seemed to favour a dilution of the reform. ' ... if we were to keep obligatory economic plans [for companies], but were to undertake certain things – e.g., we were to use a lot fewer indicators, we would ensure that there was a suitable price system, that managers and workers had suitable material incentives,' then perhaps they could improve the economy while keeping control of the process.

Nyers gave a robust reply, pointing out that if the number of plan directives were reduced, they would inexorably grow back. 'Comrade Kádár said that we still need to think this matter over. If we need to think this over, we need to think over the whole thing as to whether we send the material to the Central Committee or not … what I want to say is: there is no choice.'[31] In his summing-up, Kádár implicitly backtracked: he set out the procedures for the next meeting and did not refer either to his own comments or to those of Nyers.

He did not express such wide-ranging doubts again. At the CC meeting on 25-27 May, he once more threw his weight behind the reform, adding that, with the passing of the resolution, the debates of the previous eighteen months would be over. 'These performances, comrades, speaking among ourselves, seemed like a pack of dogs … this season is at an end.'[32] One issue that now had to be resolved was the programme's nomenclature. The economists wanted to call it 'economic reform' while the party conservatives favoured 'further development of economic direction'. The compromise – which Kádár supported – was 'the new economic mechanism' (NEM).[33] Thus was born Kádár's Hungary's contribution to the international economic lexicon.

The regime was also trying to find a more distinctive diplomatic profile. Although Hungary's international isolation had ended in 1963, its foreign policy was still characterised by an unswervingly pro-Soviet stance, captured in Kádár's fulsome declaration to the Soviet party's (CPSU) Twenty-third Congress in March 1966 that, 'There never was, is or will be an anti-Soviet Communism.'[34] With this had gone a deprecation of Hungarian nationalism: unsurprising given the long shadow cast by 1956.

Though western commentators – particularly in later years – sometimes described Kádár's Communism as 'nationalist', this was a misnomer. The regime showed – particularly in economic matters – a growing sense of national interest, but that was not quite the same thing. Kádár himself was no nationalist. As he revealingly put it to Gyurkó, 'I grew up in an age when the national flag was the symbol of the Horthy era, the concept of the motherland meant the existing social system. I hated that regime and held its symbols and system of ideas in contempt. It took time until I learnt that the red-white-and-green is the symbol of the nation, and not of Horthy and his associates.' The latter part of the comment has a dutiful ring to it, and Pozsgay noted that, when it came to patriotism, 'I never saw any intense feelings on his part. His emotional intensity focused on the working class and its struggle.'[35]

Nonetheless, circumstances began both to favour and to require a more active foreign policy. Kádár was aware that his policy, particularly regarding the Hungarian minorities, was open to criticism for its passivity, a point raised at a CC meeting in June 1967. However, his efforts to deal with the Transylvanian issue by quiet diplomacy proved ineffectual: the Romanians were intransigent, and Brezhnev had no interest in stirring up another source of conflict with them.[36] In general, however, the gradual relaxation of tensions in Europe gave a little more scope for a small country's diplomacy. The concept of 'Central Europe' was revived, with official historians even seeing merit in the Habsburg Empire (which, given

1956's echoes of 1848, had its own logic). This provided a vehicle for Hungarian interests to be pursued without incurring the charge of nationalism.[37]

Kádár had shown some interest in this a few years before – recalling long-standing ideas of a Danubian Confederation – and now he took it up publicly. 'The peoples living in the Danubian basin share a common destiny,' he said in a speech in December 1964. 'We either prosper together or perish together.'[38] Péter also took up the theme, which envisaged much closer co-operation among the ideologically heterogeneous grouping of Austria, Hungary, Czechoslovakia and Yugoslavia. Little came of this, but relations with Austria improved sharply from 1964 onwards. Péter later revived the concept of Central European co-operation as part of an overall drive for reduced tensions in Europe, including a European security conference.[39]

The regime had a strong interest in lowering Cold War barriers. Trade with the West was now growing rapidly, and it was desperately needed – both to import the advanced technology for Hungary to be able to compete, and to find markets for the exports that would pay for it. In spite of efforts to diversify, the revival of pre-war business links made West Germany the country's biggest capitalist trade partner and its fourth-biggest overall.[40] The two countries signed a trade and representation agreement in November 1963, but the division of Germany, and the disputes with West Germany outstanding from the war of Poland and Czechoslovakia, precluded formal diplomatic relations.

A new West German government, formed in December 1966 with the Social Democrat Willy Brandt as Foreign Minister, initiated secret talks with Hungary, Czechoslovakia, Romania and Bulgaria about establishing diplomatic relations. The Hungarians dutifully consulted with their partners, and on 10 January 1967 the PB resolved that official negotiations should begin. Three weeks later came the thunderclap: the Romanians, true to form, had – without consulting anyone – reached an agreement with the West Germans. At a hastily-called meeting in Warsaw, the Poles and East Germans, backed by the Soviets, steamrollered through – despite Hungarian efforts to moderate it – a protocol blocking any other Warsaw Pact country from further negotiations with the West Germans. [41]

'This text is not healthy, not good,' Kádár remarked to a gloomy PB. Some sort of holding statement would have been acceptable, 'but merely saying that the conditions for [negotiations] are not available, well, it is, to say the least, odd. They were available six months ago, but now they are not?'[42] The affair was a bruising reminder of how politically constrained Hungary was. When Brezhnev visited Budapest in September, he growled out a reminder to Kádár (in the midst of otherwise friendly talks) about the dangers of dealing with the West Germans – 'we can't sell our policies for some factories or other.'[43]

Cold war politics also hampered the development of ties with the US, especially as polemics grew over the Vietnam War and a mob attacked the US Legation in February 1965. Nonetheless, in 1967 both sides agreed to upgrade their diplomatic representation. Martin J. Hillenbrand, the first US ambassador to Kádár's Hungary on 30 October, was received by 'the undisputed leader of this country' in late November. Kádár set out at length – he spoke for fifty-five of the meeting's seventy minutes – his reflections on the Hungarian-American relationship and his belief in peaceful coexistence. Hillenbrand found him 'more personally sympathetic than I had expected', and noted his sense of humour. 'Kádár was in an obviously relaxed, good-humoured, sometimes semi-ironic mood. He seemed to enjoy playing the role of a confident leader big enough to forget the past.' Later experience, however, would bring home to Hillenbrand that Kádár was still very wary of the US.[44]

Kádár was philosophical about his limited room for manoeuvre, believing that the trends were favourable. 'If there isn't a world war,' he told the PB in June 1967, 'the West Germans' basic interest will require them to work with us.' A few months later, he was applying the same

The undisputed leader of this country': speaking at a factory meeting in Székesfehérvár, 9 August 1967

argument to the Soviet Union and its allies. If 'we want to live alongside one another in real peace', then they would have to take into account 'the capitalist world market ... and whether we like it or not, there's the Common Market too.'[45]

The government was reshuffled again in April 1967. Kállai – 'a cultural politician', 'not an economic expert'[46]– was ill suited to prepare for the NEM's introduction, and made way for Jenő Fock, who had years of experience as a CC Secretary and Deputy Prime Minister specialising in economic policy-making. A former mechanic who had first met Kádár before the war, Fock was intelligent, hard-working and quarrelsome – 'he liked a scrap' – his short fuse worsened by periodic migraines. He was a supporter of NEM, albeit a rather ambivalent one, reflecting his background in the trade unions and links with heavy industry. He worked well with Nyers, in spite of occasional clashes, Fock's capacity for picking a fight being matched by his unwillingness to bear grudges. The government now had a heavyweight leader.[47]

His main task was the final preparation of the NEM. The leadership's approach remained cautious – understandably so, since reforms in neighbouring Yugoslavia and Czechoslovakia were running into serious problems. Thus the implementation in 1966-67 built in what were openly described as 'brakes' to minimise social disruption.

The difficulty was moving from a system based on the over-full employment of cheap, inefficient resources, including labour. Kádár recognised the problem and could sound almost reactionary on the subject: 'if people are a bit worried about unemployment, that's not such a bad thing if it goes along with [the belief that] from now on we've got to work, because anyone who doesn't work will get thrown out.'[48] He knew, however, that significant unemployment was politically unacceptable. The new wage system, by putting heavy tax bills on increases in *average* wages above an approved level, gave management an incentive not to fire inefficient, low-paid workers.

If wages were to remain low, it would be difficult to raise prices, especially since price stability was seen as an important advantage of the Communist system. Only 30 per cent of producer prices would be free, the remainder being either fixed or placed under some sort of restriction. Consumer prices were still more controlled, and the differences between the two increased the need for subsidies. Furthermore, since so many prices were still arbitrary, it was easier to justify measures that protected loss-making companies.[49]

Institutional interests also slowed change. Banking reform was proposed, with an end to the National Bank's position as monopoly lender; it was deferred when the head of the National Bank, Andor László, argued that it would be excessively disruptive amid all the large-scale changes that were taking place.[50] Changes in the state bureaucracy – in particular, challenging ministries' right to appoint company directors – were similarly deferred.

The reformers' logic was that it was the implementation of the core decisions – the abolition of company-level planning and the new producer price system – that mattered. Their demonstrably positive results would make it possible to go further. Kádár too accepted the logic of gradualism. He told the CC in November 1967 that the changes that were being introduced a few weeks later had 'sufficient guarantees' that they would be orderly 'up to the limit that will still allow it to be a real reform.' Changes to prices would be gradual, but they would come – 'this is a programme for decades.' Similarly, controls on imports from the capitalist world 'may be reduced or completely abandoned in future.'[51]

In one area – agriculture - there was a more decisive breakthrough. It helped that Fehér and his supporters provided a powerful agricultural lobby. Yet heavy industry had more than its share of lobbyists too. The difference was that industry had been a favoured part of the planned economy, and its lobbying was devoted to maintaining that status. Agriculture lobbied for resources too but, building on years of experimentation at local level, also sought greater independence. The leadership, which had hesitated in 1961-64, now carried through major changes.

The financial position of the co-operatives was improved, with procurement prices raised and debts written off or rescheduled. Farms were increasingly able to own their own equipment, such as tractors, and mechanisation spread as agriculture took an increased share of funds under the third five-year plan (1966-70).[52] The shift in resources towards agriculture was made possible by some ideological contortions. Because most farms were technically co-operatives, they had been viewed as representing a 'lower form' of socialist development than, for example a state-owned factory. The PB decided to ditch the dogma. As Kádár told the CC, 'it's obvious that here we have to confront some previously proclaimed ideological propositions'; nonetheless, 'we must recognise that co-operative property too is by logic socialist property.'[53]

In the summer of 1965 – foreshadowing the thinking of the NEM – the farms were given more independence from local councils and a more equal relationship with buying institutions. The 1967 Co-operatives Law gave a further boost, recognising the role of private plots in producing, not only for families' needs but also for the market, and authorised co-operatives' industrial activities. The latter was soon reflected in rapid growth in areas such as building and food processing.

Some of these measures – notably those relating to the co-operatives' independence – did not deliver all that they promised, but the improvement was nonetheless dramatic. Grain yields rose rapidly, and by the late sixties the country was a small net exporter in bread grains. There was still more dramatic growth in the production of meats, fruit and vegetables. By the end of the decade, Hungarian agriculture was enjoying a boom.[54]

As the introduction of the NEM approached, there was another reminder of the political constraints under which Kádár operated. In early 1967, the leadership, in its continuing search for stable, longer-term borrowing, authorised exploratory membership talks with the IMF and the World Bank. The Soviets were informed, and at intergovernmental talks in June they made their reservations plain; however, the Deputy Prime Minister, Lesechko, told the Hungarians that it was their decision. In late November, on the eve of the reform and with talks with the two institutions becoming more serious, Fock led a delegation to Moscow.

This time the message was blunter. 'Lesechko was mistaken,' Kosygin told Fock and Timár. 'There is a formal view [on our part]. It would not be right for a socialist country to join.'[55] Fock demanded that the Soviets show some confidence in their Hungarian partners, but the Soviet leadership insisted that the decision was a matter of common alliance interest. On his return to Budapest, Fock was reportedly in favour of defiance, but Kádár opted to avoid confrontation.[56] The membership application was shelved, and with it a potential force for opening up the economy.

Kádár nonetheless remained optimistic. In his presentation to the expanded CC a few weeks earlier, he had congratulated his colleagues on the 'orderly, comradely debates, not personal disputes' of the previous two years. He pointed up the contrast with the Yugoslavs and Czechoslovaks, who 'were not united on the essential basic principles.' However, he believed that policies similar to Hungary's would be adopted in other socialist countries – 'this is an international necessity' – and urged those working in Comecon 'to represent the principles of our reform.' His conclusion: 'I am confident that the reform that we have decided to introduce will work well and bring about what we expect from it.'[57]

The NEM came into being on 1 January 1968. Four days later, the political crisis in neighbouring Czechoslovakia – exacerbated by the bungled economic reform – forced the resignation of Antonín Novotný as First Secretary, and his replacement by the Slovak party leader Alexander Dubček.

13

1968: 'BUT YOU KNOW THEM, DON'T YOU?'

The advent of Dubček initially seemed a happy complement to the introduction of NEM. Kádár knew him from his days as Slovak party leader; they had met in 1964 and 1966, and were on good terms.[1] Czechoslovakia under Dubček's leadership could be a useful partner in economic reform and in building trade and technological links with the West.

Reform in the Czechoslovak Communist Party (CPCS) had begun, not with Dubček in 1968, but with a process of political and economic reappraisal in 1962-63 under his disagreeable predecessor Antonín Novotný. However, the botched economic reform, standoffs with the intelligentsia and Novotný's boorish mistreatment of Slovak opinion triggered a crisis at the turn of 1967-68. Dubček took office amid rising expectations of change, but with a leadership deeply divided between moderates, radicals and a pro-Novotný rearguard.

Dubček identified Kádár as a friendly face in a bloc uneasy over Novotný's sudden fall and the two met secretly on 20 January in southern Slovakia. Aware of Dubček's difficulties, Kádár greeted him with mordant humour: 'Congratulations, and please accept my condolences.' Dubček took the joke well, and the atmosphere of the meeting was friendly. Kádár told his PB that Dubček 'showed no signs of triumph or arrogance – in fact, you might perhaps say the contrary. In a certain sense he is bitter that he's the one that they chose. He is aware of the problems and of the responsibility, and suffers a lot because of it.' He nonetheless warned Dubček of a dangerous lack of unity at the party centre. 'The people cannot be united if the party that brings them together is itself divided. The party cannot be united if the Central Committee is not united, and the Central Committee can hardly be united if there is no unity in the Politburo.'

Dubček felt that he had an ally, telling Kádár that 'there was no one else with whom he would have been able to discuss the same matters in the same way.'[2] Years later, feeling that he had been betrayed by the Hungarian leader, Dubček claimed that Kádár, probably acting on Brezhnev's instigation, had suggested the meeting. This was mistaken: it was Dubček himself who had taken the initiative. However, Kádár did report the conversation back to Brezhnev.[3]

Kádár and Dubček held a more formal but still friendly meeting on 4 February in Komárno. There and in Prague three weeks later for celebrations of the twentieth anniversary of the coup that had brought the Communists to power, Kádár urged Dubček to take the initiative by publishing the party's Action Programme quickly.[4]

However, hostility to Dubček was already mounting within the bloc. The main critics were East Germany's Ulbricht, deeply opposed both to ideological unorthodoxy and to contacts with Bonn, and Poland's Gomułka, now completing his burial of the hopes that he had raised in 1956 with an anti-Semitic purge. Bulgaria's Zhivkov later joined them. The initial Soviet response was suspicious but measured, but as the divided Dubček leadership lost control of events, and – partly in consequence of those leadership divisions – censorship collapsed, unease turned to outright alarm.[5] The Prague celebrations (22-23 February), attended by the Warsaw Pact leaders gave an opportunity for lobbying by Czechoslovak critics of reform, who warned their visitors of the impending collapse of party rule.[6]

Thus, when Warsaw Pact leaders met in Sofia on 6-7 March, the Soviets were already issuing warnings. According to Brezhnev's later report to his PB, several satellite leaders – Zhivkov, Gomułka and Kádár – lobbied him to take 'decisive steps' to get Czechoslovakia back in order.[7] Given Kádár's subsequent stance, it is most unlikely that he expressed the same strident view as the other two. However, he may have been uneasy at the degree to which Dubček was losing control of the country. A few weeks later, CC International Affairs Secretary Zoltán Komócsin warned that the Hungarian leadership 'had expected the situation to calm down after the January CPCS plenary session, but the very opposite happened' and that decisions 'were now being made in the streets rather than the CC.'[8]

Intelligentsia demands in Czechoslovakia grew more radical, securing the removal of Novotný from the presidency on 22 March. Brezhnev decided to call a meeting of the allies (excluding the troublesome Romanians) to further warn the Czechoslovak leadership. Kádár agreed that it was 'absolutely necessary to tell Comrade Dubček the truth'. He wanted to restrict the meeting to 'the Four': the Soviets, the

Czechoslovaks, the Hungarians and the Poles. He presumably hoped that, without the splenetic Ulbricht and the servile Zhivkov, the pressure on Dubček could be relatively low-key.

Brezhnev wanted Kádár to meet Dubček beforehand, since 'their relations are very good and the trust is complete … Comrade Kádár could talk about shared ideas and prepare the ground for the enlarged meeting of the Four.' As so often during the crisis, Kádár's role as honest broker shaded into that of Brezhnev's soft cop. For the Soviet leader, an indirect channel of influence on Dubček and an additional source of information were very useful. Kádár was more than happy to show his loyalty, but Dubček's later contention that he merely 'continued tamely on the Kremlin leash' was inaccurate. Kádár had his own interests to consider, and preventing a Brezhnev-Dubček collision was very much among them. He enjoyed his role as intermediary, and was well suited to its ambiguities. He did not at this point have to choose between Brezhnev and Dubček, and he must have hoped to keep it that way.

The Kádár-Dubček meeting did not come to pass, but on 19 March the Soviets and Czechoslovaks agreed that six-party talks would take place in Dresden four days later. Kádár conveyed to Brezhnev his PB's fears that the meeting would inflame passions within Czechoslovakia and weaken the party. He also made a last-ditch attempt to keep the Bulgarians out, telling Brezhnev that 'the adverse effect on Romania would exceed the favourable effect on Czechoslovakia', but was unsuccessful.[9]

The Czechoslovak delegation was ambushed at Dresden. They had expected to discuss economic matters; instead, Ulbricht opened the meeting by demanding an explanation of events in their country. Dubček sought to defend his position, but met with dire warnings from Brezhnev and more strident attacks from Ulbricht and Gomułka.

Kádár's more measured contribution helped calm the atmosphere. He thanked Dubček for his exposition, and emphasised that the Czechoslovaks' internal politics were their own affair – albeit of interest to others. He nonetheless issued a warning. There was not yet counter-revolution in Czechoslovakia, but what was happening could be the 'prologue' to it. He cited the Hungarian example of 1956, commenting that Nagy had been 'no agent, was no counter-revolutionary in the sense that he had the intention to overthrow socialism in Hungary.' He added the ominous warning that 'these events could make one of you an Imre Nagy.' The solution lay in a united party reasserting its political dominance.[10]

The meeting ended with an uneasy standoff. During the ensuing weeks, Kádár was publicly supportive of the Czechoslovak leadership, but privately he had his worries. The Action Programme finally launched on 10 April was an ambivalent document, clearly inadequate to restore the party's authority. To Kádár it was 'a big zero, it is nothing.'[11]

With new social groups mushrooming in Czechoslovakia, the Soviet leadership concluded that further intervention was essential, and that

Warsaw Pact manoeuvres on Czechoslovak soil could be used to encourage the 'healthy forces' in the country and intimidate the opposition. In April, leading KGB and military figures warned of alleged western plans for an invasion of Czechoslovakia and pressed the need for the manoeuvres on a reluctant Dubček.

The Czechoslovak leaders were summoned to Moscow for a further browbeating on 4-5 May. Reporting to the satellite leaders (again, excluding Romania) at a secret meeting in Moscow on 8 May, Brezhnev felt that the criticisms had had some effect, but urged the others to keep up the pressure on Dubček to accept the manoeuvres. Gomułka, Ulbricht and Zhivkov were again hawkish.

Kádár was the odd man out once more, though he was not against applying some pressure: 'as for military manoeuvres on Czechoslovak territory, we are for them and the longer they last the better.' However, he felt that Dubček could still be part of the reassertion of control and that external intervention should be handled carefully. He rejected intemperate and one-sided interpretations of the crisis: 'there is no counter-revolution under way in Czechoslovakia. What is going on there is a process that began with a struggle against certain mistakes committed by the previous leadership. If we're going to criticise specific individuals, then I would criticise Cde. Novotný rather than Cde. Dubček.'

He was unimpressed by his counterparts' blinkered desire to explain away unwelcome developments through *ad hominem* attacks. 'We can't sort things out by saying that Mao Zedong and co. are not quite all there, that Castro's a petty bourgeois, Ceauşescu's a nationalist and the Czechoslovaks have gone off their heads.' However, he was isolated in his familiar espousal of the two-front struggle, and came into direct conflict with Gomułka, who saw the Action Programme as a counter-revolutionary text, rather than merely confused. As Brezhnev put it in his summing-up, 'Cde. Kádár presented a somewhat different assessment' from the rest of them, even if he supported 'our general line'.[12]

Then the crisis appeared to ease. Dubček and his colleagues indicated that they would rein in the press and call a party congress to unify the leadership behind a 'centrist' line. The lull gave the Hungarian PB time to worry over a joint paper by Kádár and Komócsin, pointing out divergences between Hungary and its allies, especially the Soviet Union, over issues ranging from relations with the West to the assessment of the Czechoslovak situation.

In mid June, Dubček headed a high-level delegation to Budapest to sign a new twenty-year friendship treaty. Kádár put on a warm reception for the Czechoslovak leadership, but also discharged Brezhnev's commission 'to have a serious talk with Comrade Dubček' and help him to 'recognise the dangers'. When he reported back, the Soviet leader was pleased that Kádár was offering support to the Czechoslovaks 'while also pointing out the dangers and the tasks on the basis of the Hungarian experience.' For his part, Kádár sought to encourage rapprochement, arguing that 'the Dubček leadership can be seen to take several measures that may help them realise the correct course', and suggesting that *Pravda* tone down some of its criticisms of Czechoslovakia.[13]

The easing of the crisis proved temporary. The Warsaw Pact manoeuvres only hardened opinion in Czechoslovakia. Soviet anxiety was intensified by the publication on 27 June of the writer Ludvík Vaculík's radical manifesto, *Two Thousand Words*, and by the growing strength of reformers in CPCS local conferences. The congress in September was likely to take a radical, not a consolidating turn; if the Soviets wanted to halt the Prague Spring, they had two months left in which to do it.

Kádár began a week's visit to the USSR on the day that *Two Thousand Words* was published. At the final meeting in early July, with Fock and Aczél also present, Brezhnev and Kosygin proposed that the 'five' send warning letters to Dubček, followed by a Dresden-style multi-party meeting on the crisis – with or without Czechoslovak participation. Kádár, deploring Prague's inadequate response to Vaculík's 'counter-revolutionary document' agreed, but urged that the Czechoslovak leadership take part in the meeting if at all possible.

Thus far, the Hungarian and Soviet records of the meeting (the latter presented by Brezhnev to the Soviet PB on 3 July) agree. However, according to the Soviet – but not the Hungarian – record, 'Kádár then went on to say: the way the situation now looks, Czechoslovakia will probably have to be occupied. If this becomes necessary, we'll go ahead without any doubt ... he is certain that the Political Committee will back his standpoint on this question.' He was committing Hungary to participating in the invasion of Czechoslovakia. Some of his colleagues were apparently uneasy. 'Fock tried to say something, but Kádár cut him off by starting to speak, so he remained seated, pale and silent.'[14]

This is the murkiest incident in interpreting Kádár's role in the Czechoslovak crisis, and one that divides historians. The statement in the Soviet minutes is clearly inconsistent with Kádár's continuing pleas for restraint over the subsequent fortnight. One view assumes that Kádár's moderate line was for public consumption, the other that Brezhnev's account was mistaken or distorted.[15]

Confusion arose even at the time. On 10 July the Soviet military requested Hungarian participation in 'a military exercise from Hungary to the north', claiming that Kádár and Brezhnev had already discussed the matter. Speaking to Brezhnev on the phone that day, Kádár stated that he knew nothing of any such commitment. Brezhnev's rather stiff reply was that he had given permission for advance briefings 'for the eventuality that there should have to be extraordinary measures in Czechoslovakia, and this had been discussed [at the meetings] in Moscow.'[16] Both leaders seemed genuinely puzzled at the other's perception of what had been said.

However, Aczél's recollections of the meeting two decades later offer a possible explanation. The debate with the Soviet leaders was tense, Kádár becoming ever more weary and haggard as it wore on. 'The discussion came to an end with his saying in conciliatory fashion that in any case, ultimately, we'll be with you ...'[17] Aczél, whatever his occasional deficiencies as a source, was present at the meeting and gave his account long before the Soviet document came to light. It may be, then, that Kádár *did* give a commitment to support military action, but in much more tentative and contingent terms than those implied by Brezhnev, and that this explains the differences in their respective recollections.

If this is correct, Kádár still hoped to avoid a military solution, but signalled his willingness to participate if that was the final decision. He kept the latter part of his thinking out of the record presented to the Hungarian PB; it is possible – though this is highly speculative – that Fock, who seems to have been strongly opposed to military intervention,[18] reminded him of its domestic political costs. Kádár's juggling of sharply different courses of action would last another ten days.

On 3 July, the Soviet PB, still looking to activate the 'healthy forces' in Czechoslovakia, coordinated letters from the 'five' demanding another multilateral meeting in Warsaw. Unwilling to repeat Dresden, the Czechoslovak leadership rejected the demand, urging instead a series of bilateral meetings, including the Romanians and Yugoslavs. The Soviets were appalled by this defiance; so, for different reasons, was Kádár. He later told Andropov that 'Dubcek and the CPCS leadership took the Imre Nagy route on 8 July, when they refused to take part in Warsaw. There our ways parted.' That was with hindsight; at the time, he tried to secure a slight delay in the meeting to encourage Czechoslovak attendance, and to tone down a second joint letter.[19] However, the multilateral meeting went ahead – minus the Czechoslovaks – in Warsaw on 14 July.

Kádár and Fock had met Dubček and his Prime Minister, Oldřich Černík, in Komárno the previous afternoon. Although Dubček recalled a low-key, friendly meeting, Kádár's very different version seems more in keeping with his urgent wish to avert a crisis. He told the Czechoslovak leaders that their refusal to attend 'was the greatest mistake they had made since the January plenum' and 'created an entirely new situation'. The interpreter Károly Erdélyi later remarked that he had never seen Kádár so agitated or angry. This brutality, coming from their former ally, reduced the Czechoslovak leaders to tears.[20]

Kádár and Fock found that at Warsaw, no one would join their table during breaks: 'we sat there like some sort of scabs, and that's how the others kept looking at us,' because they had met with Dubček.[21] He was just as isolated in the conference room. Speaking 'in a noticeably quiet tone of voice' in the early afternoon session, he recounted the Komárno meeting and repeated his view that the situation in Czechoslovakia was 'deteriorating' and showed 'dangerous tendencies' – but he stopped short of calling it counter-revolution. He was still prepared to wait on events and to look for allies within Czechoslovakia.

This infuriated Ulbricht. 'In his high voice he shouted across the room' about counter-revolution and western plots, and attacked Kádár personally: 'I am amazed by the analysis that Cde. Kádár gave ... I don't know, Comrade Kádár, why you can't grasp all this. Don't you realise that the next blow from imperialism will take place in Hungary?' Bulgaria's Zhivkov was less offensive but just as explicit: 'unfortunately we cannot agree with the view offered by Cde. Kádár, nor with his conclusions.' He called for military intervention.[22]

Brezhnev spoke in the late afternoon. He quickly gave his verdict: 'counter-revolution is on the offensive ... No matter how any of us might characterise the potential consequences of the continuing offensive by the anti-socialist forces, one thing is clear: Czechoslovakia is at a dangerous phase on the path leading out of the socialist camp.' According to the Soviet PB member, Piotr Shelest, 'Brezhnev addressed this to Kádár. His name was not mentioned, but everybody understood the allusion. Kádár reacted vehemently, he began to fidget nervously in his seat, then discussed Brezhnev's words with the Hungarian delegation.' As Brezhnev continued, Ulbricht 'occasionally threw a hostile and ironically triumphant glance in the direction of the Hungarian comrades, Kádár and Fock.'[23]

Brezhnev did not call explicitly for military intervention. He urged another joint letter; if Dubček failed to respond, they would work with other Czechoslovak Communists who could 'normalise the situation in the country.' He did, however, make clear that, in support of such a group, the Soviet Union was 'fully ready to offer Czechoslovakia all necessary assistance.'

After a break, Kádár asked for the floor again. He acknowledged that 'most of the comrades criticised my remarks', and praised Brezhnev's 'profound and accurate assessment' of the situation. Most importantly, 'as far as the assessment and conclusion of the Soviet comrades are concerned, we completely agree with them and are prepared to take part in all joint actions.' Apart from some brief exchanges on drafting the joint letter, no one else spoke; rather humiliatingly, this final session of the day was solely for the purpose of Kádár's concession.

Why had he caved in? At its simplest, he felt that he could not refuse a Soviet demand. Rehearsing the course of events to the CC on 7 August, he commented, 'We could have said that we wouldn't take part in the military preparations. That would have been perfectly possible in principle. But what would it have led to? ... it's possible that they [the Soviet leaders] would have taken yet more unpredictable actions.' Speaking to Andropov a few months later, he was even less ambiguous. 'In this case, the Czechoslovak issue would have brought in a Hungarian issue too.'[24]

Romania's Ceauşescu took the opposite stance, winning plaudits at home and abroad when he denounced the invasion. Yet his decision, like

Kádár's, reflected long-standing strategic choices. While the Romanians had opted for nationalism and greater independence, Kádár had avoided direct clashes with the Soviets and pursued consumerism and low-intensity politics. To opt for defiance at this late stage would have been a much more drastic step than it was for Ceauşescu, who had been excluded from Soviet decision-making from the start.

Kádár also knew how dependent Hungarian living standards were on Soviet goodwill. He claimed later that Brezhnev had told him, 'János, just send one little unit and you can have whatever you need!' He was surely too shrewd for such a crude bribe, but vulnerability to economic pressure was another constraint on his scope for independent action.[25] In effect, his decision had been made long before Warsaw.

A few days after the summit, Brezhnev rang Kádár in emollient mood, insisting that the Soviet leadership had valued his interventions – especially his final speech. Kádár, sounding aggrieved, remarked that, 'we could have answered back certain comrades.' Brezhnev offered almost paternal reassurance: 'I would like Comrade Kádár to know that we view his situation and position with great understanding, we value his speech in Warsaw highly, and we think that the leaders of certain fraternal parties shouldn't do things like that.' He had further encouraging news: he and Dubček had agreed a bilateral meeting. Kádár, who had urged this on Brezhnev and Kosygin at Warsaw, was delighted.[26] Brezhnev had made this partial concession because the 'healthy forces' in Czechoslovakia were proving too weak to take action. Kádár had his own lines open to them and knew how isolated and frightened they were.[27]

However, the Soviets were still hoping to split the Czechoslovak leadership at the talks, scheduled for 29 July in Čierna nad Tisou on the Slovak-Ukrainian border. Once this was accomplished, pro-Soviet elements in the Czechoslovak leadership would call for waiting military support. From 20 July, the military forces of the 'five' were put on full combat alert, and the succeeding days saw large-scale troop movements and military exercises.[28]

Kádár was drawn into these preparations. On 20 July, he arranged for Vasil Biľak, the pro-Soviet Slovak party leader, and the Soviet PB member Piotr Shelest to meet in secret at his lakeside villa at Balatonaliga, where Shelest secured Biľak's promise of a letter inviting Soviet military intervention.[29] Shelest also brought Kádár confirmation that the operation was imminent. Kádár gave his support, and his more formal agreement to participate followed three days later after discussions with Fock and other senior figures.[30]

This drew an emotional response from Brezhnev in their next telephone conversation on 26 July. 'This is so invaluable for our party and our friendship that I have no words for it. I won't forget it as long as I live.' As the leaders gathered at Čierna, around twenty Warsaw Pact divisions were moving close to Czechoslovakia's borders.[31] However, the plan misfired.

Intimidated by domestic opinion, the would-be 'normalisers' dared not initiate the planned leadership split. Biľak's group failed to produce their letter. After a series of bruising confrontations, the Czechoslovak leadership seems to have quietly offered the Soviets some concessions.[32] The talks ended on 1 August with plans to convene a six party conference in Bratislava two days later.

The Bratislava Declaration – which made no explicit reference to the Czechoslovak situation – was designed to show very publicly the unity of the Communist bloc and Czechoslovakia's adherence to it. During the long haggles over the communiqué, the Czechoslovak politician, Zdeněk Mlynář, observed the leaders of the 'five'. 'János Kádár stood out far above the others, both in the political and the human sense.'

Given that Mlynář thought Ulbricht and Gomułka 'hostile, vain and senile old men', while 'observing a living Zhivkov from up close was shocking', this was faint praise. Nonetheless, he thought Kádár 'a politician who was capable of stubbornly and effectively defending an apparently hopeless minimum of national interests, a person who was uncorrupted by his own power because he had never lost sight of his real aims.' Kádár warned Dubček and Mlynář – with generous use of Hungary in 1956 as an analogy – that, if the Czechoslovak leadership did not act to rein back part of the reforms, 'someone else would.' Mlynář felt that 'his experience of 1956 remained something that affected his conscience as well as his politics.'[33]

For Kádár, Bratislava offered a welcome reprieve. Nonetheless, he told the CC a few days later that it was up to Dubček to seize the initiative and tighten up at home. ' … The internal political situation in Czechoslovakia will sharpen in the near future … If there isn't some sort of polarisation, and of course no healthy struggle, we will go back to where we were.' Under extreme conditions, he warned, 'we must choose the lesser tragedy and not the greater' – in other words, military intervention rather than 'that Czechoslovakia cease to be a socialist country.'[34]

Kádár was right to be cautious. Bratislava did not reflect a fundamental shift of Soviet view. Military preparedness was still high, Biľak's group finally handed in their appeal for intervention and the September congress was fast approaching. By 7 August, only four days after Bratislava, Brezhnev was once more on the phone to Kádár, complaining that Czechoslovakia was not following the path agreed at the conference. He also invited him to Yalta, where most of the Soviet leaders were taking their summer holidays.[35]

Kádár's visit on 12-15 August may have only partially reassured the Soviets about his reliability. True, he reportedly felt that 'Dubček – it is now clear – either does not want or is not able to control the situation – probably he doesn't want to.' However, he insisted that 'a Communist solution will be impossible if it does not dissociate itself from the pre-January state of affairs and methods.' He duly invoked the two-front struggle and praised the flexibility shown by the Soviet Union in allowing local party leaderships in Poland and – later – Hungary to find their own resolutions to their 1956 crises. The current Soviet leadership, he implied, should be similarly imaginative. The Soviet Union could not be 'the defender of yesterday … [but] must be the standard-bearer of progress in the future too.'[36]

Brezhnev asked Kádár to meet Dubček once more and 'tear him away from the rightist forces.' Kádár claimed afterwards that this was a final attempt at 'the settlement of disputed questions by political means.'[37] At this stage, this was most implausible, though Brezhnev may have wanted a last-minute assessment of Dubček's state of mind to judge whether he might be prepared to collaborate after the invasion.

The Kádár-Dubček meeting – their last – took place in Komárno on the afternoon of 17 August. Kádár may have suggested 'unforeseeable consequences' if Dubček did not take control of the situation, and commented that 'we ought to remember that these parties [i.e. the other members of the 'five'] had not changed even after the Bratislava meeting.' However, he gave no hint that the invasion was imminent.

They parted at Komárno station. Mlynář – who spoke to Dubček at some point after the meeting – had the impression that Kádár asked 'almost desperately, "Do you *really* not know the kind of people you're dealing with?"' Dubček recalled something similar but more cryptic. When Dubček complained that his programme had been subject to unfair criticism from the start, 'he [Kádár] looked at me and replied, "But you know them, don't you?"'[38]

That day, the Soviet PB made the final decision to invade. The operation would start during the night of 20-21 August, following a meeting of the Czechoslovak PB at which the anti-Dubček faction planned to seize power and ask for outside help. Kádár and the other satellite leaders were summoned to Moscow on 18 August and informed. Reporting on his 'fruitless' meeting of the previous day, Kádár concluded that 'political methods are exhausted' and pledged his support for intervention.[39]

The invasion was a short-term political fiasco. The 'normalisers' proved once more to be broken reeds, failing to carry through their coup. In contrast to 1956, the Soviets succeeded in arresting Dubček and his associates, but found themselves without a Kádár figure to provide even thin legitimacy for their presence. The 'five' met again in Moscow to debate the resolution of the crisis. Kádár favoured using the existing Czechoslovak leadership for 'normalisation' rather than the more radical options (such as a military dictatorship) favoured by Zhivkov and others. Brezhnev agreed with Kádár, and had to talk to Dubček once more, albeit on unequal and intimidating terms. The Czechoslovak leaders returned to Prague on 27 August, having signed the 'Moscow protocol' to rein in and reverse their reforms.[40]

In general, however, Kádár's advice had little effect. During the Moscow talks, the Slovak politician Dr Gustáv Husák, formerly a supporter of the Prague Spring, delighted the Soviets by emerging as a leading 'realist'. Kádár was wary of Husák's views, and disdainful of the Soviet leaders' emphasis on personalities. He told his PB on 27 August: 'We have insistently asked the Soviet comrades to be more restrained in this direction … For example in the middle of the talks they started to praise Husák a lot. They said he is so good in this way and so good in that way. We said: may God bless him, comrades, but he is our close neighbour. He's a regular Slovak nationalist – at least we have known him as such so far. May God keep him if he is good, but nonetheless we will wait.' He repeated the same point – only a fraction more diplomatically – during the Moscow summit of the 'five' on 27 September. Nonetheless, in April 1969, Husák replaced Dubček at the head of the Czechoslovak party.[41]

For Kádár and Dubček, the events of 1968 meant mutual disillusionment. Almost two decades later, emboldened by the Gorbachev era, Dubček wrote to Kádár, asking his support for a reappraisal of the invasion. Kádár did not reply, but informed Husák about the letter. Speaking to Gorbachev a couple of years earlier, he had derisively referred to Dubček as a self-styled 'national saviour' in the Nagy mould. For his part, Dubček wrote of his last discussion with Kádár, 'Now I know, of course, that he had met me on Brezhnev's instructions. In his own way, he was as much a product of "Leninist morality" as any of the others.'[42]

Kádár certainly deceived Dubček in casting himself as a more independent figure than he truly was and in reporting his discussions back to Brezhnev. Yet there was no deceit about his views. He thought that the Prague Spring should be reined in, and gave frequent warnings to Dubček; he was also deeply wary of the political costs and consequences of military intervention, and earned himself obloquy at Warsaw Pact summits for saying so. However, he found that his scope to act independently was minimal, as was his ability to influence either Dubček or Brezhnev, and the latter duly called his bluff.

Kádár's conduct can as much be criticised for lack of realism as for dishonesty. This was unsurprising: the alternatives were so unpalatable that he looked for other ways out. His sermons on the two-front struggle ignored the differences between a quiescent Hungarian society and the cauldron of rising expectations confronted by Dubček. He was also reluctant to confront the extent to which party control was collapsing in Czechoslovakia; in this respect the most accurate analyst of the crisis was neither Dubček nor Kádár, but Brezhnev.

Kádár also had illusions about the Soviet leadership. This was clear when he met Andropov – recently installed as head of the KGB – in the closing weeks of 1968. Kádár repeated many of the arguments that he had put in Yalta, urging that the Soviets avoid heavy-handed interventions in Czechoslovak decisions and taking the (retrospectively idealised) style of the late fifties and early sixties as a model. 'If at that time the CPSU had applied the Czechoslovak methods to us, it is hard to say what the consequences would have been.' The Soviet Union, he said, should show 'creative Marxism' and have 'positive answers' to new problems. Andropov was polite and friendly, but showed no sign of accepting Kádár's premises.[43]

Kádár's question to Dubček – 'but you know them, don't you?'– was one that he had reason to ask himself. Dubček had believed that for the Soviets 'times had changed' since 1956 and that 'relations within the "socialist camp" were essentially civilised.'[44] Kádár had better information, but he too had difficulty – evident in his talks with Andropov – in realising how obscurantist Soviet thinking had become.

That thinking – reinforced in its rigidity by the experience of the Prague Spring – would have implications not only for Czechoslovakia, but also for the bloc and for Hungary. As Kádár later admitted, 'the events [of 1968] had a negative influence on our reform initiatives and those of other socialist countries.'[45] He had been unable to avoid taking part in the destruction of Dubček's reform programme. Now, with no obvious ally and partner, he began to test the limits of the Soviet Union's tolerance of change, and his own.

14

CRISIS OF CONFIDENCE

By the turn of the decade, Kádár was starting to feel the burdens of nearly fifteen years at the top. He had always been physically fit, but he was a heavy smoker: a twenty a day man, rather more after a conference with Brezhnev.[1] His schedule was little different from a decade earlier. His role as First Secretary – leading the PB and Secretariat, taking a view on policy issues, managing the Soviet relationship – remained exacting, while the claims on his time of less apparently central tasks such as the work of the 'complaints office' were, if anything, increasing.

Thus we find him in January 1971 firing off an exasperated letter about the failure to meet the housing needs of an MP's widow. Shortly afterwards, he wrote to Nyers about 'a long-standing and deserving man of the workers' movement', who was depressed after having been cashiered as head of the Red October clothing factory. Would it be possible to cheer him up with a government award? Other representative cases included a payment to a veteran of 1919 now living in straitened circumstances in Romania; an old comrade's request for help for his daughter to go to medical school in East Germany; and still more officials disgruntled over their pensioning off.[2] Receiving foreign delegations also made demands on his time, including those of such vanguards of the international proletariat as the Irish and Canadian communist parties.

His weariness was apparent in a June 1970 memo to Biszku and Aczél about disputes that had arisen within his office when he was ill. 'I am thinking about how I can better organise and divide up my work, so that at least it should be physically bearable.'[3] Within a few years his health – in particular, his breathing – would start to deteriorate significantly as emphysema, a consequence of his long-term smoking, set in.[4] This was not a good state in which to confront ever more intractable political problems.

The leadership had feared the domestic consequences of the invasion of Czechoslovakia, a September 1968 report to the PB describing 'growing concern about the preservation ... of the achievements of the last twelve years.'[5] However, the consequences were limited to a handful of resignations, dismissals and the expulsion of some of Lukács' protesting disciples from the party. Aczél skilfully persuaded most of the discontented that they could serve the greater good by keeping their heads down, and there was little desire to rock what remained quite a comfortable boat.[6]

Ominous signals were coming from an increasingly conservative Moscow, where Aczél and his approach were thoroughly disliked.[7] Kádár, however, still leaned towards conciliation. This extended even to some of his old party contacts with whom there had been a breach in 1956. He had 'comradely' talks with Donáth, who raised the continuing employment problems of the former Nagyists. Kádár assessed the group as still critical in outlook 'but nonetheless loyal on the main issues'. They should be able to work and 'find their place in our society's building of socialism.' He wanted to draw Donáth back into politics and the party, but the latter was – understandably – unwilling to get involved.[8]

The leadership was also prepared to consider institutional changes, seeing a more flexible and responsive political system as a complement to NEM. However, with little willingness to challenge existing structures, a series of initiatives ran quickly into the sand. A new electoral law – intended to provide a choice of individuals if not of programmes – fell foul of local party branches' tenacious control of nominations. The separation of functions between the party (responsible for 'essential principles' and 'general orientation', according to Kádár[9]) and the state (policy implementation) was ineffectual so long as the existing lines of patronage and control remained intact. Attempts to boost local autonomy were undermined by central redistribution of funds and control of investment projects.[10] Nor did new party rules aimed at enhancing the role of grassroots members disrupt the despotic reigns of the 'little kings', long-serving County Secretaries such as Mihály Komócsin of Csongrád County.

One other area in which the leadership sought to achieve – or perhaps entrench – change was in the work of the security organs. Emphasising the difference from the Rákosi past, Interior Minister András Benkei told the November 1969 CC that matters of opinion were an issue for propaganda, not police work. Prosecutions for political crimes fell in the following years (from 207 in 1971 to 142 in 1973); however, the number of people under surveillance did not, and the focus of III/III on 'prevention' and 'social contact' justified the maintenance of a widespread network of informers.[11]

As political changes stalled, debates on the economy sharpened, testing Kádár's commitment to the NEM. He had put his authority behind it, but his commitment was much more contingent and pragmatic than that of Nyers or Fehér. His caution had coloured the many qualifications with which the new system had been introduced; if nonetheless the political alarm were to be raised, he would be prepared to make further compromises.

Initial performance was encouraging. Economic growth ran at a six per cent annual average in 1968-70, ahead of that of earlier years, and trade with the West was in surplus in 1969. Reformers pushed for further changes: the breakup of large monopoly companies, banking reform, a bond market and convertibility of the forint. They looked to a fifteen-year programme to bring prices much closer to those on world markets, and there was some progress in freeing up producer prices and reducing the number of turnover tax rates.[12]

The first sign of pressure in the opposite direction was a row in spring 1969 over companies' 'share funds', a system of workforce incentives that was attacked for favouring top managers at the expense of workers. The leadership withdrew the regulations in the autumn. The concession was cosmetic, but it emboldened the critics.[13]

The next front was increasing labour mobility, and co-operative farms' 'lending' of surplus members for factory work. Kádár was reportedly scandalised to discover that the temporary workers were paid more than their permanent counterparts;[14] the government ended the practice in August 1969. It also restricted the co-operatives' non-agricultural activities, the high wages of which were attracting workers away from the large factories. In talks with the trade union federation SZOT, price increases were added to the list of grievances.

The rapid concessions were testimony to the timidity behind Kádár's social compact: the leadership dared not ask too much of the population. Nor could it achieve real, rather than contrived, political mobilisation. '[The party was] powerless to explain to people that the necessary changes were not always going to be pleasant in the short term ... We weren't able to be a political and social driving force and so the reform came to a dead end.' The opponents of reform represented powerful interests: large but uneconomic companies and their 'core workforce', the power-base for SZOT and its leader, PB member Sándor Gáspár. Parts of the bureaucracy and party committees at factory, district and industrial sector level, their functions now in question, were also hostile. These groups had the organisation and access to the media to make their complaints count. As Nyers put it, 'The press was only producing exaggerated stories that stirred up doubt and opposition.'[15]

The complaints increased throughout 1970, many of them reaching Kádár's desk. Their political implications worried him, especially in the run-up to the tenth party congress. In a letter to his colleagues in October, his unease over the technocrats' dominance surfaced again. 'At present – and this isn't right – the personal opinions, prestige and influence of economists (Bognár, Csikós-Nagy and others) – which I do value – have exclusive influence and effect on a lot of important detailed issues.' He urged tighter wage and price controls, and worried over labour mobility and the fate of the 'core workforce'.[16] However, he did not want a complete reversal. The congress (23-28 November) saw further airing of alleged workers' grievances; Kádár took due note of them, but insisted that 'the new system of economic management is operating effectively.'[17] The fate of the NEM was finely balanced.

1971 did at least see the resolution of two long-standing problems. Some years before, Kádár had teased the American diplomat and politician Averell Harriman that Hungary had 'the assistance of the two great powers' in solving its two biggest problems. 'We handed Mátyás Rákosi over to the Soviets and Cardinal Mindszenty to you.'[18] In fact, both problems had been shelved rather than solved.

On Kádár's urging, Rákosi had been removed to austere living conditions in Soviet Central Asia (and later to the area around Gorki). He agitated to return home, and the Hungarian PB occasionally showed some willingness – notably in early 1967 – to consider it. However, the Soviets were indifferent, and Kádár stalled through bureaucratic obstacles and unacceptable conditions; time and Rákosi's deteriorating health were on his side. Kádár was the first person in Hungary to be informed of the old dictator's death on 5 February 1971. The news was announced in a deliberately low-key report in the morning papers. After a cremation in Moscow, Rákosi's relatives were permitted to have his ashes interred in a Budapest cemetery, but in a secretive ceremony attended by as many political policemen as mourners.[19]

In Mindszenty's case, the initiative came from the Americans, who saw Hungary – while scarcely central to the Nixon-Kissinger grand strategy – as a useful contact within the Soviet bloc and worried about the Cardinal dying or becoming ill on their premises. From mid-1970, they were raising the issue in both Budapest and Rome. Receiving János Péter on 16 April 1971, Paul VI indicated that Mindszenty – 'a victim of history' – should be brought out of the country. Kádár replied in an election speech in a Budapest factory four days later: concerning relations with the Vatican, 'We would like to further the settlement of certain questions.'[20] He did not wish to jeopardise the gradual improvement in relations with both the US and the Vatican, and followed his specialists' advice in making some modest concessions to ease the process.[21] Mindszenty would be granted a pardon and would not resign his post, though in practice an apostolic administrator would take over his duties.

Pressured from all sides, Mindszenty reluctantly left the US Embassy and the country on 28 September. Kádár took no direct role in the affair, but he guided its approval through the PB, desiring to minimise publicity and worrying about party members' reactions: 'if they ask why he received amnesty, we don't know what to say.'[22] In exile, the turbulent cardinal remained a thorn in his – and the Vatican's – side with high-profile speaking tours among Hungarian exiles. In February 1974, under pressure from the Hungarian authorities, the Vatican dismissed Mindszenty as Archbishop of Esztergom.[23]

The resolution of the Mindszenty issue was a rare success for Kádár; by autumn 1971, the signs of crisis were multiplying. Czechoslovakia had increased Soviet wariness of economic reform, an instinct reinforced by the Polish crisis of December 1970, when drastic price rises led to strikes, bloodshed and the toppling of Gomułka. To this closing of the Soviet economic mind was added Brezhnev's grand design to secure the bloc's western frontiers. To the extent that this meant East-West détente, the Soviet and Hungarian leaderships were in full accord. Hungarian leaders never tired of pointing out that the Warsaw Pact countries' call for a European Peace and Security Conference – without the preconditions that had previously made it unacceptable to the West – took place at the Budapest summit in March 1969. The move was, of course, driven chiefly by Soviet foreign policy objectives, though Kádár and his officials played their part through deft resolution of the differences between the participants.[24]

However, Brezhnev and his circle were anxious that détente should not mean the satellites becoming dependent on western credits or falling into Dubček-like ideological error. Instead they sought self-sufficiency through renewed Comecon integration. The Hungarians and Poles argued for integration through more market-based relations – a Comecon-wide counterpart to the NEM – but with little success. The 'Complex Programme' adopted at the Comecon summit of July 1971 did include – on paper – some vague market concepts. However, the Hungarians had to commit themselves to joint action in research and development, large energy projects and shared sector plans with partners who were all moving away from the market reforms of the sixties. 'This conference was the red light to stop reform.'[25]

Hungarian policies were still out of step, and the Soviet leadership sent ever-stronger signals of disquiet. Andropov was sent to Budapest to warn Kádár, while Brezhnev, passing through in September 1971, deprecated borrowing from the West and repeated the need for greater unity in the socialist camp. He also suggested to Kádár that he should come soon on an informal hunting trip to the Soviet Union.[26]

Soviet criticisms of NEM reinforced its opponents within Hungary. The big companies had already proved effective at using their links with County parties and the central apparatus to defend their interests and subsidies. However, they still felt that they had lost ground relative to agriculture and saw the reformers' continuing influence as a threat.[27] The different strands of the so-called 'workers' opposition' – pro-Soviet, linked to big companies and the 'core workforce' – were represented in a group that, by 1971, was taking an increasingly cohesive stance within the PB. Its spokesmen were Zoltán Komócsin, Béla Biszku and Sándor Gáspár. They represented the highest-level challenge to Kádár's authority since at least the departure of Marosán.

Komócsin was the youngest, ablest and thus – for Kádár – the most dangerous of the three. Though hitherto loyal, 'he worked under a direct line from Moscow,' an outlook probably reinforced by his role since 1965 as CC Secretary for International Affairs. He had taken the opportunity of chairing a conference of Communist and Socialist parties some years earlier to bring himself to the Soviet leadership's attention. He had shifted to an anti-NEM stance after the Czechoslovak crisis, and was seen by many as Kádár's replacement. [28]

Biszku, Kádár's deputy, had worked with him since the mid-fifties. He had been Minister of the Interior, then CC Secretary for Administrative Affairs; though closely associated with Kádár, he had always leaned towards more disciplinarian politics and had been cautious about the NEM. By now he was in outright opposition, with class-based politics his main motivation. 'He hated agriculture,' seeing developments in the countryside as the return of capitalism.[29] Gáspár's priority was the defence of his SZOT constituency in the big factories. Like Biszku, he had been at best a 'reform fellow-traveller', and had clashed early with Nyers. Unlike Komócsin, he put his opposition to the NEM in crude terms: 'Central direction is very good. The material confirms this … I tell you, there's anarchy [in the labour market].'[30]

The final element in the crisis was the overheating economy. The system's underlying pathologies, notably heavy industry's excessive and inefficient investment, remained unresolved. The leadership had added to the strains with sweeteners to accompany the introduction of NEM (improved family allowances, a shorter working week) and ambitious housing and infrastructure investments under the fourth five-year plan (1971-75). With a shortage of construction capacity in the state sector, the resulting rapid enrichment of private builders gave rise to outrage over 'unjustified incomes'.

A July PB saw a standoff between Nyers and Biszku over the state of the economy. Kádár was preoccupied by social and political tensions. 'The masses are demanding measures – because they're saying that the situation is intolerable … the working masses cannot put up with the kind of preening … that there is, and that's constantly on the increase in this country.' Soon afterwards the PB agreed further restrictions on co-operative farms' non-agricultural activities.[31] July saw the government put a stop to new investment projects. At a PB meeting in November, Fock insisted – against ominous warnings from Biszku – that the situation was under control, and Kádár seemed calm about it.[32] Nonetheless, the current account in convertible currency (essentially, trade with the West) had lurched from a small surplus to a $262 million deficit. That required further borrowing, and that was enough to set more alarm bells ringing in Moscow.[33]

Brezhnev decided to act. Had he wished to be rid of Kádár – and it is likely that at least some of his PB members did – then the Hungarian leader could not have survived. However, Kádár's standing – both domestically and within the international Communist movement – made this risky. The idea of moving him to an honorary post as party chairman was considered but abandoned. Brezhnev and Andropov agreed that the starting point had to be 'how best to support Comrade Kádár'. Policies and personnel, however, would have to change. The 'good Tsar' Kádár had to be rescued from his 'bad boyars'.[34]

Brezhnev invited Kádár 'for a friendly visit' over the weekend of 12-13 February. [35] The nature of the talks – conducted amid hunting on the Zavidovo estate – came as a shock to Kádár, even though Brezhnev sought to soften the impact of his message. His tone was one of sorrow and concern rather than of anger and threats. At one point, when the Soviet leader recalled emotionally how they had first met in November 1956, 'Kádár and Brezhnev began to weep.' (The foreign affairs specialist Mátyás Szűrös observed a similarly lachrymose incident a few years later. Perhaps Kádár shared Brezhnev's tendency towards gangster mawkishness – or perhaps he knew what was expected of him).[36]

Nonetheless, Brezhnev's 'comradely concern' embraced both Hungary's economic policy and its slack cultural and ideological stance. 'At a time like this, it is especially important that the ideological front be solid.' Kádár sought to defend his position, arguing that Hungary's problems reflected its past – 'this really surprised [Brezhnev], because he hadn't thought of it' – and that many of the issues raised were being tackled. Even so, he had to thank the Soviet leader for his advice and observations, and all round 'it wasn't the most relaxing of weekends.'[37]

Kádár was not wholly impressed by Brezhnev's critique. 'He is a pretty impulsive person. His knowledge about these economic matters is fairly uncertain.' Nonetheless, some of Brezhnev's concerns chimed with his own, and he knew better than to ignore a warning of this kind. He had to give enough ground to reduce the Soviets' incentives to remove him – yet not so much that he put his critics in a dominant position and undermined his own constituency. Much of the next three years would be dominated by getting this calibration right.

The PB divided along predictable lines, Fock arguing that the Soviets had poor information while Komócsin felt that 'what Comrade Brezhnev brought up is essentially true.' Kádár concluded that 'we must continue our general policy, our economic, cultural policy, [but] we must speed up the solution of the existing problems.' Ordinary workers who could not change jobs would share Brezhnev's views about the co-operative and private sectors. 'Economic necessities, economic policy necessities, but don't let's lose sight of political necessities!'[38]

PB debates were now 'pretty stormy … if a policeman had heard such arguments in public, he'd have intervened to break it up.'[39] Something of their flavour – and the direction in which Kádár's sympathies were moving – emerges from a May 1972 debate on the problems of the big factories:

> *Comrade Rezső Nyers:* … the capacity problem throughout the Hungarian economy has not come up now, but under the old system of economic management that Comrade Gáspár wants to bring back, I don't know why … You too had a fundamental part in the whole – *Comrade Gáspár's interruption cannot be made out.*
> *Comrade Rezső Nyers:* You're getting personal, Comrade Gáspár!
> *At this point Comrade Kádár suspended the debate.*

Summing up, Kádár remarked wearily, 'if possible, let's leave out this personal tone.' However, he picked out Nyers for criticism: 'Comrade Gáspár has a right to speak out; laymen sit here too.'[40]

By this time, however, PB members had something else to consider. On 10 May, just over a fortnight before his sixtieth birthday, Kádár had written his letter of resignation.

He had, he wrote, served as First Secretary for fifteen years – 'a significant period in the life of the party, much more in the life of an individual' – and had reached the age of retirement. The party's solid position made a peaceful handover possible, and it would set an important precedent. 'A change in the leadership of the Central Committee has always until now – recently too! – taken place amid extraordinary circumstances and convulsions.' This time, however, the change 'can take place under normal, orderly conditions.' The party and public interest demanded it 'and it is also my strongest personal wish.'

His age raised other questions. 'Now, whether I like it or not, I must face up to the fact that I have reached the stage in life in which a person's capacity for work and stamina no longer increase. On the contrary, with the passing of time, year by year and by degrees, it declines … It would be incorrect for someone to stay in place too long merely on the basis of past merits, out of reverence or because of habit, and to try to – so to speak – 'lead' with conditioned clichés and with the professional routine of political work. In no way do I want to get into such a situation.' He suggested that he retire at some point in 1973, and emphasised that there were no political disputes underlying his decision.[41]

Kádár's main purpose was surely tactical. His leadership was under question, but he probably knew that the Soviets wanted him to stay: according to the Soviet Hungarian specialist and later KGB head Vladimir Kryuchkov, he had already discussed the possibility of his retirement with Andropov and had been advised against it.[42] In any case, his meeting with Brezhnev indicated that the Soviets wanted to win him over rather than remove him. By effectively calling for a vote of confidence, he could strengthen his negotiating position with both the Soviets and his colleagues as he managed the implementation of Brezhnev's demands.

That – to use Kádár's terminology – was the 'objective' basis for the letter. Yet its 'subjective' tone makes the case for his departure persuasively and with some feeling. He knew the turbulent ends to the careers of Communist leaders in Hungary and elsewhere, and the disgrace – or worse – that awaited them if they did not die in office. There would be an innovative normality about a man simply reaching his sixtieth birthday and soon afterwards walking out of his office. His weariness and growing health problems suggest that his comments about his declining capacities were not merely formulaic. His description of someone staying in office for too long is acute – and, as it turned out, prescient.

Kádár did not seriously expect – or wish – his offer to be accepted. His self-image as a man who had merely taken on the tasks that the party had asked of him, or his dictum that 'you are not human if you're not afraid of the dentist and of power', are belied by his tenacious hold on the leadership.[43] It did, however, matter to him – internally as well as externally – to be seen to be acting as the party's servant. 'He very much identified his inner self with the self that he wanted to present to an audience.'[44] If he were now to stay on when history and his health suggested that he should not, he could justify it by knowledge that the party's leading bodies had asked him to do so.

They did. An alarmed PB rejected the proposal, and deputed a politically balanced group – Aczél, Biszku, Fock and Gáspár – to meet Kádár and urge him to withdraw it. 'Finally, we managed to persuade him to keep on working.'[45] A PB meeting on 22 May reached a 'compromise'. Kádár insisted on taking his request to the CC, the body that had officially appointed him; however, the CC would also receive a PB submission 'that, in the party's interests, it was necessary that Comrade Kádár continue to fill his current post.'[46] In following the rulebook, Kádár had ensured that he had a wider endorsement that that of his PB colleagues and rivals.

The CC of 15 June duly resolved that Kádár should stay in place. The resolution was secret, but inevitably the Soviets got to hear of it. Kádár sent a letter enclosing the relevant documents to Brezhnev 'because of the personal relations between us and the nature of the matter.' Brezhnev rang him some weeks later. 'I received Comrade Kádár's letter and read it over several times. I thank Comrade Kádár very much for his trust and care. I am pleased that he sent me this letter, but I am still more pleased with the resolution brought by the PB and the CC plenum.'[47]

On 25 May, while the resignation issue was still being resolved, Kádár celebrated his sixtieth birthday. Though he had asked for any commemorations to be low-key,[48] there was nonetheless press coverage, a fifteen minute 'historical' film, awards (including another Order of Lenin from the Soviets), congratulatory letters from the CC and other bodies, as well as from individuals. Among these were letters from Tibor Déry and from Ferenc Donáth, the latter wishing 'dear János' health and success in 'serving the Hungarian people'. Kádár replied to them as, respectively, 'my esteemed friend' and 'my dear friend'.[49] A decade and a half earlier, at the start of his rule, both men had narrowly escaped the gallows.

Kádár and Mária attended a celebratory lunch in Parliament. Replying to a speech by Biszku, Kádár set out a personal philosophy and a view of his own career that, if not always consonant with the record, was nonetheless revealing. At the beginning – and there is no reason to doubt him here – this rather isolated man expressed the importance to him of belonging. 'What is the course of a man's life? … the individual can only claim merits for certain things. For instance – and I think this is a kind of merit – when someone, at some stage of his life, realises that he is no leopard or tiger – not even a hamster – that if he wants to live he must live honestly together with the working people; and that if he wants to live better he must live better together with them. I consider myself fortunate that, at a crucial stage in my life – at the ages of seventeen, eighteen, nineteen – I came to understand that man alone can be neither human nor happy.' It was Marxism-Leninism that had helped him realise this. Thus: 'Man individually and as a social being cannot live a human life without ideas, without ideals. There are those indeed who live without ideas and ideals, but that is not a human life.'

He paid tribute to his colleagues and, in rather stilted fashion, to Mária. 'I always say that a life companion endowed with very much patience and with good nerves, and an appropriate home background, are needed if one is to be able to live and work. In this respect as well I consider myself fortunate.' The 'good nerves' probably referred to his arrest, a subject that he also touched on. 'I have even had a few things to suffer. Before Liberation they were physical; after, they were pains of the soul … For it's a pain for the soul when men ask, ask with me, whether one is an honest man or not.' In this – as in his comment that, 'if something was against my convictions, I refused to do it and suffered the consequences' – he identified with the heroic image of the Communist fighter for whom the cause and his integrity, not personal welfare or survival, are what matters. The more painful truths about his behaviour during the Rákosi era – the betrayals, the straightforward physical fear – were suppressed.

Perhaps closer to the truth was his defence of 'human commonsense and a sense of reality … in order to see how much of the [ideological] goal can be realised at the time. … Life is nevertheless in many respects a compromise. Nothing is realised the way one first envisages it. In the old world I also dreamt of liberation, socialism, Communism, and even though it was doubtful whether I would live to see the day of Liberation, there was no doubt in my mind that when the day came all that was needed were a few sensible ordinances and socialism would become a reality. That was over a quarter of a century ago, and it has since become clear that things do not get done quite that way.'

The section of the speech that drew the most attention addressed 1956 and its 'counter-revolution'. 'We know this is the learned definition of what happened in 1956. But there is also another name for it that we can all accept: it was a national tragedy. A tragedy for the Party, for the working class, for the people as a whole and for individuals as well. It was a wrong turning, and this resulted in tragedy.' However, Kádár still took the crushing of the uprising, and its subsequent acceptance, as the fundamental justification of his regime. '... I feel that, if you have nothing else to say for yourself except that in 1956, in a critical period, and in the following few years, you were of some use – you can say that you have not lived in vain ... I also consider myself happy that I have lived to see that very many people, hundreds of thousands and millions, have understood what we had to do in certain given situations which few understood at the time.'[50]

Kádár had used a formulation similar to 'national tragedy' in a PB meeting a decade earlier, and it was a deeply ambiguous term. It did not mean a fundamental reappraisal of 1956, rather a sense that the party had lost its way and that misguided individuals had therefore been caught up in disastrous events.[51] Nonetheless, for all its ambivalence, 'national tragedy' was a more conciliatory term – to individuals, if not to their cause – than 'counter-revolution'. And in contrast to 1962, Kádár was using it in a very public forum.

It seemed as though, in doing so, he was giving a further signal of social and political relaxation. In fact, he was covering a flank: policy was about to move in a very different direction.

15

A WORKER'S STATE

'From 1972, after [Kádár's] sixtieth birthday, his personality changed in many ways. He suddenly started to age rapidly. He just 'managed' his body to maintain his capacity for work. More and more, he shut himself away, he took more holidays – not for the joy of relaxation, simply to regenerate his ability to work.' On doctors' advice, he began to cut back on his workload.[1]

Yet if Kádár reduced his role as a day-to-day manager, his 'resignation' manoeuvre ensured that he remained the arbiter of Hungarian politics. He still had to satisfy the demands of Brezhnev, now at the height of his power and spreading a restrictive, defensive mentality across the bloc. There were also powerful domestic forces that had helped brake the reforms, and Kádár had reached the limits, more or less, of his own reformism. Yet he had no wish to turn the clock right back and follow the repressive orthodoxy of Hungary's archetypal Brezhnevite neighbour, Husák's 'normalised' Czechoslovakia. Such a sharp reversal would shatter the alliances on which the regime's legitimacy, and that of Kádár himself, had come to be based. His continuity as leader both reflected and reinforced the continuity with the more conciliatory policies of the sixties.

The Soviet leadership kept up discreet pressure through the summer and early autumn of 1972, deferring talks on raw materials deliveries. However, delays in a visit to Hungary by a high-level Soviet delegation, led by Brezhnev, may have come as a relief to Kádár as he hammered out a policy line.[2] The decisive CC meeting – expanded to include other top party and state officials – took place on 14-15 November. There was one notable absentee: illness prevented the attendance of Zoltán Komócsin. Kádár's putative successor had been stricken by cancer in the summer.

Kádár's long opening presentation deliberately downplayed the significance of the occasion, emphasising that this was a mid-course correction rather than a policy reversal. He also indicated that there would be no personnel changes – yet. 'It is not possible to call for heads at the start of the debate.' He defended the principle of the NEM – 'we did it together, and what we did, we did well' – and the CC resolution claimed that it must 'be developed further'. However, the measures that he presented were a 'workers' opposition' wish list: tighter price controls, especially in basic consumer goods, pay rises for factory workers, and a special examination of the country's top forty to fifty companies, accounting for around half of total output. The tools of intervention were strengthened with a new State Plan Committee serving the cabinet.

There was no direct challenge to Kádár's line in the debate, and he closed the meeting with some satisfied comments on the CC's unity. For the reformers, he sugared the pill by emphasising policy continuity and portraying the measures as a pragmatic solution to individual problems. He reiterated his familiar exasperation with the system's backwardness and inefficiency, citing factories in which problems had been evident since his time in the 13th District. 'Comrades, there's been a counter-revolution in the meantime. I ask you, comrades, can it be normal for a question like this to stay open for twenty years?'[3] But he had no new answers.

The Soviet delegation arrived a fortnight later. Brezhnev seemed happy with the resolution, though Kádár deftly deflected him from his wish to convey that happiness to a specially convened CC meeting. The visit brought one positive result: following Brandt's re-election in West Germany – 'our great joint political success' – Hungary could finally establish diplomatic relations, though it had been left to the back of the queue.[4]

When the CC resolution was adopted, 'those who took [the decision] didn't fully appreciate what it really was.' This ambiguity suited Kádár, avoiding a drastic upheaval that might agitate public opinion and call the party's steadiness and competence into question. For a while, reformers could persuade themselves that it was 'a short-term, crowd-pacifying policy … that left the door open for reform' and that their opponents had not got what they wanted.[5]

In fact, the new interventionist tools and policies took swift effect. Though Kádár claimed that official attention 'does not mean that the country's 40-50 biggest companies should now be wrapped in cotton wool', it strengthened the symbiotic relationship between these companies and their sponsoring ministries. As sole suppliers of important goods, employers of large labour forces and participants in major national (and international, Soviet-linked) projects, the companies could secure favourable price, tax and subsidy treatment, restricting still further the modest market signals that NEM had introduced.[6]

The advocates of control also had political momentum. The cabinet's Economics Committee, chaired by the pro-reform Mátyás Timár, gave way to the State Plan Committee. Its chairman, the Planning Office head György Lázár, was more a pragmatic loyalist than a doctrinaire; nonetheless, he had stood on the conservative side of some of the key debates in the mid-sixties. The same momentum carried through into shrill press campaigns with strongly conservative themes, while Biszku turned the security services against the more adventurous collective farm leaders.[7]

The anti-reform campaign opened up other fronts. Various groups – elements of the Populist movement (though certainly not figures such as Illyés and Csoóri) and the 'Populist Communist' followers of the literary historian István Király – stirred up campaigns with at least partly anti-Semitic undertones. They charged the leadership with neglecting national interests and traditions, and tied this both to the dominance of 'cosmopolitan' and 'anti-national' groups and to the allegedly corrupting effects of NEM. Aczél was very clearly the target.[8]

Letters complaining about 'anti-national' elements, especially in the media, came into party headquarters, putting Kádár under further pressure. He was no anti-Semite; Imre Pozsgay observed that 'on this question, Kádár had no prejudices. I never saw any signs of racism.' Aczél did note some minor prejudices: Kádár was not above some disparaging remarks about the 'tradesman's blood' of a relative's Jewish husband. Nonetheless, Aczél felt that Kádár 'despised anti-Semitism' and looked down on Gomułka for making use of it in 1968.

Politically, however, he treated it as a fact of life. He remembered both the appeal of the Arrow Cross in Budapest's working-class districts in the thirties and the impression left by the heavily Jewish nature of the Rákosi leadership. Thus, while some long-serving colleagues such as Aczél and Fehér were Jewish, he was careful to limit the number of Jews in senior, visible positions. Even a decade later, when considering a politician (his eventual successor, Károly Grósz) for promotion, he asked whether he was Jewish.[9]

His response to the campaigns was characteristic: he protected Aczél but made concessions, including the dismissal of some magazine editors. Though the Király campaign petered out in 1974, the more reputable Populist concerns – Hungarian minorities abroad, population problems, the regime's unease with the country's history – were growing in significance. They represented a protest against the constricted vision of politics that Kádár had promoted, although it was harder to show how an alternative could be pursued within Soviet bloc constraints.

'If any trouble starts again in Hungarian society,' Kádár remarked at a PB meeting in the early seventies, 'it will come from the intelligentsia.' Aczél airily dismissed his fears, arguing that the intellectuals were under control, but Kádár insisted on his point. Events were to prove him right.[10] In autumn 1972, three of Lukács' followers submitted for publication a densely argued political and economic case for market socialism, buttressed by civil liberties and political pluralism. The official response was sharp: the authors – and a number of other luminaries of the critical intellectual Left, including Hegedüs – were summoned before a special committee established in the Academy of Sciences. They were dismissed from their jobs and – if, like Hegedüs, they were still party members – expelled.

If this 'philosophers' trial' was in fact a disciplinary procedure, Miklós Haraszti faced a full criminal trial. Haraszti had been an irritant to the authorities since emerging as a student Leftist ultra in the mid-sixties. When a publisher turned down his account of his experiences as a worker in a tractor factory (*Piece Rates*, later translated into English as *A Worker in a Worker's State*), Haraszti circulated copies of the exposé. He was arrested in May 1973 and put on trial for 'incitement' in October.

Speaking to the PB in November, Kádár revealed just how much Haraszti – 'a man whom I can hardly describe as a writer' – had got under his skin. The trial was becoming a fiasco: 'it helped unite all opponents of the regime,'[11] providing a platform for left-leaning regime critics such as Hegedüs and Rajk's widow Júlia. It also risked undermining Hungary's relatively favourable international image. With the country increasing its western borrowing and with human rights a subject for negotiation in the European Peace and Security conference preparations, the leadership knew the constraints on its actions. Haraszti might have faced an eight-year jail term; instead, in January 1974 he was given a suspended sentence and ordered to pay costs. The trial, Kádár decided, had been 'a stupid idea' and one that should not be repeated.[12]

This conclusion was soon tested by the arrest in September of the sociologists György Konrád and Iván Szelényi. They had prepared a manuscript (*The Intellectuals on the Road to Class Power*) arguing that, under the 'socialist' system, a 'redistributive' intelligentsia was becoming the predominant social class. Given that six months earlier the CC had debated a long report submitted by Biszku 'on the development of the social role of the working class and the further improvement of its situation', this was touching a particularly sensitive spot.[13]

Kádár was in Bulgaria when the arrests took place, and they may have been ordered without his knowledge. The manuscript was circulated to PB members; Kádár reportedly asked one PB member his opinion, and was told that it was 'scientific'. 'If it's a serious, scientific work,' Kádár said, 'let them out.' Both men were released after a week; they suffered various sanctions, but there was no trial. The true significance of the decision was not Kádár's commitment to social science, but that he had learned the lesson of the Haraszti affair.[14]

The leadership had got the worst of both worlds. The alienation of the reformist Left intelligentsia was now complete. The regime had shown a thuggish side that had been played down over the previous few years, yet it had stayed its hand from a Czechoslovak scale of repression that might have truly isolated and intimidated its critics. There was still no properly organised opposition, but the conditions for its existence were being established.

Soviet pressure did not let up. Brezhnev saw the November 1972 CC resolution as merely a downpayment. Speaking in June 1973, after another visit by Andropov – 'I know that Comrade Kádár can speak completely openly with him' – he insisted that 'my feelings, my political sympathies, my personal relations with János, the Hungarian people, for Hungary are unchangeable. I will die with them.' However, he used a reference to the problems of Comecon integration to drop a hint: 'no paper will change anything if the right cadres are not in place. If there are bad cadres, that's bad; but if we leave them in place for a long time, that's still worse.'[15]

Biszku meanwhile was making effective use of a scandal involving MEGÉV, an agricultural equipment trading company. The affair was damaging to Nyers and Fehér, since they had reportedly tried to block the highly political 'investigation'. An informal PB discussion in late 1973 produced a heated row, with Kádár accusing Nyers of interference. 'And then he lost his cool. I lost my temper too – maybe I was first, then him, I'm not sure – but at the end we were yelling at each other.' In a November PB resolution, Kádár gave Nyers and Fehér serious reprimands. Their position was becoming untenable.[16]

Whether or not, as alleged, Moscow ordered Kádár to act in early 1974,[17] the Soviet leaders undoubtedly had clear ideas about dismissals. Probably top of the hit list was Fehér, because of his agricultural heresies – seen as 'much, much more dangerous' even than the NEM – and his earlier closeness to Nagy.[18] Aczél ('Zionism', cultural liberalism) and Nyers (economic deviation) ranked almost as high in Kremlin demonology. Fock – his occasional ambiguities notwithstanding – was committed to the NEM, and the Soviets had taken against his abrasive style: 'Fock negotiated with Kosygin as though Hungary were a great power.'[19] So he too had to go.

Kádár presented a list of names to a closed PB session on 26 February. Fehér received the most brutal treatment: immediate dismissal as a Deputy Prime Minister and PB member. Fock was to retire as Prime Minister, Aczél and Nyers as CC Secretaries. Komócsin, his health deteriorating rapidly, would move from CC Secretary for International Affairs to *Népszabadság* editor-in-chief.[20]

Regarding the departures of Nyers and Fehér, whose policies were causing him such trouble, 'his [Kádár's] heart wasn't bleeding … in fact, he was relieved.' Nonetheless, while the breach with Fehér was final, Kádár kept his lines open to the party's reformist wing via Nyers, reassuring him in friendly discussions that NEM would not be abandoned. He suggested a variety of new posts (Nyers became head of the Academy of Sciences'

The huntsman with the day's kill, 1981

Economics Institute) and hinted that he might one day return to the political front line.

Kádár reportedly refused Soviet demands that Aczél should be dismissed from the PB; he lost his post as CC Secretary, but was made Deputy Prime Minister and found in time that it did little to reduce his power. As he cheerfully put it: 'the word got round that Aczél can be the doorman and still run cultural policy.'[21] In that area, he was indispensable. Kádár presented Komócsin's move as a humane measure for a man too sick to travel but still wanting to work; however, it also had the political advantage of making the changes less one-sided.[22]

Further modifications in the PB meeting and in the days that followed reduced the sense of discontinuity. Fehér was allowed a more dignified exit, serving out his PB term until the congress in 1975. After a surprising intervention by Komócsin opposing Fock's immediate departure – apparently pre-arranged, probably with Kádár – it was agreed that Fock too should serve through to the congress, a timetable that he and Kádár had originally agreed in 1973. Komócsin was now keen to serve party unity. His *Népszabadság* editorial a few weeks later, emphasising that party policy was unchanged, drew a warm letter of appreciation from Fock. Kádár's letter was, characteristically, more formal, but concluded by praising Komócsin's 'outstanding and persuasive speech … a very great help to the party-spirited discussion and resolution of the personal issues that are always complicated.' Komócsin died in May.[23]

Announcing the changes to the CC, Kádár emphasised that there would be no witch-hunt: 'It must be said here that those comrades who have been criticised for some practical things are still for us esteemed comrades, the balance of whose long, long work is positive.'[24] His approach to dismissals (at least after Marosán) was a straight-faced insistence that they did not reflect political conflicts, followed by the fallen comrades' departure 'with recognition of their merits' to more junior but still comfortable posts. When Biszku and his allies tried to deprive Nyers of his seat in Parliament, Kádár stopped it, insisting that 'there is no political problem with him.'[25] He saw this as a matter of decent, 'party-spirited' behaviour. The approach also had political advantages, helping to maintain his chosen image of a calm, measured leadership pursuing a 'consistent' policy.

Brezhnev initially seemed pleased with the changes: 'I'm in full agreement with what Comrade Kádár does; my heart and Kádár's are one.' However, the kopeck eventually dropped that the purge had been relatively limited and lacked the desired ideological mood music. When they met in the Crimea in August, Brezhnev renewed his criticisms of Hungarian unorthodoxy. As for the personnel changes: 'I thought that this matter would be carried through to the end. The comrades in question have not given up their principles, which they can state freely. This worries me.' He insisted on a clear policy line for the coming congress, emphasising 'the unshakeable leading role of the working class.' He then tried to be conciliatory, explaining, 'I spoke like this because the good relations between us make this possible.'

Kádár dutifully replied, 'Thank you, I found that very helpful. I too said what I did, because the relations between us are such as to make it possible.' If, as the foreign policy specialist Gyula Horn put it, 'he could not bear being dictated to,' then he must have been biting his lip. In part, however, Brezhnev's bullying reflected his frustration: Kádár had carried out the changes as he saw fit, and there was little that the Soviet leader could do about it. However, economic negotiations between the countries were at a critical point, and on these issues he could continue to exert pressure.[26]

Oil was at the heart of Kádár's difficulties. The Soviets, Hungary's main supplier, did not pass on immediately the massive increase in the world price at the end of 1973, but proposed a 1975 price based on an average of the previous three years, and a rolling five-year average price thereafter. This would double the price that Hungary paid in 1975, with further increases in prospect unless the world price fell back sharply. Visiting Moscow in late September, Kádár asked for concessions. Kosygin was hard-edged, Brezhnev more conciliatory, interrupting Kosygin to say that 'they would have to see'.[27]

On 27 December Kádár received Nikolai Baibakov, head of the Soviet Planning Board, in an attempt to resolve the problem. His economic advisers warned that, since bilateral trade within Comecon was supposed to balance, higher oil prices would require Hungary to increase exports to the Soviet Union by 600-800 million roubles over the levels originally projected for the next five-year plan (1976-80). These would have to be diverted from western markets and would increase imports of raw materials and components, adding to the strain on a convertible currency trade balance already suffering from higher raw material prices. Kádár wanted a billion-rouble ten-year loan to tide Hungary over, but Baibakov could only offer to take the request back to Moscow.[28]

Austerity measures were politically unacceptable. The leadership leaned against price increases, and rejected a proposal from Planning Office staff to reduce the target growth rate for the 1976-80 plan from its original six per cent level. This reflected not only the predominant pro-worker ideology, but also the demands of Brezhnev's campaign for an integrated 'socialist commonwealth'. The Complex Programme and five-year plan required major Hungarian investments in Soviet raw material projects. These were an attractive source of guaranteed business for big Hungarian companies, but they required yet more western imports of components.[29]

The only way out was foreign borrowing. Like other bloc members such as Poland and Romania, Hungary had begun borrowing before the crisis, intending to use it both to participate in Soviet projects and to restructure its export base. The approach was cautious: Fock was known for his careful monitoring of debt levels and Kádár was reportedly more anxious still.[30] The oil shock changed this. Kádár was warned at the end of 1974 that net convertible currency debt – which had stood at $784 million at the end of 1973 – would rise to between $1.1 and $1.2 billion that year and to $1.6 billion in 1975 (both figures were underestimates). However, the deteriorating terms of trade provided an alibi for borrowing, as did the anticipated revitalisation of export capacity that would enable it to be repaid.

Borrowing was not a conscious choice, but reflected other decisions – or non-decisions – often justified by unrealistic assumptions. The planners were pressured to lean towards optimism, and in a system in which growth rates were a somewhat arbitrary political decision, it was hard to stick confidently to more pessimistic projections. 'Our starting point was that a certain rate of growth would destroy the balance [of the economy]. But who could tell whether this would take place at 4%, or 4.4% or let's say

4.8%?' Under these conditions, 'hope often triumphed over experience' and deficits were consistently higher than forecast.[31]

Although NEM was not formally rolled back – company-level plans were not reintroduced – the run-up to the Eleventh Congress (17-22 March 1975) saw more centralising measures affecting wages and investment. Biszku continued his campaigns against agricultural unorthodoxy, and the congress resolutions spoke of the need to 'strengthen the socialist character of the production co-operatives in agriculture'. To Biszku and others, this meant subordinating co-operatives to state farms ('the more advanced form of social ownership'), as had happened in the Soviet Union.[32]

Kádár had a weary distrust of this sort of sloganising, pointing out to the CC that the previous conference had pledged itself to 'a higher level of full socialist construction', and full socialism had not yet arrived. 'If the party does not want to get into a ridiculous situation, what are we to say now? A still higher level?'[33] In a lecture in September 1974, he commented that, of the two stages, socialism and Communism, 'obviously, we are in the first phase, socialism, and not even on a very high level.' When western politicians called Hungary a Communist country, 'we can say to them: we wish it were so.' (This *bon mot* was frequently delivered to visitors). Though he spoke dutifully of the possibilities of a 'more advanced' form of 'universal, all-people's property', he tempered it with his usual pragmatism. 'We know our own society well, and … most people pay less attention to whether it is theoretically correct than to whether the situation of the working people, of the country, and of society is improving.'[34]

Nonetheless, Brezhnev found the plans for the congress more than satisfactory and delivered Kádár's requested ten-year loan (later agreed at 800 million roubles), as well as pledges of more raw material deliveries. He clearly expected – and got – Kádár's public thanks in his congress speech. In a meeting of bloc leaders at the congress, Brezhnev spoke at length about economic coordination, international politics – and his health. Kádár assured him that the latter was a concern not only of the Soviet Union but of 'socialist countries, the international Communist movement and of progressive humanity.'[35]

With strident sloganising that seemed a throwback to another age, the congress represented the high point of the anti-reform movement. Kádár's speech, though in line with the main resolutions, struck a more cautious note; and with the congress over and a satisfied Brezhnev safely back in Moscow, he began quietly to consolidate his leadership around a more centrist position.

Fock resigned as Prime Minister in May. His successor was the Planning Office head, György Lázár: competent, hard working, unobtrusive and deeply loyal to the system and to Kádár personally. Lázár was a compromise candidate[36], and in general the departed reformers (Nyers left the PB along with Fehér) were replaced by low-key centrists rather than by ideological fire-eaters. Unusually, Kádár added two new PB members after the congress: Pál Losonczi, the pragmatic farmer and state President, and István Huszár, Deputy Prime Minister and Lázár's successor at the Planning Office, a moderate reformer. The new PB was more conservative than its predecessor, but a degree of equilibrium was maintained.[37]

Another sign that the anti-reform movement was reaching its limits came in agriculture. A cut in the buying price for pigs and, more significantly, hints of punitive taxation set off a bout of slaughtering. Around a fifth of the country's pig stock was lost in 1974-75. With the prospect of meat shortages, the leadership panicked: the Agriculture Minister was dismissed, buying prices raised and talk of swingeing taxes abandoned.[38]

The hubristic growth plans approved by the congress also came into question. It was only in June that a report full of alarming truths was presented to the PB – indicating that the subject had not been open to discussion prior to the congress. The CC finally signed off a compromise plan in November. The projected growth rate was shaved a little, while consumption and investment were projected to lag the economy as a whole, especially in the plan's first two years. Dynamic export growth would bring the external accounts into balance. Kádár was pleased with the plan, seeing it as a responsible basis for 'well-founded, unbroken development'.

Yet the planners had clearly censored themselves: this 'responsible' plan was based on unproven and heroic assumptions, and lower oil prices were factored in to make the forecasts acceptable. Even under these assumptions, net debt would 'only' increase from around $2 billion in 1975 to $4-4.5 billion in 1980. Kádár and his leadership colleagues were confronting the economic future with fingers determinedly crossed. What the banker János Fekete later called 'the age of illusions' was far from over.[39]

16

MITTELEUROPA MAN

Kádár led the Hungarian delegation for the signing of the Final Act of the Conference on Security and Cooperation in Europe in Helsinki on 1 August 1975. The summit saw a striking divergence in the conduct of the satellite leaders. While the others maintained their distance, Kádár – along with Gierek and, in very different style, Ceaușescu – projected himself strongly and favourably to his western counterparts.[1]

He drew further attention with his speech at the closing session, declaring that he and his colleagues were 'representatives of the Hungarian people, who established their state 1,000 years ago between the Danube and the Tisza, in the centre of Europe.' He followed this unusual identification with the country's historic traditions and wider, non-ideological European identity, with an equally unexpected reference to Trianon. 'In this century, following the useless sacrifices of the First World War, the territory of vanquished Hungary was reduced to one-third of what it had been.' Unsurprisingly, he welcomed the aspects of the Final Act that had been on the Soviet wish list, notably the ratification of the Europe's post-war borders. However, he also sounded conciliatory on the less congenial issues ('basket three' of the Act) of cultural cooperation and – though he did not use the term – human rights.[2]

The Hungarian government sought to maintain momentum after Helsinki, sending out proposals to nineteen Western governments (including the United States) for further improvement of relations.[3] Soon after this Kádár started travelling, visiting Vienna, Rome, Bonn and Paris. In the post-Helsinki climate, Gierek and Ceaușescu were just as active, and – because of the size of their countries – more important to the West.

Nonetheless, Kádár's 'opening to the West' would prove the most durable initiative of its kind in the bloc.

Economic benefits – the search for export markets, credits and technology licences – were a central motivation, but Kádár also needed calmer international relations to sustain the domestic policies he had pursued since the early sixties. He had already allowed a modest revival of Hungary's cultural links with Western Europe after the isolation of the Rákosi years. Further opening could conciliate groups such as the intelligentsia and religious believers, and he was still confident that the party could manage and withstand its consequences.

He also had the interest of a small country's leader in rules that constrained the bigger powers – including the Soviet Union. At Helsinki, the British Foreign Secretary, Jim Callaghan, reported to Kissinger that 'Kádár told us yesterday that they regarded it [inviolability of frontiers] as a moral and political commitment.'[4] The maintenance of 'peaceful coexistence' preoccupied him increasingly. He put his simple but persuasive philosophy to the CC: '... two countries which have mutually advantageous, lucrative, wide-ranging economic relations are much less likely to get into political conflicts or war than those that don't.' As for cultural interchange, 'This too is needed to avoid a new World War.'[5]

There may have been yet another factor in his thinking. As József Marjai, the diplomat and later deputy prime minister, put it, 'At the beginning of the seventies, he experienced a lot of shocks from the strongest alliances [i.e. the Soviet Union]. After that, he became very active ... and started travelling.'[6] In building up contacts in the West, Kádár was spreading his risks a little, above all by diversifying Hungary's economic base. He may also have reasoned that raising his international profile – though, given the country's size, it would never be that great – would give him an extra card to play.

How far was he acting in accordance with Soviet wishes? Shortly after Helsinki, the US Embassy in Budapest reported that 'one well-informed Hungarian tells us that Kádár may have made his basket three remarks as the designated spokesman on the subject for the socialist camp ... If this information is correct, fact that Soviets would assign this task to Kádár is worthy of note.'[7] It certainly suited the Soviets to have a 'soft cop' presenting a favourable image to the West, and they were interested in technology transfer – preferably with military applications. Thus, in Brezhnev's words, Kádár's travels 'served the interest of the whole socialist community.'[8]

Nonetheless, Brezhnev was uneasy about the political price of these western contacts. Kádár had no wish to detach Hungary from the Soviet Union or to defy Moscow. However, there was a grey area of policy tolerable to the Soviets in which he could operate, and a recognition on his part – which had increased over the years – that Soviet and Hungarian interests were not always identical. And, if his role in some ways suited the

Soviets, it also suited western powers to have an acceptable partner within the bloc, not least as an additional channel of communication.

A visit to neutral, neighbouring Austria in December 1976 was an easy starting-point. Kádár already knew Bruno Kreisky, the high-profile Social Democrat Chancellor, and ideological differences notwithstanding they got on 'like two gents'. Kreisky considered Kádár 'of all these Communist leaders … the most "Austrian"'. There's a fair quota of irony in his makeup and he's aware of the limits which life imposes.'[9] Both men had been born in the last years of the *kaiserlich und königlich* era. Now a journalist suggested that *k.u.k* stood for *Kreisky und Kádár*.[10]

Kádár's press conferences at the end of his western visits contrasted with the incompetence or graceless stonewalling of many Communist leaders. His language was more formulaic than that of most Western politicians, but he was a sharp and confident performer, with a nice line in self-deprecation; in Vienna, he answered a question on military issues by recalling his 'career' as a deserter in 1944, from which 'I have not advanced all that far.'[11]

He seemed different from other Communist leaders in private too. François Mitterrand, then leader of the opposition Socialists in France, visiting Budapest in May 1976, was struck that Kádár did not spout statistics 'about tonnes and kilometres, etc.' They could talk serious politics, and 'I even saw Trianon through Hungarian eyes.' Mitterrand also experienced vigorous marketing of a 'tragic' Kádár. He was given a graphic account 'by one of his ministers' (Aczél?) of the Hungarian leader's arrest and supposed tortures. Apart from musing on his prison sufferings, Kádár gave his version of 1956, which, Mitterrand thought, 'obsessed him'. He left impressed by 'this simple man with a sad countenance, dressed in ordinary-looking clothes and speaking in a soft voice.'[12]

Kádár had made a similarly strong impression on the West German Chancellor, the Social Democrat Helmut Schmidt, when they met at Helsinki. At the end of Kádár's visit to Bonn in July 1977, the two leaders showed their mutual regard in a joint press conference. They would subsequently meet a number of times, and found a style in which to communicate ideas and information. 'Kádár was not indiscreet … [but] in an indirect way he passed on a clear impression of [Soviet] views through the way in which he set out his personal conclusions … Kádár and I set out on the basis that the other could pass on tactfully to his own allies things that could be of interest to them. And each could count on not being named by the other as a source.'[13]

Kádár also met Willy Brandt – still influential as party chairman – who made a ten-day return visit to Hungary the following March. In long and congenial talks, the two mused on the tortured history of Communist-Social Democrat antagonism.[14] Some of Kádár's younger advisers, such as Gyula Horn and János Berecz, had argued for building contacts with Social Democrats, and had found him immediately responsive. He wrote to

Brandt after their discussions that 'the most fundamental problems that humanity is confronted with will not be soluble without cooperation of the two great tendencies in the labour movement.' Their joint action could 'bring us closer to a solution to the flash points that threaten the existence of human civilisation.'[15]

Had Kádár, the one-time member, one-time liquidator of the Social Democrats become more relative in his judgements? He had not become a closet Social Democrat, even if Brezhnev thought of him as such.[16] That his attitude was nonetheless different from that of the Soviet leaders was clear from the controversy over 'eurocommunism'. Kádár was much more understanding than his bloc counterparts of Western European Communist parties' efforts to adjust to local conditions by distancing themselves from Moscow and abandoning some dogmas.[17] While Brezhnev sought to draw up the political and ideological drawbridges, Kádár hoped that rapprochement with a more Social Democratic West would enable a small country's consumer socialism to flourish.

Travel apart, Kádár stuck to the lighter schedule that he had begun in 1972, though it was still fairly demanding for a man in his mid-sixties. He relaxed on Friday afternoons, watching a film along with PB members, other senior officials and their spouses. The event had a slightly downmarket feel to it. Imre Pozsgay remembered brandy, cigarettes and cold meats 'of the cheapest kind … I could never decide whether this was affected or not.' Kádár established ground rules: no Hungarian films (he did not, he said, 'wish to get involved in cultural policy') and nothing too serious. Soviet films were not much encouraged either, but light American films were. 'These films should not be taken as an indicator of Kádár's cultural level; they were his way of relaxing at the end of the week.' The choice was left to the 'representative of the working class', the elderly projectionist, 'Uncle' Szűcs.[18]

The PB member István Huszár felt that at these times, 'Kádár was longing for friendship.' If so, he was disappointed: the atmosphere was strained, with everyone on best behaviour before the boss. The same was true of Kádár's other efforts at camaraderie, such as lunches after PB meetings and small drinks parties for PB members' birthdays. Much of this distance reflected the isolation characteristic of a senior political leader, but Kádár's personality reinforced it. Though fond of telling anecdotes, 'he did not let the other person get too close … He was a lonely man. He went all over the country, but people did not get to know him, because he did not want that.'[19]

His PB and Secretariat colleagues were in no doubt about their dependence on him. In the run-up to congresses and mid-term CC meetings – the usual stage of the political cycle for appointments and dismissals – he required them to write critical assessments of their own and their colleagues' work. They also had to suggest who should be kept in place and who dismissed.[20] Though 'he expected people to speak up in debate', questioning them if they had stayed silent in discussions for some time, he always had the last word; anyone who forgot this convention 'got a bad name'.[21]

Political battles and falling out with former cronies such as Sándor and Major had narrowed Kádár's circle. The only PB member with whom he socialised was Aczél; he and his wife often joined Kádár and Mária for supper after the Friday film sessions. Aczél and Kádár also spent hours together on long walks, giving rise to a mystique about Aczél's influence. When István Huszár was suddenly dismissed from the PB and his other senior posts in 1980, Aczél told him, 'you see, Pisti, you should have come and seen me more often.' Nonetheless, 'it was Aczél himself who advertised this influence' and, while there clearly was sympathy between the two men, and friendship between their wives, it was Aczél's political uses that were the key to the relationship.[22]

Mária – cooking Kádár's favourite bread and dripping with onions, fussing over his irregular meals and heavy smoking – remained the constant in the life of the man she referred to by the old-fashioned, deferential term *úram* (my husband). Some of those who worked closely with Kádár insisted that she had little or no political influence.[23] His adviser János Berecz found it 'interesting to watch them together. If some topic came up, Kádár would start to give his opinion. Very often his wife interrupted with her view. Kádár waited politely until she'd finished, then carried on saying what he was going to say anyway, irrespective of what he'd just heard.' There were, however, persistent rumours about her role in personnel choices. Probably tongue in cheek, Kádár gave them a little encouragement: told that Elena Ceaușescu had been given 'responsibility for cadres' in the Romanian party, he muttered, 'At last – a country where they make it legal.'[24]

As Deputy Head of the Prime Minister's Information Office, Mária reportedly acted as a censor. She was an ironclad prude, and anything involving naked flesh attracted her special ire. Even after her retirement in 1980, she remained a fearsome guardian of the nation's 'prolet-Victorian' morals; if Kádár came into the office muttering about something improper on television, his staff had strong suspicions as to the real source of the complaint.[25]

Economic policy had drifted since the stalemate of 1975. The following year's summer drought hit growth and investment, with the unintended side effect of reducing borrowing needs. Kádár and his colleagues did not see this as a cause for rejoicing; in the autumn the CC Economy Secretary, Károly Németh, insisted to officials that the plan must get back on track in 1977.[26] In part, this reflected pressure from heavy industry; attempts to drain funds from companies were abandoned. Kádár also retained his conviction that the party had to deliver on living standards. This was not solely a matter of calculation: 'People always forget that Kádár was a worker – he remained one in his mentality. To raise working-class living standards was not just a question of power in his eyes, it was a core issue.'[27]

Meanwhile, hopes that convertible currency exports could outpace imports were fading as the effect of high oil prices continued to feed through. An Economics Committee report to the PB in July 1977 indicated that over the plan period unfavourable price movements in Soviet trade would cost 800 million roubles more than previously estimated. With the Soviets demanding high 'dollar content' – whether for investment projects or for consumers – this would increase imports and therefore borrowing from the West. Kádár was mandated to raise the issue in a letter to Brezhnev.[28]

The two leaders met in the Crimea on 26 July. Brezhnev offered some help with credits, while warning Kádár against dependence on the West, including debt: 'it is starting to take on political coloration.' Nonetheless, with Soviet economic problems increasing, he could offer only limited help. This left Kádár little choice: confronted with criticisms such as Brezhnev's, 'Comrade Kádár came up with the formulation that we would really like to borrow from the East, but we couldn't, because they simply did not make it possible.'[29] So he would go on borrowing from the West.

Trade and international relations dominated Kádár's talks with senior Italian politicians when he visited Rome in June 1977. However, his audience with Pope Paul VI on 9 June commanded much more attention. Church-state relations continued to improve: Mindszenty's successor, Cardinal László Lékai, was unlikely to cause Kádár difficulties and the church now had a full complement of bishops. Nonetheless, the Pope used the almost hour-long private audience to voice the Vatican's continuing concerns, notably over restrictions on religious instruction and publication in Hungary. In the formal, more public session Pope Paul, with measured understatement, described Kádár's visit as 'the culmination of a long and not uninterrupted process of rapprochement over fourteen years.' Referring to the need for both sides to respect the other's interests, he turned to Kádár and said, 'We know that you too have repeatedly expressed your readiness to do this.' At the end of the Papal statement, Kádár gave a brief extemporaneous reply.[30]

Kádár was very much alive to the political benefit of the meeting and of rapprochement with the church. He shared with the CC his delight that Lékai was willing to give the regime public support. 'Politically, that's no trifle!' He added that 'it was possible to speak very practically and realistically with the Pope about these things.' In speeches and interviews, he continued to emphasise religious toleration. He painted an idealised picture; nonetheless, though religious believers remained second-class citizens in an officially atheist state, their conditions eased steadily, especially after Helsinki. The last imprisoned priest was released in July 1977, just after Kádár's meeting with the Pope.[31]

Helsinki also reinforced the caution with which the regime treated critics. The emergence of samizdat literature in 1977 met with a fairly calm response. A letter of solidarity with the Charter 77 group in Prague, signed by thirty-four leading intellectuals, alarmed the leadership because of its 'international' implications, but the signatories experienced intermittent harassment rather than arrest. In the follow-up meetings to Helsinki in Belgrade in 1977-78, Hungarian diplomats were keen to seem constructive, distancing themselves from their Warsaw Pact colleagues' attacks on western interference. With a large-scale surveillance network and ability to pressure dissidents through employment bans, the leadership felt confident that it could contain opposition without resorting to measures that might threaten western contacts, tourism and bank credits.[32]

Relations improved with the United States as well as with Western Europe, although even after Mindszenty's departure, Kádár had taken time to overcome his distrust. In July 1972, when US Secretary of State William Rogers visited Budapest, Kádár initially claimed to be unable to see him; only when Nixon sent a personal message asking him to receive Rogers did he conclude that 'it seems there is no way to avoid this.'[33] His unease may have been compounded by the fear that, at this difficult point in his leadership, Moscow might see this as a Ceauşescu-like gesture of independence. 'Kádár appeared a little nervous at the outset' of the meeting, though he soon warmed up, teasing Rogers 'that the Secretary was in Central Committee headquarters and hoped that there would be no infection as a result.' He nonetheless emphasised that 'we should not have too high expectations' about the speed at which relations could deepen.[34]

By the mid-seventies, there were two major issues outstanding: Hungarian requests for normal trade relations under Most Favoured Nation (MFN) status, and for the return of the Crown of St. Stephen. The Holy Crown of Hungary, the medieval symbol of Hungarian statehood, had been smuggled out of the country in 1945 and was now held by the US government in Fort Knox. The Nixon administration seems to have considered its return, and in 1977 the Carter administration, keen to encourage a reformist Hungary, decided to go ahead.[35]

Nonetheless, the Americans insisted on its being a 'people to people' event, with church participation and a low profile for the party – and one party functionary in particular. The ambassador, Philip M. Kaiser, had to pass on 'a highly sensitive request … that President Carter would be politically embarrassed if Kádár were to be present at the ceremony.' Kaiser found the response relayed to him 'impressive: Kádár understood the sensitivity of the situation and would not be present.'[36]

A delegation led by Secretary of State Cyrus Vance returned the Crown in early January 1978. Carter had, however, taken a lot of political heat from émigré groups, and a Hungarian suggestion for 'a certain meeting' met with a nervy American rejection: 'we do not repeat not wish to request a meeting between the Secretary and Kádár.'[37] Nonetheless, in spring 1978

Congress passed MFN and Kádár received a congressional delegation headed by the House Speaker Tip O'Neill. In this and other meetings with American visitors, he played the part of gnarled old pol to perfection. One Senator described his two-hour meeting with Kádár as 'one of the most impressive political performances I've ever witnessed.' Guests received some heavy hints that he would welcome the chance to visit the United States.[38]

The initiatives did not all come from the Hungarian side. Kádár got on well with Ambassador Kaiser, despite the American's surprise at being presented with a Scotch and soda at their first meeting: 'not my usual drink at 10 a.m., but obviously his.'[39] (Kádár was a very moderate drinker, but often accompanied discussions with a small whisky or cognac.) In December 1978, Kaiser suggested to Péter Rényi, deputy editor of *Népszabadság*, that Kádár might visit Washington, and could be an 'interlocutor between the Soviet Union and the United States.'[40]

Both sides, however, had reasons for caution. The Hungarians were wary of the ambiguity that an 'interlocutor' role might introduce to their standing with the Soviets. For the Americans, there was still one major problem with Kádár: his past. Administration officials had already concluded that, while he was 'an innovative and successful leader ... there are still a number of emotions that he arouses among Hungarian émigrés that are best left undisturbed until after the 1980 election.'[41] The ghosts of 1956 kept Kádár from the White House lawn.

'In the international area, at least I have normal partners,' Kádár once remarked – and he did not mean his colleagues within the bloc.[42] He was understandably reticent about his views of the Soviet leadership, but thought little of Brezhnev's 'fondness for dramatics' and penchant for awarding himself ever-grander titles and medals, though he was careful to blame the latter on 'those around him. They're flattering him.' His confidence in Soviet assistance was fading, though he probably maintained an emotional loyalty to the concept of the Soviet Union, as opposed to its decadent reality.

Though he spoke, even in private, in 'comradely' terms about the other bloc leaders, he had 'extraordinarily decided opinions' about them. Bulgaria's Zhivkov he thought stupid, Czechoslovakia's Husák a political coward, East Germany's Honecker a vain womaniser. Poland's Gierek was a more natural ally, though Kádár was rightly sceptical of his grandiose industrial schemes. His relations were rather better with the semi-detached Tito.[43]

Though Kádár was circumspect in expressing his opinions about Nicolae and Elena Ceaușescu, he listened to derogatory stories about them with unconcealed approval. Mária was more outspoken. Waiting with the Kádárs at the airport for the arrival of Libya's Colonel Gaddafi in 1978, János Berecz made a passing mention of the Ceaușescus. This set off a furious diatribe from Mária – 'she went on and on' – interrupted only by the news of Gaddafi's arrival. As they set off to meet their guest, Kádár muttered to Berecz, 'If you say the name Ceaucescu once more when my wife's present, I'll kick your arse so hard you'll fly.'[44]

Kádár had good reason to disdain Ceauşescu, whose intensifying assault on the Hungarian minority in Romania was becoming a major political problem. A chilly meeting between the two leaders in June 1977 yielded the promise of cultural contacts and a Hungarian consulate in Transylvania. However, Kádár was soon disappointed in any hopes that his low-key policy would yield results: the consulate's opening was constantly delayed and conditions deteriorated further.[45]

The critiques of the early seventies had put Kádár on notice about the risks of a policy seen as 'anti-national'. A CC resolution of September 1974 cast national traditions in a more positive light; the Helsinki speech and its reference to Trianon also reflected this thinking.[46] Yet to raise an issue of minority persecution in a 'fraternal' country would be to break a major ideological taboo, and Kádár remained wary of stirring nationalist sentiment: 'if we too open the floodgates, we could be shocked by what follows.'[47] The result was a policy of inaction, at least in public. In 1978, a book by Illyés was withdrawn because it included essays dealing with the minorities, though the writer was allowed to broach the issue in general terms in two newspaper articles. Kádár knew the political damage that he was suffering, especially among Populist intellectuals, but felt that there was little that he could do about it.

Overall, however, his popularity held up. György Konrád, no friend of the regime, wrote a few years later, 'In the tavern I hear, "God watch over Jani!" and "We'll be all right so long as he's in charge!"' An émigré leader who protested against Kádár's visit to Paris in 1978 heard from his visiting mother, who still lived in Hungary, 'believe me, that we can be considered a half-way western system by comparison with the Czechs, the Poles and the Romanians – we've got Kádár to thank for it.'[48]

Although there was quite widespread acceptance of some official values – such as full employment, state ownership and egalitarian incomes policies – Kádár achieved only 'a partial legitimacy'.[49] Given the historically strong desire in Hungary to be part of the European mainstream, from which adherence to the Soviet bloc excluded it, this was probably the best that he could hope for. Western commentators' frequent (and unverifiable) claim that Kádár could have won a free election missed the point: much of his popularity rested on his seeming the best option under any *realistic* circumstances. Compared with Hungary's recent past, and with figures such as Brezhnev, Husák and Ceauşescu, he did seem benign. The intermittent fears in 1972-75 of a reversion to the past, and their gradual dispersal, added to his standing. He seemed to be the personal guarantor of a modest but bearable existence.

He was buttressed by a general sense of improvement, with rising incomes, a continued expansion of white-collar employment and improvements in housing and transport infrastructure. Yet its foundations were increasingly insecure. The economy boomed in 1977, growing by eight per cent, but surging investment sucked in imports from the West; net debt rose from $2.2 to $2.8 billion. However, when some Planning Office staff urged that the five-year plan should be modified, they found the PB hostile: 'they said that our growing more slowly wouldn't solve anything.'[50]

Unwilling to adopt painful measures, Kádár and his colleagues looked to longer-term structural change. A policy paper brought to the CC in October emphasised selective growth of exports to the West in place of import substitution and overwhelming reliance on Comecon. The CC resolution also mentioned bringing producer prices closer to the realities of the world market. Debating the report, Biszku urged 'the importance of consultation with the Soviet Union and with Comecon countries.' Kádár was dismissive: 'I recommend that we don't consult with anybody, because there's nothing to consult about; these are Hungarian economic problems and unfortunately no one is interested in them.'[51]

More immediate pressures, however, could not be ignored. The CC's December resolution urged a tougher approach to subsidies and investment credits and (in an unpublished section) looked to some increases in consumer prices. By early 1978 the external financial position was deteriorating more rapidly than ever; by year-end, net convertible currency debt would exceed $4 billion. Projections generated by National Bank economists were so alarming that 'we scarcely dared write them down.' The Bank's leaders knew, however, that Kádár was reluctant to confront the problem, and officials' warnings went no higher than the Economics Committee prior to the major 'half-term' CC of April 1978.[52]

Thus Kádár's lengthy presentation to the CC still looked for a very gradual correction.[53] Nonetheless, he set a clear general direction that drew together the new economic policy with the domestic and international initiatives of the previous three years. He reiterated his 'policy of alliances', rapprochement with the church and peaceful coexistence with the West: 'this means economic links, social links, cultural links, travel.' For the benefit of the simpler souls on the CC, he explained the need for economic links with the West. 'In every Hungarian shipment that goes to the Soviet Union or to other socialist countries there is ... a particular amount – whether it's 5 per cent, whether it's 15 per cent, whether it's 24 per cent, sometimes a bigger percentage – that is Western imports ... and these we have to pay for in the West. So there's the secret of our economic contacts!'

The second item on the agenda was 'redeployment of cadres'. As early as 1976, Kádár had quietly removed the CC Secretary Árpád Pullai, who had been a forceful operator within the 'workers' opposition'. Now Biszku was sent into retirement. It was rumoured that he had again plotted against Kádár, trying to turn the Soviet leadership against him; years later, Kádár indicated that there was some truth in this. In any case, Biszku's dour crusades against economic unorthodoxy and against agriculture in particular were incompatible with the new policy line.[54]

Kádár made clear – without, of course, giving any suggestion of the link – the lessons that he wanted drawn from Biszku's ouster. Everyone, he said, should support Hungarian-Soviet friendship, but 'no one should over-achieve with 130 per cent Hungarian-Soviet friendship.' He went on, 'Allow me to emphasise this, and let everyone in the party understand it: with the Soviet Union, with Hungarian-Soviet friendship, it is not X or Y who is the friend, and no one should try to present himself as the Soviet friend in a particular area. That cannot be allowed. The ally, the friend of the Soviet Union in Hungary is the Hungarian Socialist Workers' Party, the Hungarian working class and the Hungarian people, and everyone must act in this spirit.' So much for the plotting of the early seventies.

Lest the point be missed, he also warned against those who set themselves up as representatives of particular social groups, such as the working class. 'The resolutions are binding on everyone, and no one should be more Catholic than the Pope. I'm not just saying that because I was in Rome ...'

17

CREDIT CRUNCH

Kádár's installation of a new economics team at the April 1978 CC meeting was a signal both of policy direction and of seriousness about implementation. The new CC Economics Secretary, Ferenc Havasi, was an experienced operator, a former Secretary of Komárom County who had been Deputy Prime Minister since 1975. He was not a reformist technocrat in the Nyers mould, but was nonetheless critical of excessive subsidies and the inconsistent implementation of NEM. The new Deputy Prime Minister was the former diplomat and ambassador to Moscow, the clever and abrasive József Marjai. He and Havasi would later be rivals, but they initially worked together effectively as a force for economic realism.[1]

The new team delivered more than Kádár had perhaps bargained for. Officials soon convinced Havasi of the need for austerity, and at a PB meeting in early June, Kádár admitted that 'we've got to make a fresh effort' to contain the debt. Nonetheless, it took a series of meetings and modifications of the original proposals before he and many other PB members would truly accept it.[2] Even with tough measures, more credit was needed, and the CC Economics Committee urged a renewed application to join the IMF and World Bank. Kádár was cautious, knowing that Moscow would object. He proposed writing to the Soviet leadership – which had still not paid in full the credit promised by Brezhnev in 1975 – raising the IMF-World Bank issue, but also highlighting Hungary's financial problems and asking for help.[3] Though the auguries for Soviet generosity were scarcely encouraging, he still hoped to raise a loan; he may also have reasoned that, if he were finally constrained to join the Washington institutions, he could show that he had exhausted every more palatable alternative.

Kádár wrote to Brezhnev on 17 July, asking for a meeting and for additional loans, deferment of payments and an expansion of Soviet raw material deliveries in the coming 1981-85 plan.[4] However, their meeting was fruitless. Brezhnev indicated discouragingly that financial matters would be left in the hands of the respective Prime Ministers and specialists, while warning that, 'these days we were hearing again about the IMF and the World Bank. In these financial institutions the USA's political ambitions carried the day.' He added that US gestures, such as MFN and the return of the Crown, were part of a western plot to 'Romanianise' the socialist countries.[5]

After prolonged debates within the party, a CC resolution in December prepared the way for increases in both consumer and producer prices, and for cuts in investments. Reluctantly, Kádár accepted that living standards would have to stagnate. Even so, he cast policy in deliberately gradual terms, with the 'double aim' of 'underpinning our achievements up to now' in production and living standards while securing the future. Living standards would stagnate but not fall while industrial competitiveness was improved. A financial crisis, he said, must be avoided, because Hungary 'would then hand itself over to the West.'[6]

Brezhnev's warning notwithstanding, the IMF-World Bank issue came back onto the PB's agenda in February 1979. Most members were at least open to the idea; Kádár agreed in principle, though subject to yet further consultations with Brezhnev. These took place in early March, with a predictable further rejection.

However, if Kádár's thinking was to use the Washington institutions as a lever to extract more money, he succeeded. Brezhnev offered to top up the long-term loan to Hungary to one billion roubles. Kádár declared that Hungary 'does not intend or want to sponge off the Soviet Union', and gratefully pocketed the concession. If he had to sit through a sermon from Brezhnev on socialist cooperation and the dangers of links with capitalism, doubtless he thought it a price worth paying. Shortly after his return to Budapest, the PB took the issue of IMF and World Bank membership off the next CC meeting's agenda. If he could ease financial pressures without confronting the Soviet leaders, so much the better: 'he kept putting off the [IMF] decision because he suspected that they didn't [understand it] in Moscow and that it would have unforeseeable consequences.'[7]

With the application to the Washington institutions dropped, Brezhnev's three-day visit to Budapest, starting on 30 May, went smoothly. He was now very frail, an ambulance accompanying his motorcade. Kaiser, the American ambassador, noticed 'the anxiety that permeated the airport' at his arrival, reflecting uncertainty over his attitude towards Hungarian policies. Brezhnev endorsed them, and the atmosphere on his departure was very different, with a 'sense of relief ... smiles rather than strain on the faces of the Hungarian leaders. Kádár was noticeably bouncy and talkative, and with a big grin on his face gestured to several of us Western ambassadors.'[8]

While changes to the producer price system were planned for introduction in 1980, the PB decided in March that major consumer price increases should be brought forward to the summer.[9] The leadership was understandably nervous of the reaction to sharp price rises for basic goods and sought to draw some of the sting by increases in incomes. Outward protests were limited, but the message that the easy days were over got through; from then on, public economic pessimism was on the rise.[10]

As the banker János Fekete recalled, when the austerity programme was planned, 'it was possible to expect that we could make a nice peaceful recovery from our difficulties.'[11] However, external pressures worked against Kádár's gradual approach. Oil prices surged again in the aftermath of the Iranian Revolution, and the Soviets were becoming reluctant to forgo revenue by supplying oil and gas on Comecon terms, which – because they lagged behind movements in world prices – still had an element of subsidy. Kádár initially believed that this could be overcome by more determined negotiation: 'we must fight, Comrade Huszár, we must fight.' Gradually, however, he realised the scale of the problem, and became increasingly alarmed, especially when there was no sign of the credits promised by Brezhnev in March.[12]

His frustration boiled over when he met the visiting Soviet PB member Andrei Kirilenko on 22 October. He recalled past Soviet promises and the

Farewell to Brezhnev, June 1979. Relations had not always been so close.

hopes that Brezhnev had raised in March. 'But what followed did not match up with that. The detailed talks are exactly the same as they were before the 6 March message ... We need a five per cent annual increase in Soviet raw material and energy deliveries to be able to achieve minimal development. Comrade Baibakov has so far promised two per cent. That's not enough for us.' He had also had enough of carping over Hungary's western links. 'Some Soviet economists worry away over that. According to some of them it's a result of our [economic] management system. That's fundamentally wrong. The truth of the matter is that to live, work and produce in Hungary, we have to import materials and energy.' Hungary could solve its problems, but 'let us build on the platform stated by Comrade Leonid Ilyich Brezhnev on 6 March.'[13]

Another precondition of Kádár's strategy, continuing détente, was also eroding as NATO considered installing medium-range nuclear missiles to counter a Soviet build-up. In September, with Schmidt visiting Hungary, Brezhnev urged Kádár to use his influence on the German chancellor to stop the decision.[14] It was far too late for that; on 12 December NATO ministers voted for deployment if missile reduction talks with the Soviets proved unsuccessful. Nor was this the end of 1979's shocks. One senior colleague had noted Kádár's punctiliousness in not telephoning people in their private time at home. That Christmas Kádár broke his rule, since he had urgent news: the Soviets had invaded Afghanistan.[15]

Initially, the Hungarian leadership hoped to avoid the fallout of the 'second Cold War'. However, in late January Moscow 'requested' bloc members to freeze contacts with the West. This would mean cancelling visits to Bonn by Foreign Minister Frigyes Puja and by a delegation to the United States. When the PB debated the issue on 29 January, many members – some of them normally conservative in outlook – felt that Hungary's interests were being discarded and were willing to defy Moscow. Kádár was not; as over the Washington institutions, he shied away from open conflict. His speech was rather incoherent, but he made his point about the Soviet-Hungarian relationship with visceral force. 'How long do you think they'll be polite with us? Why with us ... forgive my putting it like this, with our lousy little lives, and country and everything ... how long will they be polite with us?'

As usual, he got his way, but wrote to Brezhnev to urge regular consultations within the bloc and the need to keep lines open to Western Europe. Seeking to limit the damage with West Germany, he also wrote to Brandt and Schmidt.[16] A Moscow conference of CC Foreign Affairs Secretaries at the end of February agreed that bloc members should maintain links with Western Europe in the hope of diluting US influence. As before, Kádár's policy was ambiguous. His cultivation of the West Germans matched with Moscow's desire to create divisions within NATO, but also reflected Hungary's pressing financial and economic interests. Those interests also, however, encouraged initiatives that challenged bloc taboos. In early 1980 an Economics Committee report proposed that Hungary establish direct relations with the EEC.[17]

The beginning of 1980 also saw the austerity programme continuing, with the introduction of a new producer price regime. This meant sharp one-off increases in energy and raw material prices, but there were also longer-term reforms. Domestic energy prices were linked to the world market, manufacturers exporting to the West had to align their domestic and international pricing and in 1981 the forint exchange rates were unified. Kádár muttered disapprovingly that imported inflation might slip in 'like an American pancake', but let it pass.[18]

Similarly, cuts in subsidies and investments were accompanied by attempts at institutional change. The 'branch' ministries serving different sectors were merged into a single Industry Ministry, large monopoly companies were broken up and a revival in agricultural co-operatives' non-farming activities promised some competition. Liberalisation of private initiative in the service sector – the 'second economy' – had been under consideration since 1978. The PB approved the general concept in February 1980, and detailed policies were implemented two years later.[19]

Kádár did not intervene heavily in economic policy-making. When it came to austerity measures, 'Kádár let us do it.' He nonetheless shepherded the important measures through the PB and CC, indicating, for example, his support for the liberalisation of small-scale services and the sector's need for a stable tax system and raw material supply. At the low-key Twelfth Congress (24-26 March 1980) he admitted that the 1976-80 plan would not be fulfilled, and that during the succeeding plan 'there will be [only] moderate growth, but conditions for further progress in the years ahead must be ensured.'[20]

Many policies, however, were inadequate to ensure those conditions. Fundamental relationships did not change; company managers were still appointed by the state, albeit by a different ministry. The policy mix strengthened 'functional' ministries, such as Finance, whose main priority was austerity, not corporate independence. In addition, cuts in investment fell disproportionately on agriculture and infrastructure, while many big and uneconomic projects with powerful lobbies were protected. And with large companies' loss-making exports keeping the current account afloat, the leadership's willingness to sustain pressure on subsidies was questionable.[21]

These tensions and ambiguities were apparent in the sixth (1981-85) five-year plan. This projected annual real income growth of just 1-1.2 per cent, while net convertible currency debt would still grow, albeit slowly. This was compatible with the growth of a dynamic, competitive export sector only if weaker branches of the economy were being drastically scaled back. Yet the leadership dared not move beyond its forlorn efforts at slow motion restructuring.[22]

The next blow came from Poland. Kádár was not alone in having relied on western borrowing; so had much of the rest of the bloc, and Gierek had pursued the primrose path with particular recklessness. Now his efforts to resolve a deepening economic crisis through meat price increases brought about strikes, the occupation of the Lenin shipyard in Gdańsk in August and the creation of the Solidarity trade union in September.

Kádár was angry and contemptuous of the Polish leadership, remarking that 'Poland reminded me of a drunk who staggers from side to side, but thanks to the grip of his guardian angel doesn't actually fall.'[23] He was also disorientated by the rise of Solidarity, a clearly working class movement linked to the Catholic Church. Sitting by Lake Balaton with the Culture Minister Imre Pozsgay, Kádár talked about Poland. He did not show strong emotions – 'he was rather tired by that time' – but his final remark betrayed his perplexity. 'Even their leader is from the working class!'[24]

Though carefully watching domestic reaction to the crisis, Kádár's bigger worries were its impact on western lenders' confidence in the region – Hungary duly experienced its first net outflow of funds in 1980 – and the damage that a Soviet intervention might do to East-West relations. Though hostile to Solidarity, he quickly emphasised to Brezhnev the need to avoid 'interfering from the outside'. As he put it to the CC, 'this is a Polish problem, they must deal with it; we should use every opportunity to help them, and sometimes this is done most intelligently by not interfering in their disputes.'[25]

Even if Kádár was as cautious over intervention in Poland as he had been over Czechoslovakia in 1968, he was less isolated – and therefore, paradoxically, less important – than he had been in the previous crisis. In much more dramatic form, Poland would reinforce the lesson of Kádár's constant haggles with Brezhnev: the Soviet Union was starting to count the cost of empire, and its leaders were extremely reluctant to get directly involved. A bid by Honecker, Husák and Zhivkov for a military solution in November and early December seems to have failed for lack of Soviet support.[26]

Thus, when the leaders gathered in Moscow on 5 December, they could only put their own variants of a loose agreement that the Polish leadership should – somehow – 'restore order'. Kádár's speech – in many ways the most practical and detailed at the meeting – typically focused on the political preconditions for re-establishing control: a united leadership, a clear platform and a firm grip on radio and television ('these media are integrally linked to the question of power'). Seeking perhaps to underline the lack of need for external intervention, he drew encouragement from some of the initiatives of the new Polish leader, Stanisław Kania. Recalling his experiences after 1956, his watchword for the Polish leaders was: 'you are stronger than you think.'[27]

Shortly after the summit, at the turn of 1980-81, Kádár suffered severe pulmonary oedema (a buildup of fluid in the lung, usually caused by weakness of the heart's pumping mechanism, which may in turn have been a by-product of his emphysema). His doctors thought his condition 'close to life-threatening', and after hospital treatment he took two weeks' rest at a party resort. With other health problems growing – in particular, narrowing of the arteries, another smoking-related condition – he had to reduce his work commitments further and began to take longer, more frequent holidays.[28] However, there was a limit to how far he could step back: the pressure of events was relentless.

He was in demand as an expert consultant on 'normalisation', receiving three visits from senior Polish figures in the first seven months of the crisis. By the time that Kania came to Budapest in March 1981, conflict with Solidarity was sharpening. Kádár's advice is an interesting measure of how far – when confronted with a crisis – he had truly mellowed over the years. 'When the class enemies launch a general attack, there can be no clemency. In the fight against class enemies the laws of humanitarianism are suspended ... fight to the finish, preferably using political means but, if necessary, using any other means available to authority; the basic requirement is that Poland remain a socialist country.'[29]

Unsurprisingly, the leadership turned its attention at this time to opponents inside Hungary. A more organised critical movement – the 'Democratic Opposition' – had come into being since the first open act of defiance, the statement of solidarity with the Charter 77 group in January 1977. János Kis and György Bence, veterans of the 1973 'philosophers' trial', gave the grouping its main intellectual motor. Other key figures included Haraszti, Konrád and – in the background, contributing his long political experience – Donáth. Like its Polish counterparts, the Democratic Opposition sought to build an independent society from the bottom up through the creation of 'parallel' media and organisations that broke official taboos. Early initiatives included samizdat writings, a 'flying university' giving unofficial talks and seminars in private apartments and an independent charity highlighting the problems of the poor.

Kádár initially stayed his hand, and with reason. Though the PB's discussion of the opposition, on 9 December 1980, took place in the shadow of the Polish crisis, Hungary lacked the linkages of opposition intelligentsia, discontented factory workers and a strongly independent church that had proved so dangerous in Poland. So long as this continued, Kádár saw no need to change policy; however, he warned the PB, 'should the opposition try to join up with the workers, then there will be no quarter given.' He saw the problem as one of intellectual underemployment: 'there are more writers than really write; it's the same situation with film directors. The intellectuals are discontented because there are more of them than society needs.' The PB agreed that it was 'a political rather than an Interior issue'; nonetheless, there was an increase in measures such as publishing bans on writers linked to the opposition.[30]

When the PB revisited the issue in March 1982, the opposition – emboldened by the Polish example – had made the important shift from independent writing to independent publishing. The first edition of the leading Democratic Opposition periodical *Beszélő* (Speaker) was published in October 1981. Distribution started with a 'boutique' in the flat of the architect László Rajk the younger, Kádár's godson. For historical reasons, the leadership remained wary of victimising him; Kádár reputedly commented that 'we don't want another Rajk trial.'[31]

Nonetheless, his mood had hardened. Although he still saw a partial solution in trying to tackle the problems raised by the critics, he now favoured a more vigorous use of 'administrative measures'. This still did not mean large-scale arrests and trials on the Czechoslovak model, but a 'step by step' approach, applying pressure through house searches, withdrawal of passports and blacklisting from employment.[32] Use of these measures increased during 1982.

Even if constrained by its external image and obligations, the leadership held a strong hand. Its sanctions could deter all but the most determined, and it was fully aware of opposition activities through surveillance and informers. Though the scale of the latter network has not been fully clarified, it was probably on a smaller scale than that which served East Germany's Stasi or Romania's Securitate. Kádár's Hungary was a lighter-touch police state than these more infamous counterparts: but it was a police state nonetheless.

However, these measures could not resolve the growing estrangement of the intellectuals. The generation with which Aczél had struck his bargains was passing from the scene, and younger writers from a variety of traditions were less responsive to his blandishments. A sign of the changing mood was the elections to the leadership of the Writers' Union in December 1981, in which a number of figures close to the regime were voted out. As before, the writers had significance beyond their numbers; their alienation spoke of a loss of intellectual ground by the leadership, leaving a gap which critics – whether the Democratic Opposition, or 'semi-opposition' figures such as Sándor Csoóri, the leading heir to a Populist tradition increasing alienated over the minorities issue – might fill.

These, however, were long-term worries; it was the financial pressures that were immediate, and they were intensifying. The austerity measures and an export drive had turned a convertible currency trade deficit of $782 million in 1978 into a surplus by 1980, and that surplus was rising. However, world interest rates had risen steeply, and Hungary's credits, unlike those of most of its neighbours, were predominantly floating-rate syndicated loans from the euromarkets. The average interest rate stood at 5.9 per cent in 1979, but 9.7 per cent in 1980 and 14.0 per cent in 1981, and the much higher interest costs kept the current account deep in deficit. Hungary was on a debtor's treadmill.[33]

Worse, many loans taken out in the mid-seventies were coming due just as western credit dried up. The region was tipping into crisis: Poland had put a moratorium on its debts in March, and Romania subsided into rescheduling later in the year. East Germany and Yugoslavia were also struggling with their borrowings. Tainted by its neighbours' problems, Hungary could not raise money from the markets after May.[34]

Kádár's usual summer meeting with Brezhnev (27 July) brought another blow. The Soviets had already cut oil supplies the previous November, selling oil for hard currency and using the proceeds to aid Poland.[35] Now Brezhnev said that the Soviet Union could not deliver all the oil and gas pledged to Hungary for the remainder of the 1981-85 plan. He confirmed this by letter six weeks later.[36] Hungary would need either to squeeze economic growth still further, or borrow more to make purchases at world market prices.

The July meeting had a further significance. Kádár gave his usual account of Hungary's credit difficulties, and remarked that, supportive as he was of the idea of Comecon integration and a 'socialist commonwealth', it would not be a practical proposition for ten years. To fulfil its already modest economic plans, Hungary would need to widen its sources of western credit – and he made a passing, rather cryptic reference to the World Bank. Brezhnev, it seems, did not respond.

Not long afterwards, the Hungarian leadership re-activated plans to join the Washington institutions. Havasi brought the proposals forward in the PB of 15 September. After his meeting with Brezhnev, Kádár had changed his stance: Hungary, he said, must join even if the Soviet Union were to repeat its opposition. He urged discretion, worrying about the enthusiasm of 'somewhat right-leaning economists. They like to broadcast things and chatter all over the place, and they'd spoil this thing just as in its time they spoiled our economic reforms. We'll have to warn them off, won't we?' Similarly, he told János Fekete, deputy head of the National Bank and his chief negotiator, 'Fekete, don't make a big noise about this.'[37]

With exploratory talks already under way in Washington, the CC approved the decision on 22 October with one dissenting vote. The application was announced on 4 November. Formally, the Soviets had been informed only in a letter from Lázár to his counterpart Nikolai Tikhonov two days previously.[38]

What did the Soviet leaders know, and when did they know it? There is no definite answer, and some of those involved in the decision are convinced that they were taken by surprise.[39] Hungarian officials gave contradictory impressions. One told an American diplomat of the decision quite early in October (well before the CC's vote), adding that Moscow had been consulted. Shortly afterwards, however, other spokesmen gave quite a different impression, playing up Hungary's independence and Soviet disapproval.[40]

Kádár had given Brezhnev a broad indication of his intentions during their summer talks and probably took his reaction – or lack of it – as tacit acceptance. Aczél's formulation of what happened may be significant: Kádár 'only gave the green light when the voices from outside in opposition were already stilled.' When the decision was announced, some Hungarian officials told American diplomats that Soviet objections had been easing over the previous year, and other sources confirm this.[41] Confronted with the intractable Polish problem and with mounting economic difficulties at home, the Soviet leadership had been unable to fulfil its past role of subsidising Hungarian living standards. With their final retrenchment on energy supplies, they had effectively cut Kádár loose to find his own salvation.

Most probably, the Soviets simply 'didn't say no'. Kádár's low-profile approach enabled both sides to operate on a 'don't ask, don't tell' basis. If the Soviets were not asked their opinion again, they would not have to object; and if they did not express a view, the Hungarians did not have to defy it. Nonetheless, when Mátyás Timár, head of the National Bank, informed his Soviet counterpart, 'he was not surprised. There was no response.' Valeri Musatov, then serving in the Soviet Embassy in Budapest, believed that 'Moscow knew. Not the details, but the direction was clear.'[42]

Kádár had stayed ahead of events – just. The crisis in Poland continued to deepen, and on 18 September the Hungarian CC sent a letter under his signature to its Polish counterpart. This demanded that the Polish leadership should show 'a definite sense of direction' and 'drive back the open attack of anti-socialist forces.'[43] A few weeks later Kania was gone, with General Wojciech Jaruzelski the new strongman of the party and government.

Awareness of a looming confrontation in Poland may have given Kádár an extra incentive to move quickly with his IMF-World Bank application: Jaruzelski declared martial law on 13 December. The general cast himself as a reluctant dictator, and was deeply interested in Kádár's experiences. When at his request a Hungarian delegation visited Poland in late December, Jaruzelski asked his visitors whether Kádár had felt so isolated in November 1956. He was to try to copy the Hungarian formula of repression followed by reform, and became one of the few bloc leaders whom Kádár respected.[44]

The IMF-World Bank application was just ahead of events in another sense. At around the turn of the year there was a run on deposits at the National Bank of Hungary. During the first quarter of 1982, Hungary's foreign exchange reserves fell by three-quarters to $400 million, barely a month's imports. Kádár had been determined that Hungary would remain a good creditor; now the risk of having to reschedule debt was very high. However, years of steady contact with Western central banks paid off: the Bank for International Settlements raised an interim credit that saw the country through until it joined the Washington institutions in May. Though there were still some alarms, IMF credits and a gradual return to the commercial markets enabled reserves to be rebuilt.[45]

The rescue package was mostly handled by specialists such as Fekete, but Kádár was also involved. In mid-April, he received a delegation of thirty western financiers. When he travelled to Bonn later in the month, he discussed financial help for Hungary with the Bundesbank President, Karl-Otto Pöhl, and met with business leaders, who warned him that Hungary risked being sucked into Poland's deep financial crisis. Kádár reacted to this 'very thoughtfully'.[46]

The Bonn visit, however, brought disappointment over Kádár's hopes for a closer relationship with the EEC. The idea had been raised in talks between Hungarian and German officials in the latter part of 1981. However, in November Schmidt wrote to Kádár, ostensibly raising issues for the Hungarians to consider before making such a step, but clearly warning him off. The issues the chancellor raised were practical, but he may also have been influenced by his priority of good relations with Moscow; however much he respected Kádár, a deal with Hungary had by comparison little weight in the scales.[47]

Schmidt was taken aback by his discussions with Kádár in Bonn: 'for the first time I could clearly see signs of his old age, and of his political judgement falling off.' He was also surprised when Kádár again raised the issue of a Hungary-EEC agreement. Schmidt now actively dissuaded him, arguing that news of the talks would soon leak and that the Soviet reaction might undermine Kádár's position. Kádár realised that the scheme would have to be shelved. As is clear from their subsequent correspondence and informal meetings after Schmidt had left office, the incident did not diminish his admiration for the German. However, advisers such as Havasi and Horn who had, he felt, misjudged the situation, felt the edge of his anger. 'We started something that bore no relation to reality. This Schmidt, he knows what's going on in the world!'[48]

On 25 May, Kádár celebrated his seventieth birthday. In a reflection of the changes of the past decade, his guests at the celebratory reception included Cardinal Lékai. As at his sixtieth birthday, the celebration followed a period of high tension. In his speech, Kádár emphasised national unity: 'we can thank this policy and this consensus for what we have achieved.' He was starting to sound like a One Nation Communist. 'Regardless of our worldviews, our party affiliations, our offices, all of us [present] have a common characteristic: in our lives, we look beyond our personal affairs … [for the] Hungarian working people, the fate of the country and the prosperity of the nation.' He also reflected ruefully on age. 'The longer a man lives, the more remarkably useful experiences he can gather. That's the good side of old age. Unfortunately, what also comes with old age is that the capacity to make use of those experiences declines with time ... I'm seventy. At this age a man doesn't change his view of the world.'[49]

He also commented that 'we now live at a turning point in history, and that won't last long.' Some saw this in terms that Kádár would not have welcomed. Visiting Washington for the first time at the end of April, Árpád Göncz – writer, translator and former political prisoner – told his American hosts that 'the tendency toward democracy in Hungary is now irreversible.'[50] Certainly the problems confronting Kádár were looking ever more intractable. Yet hindsight – the knowledge that events would vindicate Göncz's assessment, and would result in his becoming the first President of a democratic, post-Communist Hungary – should not distort the degree to which Kádár and his system were still, indisputably, *there*. The regime had significant coercive resources at its disposal. The Soviet Union had somewhat reappraised its stance towards the satellites, but it had not abandoned them. Mass opinion was probably uneasy rather than rebellious, seeing little alternative to the regime – indeed the fate of Solidarity in Poland seemed to reinforce Kádár's standing as the best available option.

Above all, a collapse had been averted. By spinning the decision out, Kádár had taken Hungary into the IMF and the World Bank without provoking a Soviet reaction. The master of political escape had, it seemed, bought himself more time. It remained to be seen what he would do with it.

18

LIMITS

The stagnant economy confronted Kádár with difficult choices of policy and strategy. Writing in *Beszélő* in May 1982, the opposition leader János Kis summed up the dilemma. 'If [the regime] wishes to carry out the reforms, it must make political concessions, and the public support that it gains could be used to break down the resistance of the apparat. Or, if it does not wish to take a chance on political concessions, it must rally the apparat to show its strength towards society.'[1]

The PB elected in March 1980 was unlikely to make radical choices; its main feature – seen in the departures of Fock and Biszku – was its distance from the battles of the early seventies. Shortly before summoning István Horváth back from a county secretary's post to become Interior Minister in 1980, Kádár told him that 'things are not the same as you remember from your time in Budapest.' The PB of the early eighties was easy for him to manage, but the price was uniformity and dullness; in contrast to the protagonists of a decade earlier, the only strong personalities were Aczél and Havasi, and the latter was in the last resort a Kádár loyalist. In terms of policies and style, Havasi was the characteristic figure of the period; he was genuinely committed to reform, but was also a pragmatic man of the apparatus whose past as a county secretary gave him strong links to heavy industry. Under his and Kádár's leadership, policy would only inch forward.[2]

Kádár's health had recovered somewhat, but he was 'absolutely frustrated' with apparently insoluble problems and had lost his interest in policy. The atmosphere that he created in the PB and CC was to deal with routine matters and shy away from the new and the difficult. 'Whenever drastic or shocking economic news arrived, the slogan was that we shouldn't trouble Comrade Kádár with this.'[3]

Though the worst of the financial crisis had passed, economic policy had to be tightened further. Reserves were still low, debt repayments high and the prospects for fresh borrowing uncertain. Policy now aimed to start reducing debt levels in 1983, three years ahead of earlier plans; living standards would fall rather than merely stagnate. Kádár nonetheless insisted that the plan targets could still be met, and that publicity about the 'negative programme' should be kept to a minimum.[4] The forint was steadily devalued, prices raised and tough import controls imposed. The latter measures – centralising company-level decisions in the hands of senior officials such as Lázár and Marjai – ensured short-term solvency, but undermined corporate independence and stifled the import of machinery and technology needed to modernise Hungarian industry.

The arguments over structural economic change were becoming ever more pressing. Havasi had set up an Economic Policy Consultative Committee to examine the issues, but the debate also took on an outspoken life of its own in the specialist press. Some of the arguments trod on very sensitive ground, with a recurring emphasis on the need to re-examine the political and institutional background to economic reform.[5]

Meanwhile, there was a new factor to take into account: change in the Soviet leadership.

Brezhnev died on 10 November 1982, and was succeeded by Andropov. For Kádár, this was 'a great moment of his life'; he had long boasted of his friendship with the one-time ambassador, and 'he considered Andropov a conservative reformer like him.'[6] The new leader projected drive and determination, though age and ill health were already telling against him; the American Secretary of State George Shultz was reminded 'of Sherlock Holmes' deadly enemy, Professor Moriarty, all brain in a disregarded body.'[7] Andropov began by purging corrupt officials and stepping up industrial discipline, but he was also open to some economic reform measures. Politics was another matter. His spin doctors' portrayal of a liberal-minded, whisky-quaffing jazz enthusiast notwithstanding, he ordered a tougher ideological line and a squeeze on dissent.

Andropov's programme reinforced Kádár's instinct to step up pressure on the opposition. Rajk's 'boutique' was raided in March 1983; not long afterwards, he was forced to leave his flat. The authorities also tried to nail the opposition for evading tax on their publishing activities.[8] Speaking to the mid-term April 1983 CC, Kádár warned that 'If someone ultimately proves to be incorrigible … [we] will defend our people's interests and socialist gains by every means and against anyone in the manner required by the circumstances.'

The leadership also drew a line in the economic debate. Economists had been debating new forms (albeit still 'socialist') of company ownership; by the end of 1982, Havasi had made it clear that this was off the agenda.

Kádár used his CC talk, and a high-profile radio and television interview a fortnight later, to reinforce the point. He endorsed a continuation of the 1968 reform, but emphasised that the state would not withdraw from the direction of the economy. 'We've heard views that we now have to reform the reform. We have no such ideas ... We are not going to make some radical change from this management system to another.'[9]

Kádár forwarded his CC speech to Andropov; the Soviet leader replied that he had paid particular attention to Kádár's comments on economic reform. The experiences of different countries – including, by implication, Hungary – were 'our collective riches'. After long years of ambivalence or hostility, Brezhnev had towards the end of his time taken a more favourable view of Kádár's policies. Andropov was now reinforcing this approval.[10]

When Kádár visited Moscow in July, there was more talk of a shared fund of experience as socialist countries sought 'a more intensive path of development'. Kádár explained at a press conference, 'I have known Yuri Andropov for a long time ... Old acquaintances need fewer words to understand each other.'[11] Yet the trip yielded only some warm words and a few economic cooperation agreements. Overall, though 'Kádár thought a great deal of [Andropov]', from a Hungarian point of view 'his time in office did not turn out to be so special.'[12] This was not solely a result of the rapid deterioration in Andropov's health. Whatever his and Kádár's opinions of each other, their countries' economic difficulties were creating a growing divergence of interests.

The CC International Affairs Secretary, Mátyás Szűrös, and the head of department, Gyula Horn, both 'had very good first hand information on what was happening in the Soviet Union.' This led them and many of their colleagues to conclude that the regime had to keep building links with the West. Kádár knew of the unorthodoxies being discussed within the department, and tolerated, even encouraged them – so long as they did not frighten the Soviet horses. [13]

This was not always easy to achieve. In mid-September, Kádár received the US Vice-President, George Bush. Despite awkward timing, with superpower relations at a nadir, the meeting was very successful. Less happy from Kádár's point of view was Bush's subsequent speech in Vienna, in which he set out the administration's strategy of 'differentiation' towards the bloc, mentioning Hungary by name (and, worse still, bracketing it alongside Romania). This was the kind of praise and publicity that Kádár did not want; when George Shultz visited in late 1985, Kádár urged him, 'Don't come here with your big trombone.'[14]

Worse followed. Some unorthodox remarks by Szűrös in a talk on 6 October were leaked to Moscow. From his sickbed, Andropov wrote to Kádár to express his 'incomprehension and distress ... What is this – boundless political naivety, or something worse?' Kádár defended Szűrös' general conduct but promised to take him to task, and gave the CC

Secretary a humiliating rebuke during a PB meeting. Afterwards, however, Aczél told Szűrös, 'Mati, don't take it too seriously. Kádár put on an act, so that the Soviets will get to hear that he's done what he promised.' When Szűrös continued to float trial balloons in speeches and articles, Kádár turned a blind eye. 'More than once [Szűrös] was given a dressing-down for his speeches, but he wasn't dismissed for it. This shows that Kádár, who had very good instincts, in broad terms agreed with the policy.'[15]

Kádár still wanted an agreement with the EEC, and for western leaders he was an increasingly attractive interlocutor. Jaruzelski's coup against Solidarity made him unacceptable in polite international society, at least for the present, while Ceaușescu's human rights violations were a growing embarrassment. That left Kádár, and his well-known links to Andropov increased his value as an indirect conduit to the Soviet leadership at a time when direct contact was very limited.

Thus Britain's Margaret Thatcher, West Germany's Helmut Kohl and Italy's Bettino Craxi (all of whom had just taken delivery of the intermediate-range missiles that so outraged the Soviets) visited Kádár in the first half of 1984. If Bush's visit is any guide, this took place neither in defiance of the Soviets, nor at their urging; Kádár's letter to Andropov indicates that he had consulted with the Soviet leaders about it and, getting no response, decided to go ahead.

Kádár was still able to make a good impression on visitors. When Margaret Thatcher visited Budapest in February 1984, she found him 'still

Opening to the West: welcoming Margaret Thatcher to Budapest, February 1984

vigorous and very much in charge. He was a square-faced, large-boned, healthy complexioned man with an air of easy authority and an apparently reasonable frame of mind in discussion.' Their conversation was wide-ranging; Kádár even talked about Nagy's fate, claiming that he had had an undertaking from the Soviets that he would not be executed. Similarly, George Shultz reported to President Reagan that Kádár 'provides the sense of duration and the steady hand' in politics, and that Hungarian history had produced 'a great deal of experience and learning, a description that fits Kádár as well as the Hungarian people.'[16]

Kádár had developed an enthusiasm for foreign affairs[17]; he was not the only leader to find them an attractive alternative to intractable domestic problems. The economy gave little cause for celebration. Though Hungary's net convertible currency debt fell from just under $5 billion to $4.6 billion during 1983, its second consecutive year of decline, growth was stagnant, with real wages falling and consumer price inflation running at over seven per cent. The balance of trade was in surplus, but this reflected import controls, sales to the West of Soviet oil refined in Hungary and sales of surplus agricultural product for dollars within Comecon.[18]

There was no sign of the dynamism that would enable growth to be combined with financial stability. The attempts to break up monopolies had had little effect on the biggest companies. The effect of the 1980 producer price system was similarly blunted; one study showed relief being provided to two-thirds of companies. Most convertible currency exports were only profitable with subsidies; once again, the need to protect short-term financial stability was thwarting structural change.[19]

While real wages fell, incomes were sustained by welfare payments and by the growth of the private sector following its liberalisation in 1980-82. By the mid-eighties, around a third of all working time was committed to the 'second economy' (including household farming). The figure would be higher still if it included 'enterprise-based economic work partnerships' in which employees of large companies carried out extra work (operating as a partnership and usually demonstrating sharply higher productivity) on company premises after hours.[20]

The second economy supplied goods and sustained incomes, but at the price of the longest working hours in Europe. This combined with other problems, such as the pressures on family life resulting from the shortfall in the housing programme, to produce growing symptoms of social distress: cancers, heart disease, alcoholism and suicides all rose sharply. These phenomena were not unique to Kádár's Hungary; much of the Soviet bloc saw falls in male life expectancy in the seventies and eighties. Nonetheless, by many measures the strains in Hungarian society were particularly severe.[21]

For the leadership, the situation was not yet critical, but it was disquieting. Polling evidence suggested that in the first half of the eighties public opinion became considerably more pessimistic.[22] Kádár could see the need for safety valves, and revived a neglected element of sixties reformism. In spring 1983, the leadership agreed to institute contested parliamentary and local elections in all electoral districts. The intention was to give some new life to very stale institutions, and to allow grievances to be voiced without a fundamental challenge to the system. These proposals were to take effect in the 1985 elections.[23]

A similar desire to separate out 'legitimate' criticism from outright opposition influenced the approach to the increasingly fractious intelligentsia. In a reshuffle of senior posts in June 1982, Kádár restored Aczél to the Secretariat, with responsibility for culture and ideology. This merely formalised the influence that Aczél had maintained informally since 1974, but Kádár wanted him to win round the intellectuals as he had in the early sixties and so isolate the opposition.[24]

The difficulties of Aczél's task soon became apparent. The first challenge was the publication in the United States in early 1983 of a book by Miklós Duray, an intellectual leader of the Hungarian minority in Slovakia, with a forceful foreword by Sándor Csoóri. Not only did this raise the intractable minorities problem, Csoóri's essay was also a wide-ranging critique of the one-party state. Official attacks on Csoóri, coupled with restrictions on his ability to publish and to travel in an official capacity, enraged much of the intelligentsia.

The damage was compounded with the dismissal in October 1983 of the editorial team of the outspoken magazine *Mozgó Világ* (World in Motion). Aczél had taken a moderate line during an earlier crisis in 1980, but the magazine had continued to test the limits of official tolerance, providing a forum for opposition ideas and spokesmen. When the PB debated the issue on 26 June, Kádár made clear his growing disenchantment with Aczél's approach. He recalled that when 'we came across this bloody paper two years ago,' Aczél's people had concluded that the editorial team could get it under control. 'So our [cultural] direction is inefficient, it's slow and we've got to sort that out.' As for *Mozgó Világ*, 'the country would be none the poorer if one, two or three of these trashy papers were not around – there'd still be enough left over.'[25]

The purge at *Mozgó Világ* triggered protests from university students. The new editorial team, keen to establish its credibility, included in its first (January 1984) issue an interview with Nyers, who gave an outspoken account of the events of 1974. Aczél, wishing to show that meaningful debate was still possible, had asked Nyers to give the interview. Kádár took a less convoluted view of things: at the next CC, he criticised Nyers by name for speaking out of turn.[26]

Kádár was doubtless more sensitive to mass living standards than to the critiques of dissenting intellectuals, but he was certainly aware that attacks were more effective at a time of economic stagnation. In late 1983 or early 1984, he came to the conclusion that economic stimulus was needed to rally the party and isolate the opposition. Policy was at this point up for grabs; Lázár, Timár of the National Bank and, most outspokenly, Marjai advocated continuing austerity, but the political pressures against them were building.[27] Kádár had grown weary of justifying restraint to grumbling representatives of local parties. 'At the start, Kádár explained the facts to them, but as years went by and nothing happened, they were less and less enthusiastic about it.' So was he. The advocates of austerity 'had a growing sense of dislike coming from the top.'[28]

The first line of debate concerned a new reform package. Many of the more radical proposals put to Havasi's committee had already been jettisoned. When, in a presentation to the PB in late 1983, Planning Office staff ventured into what he considered political territory, Kádár 'really tore us off a strip.' Nonetheless, the April 1984 CC agreed a government-led Action Programme for 1985-87, focusing on subsidy reductions, banking reform and greater legal and financial independence for companies.[29]

There were more bruising battles over economic growth targets for 1986-90. The Planning Office set out three projections, with an austere central forecast of a two per cent annual rate. The industry lobbies weighed in with demands for four per cent. At the 10 April PB, and at the CC a week later, Kádár emphasised the need for growth. They had told the people that living standards would have to mark time while the balance of payments was corrected. 'But this was five years ago. Do you think that this can be the programme for the next congress too, and can win credit with the people? No! That's not enough! We need something else, we need more than this … We must aim for an annual growth in national income of 2.5 to 3 per cent.'[30]

Kádár's argument was political: there had to be an encouraging message to rally party and public at the 1985 congress. Nonetheless, he could argue that the targets were relatively modest and would be driven by the reform package adopted by the CC; indeed, some level of growth was needed to make structural changes. Havasi, who supported his leader in abandoning the austerity camp, argued in those terms both then and later.[31] Nonetheless, the brakes were being taken off.

To use the terminology of the Kis analysis, Kádár was opting to 'rally the apparat'. Soviet developments reinforced this choice. When Andropov died in February 1984, Kádár apparently hoped that his protégé Mikhail Gorbachev would succeed him. The two men – almost a generation apart – had got on when they first met in 1974. In September 1983, Gorbachev visited Hungary and his praise of the star performers of the Hungarian agriculture sector had reinforced Kádár's favourable view of him.

However, it was the stolid Brezhnevite, Konstantin Chernenko, who became the new General Secretary. Kádár shared the almost universally low opinion of Chernenko's abilities; although he kept photos of his meetings with successive Soviet leaders on his office wall, he delayed for some time putting up a picture of a man whom he considered an accidental and transitional Soviet leader. At Andropov's funeral, he greeted

Gorbachev before Chernenko and bluntly told Andrei Gromyko that 'things should have been thought through better, there should have been rejuvenation.'[32]

Chernenko's elevation encouraged the more conservative forces throughout the bloc, Hungary included. The atmosphere of orthodoxy, coupled with still distant superpower relations, also helped scupper the possibility – which emerged suddenly and unexpectedly in early 1985 – of Ronald Reagan coming to Hungary after European visits commemorating the fortieth anniversary of the end of the Second World War. Nervously recalling Bush's visit, the Hungarians sought assurances that Reagan would say nothing to embarrass them. This was unacceptable, and a Reagan-Kádár meeting – two septuagenarian anecdotalists – did not come to pass. Kádár remarked afterwards to the American ambassador Nicholas Salgo that the publicity surrounding a visit 'is not good for Hungary today ... certain people who have negative reasons for doing so would have definitely remembered it.'[33]

'Rallying the apparat' involved not only economic expansion, but also regaining the political initiative from the opposition, and here too the approach started to harden. Aczél had enjoyed little success in winning round the critics. He met Donáth at the turn of 1983-84 but found him willing only to debate with the leadership in public rather than to reach a private deal. Kádár, revealingly, thoroughly disapproved of the initiative. He was losing faith in Aczél's strategy, while Aczél was starting to criticise him during his private talks with opposition figures. In October 1984, Aczél submitted his resignation as CC Secretary, knowing that it would be accepted. He remained in office until the congress, and in the PB thereafter; for the present at least, he and Kádár remained on good personal terms; but their quarter-century long political collaboration was over.[34]

The appointment of János Berecz as Aczél's successor was revealing of Kádár's more conservative policy turn, as was that of Berecz's contemporary Károly Grósz, who was made Budapest party secretary in December 1984 and joined the PB soon afterwards. Both had reputations as tough authoritarians: Aczél in particular held them to have been foot soldiers in the anti-reform campaign of the early seventies, though both denied it.[35]

The other outstanding member of the younger (though now middle-aged) political generation, the former Culture Minister Imre Pozsgay, was suspect because of his outspoken style and links with Populist intellectuals, though his public profile and western contacts made it worthwhile to keep him within Kádár's political tent. He had been parked in what Kádár hoped was the powerless role of chairman of the Patriotic People's Front. Kádár had already blocked a proposal to bring Pozsgay into the PB once (in 1980), and kept him out in 1985.[36]

Grósz and Berecz were both in their early fifties, and could be seen as long-term leadership contenders. Kádár may have thought similarly – with the emphasis on the long term. He had no intention of stepping down before – at the earliest – a further congress in 1990; he would sometimes justify himself by reference to the rejection of his resignation in 1972. The only possible successor within the existing PB, Havasi was a loyalist who was taking a battering over the economic crisis. Kádár's low-key deputy, Károly Németh, had been spoken of as a possible successor for a decade. However, Kádár explained to Salgo 'with a large grin on his face' that Németh was there solely to cover him on protocol duties. As far as the succession was concerned, Németh was a convenient non-answer to the question.[37]

The drive towards expansion continued. During the summer, Marjai was overruled when he advocated undertaking a further programme with the IMF. This would have required more austerity and there were now other, easier options. Hungary's hard financial slog and honouring of its debts differentiated it from many of its neighbours in the eyes of financial institutions. New loans taken on more than doubled in 1984 to $2.4 billion.[38]

CC meetings in November and December ratified the direction set in the spring. The planners tried to argue against a three per cent growth target, and to ensure that the economy did not outpace the growth in exports. However, they were required once again to fudge their forecasts about international economic conditions.[39] When Marjai warned in the press in January 1985 that 'we are still not out of economic difficulties', Kádár turned on him in private, claiming that he wanted to enforce more of the 'policy of misery', and that the congress, the people and the working class would not stand for it.[40]

The somewhat traditionalist feel of the Thirteenth Congress (25-28 March) was underlined by Kádár's election, not as First but as General Secretary, the more Soviet-style (and Stalin-era) title. Reform proposals were not disavowed, but they took a distant second place to expansion. The tone was, however, less strident than that projected a decade earlier: less a neo-Stalinist restoration than a jumble of crowd-pleasing measures and gifts to interest groups. The economic platform allowed for only moderate expansion, especially in consumption, but even this was unrealistic – especially when combined with projections for lower inflation, higher investment, better infrastructure and an improving balance of trade.[41]

Kádár's speech was reflective of the jumble. This was 'not reassuring to party members or to others … because Kádár was almost incoherent. His speech was jumping from one problem to another without any clear train of thought.' Nor was it only his public appearances that could be disquieting. A few weeks before the congress, he met with the former PB member István Huszár, who now had to make way for Aczél as head of

The ill-starred Thirteenth Congress. In the background –
in more senses than one – György Aczél

the Institute of Social Sciences and to take a lesser post. They started talking about social issues, and then, 'as I looked up, I saw that Kádár was shedding tears ... He said, "Well, you know, I have a bad conscience about you."' Huszár was astonished – 'he was behaving like a small child' – and concluded that Kádár was no longer up to being a statesman.[42] His weariness with intractable problems seemed to be getting the better of him.

Aptly enough, the main Soviet representative at the congress was the orthodox Leningrad party boss, Grigori Romanov, who had been seen as a possible successor to the fast-ailing Chernenko. The rather conservative attempt to mobilise the party at the congress appeared to match not only internal pressures but also the prevailing Soviet mood. However, Romanov attended the Congress not as an heir apparent but as a defeated contender. Chernenko had died on 10 March. By the time that Kádár attended his third Soviet funeral in little over two years, it was clear that the new leader was Mikhail Gorbachev.

19

'THE BRUTUSES SHOWED UP'

At the Warsaw Pact leadership meeting in the Kremlin following Chernenko's funeral, Kádár offered his congratulations – to Andrei Gromyko, who had made 'a proposal that looked to the future'. It was Gromyko who had proposed Gorbachev as General Secretary.[1]

With his drive for economic 'acceleration', Gorbachev seemed initially to be the younger, more vigorous version of Andropov that Kádár had hoped for. If Gorbachev moved quickly to thaw superpower relations, this too was thoroughly welcome to the Hungarian leader. Gorbachev's early stance towards the bloc was one of cautious non-intervention, but he was clearly well disposed towards Kádár's Hungary.[2]

When Kádár visited Moscow in late September, his talks with Gorbachev lasted four and a half hours. In the generally harmonious atmosphere, there was just one jarring note: Gorbachev offered some 'friendly advice' on Kádár's age and health. 'You have given yourself over completely to the revolution, but you must manage your energies and prepare a worthy successor.' Kádár rapidly fell back on the rejection of his resignation in 1972. 'I can't go into retirement yet.'[3]

Gorbachev's statement was clumsily sincere. Given the age of most of the satellite leaders, 'the leadership issue was on the agenda.' Nonetheless, his non-interventionist ideology precluded any attempt to force them into retirement, least of all Kádár: problems in Hungary would undercut the arguments for change within the Soviet Union, and he saw Kádár as the guarantor of stability in the country. In suggesting that Kádár should prepare for a gradual handover, he was saying exactly what he thought.[4]

In the aftermath of the Thirteenth congress, there was little to suggest to Gorbachev, or to other observers, that a crisis was imminent in Hungary. Nonetheless, critical voices were increasingly being heard. The first sign of this came with the multi-candidate elections for Parliament and for local councils in spring 1985. The process was, of course, carefully controlled. All candidates had to sign a declaration accepting the 'leading role' of the party and friendship with the Soviet Union, and those opposition figures who swallowed hard and signed were still screened out.

Nonetheless, seventy-eight independent candidates were nominated and forty-one elected in the polls on 8 June, making up just over a tenth of the new Parliament. More than a third of the incumbents who ran for re-election were defeated. Perhaps the most striking result was the defeat of Mihály Komócsin, who had run Csongrád ('Pol Pot county') as a personal fiefdom, at the hands of a local television presenter, Zoltán Király, who went on to become an outspokenly critical parliamentarian. The elections brought some new voices, representing local interests, into the political system – albeit at some distance from the real centres of decision-making.[5]

The elections also gave a platform to Pozsgay, who met offended supporters of independent candidates whose nominations had been refused. Kádár's attempt to sideline him at the PPF had backfired. Interpreting the powers given under the front's statutes with dogged literalness, Pozsgay used the post to extend his following among non-party groups, especially Populist intellectuals.[6] He also gave a semi-official platform for critics, including in early 1986 a number of dissatisfied reform economists. The document that they produced in the autumn, *Turnabout and Reform*, was a thorough critique of existing policies and a radical programme for action.

Shortly after the June 1985 elections, forty-five intellectual leaders held a three-day conference to discuss the national crisis at Monor, just outside Budapest. It drew together representatives of different critical groups: Populists such as Csoóri; Kis and other spokesmen of the Democratic Opposition; veterans of 1956, such as Donáth, the organiser of the gathering; and reform economists still with one foot in the official camp. The meeting would prove a false dawn in overcoming the opposition's divisions; however, Budapest gossip reported accurately that an alarmed Gorbachev had raised Monor during his September discussions with Kádár.[7]

The Gabcikovo-Nagymaros dam, a vast hydroelectric project to be built in cooperation with Czechoslovakia on either side of the Danube, had roused yet further opposition. After considerable delays Kádár – mindful of relations with Czechoslovakia and the demands of domestic energy lobbies – decided in October 1983 to push ahead. The resulting protest movement, the Danube Circle, founded in February 1984, provided a model of a grass roots movement independent and critical of the authorities.[8]

Faced with this loss of initiative, the leadership, as János Berecz put it, 'launched a rather conservative counter-attack that lasted until the end of '86.' Berecz was the most visible exponent of this strategy: however, he did so with Kádár's full support.[9] The holding of the European Cultural Forum – part of the Helsinki process – in Budapest in October cramped the authorities' style for much of 1985. Afterwards, however, troublesome writers and magazines were suppressed, samizdat activists experienced more house-raids and harassment and – after some years of official tolerance – 1986 saw a brutal police response to an unofficial demonstration on 15 March, the anniversary of the outbreak of the 1848 uprising.[10]

The measures represented a hardening of the official line, reflected in a July 1986 report to the PB and a subsequent resolution identifying dissent with hostile activity. Yet they were still constrained by western reaction and at best slowed the growth of the opposition's influence, which was spreading even to official circles. *Beszélő* could no longer be bought from László Rajk's 'boutique', but runners were taking more than twenty copies to the State Planning Office.[11]

By this time, Kádár was starting to have doubts about Gorbachev, questioning his ability to stay the course and how thoroughly his domestic policies had been thought through.[12] Gorbachev's visit to Hungary in June 1986 got off to a poor start at a meeting with the Hungarian PB and Secretariat. Knowing full well about Gorbachev's strict (and unpopular) anti-alcohol campaign, Kádár brought out the cognac. 'I don't know, Comrade Gorbachev,' he said, 'whether your religion permits alcohol, but ours certainly does. So I raise my glass to your health, and let's toast the good old days, when we could still have a drink.'

Kádár may have been in delinquent mood because he had not wanted the meeting to take place. Dealing with the Soviet General Secretary was, he felt, his prerogative, and he probably nursed the suspicion that Gorbachev was checking out that 'worthy successor'. Nonetheless, Gorbachev insisted on the meeting. He eagerly asked his hosts' opinions on a range of major issues ('we're here to listen'); the Hungarians, conscious of the glowering presence of their boss, stayed uncomfortably silent. After half an hour – 'the most ghastly minutes of my life,' according to Grósz – Gorbachev gave up in frustration.

Yet the significance of these incidents can be overstated: Gorbachev had very warm recollections of the visit. He found Kádár enthusiastic about his ideas, and his only doubt as he left Budapest was whether the Hungarian leader still had the energy to do what was needed. Yet Kádár had always been skilful at making others feel that he was fundamentally sympathetic to their aims. Grósz thought that he liked Gorbachev, but 'the basis of this fellow-feeling was towards the man – towards the politician, he had reservations.' Reportedly, Kádár was soon saying to his associates that the Soviet leader was a dangerous man.[13]

Gorbachev's advice that Kádár should ration his energies became ever more pertinent from early 1986. The change was relatively sudden. Visiting Britain in late 1985, he had struck the British ambassador to Hungary, Peter Unwin, who had accompanied him, as being in good shape for his age. He could still be deft in conversation. When Unwin mentioned Cardinal Mindszenty, Kádár deflected the issue, asking whether Unwin was a Catholic or an Anglican. A Catholic, Unwin replied. Kádár responded, 'We won't tell them that in Whitehall.' Margaret Thatcher asked him about Hungary's relatively open travel policy; Kádár explained that 'when a Hungarian travelled abroad for the first time, he would ask himself: why should I defect this year, when I can always defect next year?'[14]

During 1986, however, he started taking month-long holidays; he was in his office for less than half the year. He spent more time with Mária, whose increasingly severe hip problems restricted her mobility. For some years there had been a stiff, impassive quality to his official appearances. Now his poor breathing made public speaking a trial, as did difficulties in concentration; the latter may have reflected narrowing arteries reducing blood flow to the brain, whether as a result of general ageing or of his other health problems. Mária – without his knowledge – would ask his staff to ensure that his speeches were no longer than fifteen or twenty minutes. In any case, their rambling content led officials to warn radio editors, 'don't broadcast it because Kádár was not at his best.'[15]

Increasing economic worries left no room for absentee leadership. The stimulus had little effect on output but fed through to a rapid deterioration in Hungary's financial position. In the absence of real financial discipline, big companies used their increased independence to expand investments, grant wage increases – and demand more subsidies, increasing the government deficit and external debt. In November, the head of the IMF, Jacques de Larosière, wrote to Kádár about 'my concerns regarding some recent trends in the Hungarian economy'; Kádár's reply was polite but non-committal.[16]

Economic problems and his growing infirmities were bringing forward the issue of Kádár's replacement. Horst Teltschik, adviser to Helmut Kohl, had visited Budapest in the mid-eighties. He found Kádár friendly but 'really old, not ready to change things' and grumbling that 'things had got worse because of the reforms.' He also met Gyula Horn and Miklós Németh, of the CC's International and Economic Policy departments, who were insisting that Kádár had to go. Meanwhile their ally István Horváth, Hungarian ambassador in Bonn since June 1984, was urging the German government to use its economic leverage to push for further reforms in Hungary (and the advancement of his patron, Ferenc Havasi). Economic issues, Hungary's western links and the succession struggle had become connected. Brezhnev would surely have felt that his warnings about western contacts had been vindicated.[17]

Kádár's steadily growing problems – political, economic and international – came together at the end of 1986, pushing his leadership close to crisis. The first went back to the regime's origins: October would mark the thirtieth anniversary of the 1956 revolution. The opposition had begun to challenge official taboos on the topic, making Kádár's preferred strategy of amnesia difficult to sustain. Berecz launched a series of newspaper articles and television programmes setting out a strictly orthodox counterblast. The crudity of the approach – an apparent regression from the ambiguities of Kádár's 'national tragedy' formulation fifteen years earlier – proved devastatingly counter-productive.

Berecz followed this up a few weeks later with a confrontation with the Writers' Union, which Kádár was querulously demanding be brought to heel. Berecz's abrasive address did not impress the writers, who again voted pro-regime members out of their leadership. Efforts to split the writers and create a new, tamer organisation got nowhere; the leadership was left looking foolish and impotent.[18]

The writers and other critics were emboldened by Gorbachev's increasing radicalism, which was now also applied to relations within the bloc. At a summit of Comecon leaders in Moscow on 10-12 November, Gorbachev took a tough line on economic aid to the satellites; after the oil price collapse of 1986, the Soviet Union had little to give. He also made much clearer than before that the Soviet Union would not intervene in their affairs. Unintentionally, Gorbachev was undermining a major basis for Kádár's support – the belief that he was the best option available within the limited possibilities allowed by a conservative and threatening Soviet leadership. Kádár responded 'with a kind of nostalgia', remarking, 'the time of change comes at last. But I'm old now, I can't carry them through.'

This was a diplomatic way to distance himself from Gorbachev's increasingly alarming radicalism. When his long-standing associate Ernő Lakatos took a delegation to Moscow and wrote an upbeat report, Kádár dropped in to Lakatos' office. 'You were very enthusiastic writing this report, weren't you?' he asked. Lakatos said that he was. After a long silence, Kádár said, 'listen, never trust someone who can destroy things, but cannot build them.' What Gorbachev offered was slogans, not a programme: 'believe me, it will come to a bad end.' Gorbachev's encouragement of intelligentsia critiques of his opponents, the agitating of public opinion rather than the hammering out of a centrally agreed programme – these may have awakened Kádár's bad memories of Dubček, even of Nagy.[19]

The third feature of the crisis was the continuing economic deterioration. With wages and investment slipping out of control, the convertible currency trade balance, which had been in surplus since 1980, plunged into deficit. The rapid growth of foreign debt – from $4.1 billion at the end of 1984 to $7.8 billion two years later – was exacerbated by the

National Bank's borrowing in low interest rate currencies such as the yen and deutschmark, while holding its reserves in the now-depreciating dollar.[20]

The crisis was the major item for the CC of 18-19 November. There would have to be personnel changes, and there were even rumours that Kádár would soon step down. In the event, 'Kádár didn't want big moves'; there were no changes at the CC meeting, though some government economic policymakers were sacrificed a month later. The CC resolution admitted that both the government and, more strikingly, the PB bore responsibility for policy errors. It did, however, seek to diffuse blame by use of the vague formula – favoured by Kádár – that 'the country has consumed more than it has produced.'[21]

Seeking to regain the initiative and to dispel any talk of his retirement, Kádár gave an hour-long television interview on 12 December. It did him little good. He spoke 'in a low and often mumbling voice', and his 'we have consumed more than we have produced' formula probably alienated many viewers, who were aware of working very hard, and of having rather little consumption to show for it.[22] It was from around this point that the true crisis of legitimacy – for Kádár and for his system – can be dated: polls show a collapse in economic expectations and increasingly unfavourable comparisons of Hungary's system with that of Western Europe.[23]

Though incremental changes continued, Kádár acted as a brake on more drastic options. When the CC's Economic Policy Department under its new head, Miklós Németh, brought before the PB one of a series of challenging position papers in the early months of 1987, 'the only person who understood the gist of the paper was Kádár. He posed one question: tell me, team at the other end of the table, what do you want? Do you want to bring back the small Fischers – from the past?' Németh had to have the reference explained by an older colleague: Fischer had been a famous stock market speculator from the thirties. Kádár was worried about the return of capitalism. [24]

The issue of responsibility for the crisis – touched on at the December CC – would not go away. Havasi and Lázár were particularly vulnerable, and the latter, weary after a dozen years as Prime Minister, was ready to go. Kádár replaced him with Károly Grósz: younger than most of his PB colleagues, formidably energetic and with excellent contacts across the party and large companies. Grósz's working-class origins were a point in his favour in both Kádár's eyes and those of party members. His past associations and many of his statements suggested an orthodox, even conservative viewpoint. Nonetheless, he was critical of policy shortcomings, and had cultivated a fashionably sub-Thatcherite brutality in stating unwelcome truths.[25]

Kádár seems to have had some fellow feeling with Grósz. He promoted him to Budapest and the PB following a visit to Grósz's Borsod County fiefdom in 1983, during which they had hunted together and held long discussions about the country's problems. He nonetheless had a clear-eyed understanding of Grósz's ambition, and could see that he was a potential threat. He must also have known that many in the Soviet hierarchy saw Grósz as his natural successor: Yegor Ligachev, later to be Gorbachev's conservative deputy, had checked him out in 1984, and subsequently Soviet officials were given to praising Grósz's energy and commitment to strong party rule.[26]

Kádár presumably calculated that Grósz could take the blame for harsh economic decisions and, if necessary, failure; if, however, he succeeded, Kádár could share the credit. Grósz, naturally, made the same calculation, and was reluctant to take on the premiership: he accepted only after ensuring appointments for key allies and extracting assurances that the government would be free from PB meddling.

Lázár and Havasi could not simply be dismissed, since that would be too open an admission of failure. Lázár was made Deputy General Secretary, which as 'a disciplined man' he took on out of loyalty, but with little enthusiasm. Havasi, with no background in the capital, was foisted on an unwilling Budapest party. To placate domestic reformers and foreign creditors – the Bonn Embassy warned that a major German loan might be in jeopardy if the wrong appointment were made – the young technocrat Miklós Németh replaced Havasi as Economics Secretary.[27]

The piecemeal changes were badly received at the 23 June meeting of the once-compliant CC. Fock argued – to Kádár's considerable irritation – that he should stand down as General Secretary and take an honorary role. Kádár still got his way, but with his prestige impaired.[28] Others too were saying the previously unsayable. Shortly before the CC meeting, a special edition of *Beszélő*, entitled 'The Social Contract', had included in its analysis a simple demand: 'Kádár Must Go!'

Grósz had to seize the initiative: he was now the front-runner for the succession, but time and the difficulties of his task would probably work against him. By September he had austerity measures ready, and in the middle of the month he and Kádár both addressed Parliament. While Grósz set out his programme in brisk, businesslike fashion, Kádár's performance was disastrous. His speech was slurred, and he meandered from topic to topic. Most damagingly, he bumbled his way to an admission of error. '…since you can portion out who's been on these bodies for such a long time, then probably I have the biggest share of responsibility, because in some way or other I was always there. I accepted these plans, and I voted for them.' The contrast, captured on national television, was painful. Kádár had done Grósz's work for him.[29]

Aczél, still uneasy about Grósz, wanted Kádár to follow the example of Deng Xiaoping, and step back from day to day politics, while acting as patron and adviser to the reformers of the next generation.[30] With this in mind, he arranged for him to meet Pozsgay during September. But Kádár's thinking was running in the opposite direction. With new currents coming from Moscow, the economy in crisis and his own authority crumbling, he saw more and more parallels with 1956. He had particular venom for those who exacerbated the crisis by dividing the party, and was beginning to see Pozsgay as another Nagy. He went on the attack, angrily demanding that Pozsgay follow the party line. Pozsgay realised that 'there was nothing more to discuss with Kádár' and, his previous misgivings notwithstanding, edged towards Grósz. Kádár had helped bring about a dangerous combination: Pozsgay's links outside the party and Grósz's strength within it.[31]

The two worked together over another opposition intelligentsia conference in the village of Lakitelek on 27 September. This was a largely Populist affair, with a smattering of reform Communists: rather than go along with the radical postures of the Democratic Opposition, the Populists were creating their own force and allying – for the present, at least – with the party's reform wing. Pozsgay attended the conference and brought a supportive message from Grósz. The participants resolved to create a Hungarian Democratic Forum – cast for now as an independent intelligentsia movement that would bring added pluralism to the political system, but soon to become a Populist-influenced political party.

Kádár, meanwhile, was travelling. A visit to China on 10-13 October – his first in thirty years – yielded a 'cordial, emotional reunion' with Deng. In spite of his negative reaction to Fock's proposal, Kádár may have begun to see some attractions in Deng's example of withdrawing from formal leadership positions but maintaining a guiding role in the background.[32] Power and prestige were certainly slipping away from him. In Moscow in early November for the seventieth anniversary celebrations of the Bolshevik revolution, he was reportedly snubbed and given the worst seat for a Moscow theatre performance. Even if this was exaggerated, Soviet enthusiasm for Grósz was growing and Kádár's talks with Gorbachev were brief and insubstantial.[33]

His authority was also weakening at home. The November CC saw a paper on ideology by Berecz – developed with Kádár's blessing – come under sustained attack. Meanwhile, pressure was growing for Hungary to imitate Gorbachev's plans for an extraordinary conference of the Soviet party in 1988. 'Of course, Kádár was the person who wanted it least.' There had not been such a conference since June 1957 and at the very least Kádár wanted to delay it until year-end. However, Grósz and his allies were pushing for an early date and on 8 December the CC agreed to call the conference for May.[34]

Some of those close to Kádár felt that 'he pretty much gave up' after Grósz became Prime Minister. Certainly, he had lost a lot of political ground. On New Year's Day 1988, Grósz gave a very personal, outspoken television interview, moving his campaign up a further gear. Soon afterwards, Kádár went for a month-long rest at the Dobogókő party resort, just north of Budapest. It was clear that he was seriously considering quitting.[35] However, when he returned in early February, he was ready to fight to stay in place.

He had strong reasons to stay. Vadim Medvedev, head of the Soviet CC's department for relations with ruling Communist parties, warned Gorbachev that 'Kádár does not want to retire as a defeated politician.' The New Year had seen articles in the reformist, Pozsgay-influenced sections of the press commemorating the twentieth anniversary of NEM. Some had been explicitly critical of the 1972-74 reversal, for which Kádár knew that he would take much of the blame. He also feared that, once he left office, 1956 and Nagy's execution would be re-examined.[36]

He visited county and local party leaders to drum up support, starting with leading figures from the Budapest party on 8 February. Within the leadership, he held 'closed meetings in the Kádár style', requiring recommendations for appointments and dismissals, and extracting from his colleagues a two-thirds majority in favour of his staying on.[37]

He also put pressure on his critics. At the end of February, the PB reprimanded Pozsgay for his links to the Hungarian Democratic Forum, while Nyers came under attack for his involvement in the New March Front, a reform socialist pressure group set up with Aczél's support at the end of 1987. The group had still not given up on Kádár: they sent him a copy of their manifesto, and Nyers met him on 13 February. He found Kádár polite but evasive, still denying that there was a crisis. In late March Nyers was instructed to stay silent on controversial issues for the next two months. Some within the apparatus may have envisaged much harsher methods: there were reports of plans, later aborted, to create an elite army-police unit and to issue ammunition to the Workers' Militia.[38]

However, Kádár's counter-attack quickly ran into difficulties. The first sign, in mid-February, was the angrily critical responses by party committees to Berecz's ideological formulations. Some called for the resignation of senior figures by name, including Kádár; 40,000 members, almost five per cent of the total, resigned from the party between December and March. Kádár was shaken by the responses, and his tours of the local parties gave him little encouragement either. 'It was quite clear to those of us who were organising his tour that his line had no more support at any level of the party workers.'[39]

Grósz also toured the local parties pitching for support, and his supporters found other ways to undermine the party leader. When Kádár made a 'very ugly speech, very anti-reformist' at a Budapest factory in February, the radio editors called party headquarters to ask whether they should engage in their usual protective censorship. 'And we got the answer: broadcast it fully. And we realised that these must be the final days of János Kádár.'[40]

The Soviet leadership was also making its preferences clear. Early in 1988, Grósz sent the Soviet specialist Gyula Thürmer to Moscow to test opinion. Gorbachev told him that Kádár was greatly respected but 'knows what he should do in such [a] historical situation.' Armed with this 'unofficial message to Mr. Kádár', Thurmer returned to Budapest. Kádár 'heard my words without any comments.' When Thurmer asked whether he should make a written record, 'he told me you should forget it.'

Kádár tried to forget it too: when Gromyko, now Soviet President, visited Hungary in late February, Kádár told him that he would stay on until 1990. A worried Medvedev warned Gorbachev that Kádár 'does not sense the changed mood in the party and society' and that there was the risk of 'serious social and political convulsions'. Medvedev urged that Kádár be persuaded to go, and that Grósz be given support, although all this was to be done within 'the accepted norms of the relations between our parties.'[41]

Two days after the biggest-yet 15 March demonstration, Kádár made another television broadcast, insisting again that there was no crisis. As before, it all too effectively conveyed the image of 'a tired and haggard old man' repeating stock phrases. His final throw was the expulsion of four leading reformers from the party on 9 April. This quickly backfired: academics on the reforming wing threatened to quit, and there was little support from the party officials, whose main concern now was to support Grósz. The CC of 23-24 March had already shown the direction of the party hierarchy's loyalties, failing to back Kádár's chairmanship of the steering committee coordinating the conference. [42]

Whatever determination Kádár had mustered in early February was now shaken. A visit by the Soviet Prime Minister, Nikolai Ryzhkov, in mid-April must have underlined Moscow's desire for change. Aczél and other old associates were urging him to recognise reality, and for some time, Kádár had been holding lengthy talks with Grósz. When the Prime Minister, asked by Kádár what he should do, said that he should retire, he met with a wounded Caesar's response: 'You too say that!'[43]

At the end of April, Grósz made his bluntest public statement yet, referring to the 'biological laws' that affected leaders, however eminent. On Sunday, 1 May, Soviet TV broadcast a profile of Grósz. On the evening of 2 May, Kádár called Grósz into his office. He told him that, at the following day's PB meeting, he would announce his resignation as General Secretary, and recommend Grósz as his successor. Németh remarked afterwards, '[all] credit to Grósz's political ability and skill, he managed to force Kádár out of power. None of those who worked in the party would have been able to do this, only Grósz with his skills and network.'[44]

The terms of Kádár's departure had yet to be resolved. A degree of continuity – the continuing presence of his supporters in the party's main bodies, some role for himself – would safeguard him against becoming a scapegoat for all that had gone wrong. There were some initial suggestions that he might serve as an adviser to the leadership; however, Grósz favoured his taking the new, specially created role of Party President. Kádár, meanwhile, may have wavered over his decision to go: he passed a message to Gorbachev that he was still thinking things over and 'I don't want Mikhail Sergeyevich to learn my decision from the newspapers.' At Kádár's request, Gorbachev sent an emissary: aptly, it was Vladimir Kryuchkov, head of the KGB, an Andropov protégé and veteran of the Soviet embassy in Budapest in 1956. [45] He met Kádár at Dobogókő on 17 May. It was probably there that a deal was brokered: Kádár would go, but the changes would be under his supervision and would 'protect his position within the party'.[46]

Under this agreement, Kádár would be Party President, and, while not a member of the PB, would have the right to attend its meetings and those of other bodies. There would be no reckoning for past actions and, to guarantee this, the party's disciplinary bodies would remain in reliably Kádárist hands. Only one-third of the CC would be replaced; the PB would be a mixed bag of Grósz supporters, reformers – represented by Pozsgay and a politically resurrected Nyers – and guarantors of continuity from the Kádár era such as Havasi and Gáspár. Kádár seemed assured of a dignified and influential retirement.

On 19 May, Kádár formally submitted his resignation to the PB. He also informed Gorbachev, who was full of praise for his decision. 'This demonstrates the political wisdom of the Hungarian leadership, and of my friend János Kádár ... This isn't an easy situation – not for you, not for us.' He politely briefed Kádár on the latest policy developments, and assured him that 'our political and personal relations continue. I'd very much like that. I'll be happy for us to meet and exchange opinions.'[47]

Opening the conference the next morning, Kádár did not mention his resignation which, though widely forecast, had not been officially announced. His fifty-minute speech, delivered in 'a firm but monotonous voice', struck a conservative, sometimes strident note: he spoke of 'our opponents, our enemies', language which seemed to belong to another age. He warned both the press and the PPF to represent the party line.[48]

He had made a bad misjudgement. The mood of the three-day conference was captured by speakers who called for 'new words, new faces, new political intentions'. Grósz and Pozsgay both emphasised the crisis and identified themselves with radical change. 'Decency is not enough,' Grósz told the conference. 'Decency is not appreciated by the market.' Perhaps the only encouragement for Kádár came when Aczél, to strong applause, hailed his achievements as 'the greatest work in our country's history'. But this was valedictory praise.[49] Kádár sat gloomily through the debates, but after his speech he was 'utterly passive'. He spent time in a private room or in the buffet area with Mária, who most unusually had accompanied him. She too cut a forlorn and isolated figure.[50]

On Sunday 22 May, the last day of the conference, Kádár gave a summing-up speech that lasted for over an hour. It was more conciliatory than his opening contribution, but offered no new solutions. He did, however, claim a surprising endorsement for his policies: 'Not so long ago, Mrs Thatcher pointed out … [that] the Hungarian government is pursuing a realistic policy and going in a good direction.' It would be good, he suggested, if the Hungarian press were equally supportive. The speech rambled, and his efforts to enliven it with folksy humour, peasant proverbs and stories from his childhood fell flat. Delegates 'looked appalled and sad' and were clearly longing for him to finish: the only time that they applauded was when he sat down.[51]

They did, however, get one last glimpse of his old authoritarianism. When a draft document was put to the conference for approval, some delegates tried to put forward individual amendments. Kádár seized the microphone to shout them down, banging his fist on the table, and forced through a vote on the entire document.[52] After that, the conference went into closed session to elect the new CC by secret ballot.

When the votes were counted that afternoon, Kádár was stunned. To be elected to the CC, it was necessary to secure support from just over half of the 984 voting delegates. Normally this was a formality. Now five of Kádár's PB loyalists – Lázár, Havasi, Gáspár, Károly Németh and Miklós Óvári – had been ousted, making them ineligible to serve in the PB. The leadership on which Kádár had counted to maintain continuity and his influence had been decapitated. His position of Party President would be a

Down and almost out: with Mária at the party conference, 21 May 1988

title, nothing more. His fallen colleagues were equally shocked by their humiliation: Havasi broke down in tears.[53]

Kádár smelt a conspiratorial rat, and he was right to do so. Grósz had no wish to have his power diluted or second-guessed by a Kádárist rearguard. He had already sought to pack the conference with his supporters, and after the exasperation caused by Kádár's opening speech, his backers had contacted delegates, urging them not to vote for the old guard. A third of the CC was entirely new, many of them technocrats and industry leaders loyal to Grósz, and another third had served only since 1985. They in turn elected an eleven-member PB, more than half of them newcomers. This, not Kádár's resignation as General Secretary, was the real coup at the conference.[54]

When Kádár's appointment to his new post was announced to the congress that evening, the delegates, perhaps shaking off guilt over political parricide, gave him a standing ovation. A young woman who had earlier made a strongly critical speech presented him with a bouquet. He looked tired and disoriented, but in a brief speech, more gracious and effective than his two earlier contributions, he paid tribute to the departing PB members and wished the newcomers success. Of his appointment as Party President, Berecz told reporters that it was 'to give respect and appreciation to a man who, for more than 30 years, has been linked to all of our results and achievements.'[55]

However, neither compliments nor bouquets, neither an impressive title nor a few other perks – such as keeping his old office – could mask the fact that Kádár had been stripped of power. On the day after the conference, his associate István Katona found him slumped in his chair. Without even greeting him, Kádár gave his interpretation of the weekend. 'Comrade Katona, the Brutuses showed up.'[56]

20

GHOSTS

Kádár was criticised for staying in office too long, and most of what happened after his seventieth birthday was bad for the country and his reputation. He seems to have realised it, telling Grósz, 'You know when I got it wrong? When I didn't retire in 1972.' On another occasion, he suggested that he should have gone in 1978.[1]

Nonetheless, the events of the year after he lost office suggested that there had been good reasons for him to want to stay. Power had allowed him to conceal things, sometimes even from senior colleagues: his successors were shocked to discover, for example, that he had agreed (with the knowledge only of the Defence Minister) to the stationing of Soviet nuclear weapons on Hungarian territory.[2] Above all, he could suppress any assessment of the murkiest events in his career: Rajk, 1956 and Nagy. Now the past came back to haunt him.

Kádár drew the obvious conclusion from the May conference and 'radically withdrew' from day to day politics. Grósz, wary of an alternative court springing up, made clear that dealing with the Party President was his responsibility. 'He was not exactly cordoned off, but almost.' Nonetheless, for some months Kádár tried to act out his new role. He had quite frequent and 'worthwhile' conversations with Grósz. He presided at several CC meetings, received foreign visitors and gave a few interviews.[3] To the American journalist Flora Lewis, 'He spoke with an air of nostalgia, almost whispering to himself, his craggy face crinkling with emotions of memory.' He insisted that socialism would survive. 'I'm deeply convinced that there will be no capitalist system in Hungary again. This system is capable of defending itself with its own strength.'[4]

His successors, however, were riven by differences of outlook and personal rivalries. The economy remained in crisis, and one of the system's pillars crumbled when a law making company privatisation possible was passed in the autumn. The leadership responded uncertainly as new political parties sprouted into life and independent MPs urged radical constitutional change. There had been talk of 'socialist pluralism' in the run-up to the conference, but no agreement as to what this meant. Grósz (and Kádár) were determined to maintain the one-party system; as late as November 1988, Kádár was intervening with his colleagues in an effort to excise references to a multi-party system from policy documents.[5] Pozsgay, however, with one foot in the Populist camp, favoured at least a form of multi-party politics.

Meanwhile, ominously for Kádár, Pozsgay – as part of an attempt to build broader alliances – was heading up a series of committees examining the party's record in power since 1956. Pressure was building up from other sources. For years, relatives and friends of those executed in the Nagy and other trials had braved political police harassment to tend and place tributes at what they believed – on the basis of rumour – to be the graves. Early in 1988, Miklós Vásárhelyi, the last surviving defendant of the Nagy trial living in Hungary, applied for the case to be retried. In June the Historical Justice Committee was formed to press for reassessment of cases and the decent reburial of those who had been executed. Although the police aggressively broke up a demonstration on the anniversary of Nagy's execution, the leadership later indicated its willingness to accept the reburial of his remains in a private ceremony.[6]

There was not yet any official reassessment of Nagy or of other cases, which would be inseparable from that of 1956 as a whole – and with it, Kádár's reputation. Even after his downfall, this had held up relatively well: polls gave him the lion's share of the credit for the regime's successes, while blame for its failings was diffused among the political and economic establishment.[7] 1956 was not forgotten, but the decades of Kádár's dominance had helped to suppress and obscure it. A full reappraisal could be devastating for his standing.

Kádár's health deteriorated further, and he had to take a two-month holiday over the summer. He also had cataracts on both eyes that made reading difficult. A more immediate problem was his growing difficulty in using his right hand, owing to the shortening of a tendon; in early September the doctors recommended surgery, but Kádár put it off until mid-November. By that time, he could barely write; after the operation, he lost ten kilos in weight, and his recovery took longer than expected.[8]

The Christmas period was quiet and lonely. 'I sat there with my wife, she can't go [anywhere], neither can I.' A few weeks later, on 28 January, came the bombshell. Anticipating the conclusions of a committee of historians reporting to him, Pozsgay used a radio interview to describe the 1956 events as 'a popular uprising'. His statement threw the party leadership into anguished confusion. Kádár wanted to take part in PB meetings on the issue, but Grósz kept him out. Kádár retreated to Dobogókő for the first two weeks of February.[9]

There were good reasons for Grósz not to want Kádár's participation. Pozsgay's popularity made him hard to dismiss, and Gorbachev was looking to a reformed socialism to shore up the Warsaw Pact regimes, especially in Poland and Hungary. Thus, at the CC on 10-11 February, Grósz criticised Pozsgay's statement, but stated his confidence in him as a member of the leadership. With some qualifications, the CC resolution accepted the new interpretation of 1956. The same resolution approved the principle of a multi-party political system, albeit in a form that the MSZMP still – for the present – expected to dominate.[10]

Not only had Pozsgay broken with the official past, the party's highest body had effectively endorsed him. The effect on Kádár was traumatic: from this time can be dated a faster decline in his physical and mental condition. 'He feared that if Imre Nagy and his associates were rehabilitated, then he was the criminal.' Guilt, fear of being called to account and a crumbling of self-belief would haunt him in the coming months.[11]

The dam was now breaking about discussing the recent past. More and more aspects of 1956 were debated in the press. Early February saw the broadcast of *Right to Asylum*, a series of television interviews with surviving members of the Nagy group in the Yugoslav embassy. In the 3 February issue of the weekly *Élet és Irodalom* (Life and Literature), István Tamás, a former editor of *Népszabadság*, produced the full charge sheet against the former leader and asked, 'What does János Kádár say?' In the middle of the month, the Justice Ministry and the relatives of the executed Nagy trial defendants reached agreement that their remains would be reburied on 16 June, the anniversary of the hangings. It had originally been envisaged as a private ceremony, but after Pozsgay's statement pressure built for a more public act of commemoration.[12]

Kádár's lengthy absences sparked rumours that he was either being kept in seclusion, or planning a comeback. To dispel this, he was encouraged to make some brief, televised comments at the start of a CC meeting on 20 February. He emphasised that, while he had taken no part in recent decisions, 'I hold every decision of the Central Committee to be binding on me.'[13]

Soon afterwards, he began giving interviews to the *Népszabadság* journalist (and former ÁVH officer) András Kanyó. This too seems to have been at the leadership's instigation: something would have to be said about the Kádár era, and it was probably felt best that Kádár should do this with a trusted journalist under controlled conditions. Preparing for the first interview on 10 March gave Kádár something of a lift: he had a project and he was 'in his element' as he gathered his thoughts and materials. Though wary at the start, Kádár seemed later to relax, talking well into the evening; he told Kanyó that 'it wasn't work that bothered him, but passivity.'[14]

Nonetheless, the interviews addressed all the most neuralgic subjects of his career and his answers were often evasive or dishonest. On Nagy, whom he portrayed as weak rather than wicked, he sounded regretful: 'we were on the same track, we struggled together, but later our ways parted … Imre Nagy's tragedy is my personal tragedy too.'[15] He soon found the painful subject matter exhausting and his suspicions of Kanyó increased. He sought to restrict the journalist to submitting written questions, and the discussions petered out in early April. At their last meeting on 10 April, Grósz was present. Kádár had decided that he would put his case in a more public forum and hoped to take part in the next CC in two days' time. He repeatedly asked Grósz, 'You won't forbid me to be there?'[16]

At lunchtime on 12 April, after a distracted conversation with his doctor, Kádár rushed off 'like a madman' to the CC meeting. Warned that he was coming, the CC press spokesmen met him as he entered the building. Sitting with them, Kádár gave a foretaste of what he planned to say. The man who for decades had maintained such a stolid reserve now 'just talked and talked … There was this enormous hunger in him to communicate.'[17]

Grósz may have deliberately set Kádár up to discredit himself, either because he still felt threatened by his presence or to make him a scapegoat for the party's past crimes. Whatever his motives, Grósz could surely have prevented Kádár from speaking had he really wished to. When Kádár joined the CC session in the late afternoon, his appearance shocked many members. He had lost more weight, and his face was drawn; his gaze was vacant, sometimes frightened; he wore an open-necked shirt, since he could no longer tie his tie; his clothes were crumpled and hung loose about him.[18]

He was welcomed to the meeting; invited to speak first, he stood and talked for more than an hour.[19] It was clearly an enormous effort, but he was determined to give his account of his life and career. As he had told those who had tried to dissuade him, he did not know when his health might allow him to do so again. The audience's apprehensions must have been stirred when he began by talking distractedly about his and Mária's health problems. He was unable to concentrate, and rambled from point to unrelated point. 'There were some clear moments, but at other times it was just fog.'[20]

Yet through the fog, certain themes emerged: guilt mixed with a sense of victimisation, attempts to justify the past, fear of the future, despair at his failing physical powers. One question tormented him: 'What is my responsibility? … the doctor said that my problem is that I am forever thinking about my responsibility … day and night – and this too demands energy – my head spins as to what my responsibility is.' The CC members were a captive audience as the man who had dominated their political lives exposed both his senility and his anguish; the speech was 'the product of a mind that had gone astray ... it was terrible to listen to.'[21]

His answers about his 'responsibility' were elliptic, muddling up eras and events. One 'wasn't used by me, but by another man, a westerner, who didn't say it when Soviet tanks were present. He said that the Danube flows too fast.' He may have been thinking of Schmidt, and his warning against a precipitate move towards the EEC[22]; but it surely also reflected a sense of helplessness in the face of events, of being the object, not the subject of history – and of the moral excuse that this almost provided.

He let slip his resentment over his downfall, directed towards Grósz and Gorbachev. He complained that he could not speak out, and that he wanted to give the benefit of his experience, yet no one would make time for him 'because I am older than everyone.' He was a figure of abused loyalty: 'I am a scapegoat in the biblical sense, because they elected me president and think that, after all, I'll defend the party and the system.'

He feared for the future, hinting at a coming persecution of those who had collaborated with the Communists. He had much more to say about the past, above all about 1956 and about the fate of 'the man who later died'. He had no coherent argument, but strained to justify what he had done. '... the first charge against me after I changed sides in '56 is that I was a Soviet agent. But I was not a Soviet agent, I tell you that in all seriousness, and I can prove it ... I didn't call any element counter-revolution. Not that. I only said that they opened the way to counter-revolution.'

He recalled his fears that 'the Russians perhaps wanted to do me in,' saying that he was 'set free' when he got to Szolnok and yet 'the interpreter was there too.' He had worried – referring perhaps to his talks in the Kremlin, perhaps to later meetings with the Soviets – what to do 'if the first question wasn't the one that I was prepared for? I can't be proud of that, I can't be proud. When – perhaps everyone knows what this responsibility means. Hours, minutes – it wasn't just my fate that was at stake, it was the fate of God knows how many people.'

His defence rested on the threat of a Rákosi-ite alternative and more on the relatively moderate interpretation of events with which he had returned to Budapest: 'a peaceful student demonstration, an uprising, I in no way characterised it as counter-revolution.' This, he apparently wanted to believe, had been his 'real' approach, not the subsequent hardening of the line that paved the way for the reprisals. On the Nagy group kidnapping, he offered a vague and convoluted explanation blaming the refusal of Nagy and Losonczy to resign as ministers. He did not mention Nagy's execution, but touched on Rajk's, apparently putting in a plea of gullibility: 'I must ask you whether it's good that I am an idiot, I can accept that too.'

By now, much of his audience was uneasy and distressed: some CC members were in tears.[23] He seemed aware of the effect that he was having, and was almost overcome with pain and frustration at his own incapacity. 'How long have I been speaking? I will finish. I can't, I can't bear it that I'm inactive and can't respond to things. I can't bear it!' His doctor had recommended against his making a speech like this, but 'I said that it's at my own risk, because if I'm wrong, I can say that I'm already a really old man and so ill that I don't care if someone shoots me. I'm sorry.'

Grósz suggested a break, but Kádár was determined to finish. Asking ironically if he could still address them as 'comrades' – 'because you can't any more in Parliament'– he tried to reach a conclusion. He went back again to 1956, justifying the intervention by the 'pogrom' that was developing against Communists. 'But if I don't look at things historically, then I can truly say that, looking back over thirty years, I'm sorry for everybody.' He hinted that he could no longer view things with 'the tone of incorrigible optimism' that had characterised him in the past, and promised that he would answer everything 'for which I am now tormented for not speaking out. Thank you very much.'

It was over, and his shaken audience applauded. Grósz called a break in the meeting. Kádár returned to his office and asked urgently for Nyers to see him. He seems still to have wanted to explain himself, in this case to a colleague whom he regarded as an honest critic. He was much more lucid than he had been in his speech. He admitted to errors in some of his appointments, insisted again that 'the tragedy' could have been avoided had Nagy (whose name he did not mention) resigned and admitted ruefully to suffering from 'persecution mania'. Nyers had the impression that 'Kádár was not only haunted by the past, but also quite worried about his own future ... [though] Kádár was not the sort of person to voice this.'[24]

There was still no escaping the ghosts of the past. Exhumation and identification of the bodies of the Nagy trial victims in the increasingly famous Plot 301 of the suburban Rákoskeresztúr cemetery began in late March. Details of the attempts to insult and obscure the memory of the dead – the bodies buried face down in unmarked graves in an overgrown corner of the cemetery, reserved for criminals and the remains of animals from the zoo – emerged and added to the horror of what had happened.[25]

There were other visitations. On 17 April, after nearly twenty years' purdah in the Slovak Forestry Commission, Dubček appeared in a Hungarian television interview to denounce Kádár's role in 1968. 'You say that Kádár was protecting Hungary. But what did he protect? The preservation of the Brezhnev system.' In early May, a conference of historians picked over 1956 and the Nagy kidnapping, while on 7 May a newspaper published a document in which Mihály Farkas recounted Kádár's approval of the beating of Rajk.[26]

Kádár was clearly in no state to continue as party president; the flow of revelations added a political imperative for the party to be rid of him. While his doctors briefed the PB at the start of May, Grósz visited him to tell him of the leadership's thinking. Kádár did not resign, but asked that the CC should decide the outcome. The answer soon came. On 8 May, the

CC sent him a letter discharging him from both the party presidency and from membership of the CC itself.

The letter paid tribute to his accomplishments, though also referring to 'a number of mistaken decisions' over the previous decade and a half. In reply, Kádár admitted to mistakes but emphasised that his intentions had always been good. Others would have to take his work on. 'These days I am instead occupied with thoughts of my own responsibility. I hope that you are right: that coming generations will judge more objectively the accomplishments and mistakes of the last three decades.'[27]

His removal hit Kádár hard, and he became convinced that he would have to leave his home in Cserje Street. This was not wholly irrational – ousted party dignitaries had often had to accept smaller homes after loss of office – but nonetheless reflected his consciousness of how far he had fallen. He even packed some belongings in a bag before Mária – or, by another account, Grósz, who was called and hurried to see him – persuaded him that he could stay.[28]

Aczél wrote to Mária at the end of April, offering help 'on the basis of many decades of friendship'. Kádár was reluctant to see him, viewing his actions after 1985 as a betrayal. A month later, Aczél wrote to him, wishing him a happy birthday and almost begging for a personal meeting.[29] He got it, but it was 'not agreeable'. Kádár kept him waiting for more than an hour, and though he began by saying that 'now we're once more on a level, we're just friends,' what followed was far from friendly. 'Gyuri, on three things you stabbed me in the back. I didn't expect that from you, my one friend.' He blamed Aczél for pushing an over-liberal interpretation of 1956 – 'you shouldn't quote me that it was a national tragedy … Berecz was right, it was counter-revolution' – and for his role in the New March Front. 'You were always an aristocrat. You always looked down on anyone who wasn't cultured.'

Aczél may have exaggerated some aspects of the conversation, but Kádár was undoubtedly resentful towards him. It also seems that in private Kádár held to the harsher view of 1956 to which he had reverted in his final years in power, rather than the more complex, defensive line that he took in his last speech to the CC. Yet it is probably a mistake to look for consistent thinking at this stage. Aczél's last picture was of someone who was 'barely the old Kádár', a querulous old man snapping at his secretary when his tea was late and cold.[30]

As Nagy's reburial approached, the Hungarian and Soviet leaderships, worried about its effect on Kádár, sought to shield him from it. In early April, Gorbachev, Jaruzelski and Honecker had all offered their hospitality. In early May, his doctors suggested that he go to the Crimea. Kádár refused them all, fearing that he would repeat Rákosi's fate and die in exile.[31]

However, the tenor of the Nagy reburial was getting dramatically worse for him. The opposition – now unified into an 'Opposition Round Table', with which the party leadership was preparing to negotiate – demanded that the funeral be preceded by the coffins lying in state in one of Budapest's grandest public spaces, Heroes' Square. Once again, the MSZMP leadership split; the ceremony was approved on 22 May, and it was later agreed that senior party reformers would take part, officially representing the government rather than the party.[32] The reburial of an executed leader, with devastating effect on the party's moral standing, had foreshadowed the start of the Kádár era; now another would mark its rejection.

Isolated and very weak, Kádár wrote again to the CC, demanding a judicial investigation of the Nagy case. He insisted that a duly constituted court had condemned Nagy and it had not been his business to intervene. 'Did I interfere with the investigation, did I interfere with the sentences etc.? ... If I am not [guilty], I ask the Central Committee to ensure that insinuations and hints about me cease.' Below his signature, he scrawled, 'The wife wrote the letter.'[33] A judicial review was already being prepared; on 6 June, ten days before the reburial, a remedial petition to overturn the Nagy judgment was submitted to the Supreme Court.

On the sunny morning of 16 June, the columns of Heroes' Square were draped in black. National flags flew with holes cut out of them, recalling those of 1956. Amid a setting designed by László Rajk, thousands of people filed past the six coffins: those of Nagy, Losonczy, Maléter, Gimes and Szilágyi, as well as an empty coffin representing the Unknown Insurgent. Sombre music played; name after name, the list of the three hundred victims of Kádár's reprisals – giving their occupation, date of execution and age at which they were killed – was read out. Later, official delegations laid their wreaths, and at 12:30, there was a national minute of silence. One of Nagy's radio addresses from 1956 was broadcast, his voice echoing round a square now filled with some two hundred thousand people. Speeches were made and then the coffins were taken back for reburial in Rákoskeresztúr.[34]

The British journalist and academic Timothy Garton Ash noted, 'One name is not mentioned in any of the speeches. One name is in everyone's mind. It is the name of János Kádár ... Where is he today, that sick old king? Is he watching on television? He is Macbeth, and Banquo's ghost lies in state on Heroes' Square. This is not the funeral of Imre Nagy. It is the resurrection of Imre Nagy, and the funeral of János Kádár.'[35]

After the reburial, there were rumours that Kádár (and perhaps Mária) had committed suicide, or that he had fled to Cuba. This was melodramatic, but party officials had been worried as to how he would get through that day, and the CC spokesman Emil Kimmel used the pretext of needing his signature on a letter to visit him. Struggling with his illness and his memories, Kádár 'writhed powerlessly in his sick-bed'. He gave away little of his feelings, but asked at a couple of points, 'Is the funeral really today?' and 'Is today the day?'[36]

Kádár did not want to go into hospital, and Mária tried to nurse him at home. Yet she was unequal to the task, and he had ceased to take his prescribed medication; he continued to deteriorate. On better days they talked of moving to a smaller house and living a tranquil private life. 'The next day though, things were completely different. My poor husband, when I tried saying to him, "Don't shout, dear, don't talk in that coarse way," would reply "It isn't me; it's my illness."' Towards the end of June, he asked, 'Mária, how long do I have to endure this?' Making up an answer, she said 'until Christmas.' After that, he ceased to complain; he had a target to work towards.[37]

Soon afterwards, probably at the start of July, he telephoned a surprised Jenő Fock. He thanked him for having always acted with his best interests at heart, and asked his pardon and that of 'my former boss' (Grósz) for having interrupted the CC's work in April: 'I wanted to make my farewell to the body that I belonged to for decades.' At this point Kádár was overcome with emotion, yet was clearly reluctant to hang up. 'Instead he thanked me again for having protected him against the extremists in the CC meeting. He said that he wanted to thank his successor too for never having turned against him. The last sound that could be heard from the phone was of János Kádár sobbing.'[38]

Fock felt that Kádár was preparing for the end, trying to sum up his life and career. How did the record stand? What had he achieved?

Not even Kádár's critics could deny his political skills. For three decades he had been a great tactician and survivor, patiently building his authority after 1956 and rebuilding it when it was challenged in the early seventies. He had the cunning and ruthlessness required for high-level political survival: he was tenacious in defence, and deadly on the rebound. In dealing with the Soviets, with the party and with the mass of Hungarians he had a strong sense of the minimum that had to be conceded and the maximum that could be enforced at any time.

He was no intellectual, and would have recoiled at the accusation, but he was shrewd, with a quick grasp of issues and an ability to impress those he met. He could also persuade many of his interlocutors that he had some sympathy for their viewpoint without fully showing his hand. His capacity to create a useful ambiguity served him well in persuading the Soviets of his essential loyalty without seeming – as Rákosi had – to be an international Communist operator who merely happened to be Hungarian. 'He could switch guises – sometimes the Hungarian, sometimes the international Communist; he was the master of this.'[39]

There was, however, a long charge sheet against him. He was at least an assistant gravedigger of Hungarian democracy in 1945-48. His involvement in Rákosi's terror and in the Rajk affair was bigger than he later admitted. In 1956, this time playing a central role, he helped for a second time to destroy Hungarians' hopes of choosing their own future. He bore heavy responsibility for the brutal reprisals that followed, ranging from the cold-eyed realpolitik of Nagy's execution to the vindictive hangings of teenage insurgents. Even if the reprisals exceeded what Kádár had planned when he returned to Budapest in early November, he adapted quickly and made calculated use of terror to secure his leadership. If, at the end of his life, Kádár brooded on his 'responsibility', he had a lot to brood about.

Furthermore, Kádár was the central figure in a system that for forty years wrenched Hungary away from the paths of development taken by its western neighbours, doing damage that is only slowly being repaired. He left a legacy of industrial backwardness, foreign debt, environmental damage and the corrupting effect on society of years of official mendacity. Eventually the drain of debt service and industrial subsidies undermined even the regime's central aim of an expanded welfare state. The results were seen in a housing shortage and in inadequate health and education services.[40]

Yet external forces and constraints shape any political life – Kádár's perhaps more than most. In pre-war Hungarian society, he was a marginal man – as much underclass as working class – who had joined a marginal party, little more than a persecuted sect. The Soviet victory of 1945 made him, almost overnight, a significant political figure. In every major step in his career thereafter the Soviet leadership and its wishes were a powerful, often dominant factor. The case for his defence is that, as an admiring Willy Brandt put it, 'he did the best possible, given his knowledge of the realities as they were then.'[41]

This argument has to be handled very carefully. Kádár was not simply an object of external, Soviet constraints: he had very much willed them into being and supported them. After 1945 and again in 1956 he made his choice. The primary assessment of his role must view him and his system on their own merits, and that judgement has to be a harsh one. Nonetheless, it is also possible – always bearing the primary verdict in mind – to take a secondary, more relative view, comparing him and his system with those of the other Soviet satellites.

Even this has to be qualified. The bloc's post-Stalinist states were structurally very similar. Kádár's apologists played up the distinctiveness of his system. Western commentators sometimes did the same, particularly in over-optimistic early assessments of the NEM. The Hungarian leadership was relatively subtle in its treatment of dissent; however, the constant drip of revelations about the informer network of the political police is a reminder that 'though the Hungarian "barrack" may have been the "jolliest" in the socialist camp, it was a barrack nonetheless.'[42]

Kádár's Hungary was, then, a point on the post-Stalinist spectrum rather than a fundamentally different system. That said, in most respects it was if not more 'liberal' than other Communist countries, certainly 'more cautious, circumspect, indirect, subtle, velvet-gloved in the way it treated its own people.'[43] That owed a lot to Kádár, and a lot to 1956. Two individuals, Rákosi and Nagy, and two experiences – his imprisonment in 1951, and the crisis of 1956 – served as negative reference points, the objects of Kádár's long-running 'two-front struggle'. From this, he drew a series of simple but fundamental maxims.

The party must not be divided or factionalised. Party policy should develop in a stable, predictable fashion. There should be clear leadership, but developed through the party's constitutionally ordered bodies, not personal dictatorship (though in practice this 'Leninist' style did allow for Kádár's dominance). Rising living standards should be central to policy. No major social group should feel itself isolated or victimised. Passive obedience was expected from a de-politicised population, not mobilisation in pursuit of grand political ambitions. A less confrontational style of politics could ensure that the political police remained under party control and did not threaten the security of senior figures. These concepts, added to the party-state structures inherited from Rákosi, would be the constants of the Kádár years. Most of the variations on these themes would reflect the vicissitudes of bloc politics.

Much of this was common currency as the leaderships of the 'people's democracies' absorbed Khrushchev's assaults on Stalinism and searched for new sources of legitimacy.[44] However, under the shadow of 1956, it was Kádár's Hungary that made the most consistent, durable efforts in this direction.

Kádár's greatest successes came in the early sixties, as he achieved both personal dominance and political easing. He was well suited to the times. He had few visions of making a new heaven and a new earth; to a society that had undergone successive traumas, and which had lost many of its remaining natural leaders after 1956, he offered stability, a less intrusive form of authoritarianism and the hope of a modest prosperity. It was a restricted vision, but Hungarians had plenty of experience of the alternatives. As the economist and writer László Lengyel put it, 'The only thing that János Kádár said to history was that he had nothing to say. But what a novel thing this was: someone who could remain silent in this garrulous, chattering country.'[45]

Yet Kádár was at this point committed to the path of renewal set out by Khrushchev rather than merely a shopworn pragmatism. If his embrace of economic reform was more a practical response to problems than a thorough commitment to and understanding of the concept, he nonetheless saw it as part of a wider reappraisal going on within the Communist world. In his most optimistic moments, he hoped that Hungary could contribute to that rethinking. He also hoped, up to the invasion of Czechoslovakia and even beyond, that relations between Moscow and other Communist countries could be put on a different, less domineering basis.[46]

After 1968, however, it became increasingly clear that in Moscow no one – certainly no one that mattered – was listening. Kádár managed the crisis of his leadership and of the fate of the NEM in 1972-75 with great skill, but thereafter his reduced appetite for innovation and physical decline made policy-making a weary matter of brokerage and survival. Material changes still took place, but slowly and under force of circumstance.

However, even before Brezhnev's intervention, pressures to water down the reforms were mounting and subsidies stayed stubbornly high. Kádár was willing neither to risk social tension nor to challenge the established patterns of power within his system. In his emphasis on stability of personnel, he was closer to the antagonistic Brezhnev than to his mentor Khrushchev. The long-serving heads of major companies, often also members of the CC, along with their equally durable counterparts in the county and central party apparatus were formidably entrenched lobbyists for particular interests. An ability to lock in to Soviet-favoured projects added to their muscle. Kádár often emphasised that gains in living standards had to be soundly based in economic progress, but the capture of resources by favoured groups made this impossible. Borrowing made up the gap.

Thus, even if the Hungarian economy under Kádár had more market elements than did those of the other Comecon countries, it was not different enough to mark a real breakthrough. There were some positive features, notably the greater availability of food and consumer goods and the growth of smaller private enterprises during the eighties. It is also likely that Hungary's western orientation and experience of partial market mechanisms were of some value in adjusting to the new economic regime after 1989, helping make the country the early destination of choice for foreign investment in the region. But the bulk of Kádár's economic legacy was, like that of the other bloc countries, wretched.

Agriculture provided an interesting exception. Conditions after 1956 and the desperate need to sustain production during collectivisation created a political constituency for more efficient and flexible methods of production and remuneration that had no counterpart in industry. Even this success was strictly relative, and was vitiated by the squeeze on investment budgets during the eighties. Nonetheless, Hungarian agriculture had performed markedly better than that of other bloc countries, and Kádár had at the very least allowed it to happen.

If there were limits to the economic change that Kádár was prepared to countenance, the same was true of the political sphere. He won plaudits at home and abroad for his softening of the party's dictatorial rule, but he never confused this with the dilution of its power. If there was one thing that Kádár believed in, it was the party as an institution. It had given identity and meaning to a clever but alienated and disoriented young man, and he never abandoned it. In a rare moment of relaxation, he remarked to

Nyers that 'perhaps the most productive form of government is enlightened absolutism.'[47]

In this, he could draw on historical precedent. As has often been pointed out, for most of the period from 1848 to 1988, the last word in Hungarian politics rested with one of three men: Emperor and King Franz Joseph, Admiral and Regent Miklós Horthy and First Secretary János Kádár. All three came to power amid revolution and foreign intervention and used brutal methods to confirm their authority, but later established themselves as benign autocrats, guarantors of stability and of authoritarian but relatively restrained systems. Consciously or not, Kádár put these earlier patterns of leadership into a low-key modern dress.[48]

To Kádár's strongest critics, his system was more corrupting than Rákosi's.[49] With its blandishments of small concessions, its encouragement of writers' self-censorship, its network of informers and array of 'soft' sanctions – its control over jobs, housing, the right to travel – there was something quite insidious about the Kádár system. Miklós Haraszti described the intellectuals' 'velvet prison', but the same could be said for society as a whole. The system's lack of legitimacy and the constriction of the civic sphere also had a corrosive effect on attitudes. Late in the Kádár era, the European Values Systems Survey found Hungarians to be at the extreme individualist end of the spectrum.[50]

It would, however, be an excessively purist and morally bracing argument to conclude that a 'harder' system such as Rákosi's was somehow preferable. The destruction of many social values was a common feature of the systems imposed across the Soviet bloc, not merely of a 'soft' one such as Kádár's. While there are intractable dilemmas over 'how a successful effort to make oppression comfortable for the majority of the oppressed is to be judged'[51], it still – to this author at least – seems preferable to the most obvious alternative. Kádár can still be given a little credit for his 'little freedoms'.

Did the relative tolerance under Kádár help pave the way for Hungary's breaking away from Communism? Or was this simply a result of the withdrawal of Soviet support from an essentially unchanged regime?

The change in Soviet policy under Gorbachev was certainly the necessary condition for Hungary's regime change in 1988-90. Nonetheless, Kádár contributed – unintentionally – to the outcome in two respects. The first was the failure of his economic policies. As the dour normalisers of Prague had always warned, the two least orthodox members of the bloc, Poland and Hungary, proved to be its weakest links. Their intractable economic crises led Moscow to sanction political changes that had a knock-on effect elsewhere – in Hungary's case, the decision by Kádár's successors in September 1989 to allow East Germans to travel to the West, thereby destabilising the East Berlin regime.

Secondly, Kádár affected the *form* if not the *fact* of the transition by moderating the policy reversal of the mid-seventies. In the Brezhnev era, the resurgence of party bureaucracies, a renewed emphasis on recruiting workers as party members and the purging of reformist technocrats were bloc-wide phenomena. In Hungary the process, though not absent, was relatively limited: the shift back to 'worker-cadres' within the party was more modest than elsewhere, and in any case the intelligentsia was able to colonise the state apparatus.[52] The reform Communism of the sixties had lost its impetus, but it had a long half-life, leaving the Hungarian party relatively porous to external influences. The western orientation of Kádár's foreign and economic policies had a similar effect.

Thus, even as the economic and political crisis deepened, the leadership held back from the harshest measures against dissent, while the reactions of western governments became an ever more important factor in decision-making. There had long been contacts and a sort of continuum between the leadership and at least its moderate critics in a way that would have been unthinkable in Husák's Czechoslovakia. Now some aspects of opposition thinking carried over to policy-makers, and a wing of the party found that it had an incentive to bargain and form alliances with outside critics.[53] In the sixties, Kádár had felt strong enough to hand down concessions from above: now his leadership was too weak to stop others taking them.

After 1985, Kádár tried to seize back lost ground, especially when the opposition revived the issue of 1956. But with Gorbachev sending out a very different message, it was too late. Neither the opposition nor the West toppled him, and even Gorbachev's role was secondary: Kádár was removed when the economic crisis and his declining powers led the party apparatus to lose faith in him. However, the step-by-step transition under his successors reflected political forces that had developed during his tenure. Kádár was emphatically not the father of Hungarian democracy, but it might well have come about differently without him.

Some of his influence lingered on in post-Communist Hungary. Not least because of the very gradual transition, many of the values and not a few of the elites of the Kádár era carried over into its successor. Polling almost a decade after Kádár's death indicated that 58 per cent of Hungarians took a positive view of the Communist era, a markedly higher figure than that for Slovaks, Czechs and Poles. A comparison of attitudes of Hungarians with those of East Germans suggested that, since Hungarians had 'gained less' in terms of personal freedoms from the transition, their view of it focused more on the difficult economic transformation. However, only a minority of Hungarians would have wished to return to the old regime: the central current of opinion was 'nostalgic but realistic'.[54]

A positive assessment of Kádár's rule also influenced judgements of his role in 1956. Looking at survey evidence fifteen years after the regime change, the sociologist Mária Vásárhelyi diagnosed a 'national schizophrenia' over the issue. Although only 16 per cent of Hungarians accepted Kádár's assessment of the events as 'counter-revolution', less than a third believed that he had betrayed the revolution. More than half saw him as a victim of circumstances, and most held the Soviets primarily responsible for the reprisals. Respondents' views varied by social group – more educated Hungarians tended to take a harsher view – and, predictably, by political alignment, but the overall outcome was strikingly favourable to Kádár. His generally high standing was confirmed in the 1999 'greatest Hungarians' poll.[55]

However, the system that emerged in Hungary after 1989-90 was very different from that to which Kádár had devoted his life and for which he had so bloodied his hands. The marginal man had the realism to recognise that he and his marginal party had been very much imposed on his countrymen, and to seek to overcome this through concessions and co-opting of major social interests. His long-term bet – perhaps more implicit than explicit – was that economic success and the dominance of party ideology would reshape attitudes, giving the party a more secure base. He lost his bet: the system proved incapable of economic dynamism, and instead of the party successfully projecting its ideology onto society, outside influences came to bear on parts of the party and state apparatus. The dominant influence to which his successors have had to adjust has been that of the global capitalist market.

Kádár did not live to see the system's fall, but he must have realised that it was tottering, and that harsh judgement was being passed on much of his record. In his final months, he invited tragic, Shakespearean analogies. To some he was Macbeth, haunted by his crimes; to others he was Lear, the mad old ruler abandoned by his court.[56] He perhaps lacked the grandeur to quite sustain such comparisons. However, even if not in the strict sense a tragedy, there is poignancy and frustration about his career, and about its consequences for Hungary. Kádár's personal and inner life does not seem to have been as empty as that of a Hitler or a Stalin, but it was limited nonetheless: he was truly *homo politicus*, and as such he would have expected to be judged. Despite his abilities, and with serious crimes on the other side of the account, the positive results of his efforts were relatively meagre.

This reflected both the huge constraints on Hungary's freedom of action during the Soviet era and the inherent failings of the Marxist-Leninist project. In Kádár's career, the two were inextricably linked. Pragmatic as he was in day to day operation, Kádár was a man who had committed himself to a cause, one that by 1989 was ceasing to be viable. It is apt that his lifespan matched almost precisely 'the short twentieth century', 'the age of extremes.'[57] That time – his time – was now over.

Kádár was admitted to Kútvölgyi hospital during the morning of Monday, 3 July. His extremities were swollen by peripheral oedema; he was also suffering from pneumonia, and from severe circulatory and respiratory problems. He could barely speak coherently, and as he wheezed and gasped for breath, he sometimes muttered, 'Kill me.' Late on the first day, he asked the nurse how long he would stay in hospital; she told him that it would be until he got better. 'He replied that he would never return home because he was ga-ga.' The nurse soon concluded that 'he almost took a conscious decision to die.'[58]

During his first twenty-four hours in hospital, Kádár's condition deteriorated further. Mária stayed at his bedside. On 4 July, he had brief visits from Grósz and from Nyers, who had succeeded him as party president. On that day and the next, radio reports described his condition as critical and not improving.[59] At 7 a.m. on Thursday, 6 July, radio broadcasts repeated that Kádár was in critical condition. At 9 a.m. the Presidential Division of the Supreme Court began its session that would overturn the verdict in the Imre Nagy case.

Kádár died peacefully at 9.16 a.m., Mária sitting by his side. Overwhelmed with grief, she had to be given tranquillisers. A little over half an hour later, the news was broadcast in a terse radio statement. A longer announcement from the leadership, released shortly afterwards, spoke of 'shock and sorrow' at his passing and said that his name would live in the memory of Communists and Hungarians.[60]

The reaction to Kádár's death marked a sharp reversal from the sense of rejection and disgrace that had filled his final weeks. In one poll, three-quarters of those asked agreed that 'with his passing Hungarian political life has lost one of its greatest figures.'[61] As usual at such times, those with a harsher view of Kádár stayed relatively quiet, but there was nonetheless quite a widespread sense of loss. Many Hungarians were already looking back on the sixties and seventies through a roseate folk memory of easing political pressure and rising living standards. In any case, Kádár was the only national leader that many people could remember. One interviewee said that it was as though his father had died; another, more nuanced, said that it felt like the loss of 'some not particularly close acquaintance' and that it was the end of an era, the era of her youth. Nonetheless, she hoped for better times ahead.[62]

Kádár's funeral had to be delayed, since US President George Bush was about to visit Hungary. Before leaving the US, Bush paid a handsome tribute to his former host: 'I look at him as a man who served his country … in death, give the man the credit for what he did accomplish.'[63] Nonetheless, it was easier for everyone for Kádár's funeral to take place after Bush had left. And so it was on 14 July, the Bastille bicentenary, that János Kádár was buried in the 'Pantheon of the Workers' Movement' in Budapest's Kerepesi cemetery.

At 3 p.m. on the eve of the funeral, hours after Bush's departure, party officials opened the doors of the White House to those who wished to pay their respects to Kádár's coffin. They were taken aback by the response.

Long queues formed, and plans to close at 8 p.m. had to be delayed until the early hours of the morning, with a re-opening at 6 a.m. for those still determined to come. Even in the early afternoon of the 14th, after the paying of respects by party, state and international representatives, more time had to be set aside for the unexpected tributes. Altogether, some sixty thousand people filed past the coffin. Once again, there was a sense for many of commemorating the end of a chapter, both in their own lives and in Hungarian history. Some had attended the Nagy lying-in-state four weeks earlier 'and could not quite rationalise what they were doing.'[64]

Flanked by motorcycle outriders, the cortège set off at 4 p.m. It passed slowly through the streets of Pest, lined several deep with onlookers. The atmosphere was tense; like Nagy's reburial, this was also a political demonstration, and many of those watching were party stalwarts mourning the passing not only of a man or of an era, but of a system that had nourished them and in which they believed. There was, however, no disorder.[65]

Up to a hundred thousand people attended the final ceremony in Kerepesi, while just over a quarter of the non-party population watched it on television. The Pantheon, a section of the cemetery dominated by a socialist-realist monument, already housed the remains of, among others, Imre Mező and László and Júlia Rajk. After speeches by Nyers, the state President Bruno F. Straub and an Angyalföld locksmith and party activist, Pál Kollát, the coffin was lowered while the patriotic *Szózat* (summons) was sung, followed by the *Internationale*. The grave was soon covered with wreaths and bouquets.[66]

Tributes in the aftermath of Kádár's funeral, Kerepesi cemetery, 14 July 1989

Kádár is buried in a separate plot to one side of the main Pantheon monument and graves. Mária joined him there in 1992. The inscription recalls his self-justification before the UN General Assembly in 1960:

I WAS WHERE I HAD TO BE

I DID WHAT I HAD TO DO

1956 was, in effect, carved on his tombstone.

Notes

The following are the abbreviations used for the major primary sources consulted for this book.

MOL = Magyar Országos Levéltár (Hungarian National Archives). Transcripts of meetings of the major party bodies (Central Committee, Politburo, Secretariat), as well as documents from Kádár's personal secretariat. Documents are classified by fonds, file and storage unit (*őrzési egység*, or *ő.e.*).

PIL = Politikatörténeti Intézet Levéltára (Archives of the Institute of Political History). Material related to the Hungarian Left, including the Hungarian Communist Party prior to 1948. The classification system is similar to that of MOL.

HU OSA = Open Society Archives. This incorporates the former collections of Radio Free Europe/ Radio Liberty. Section HU-OSA 300/40/6 includes the confidential files of RFE/ RL, based on unofficial sources within Hungary. HU-OSA 300/40/5 includes more publicly available sources, such as newspaper cuttings. Many of these are available elsewhere, but I have included the references, since they provide an easily accessible source of information on Kádár.

1956 OHA = Oral History Archives of the 1956 Institute. A number of these interviews are quoted direct; in addition, many sections of the archive relevant to Kádár were reproduced in a special edition of the historical magazine *Rubicon* and in the related book, *Ki volt Kádár?* (Who Was Kádár?), edited by Árpád Rácz.

MK 1-10 = interviews given by Mária Kádár (Mária Tamáska), Kádár's widow, in *Magyarország* magazine between October and December 1989 (editions 40-49).

NARA = National Archives and Records Administration, Washington DC. Material consulted from Department of State archives and Nixon Presidential Materials.

JCPL = Jimmy Carter Presidential Library, Atlanta, Georgia. State Department and NSC materials relating to Hungary 1977-81.

FOIA = US State Department documents requested under the Freedom of Information Act.

Baráth = several Soviet documents made available to me by Dr. Magdolna Baráth. These are from the Foreign Policy Archive of the Russian Federation (AVPRF) and the Russian State Archive of Contemporary History (RGANI). They are classified by fonds, inventory (opsis), folder (papka) and document (delo).

Révész (ed.)/Aczél = Sándor Révész's article, 'Aczél György: Egy Kádár-portré töredékei' (*Beszélő*, October 1999) draws together comments on Kádár from various essays and interviews by his long-term political collaborator. Aczél intended to use these as raw materials for a book on the Kádár era, but the project was far from complete at the time of his death in 1991. The original documents are held in the Hungarian Academy of Sciences.

Acknowledgements
[1] Alison Hanham (1975), *Richard III and his early historians 1483-1535* (Oxford: Oxford University Press, 1975), p. 195 n. 2.

Introduction
[1] http://hirek.prim.hu/cikk/5698/; János Berecz, *Vállalom* (My undertaking), pp. 345-6.
[2] John Dunn, *The Cunning of Unreason* (London: HarperCollins, 2000), p. 165.

Chapter 1: 'We Are Not Beggars'
[1] László Gyurkó (1985), *Introductory Biography*, in János Kádár (1985), *Selected Speeches and Interviews*, p. 11.
[2] William Shawcross (1974), *Crime and Compromise*, p. 20; Tibor Huszár (2001), *Kádár 1912-1956*, p. 8.
[3] Gyurkó (1985), p. 13; Piroska Döme, interview with the author, Budapest, 25 June 2002.
[4] Huszár (2001), pp. 7-8.
[5] Huszár (2001), p. 10; Shawcross (1974), p. 22; Gyurkó (1985), p. 13.
[6] Gyurkó (1985), p. 10 for the 'beggar' story; for a refutation, see Huszár (2001), p. 9 and pp. 349-50, n. 13.
[7] Shawcross (1974), p. 22.
[8] László Kontler, *Millennium in Central Europe*, pp. 302-18.
[9] Huszár (2001), pp. 9-10, 14; Mr and Mrs Zoltán Bognár (local historians, Kapoly), interview with the author, 23 October 2003.
[10] Gyurkó (1985), pp.10-11, 13; Huszár (2001), pp. 13-14.
[11] Gyurkó (1985), p. 11; Paul Lendvai (1988), *Hungary*, p. 60.
[12] Gyurkó, (1985), pp. 11-12; Huszár (2001), p.16; Sándor Révész (ed.), 'Aczél György: Egy Kádár portré töredékei' (György Aczél: Fragments of a Kádár portrait), *Beszélő*, October 1999, p. 103 (hereafter Révész (ed.)/Aczél); Bognár interview.
[13] Bognár interview.
[14] Huszár (2001), pp. 12-17.
[15] Révész (ed.)/Aczél; 'March 1 conversation between János Kádár and Ambassador Salgo', Telegram 2230 from US Embassy Budapest to Secretary of State, 21 March 1985 (FOIA).
[16] 'Kádár János látogatása Mesterházi Lajosnál 1967. jan. 26-án' (János Kádár's visit to Lajos Mesterházi, 26 January 1967), PIL 867.f. K-2 ő.e.
[17] 'János Kádár's visit ...'; Gyurkó (1985), p. 17.
[18] Gyurkó (1985), pp. 13-14, drawing on 'János Kádár's visit ...'
[19] 'János Kádár's visit ...'; Döme interview.
[20] János Kádár, 'Első lépesek' (First steps), 1 February 1956, PIL 867.f. K-2 ő.e; Gyurkó (1985), p. 13; Döme interview.
[21] Kádár-Salgo conversation.
[22] 'János Kádár's visit ...'
[23] Huszár (2001), p.15; Bognár interview; 'János Kádár's visit ...'
[24] Révész (ed.)/Aczél, p. 103.
[25] Révész (ed.)/Aczél, p. 103; Mária Kádár, interview 3 (of 10) in *Magyarország*, editions 40-49, October to December 1989 (hereafter MK 1-10).
[26] Kádár speech, 25 May 1972, in János Kádár (1974), *For a Socialist Hungary*, p. 394.
[27] János Kertész letter to Kádár, 9 June 1958, in Tibor Huszár (ed.) (2002), *Kedves, jó Kádár elvtárs!* (Dear Comrade Kádár ...), pp. 740-1; Shawcross (1974), p. 30; Bognár interview; Huszár (2001), p. 350, n. 22.
[28] 'János Kádár's visit ...'
[29] Szonya Szelényi, *Equality by Design*, p. 23; 'János Kádár's visit ...'; Huszár (2001), pp. 8, 23, 351-2, n.55.
[30] Gyurkó, pp. 18, 64; Döme interview; Kádár, 'First Steps.'

[31] 'János Kádár's visit …'; police report on interrogation of János Csermanek, 10 November 1931, in András Kanyó, *Kádár János: végakarat* (János Kádár: Last Will and Testament), pp. 9-10; Huszár (2001), p. 25.

Chapter 2: Becoming Comrade Kádár

[1] Kádár, 'First steps'; 'János Kádár's visit …'; Levente Sipos, 'Kádár János visszaemlékezései' (János Kádár remembers), in Árpád Rácz (ed.), Ki volt Kádár? (Who was Kádár?), p. 33.
[2] Kádár, 'First Steps'; Gyurkó (1985), p. 19.
[3] 'János Kádár's visit …'; police report on interrogation of János Csermanek, 10 November 1931, in András Kanyó, *Kádár János – végakarat* (János Kádár: Last Will and Testament), pp. 9-10; Kádár, 'First Steps'; Gyurkó (1985), p. 25.
[4] Döme interview; Kádár, 'First Steps.'
[5] Kádár, 'First Steps'; Bennett Kovrig, *Communism in Hungary*, p. 112.
[6] 'János Kádár's visit …'; Kádár speech at the Ganz-Mávag works, 29 January 1963, in János Kádár (1965), *On the Road to Socialism*, p. 154; Kovrig, p. 112.
[7] Kádár, 'First Steps'; 'János Kádár's visit …'; Kádár letter to Sverdlov Museum, Sverdlovsk, 8 October 1958, MOL M-KS 288.f. 47/721 ő.c. For an analysis of the circumstances in which Csermanek joined the party, see Huszár (2001), pp. 28-31.
[8] Kádár, 'First Steps.'
[9] Révész (ed.)/Aczél, p. 104.
[10] Reproduced in Sipos in Rácz (ed.), p. 29.
[11] 'Adatok Kádár elvtárs életrajzához' (Materials for Comrade Kádár's biography), unsigned, 31 January 1963, PIL 867.f. K-2 ő.e.; police report in Kanyó, pp. 9-10.
[12] 'Materials for Kádár biography'; 'Court sentence in case of 'János Csermanek and his associates', in PIL 765.f. 2 ő.e.; Kádár speech to CC of 14-15 June 1972, MOL M-KS 288.f. 4/117 ő.e.; Kádár-Salgo conversation.
[13] Kádár statement at rehearing of his trial, 22 July 1954, in László Varga (ed.) (2001), *Kádár János bírái előtt.* (János Kádár before his judges), p. 468; 'Materials for Kádár biography'.
[14] Kádár rehearing statement in L. Varga (ed.) (2001), pp. 467-70, 480, also commentary p. 85 and n. 360; 'János Csermanek and his associates.'
[15] Kanyó, pp. 20, 22-27; Kasa Istvánné (Mrs. István Kasa), 'Emlékeim Kádár Jánosról' (My memories of János Kádár), *Népszabadság*, 17 July 1989, HU-OSA 300/40/5, Box 87; 'Materials for a Kádár biography'; Révész (ed.)/Aczél, p. 104.
[16] 'Materials for a Kádár biography'; Gyurkó (1985), pp. 38-40.
[17] Kádár rehearing statement in L. Varga (ed.) (2001), pp. 469-70.
[18] 'Materials for a Kádár biography'; Gyurkó (1985), p. 39; János Csermanek prison record, PIL 765.f. 2 ő.e.
[19] Gyurkó (1985), pp. 39-40; Kanyó, p. 20; Révész (ed.)/Aczél, p. 104; György Aczél, interviewed by András B. Hegedűs, Gyula Kozák and György Litván (1989-91), 1956 OHA (no. 162), in Rácz (ed.), p. 175; Piroska Döme, 'János', PIL 942 f. 2 ő.e.
[20] Kádár rehearing statement in L. Varga (ed.) (2001), p. 470.
[21] Kádár rehearing statement in L. Varga (ed.) (2001), p. 470; Lajos Gallai, 'Önéletrajz' (Autobiography), PIL 867.f. 1/G-146 ő.e.
[22] I am grateful to Professor Rudolf Tőkés for this anecdote.
[23] Döme, 'János.'
[24] Éva Bozóky, interview with the author, Szigliget, 26 June 2002.
[25] József Marjai, interview with the author, Budapest, 19 February 2004; György Fejti, interview with the author, Budapest, 14 September 2004.
[26] Gyurkó (1985), pp. 33-4; Shawcross (1974), p. 43; see also Béla Kelen, interviewed by Gábor Murányi (1987), 1956 OHA (no. 101), p. 300.
[27] Kádár speech to CC of 14-15 June 1972, MOL M-KS 288.f. 4/117 ő.e.
[28] Miklós Molnár (1990), *From Béla Kun to János Kádár*, pp. 65-68; Kovrig, pp. 123-7.
[29] Kasa, 'My memories of János Kádár.'

30 Rudolf L. Tőkés (1996), *Hungary's Negotiated Revolution*, pp. 19-20, and author's telephone conversation with Professor Tőkés.

31 Júlia Rajk, interviewed by László Rajk and László Bokor (1980), 1956 OHA (no. 142), p. 20 (B).

32 Sources for this and subsequent paragraphs: Döme, 'János'; 'Kedves Piroska!' (Dear Piroska), *Képes* 7, 30 June 1990, HU-OSA 300/40/5, Box 87; Döme interview.

33 'Memoir' (16 July 1979) by Miklós Szinai, PIL 867.f. 1/ SZ –144 ő.e.

34 Kádár rehearing statement in L. Varga (ed.) (2001), pp. 470-1.

35 Gallai, 'Autobiography.'

36 Miklós Szinai, 'Recollections', 24 January 1958 and 16 July 1979, PIL 867.f. 1/ SZ –144 ő.e.; recollections of István Sági, 21 August 1961, PIL 867.f. 2/ S –136 ő.e; Kádár rehearing statement in L. Varga (ed.) (2001), p. 471; 'Materials for a Kádár biography'; Huszár (2001), p. 49.

37 Döme, 'János'; Döme interview.

38 Kasa, 'My memories of János Kádár'; Gyurkó (1985), p. 45.

39 István Sági, 'Visszaemlékezés' (Recollection), August 1977, PIL 867.f. 2/ S –136 ő.e.; Gyurkó (1985), pp. 46-7.

40 Döme, 'János'; L. Varga (ed.) (2001), pp. 90-1.

41 'Kádár János feljegyzése a Béképárttal kapcsolatban' (János Kádár's memorandum concerning the Peace Party), 20 June 1956, PIL 867.f. K-2 ő.e.; 'Materials for a Kádár biography.'

42 István Kovács, interviewed by János M. Rainer (1988) 1956 OHA (no. 158), pp. 215-6.

43 Ferenc A. Váli, *Rift and Revolt in Hungary*, p. 33; Kádár rehearing statement in L. Varga (ed.) (2001), pp. 471-2; 'Materials for a Kádár biography'.

44 'Schifferné Szakasits Klára emlékezik' (Recollection of Klára Schiffer, née Szakasits) in Kanyó, pp. 91-2; Haraszti statement at rehearing, 22 July 1954, in L. Varga (ed.) (2001), p. 508; for Kádár's view, see pp. 472, 512.

45 Kádár rehearing statement in L. Varga (ed.) (2001), p. 472.

46 'János Kádár's memorandum' (1956).

47 Kádár rehearing statement in L. Varga (ed.) (2001), p. 473.

48 'János Kádár's memorandum' (1956); Kádár rehearing statement and 'Donáth Ferenc gyanúsított kihallgatása' (Questioning of the accused Ferenc Donáth), 15 June 1954, in L. Varga (ed.) (2001), pp. 302, 473-4.

49 L. Varga (ed.) (2001), pp. 78-9; 'Szirmai István bejelentése Kádárról' (István Szirmai's declaration about Kádár), 22 May 1951, in L. Varga (ed.) (2001), pp. 255-6; Questioning of Donáth, in L. Varga (ed.) (2001), p. 301; Donáth rehearing statement in L. Varga (ed.) (2001), pp. 485-6, 490-3.

50 'János Kádár's memorandum' (1956).

51 'János Kádár's memorandum' (1956).

52 György Aczél, 1956 OHA interview, in Rácz (ed.), p. 188.

53 Kádár rehearing statement in L. Varga (ed.) (2001), p. 480.

54 This and succeeding paragraphs: MK2.

55 Huszár (2001), p. 113.

56 Kádár letter to Mária, 30 November 1955; Ottó Róna letter to Kádár, April 1957; in Huszár (ed.) (2002), pp. 85-7, 702-3.

57 'János Kádár's memorandum' (1956); Kovrig, pp. 143-4.

58 'Materials for a Kádár biography.'

59 Kádár rehearing statement in L. Varga (ed.) (2001), p. 474; 'János Kádár's visit ...'; Kádár, 'Memoir' for Party History Institute, 20 November 1984, in Kanyó, p. 32. See also the analyses in Huszár (2001), pp. 63-5 and L. Varga (ed.) (2001), pp. 89-90.

60 Kádár letter to Dr. Mihály Perneki, 13 December 1978, PIL 765.f. 3 ő.e.

61 Kádár rehearing statement in L. Varga (ed.) (2001), p. 474; MK2.

62 Kádár rehearing statement in L. Varga (ed.) (2001), p. 474-5; Kádár, 'Memoir' (1984), in Kanyó, pp. 32-3.

63 Szirmai declaration about Kádár' in L. Varga (ed.) (2001), p. 255; Vladimir Farkas, *Nincs mentség* (No excuses), pp. 342-3; Winckelmann telegram, 28 July 1944, PIL 765.f. 2 ő.e.; L. Varga (ed.) (2001), pp. 89-92. The example of the late Gyula Schöpflin indicates that the authorities were less than omniscient. A party member since 1933, with a fat police file to his credit, he expected to be arrested in 1941 and sent to the front. However, a friend in counter-intelligence destroyed the file. There seems to have been no copy, and Schöpflin was not arrested. I am grateful to George Schöpflin for this account.

64 MK3; Révész (ed.)/Aczél, p. 106.

65 Kádár, 'Memoir' (1984), in Kanyó, p. 34.

66 Kádár, 'Memoir' (1984), in Kanyó, p. 34.

67 Kádár memorandum to Rákosi, 1 February 1951, in L. Varga (ed.) (2001), p. 178; Kasa, 'My memories of János Kádár.'

68 Kádár rehearing statement in L. Varga (ed.) (2001), p. 475; Kádár, 'Memoir' (1984), in Kanyó, p. 35.

69 Kádár, 'Memoir' (1984), in Kanyó, pp. 35-6; Djorde Herceg letter to Kádár, 24 November 1977, and Kádár reply, 5 December 1977, in Huszár (ed.) (2002), pp. 765-7.

70 Béla Kelen, 1956 OHA interview, in Rácz (ed.), p. 173; Shawcross (1974), pp. 47-8; Gyurkó (1985), p. 49.

71 'János Kádár's visit …'; Kádár, 'Memoir' (1984), in Kanyó, pp. 36-7; MK3; Huszár (2001), pp. 66-8.

72 Krisztián Ungváry, *Battle for Budapest*, p. xi.

73 Kádár rehearing statement in L. Varga (ed.) (2001), pp. 478-9; interrogation of János Kádár, 18 May 1951, in L. Varga (ed.) (2001), p. 238; Kádár memorandum on the Rajk affair, 20 July 1954, in Rácz (ed.), pp. 47-8.

74 Miklós Vásárhelyi, interviewed by Gábor Murányi (1994), 1956 OHA (no. 3.2), in Rácz (ed.), p. 173.

75 Miklós Vásárhelyi, 1956 OHA interview, in Rácz (ed.), p. 173; István Kovács, 1956 OHA interview, p. 97.

76 Shawcross (1974), p. 44; Kanyó, p. 19; Béla Kelen, 1956 OHA interview, p. 301.

Chapter 3: Salami

1 CC, 19 January 1945: PIL 274.f. 2/11 ő.e; Tibor Zinner and Sándor Szakács, *A háboru 'megváltozott természete'* (The 'changed nature' of war), pp. 77-78; István Kovács, 1956 OHA interview, p. 112; Molnár (1990), p. 251, n. 39.

2 In its earliest days it was known as the PRO (*Politikai Rendészeti Osztály* – Political Police Department).

3 Szakács and Zinner, p. 82.

4 Döme, 'János'; Huszár (2001), p. 17.

5 Huszár (2001), pp. 78-9.

6 Szakács and Zinner, pp. 86-8.

7 Paul Ignotus, 'János Kádár – Hungary's Quisling Redeemed' in Rodger Swearingen (ed.), *Leaders of the Communist World*, p. 320.

8 Váli, p. 45.

9 István Kovács, 1956 OHA interview, pp. 202-3.

10 Charles Gati, *Hungary and the Soviet Bloc*, p. 104.

11 Ignác Romsics (1999), *Hungary in the Twentieth Century*, pp. 222-4; Gati, p. 21; George Schöpflin, 'Hungary after the Second World War' in György Litván (ed.), *The Hungarian Revolution of 1956*, pp. 11-12.

12 Shawcross (1974), p. 54; Molnár (1990), p. 110.

13 György Gyarmati, 'Rendőrfőnök és belügyminiszter 1945-1950' (Police chief and Interior Minister) in Rácz (ed.), p. 36.

14 Szakács and Zinner, p. 230; CC, 18 March 1946, PIL 274.f. 4 /123 ő.e; PB, 20 March 1946, PIL 274.f. 3/30 ő.e.

[15] Szakács and Zinner, pp. 245-6; Sándor Kopácsi, *'In the Name of the Working Class'*, p. 45.

[16] 'Notes of the conversation with Comrade Kádár', in Lajos Iszák and Miklós Kun (eds), *'Moszkvának jelentjük ...' Titkos dokumentumok 1944-1948* (Reporting to Moscow: secret documents), pp. 186-7.

[17] György Gyarmati, 'Kádár János és a Belügyminisztérium Államvédelmi Hatósága' (János Kádár and Interior Ministry's State Security Authority), *Trezor* 1. (1999), p. 118 n. 8.

[18] Discussion of 1945 election (November 1945), PIL 274.f. 7/50 ő.e.

[19] Expanded meeting of Budapest party Secretariat, 2 January 1947, PIL 274.f. 16/130 ő.e; Kovrig, p. 206.

[20] György Aczél, 1956 OHA interview, in Rácz (ed.), p. 173.

[21] Gyurkó (1985), p. 56.

[22] Miklós Vásárhelyi, 1956 OHA interview, in *Rubicon* 2000/7-8, p. 76; Valeri Musatov, interview with the author, Budapest, 24 September 2004.

[23] György Aczél, 1956 OHA interview, in *Rubicon* 2000/7-8, p. 76.

[24] 'Az MKP listavezetői: Kádár János' (Leaders of the MKP list: János Kádár) (*Szabad Nép*, 23 August 1947), HU-OSA 300/40/5, Box 80; László Gyurkó, interview with the author, Göd, 13 December 2002; György Aczél, 1956 OHA interview, in *Rubicon*, 2000/7-8, p. 76.

[25] Jenő Széll, interviewed by András B. Hegedűs, Gyula Kozák and Mrs Szabó, née Ilona Dér (1981-82), 1956 OHA (no. 4), in Rácz (ed.), p. 174.

[26] Éva Bozóky, interviewed by Péter Pál Tóth (1987), 1956 OHA (no. 80), in Rácz (ed.), p. 174.

[27] Szilárd Ujhelyi, interviewed by Péter Pál Tóth (1982-85), 1956 OHA (no. 40), in Rácz (ed.), p. 174; Ignotus in Swearingen (ed.), p. 318; 'Leaders of the MKP list: János Kádár'.

[28] Szakács and Zinner, pp. 366-7.

[29] PB, 21 February 1948, PIL 274.f. 3/133 ő.e.; István Kovács, 1956 OHA interview, pp. 184-5.

[30] PB, 26 February 1948, PIL 274.f. 3/134 ő.e.

[31] Rezső Nyers, interview with the author, Budapest, 5 December 2001.

[32] 'A párt feladata a termelés előmozdítása, a dolgozók nevelése: Kádár János elvtárs kongresszusi beszéde a pártmunka kérdéseiről' (The party's task is to boost production and educate the workers: Comrade János Kádár's speech to the congress on issues of party work) (*Szabad Nép*, 20 June 1948), HU-OSA 300/40/5, Box 80.

[33] Kádár memorandum on the Rajk affair, in Rácz (ed.), p. 48; Gyarmati in Rácz (ed.), p. 36.

[34] Kádár, letter to Rákosi, Gerő, Farkas & Révai, 11 February 1951, in L. Varga (ed.) (2001), p. 184. The letter, written a couple of months before Kádár's arrest, has a 'confessional' quality.

[35] Jenő Széll, 1956 OHA interview, in Rácz (ed.), p. 174.

[36] Farkas, p. 91; Júlia Rajk, 1956 OHA interview, p. 34 (A).

[37] Kádár talks with Gorbachev, 25 September 1985, in Magdolna Baráth and János M. Rainer (eds), *Gorbacsov tárgyalásai magyar vezetőkkel* (Gorbachev's talks with Hungarian leaders), p. 45.

[38] MK3; Gyurkó (1985), p.50; Huszár (2001), p. 112 and p. 366 n. 146.

[39] Szakács and Zinner, pp. 384-86; Kádár report on Pócspteri, PIL 274.f. 11/79 ő.e.

[40] Gyarmati (1999), p. 136.

[41] Gyarmati in Rácz (ed.), p. 38.

[42] Kádár letter to Rákosi, 21 July 1954, in L. Varga (ed.) (2001), p. 639; Gyarmati (1999), pp. 142-4.

[43] Gyarmati in Rácz (ed.), pp. 37-8.

[44] Peter Kenez, 'The Hungarian Communist Party and the Catholic Church 1945-1948', *Journal of Modern History*, Volume 75, number 4 (December 2003).

[45] 'Notes of the discussion between Comrade L.S. Baranov and Comrades Rajk and Kádár, members of the Political Committee of the Hungarian Communist Party', in Izsák and Kun (eds), pp. 263-4; Gyurkó (1985), p.67.

[46] 'Eltemették Kádár János édesanyját' (János Kádár's mother buried) (*Szabad Nép*, 5 February 1949), HU-OSA 300/40/5, Box 80; Döme, 'János.'

[47] MK3.

Chapter 4: 'You're the Enemy's Man'

1 Kádár testimony to 1954 rehearing of his trial in L. Varga (ed.) (2001), p. 476; Júlia Rajk, 1956 OHA interview, p. 50 (A).

2 Kádár letter to Kovács committee, 3 April 1956, in L. Varga (ed.) (2001), p. 654; Gábor Péter confession, 10 July 1956, in Gábor Koltay and Péter Bródy (eds.) (1990), *El nem égetett dokumentumok* (Unburned documents), p. 24.

3 For the effects of the Soviet purges, see Robert Conquest, *The Great Terror*, pp. 445-7; on 'incipient diversity' in international Communism, see Gati, p. 110.

4 Farkas, p. 159; Ferenc Donáth (1992), *A márciusi fronttól monorig*, p. 288; Árpád Pünkösti (2004) *Rákosi, Sztálin legjobb tanítványa* (Rákosi, Stalin's best disciple), p. 224.

5 Tibor Hajdu (1992) [b], 'A Rajk-per háttere és fázisai' (The background to and phases of the Rajk trial), *Társadalmi Szemle*, 1992/11; L. Varga (ed.) (2001), pp. 41-57.

6 L. Varga (ed.) (2001), p. 60 and n. 243.

7 Kádár letter to Kovács committee, in L. Varga (ed.) (2001), p. 655.

8 Révész (ed.)/Aczél, p. 107.

9 Farkas, p. 195; Pünkösti (2004), p. 230.

10 Tibor Hajdu , 'The Party Did Everything For You', *The Hungarian Quarterly* 37, no. 141 (1996), p. 82.

11 This and other citations from the transcript are from the translation given in Hajdu (1996), pp. 87-99.

12 Béla Szász, *Volunteers for the Gallows*, pp. 146-7; see also Shawcross (1974), pp. 66-7. The earliest published version of the story appears to be in an article by György Paloczi-Horváth in the *Sunday Times* (24 March 1957).

13 See, for example, the insistence of Gletkin, Rubashov's interrogator, that, 'Your testimony at the trial will be the last service that you can do the Party.' (Arthur Koestler, *Darkness at Noon*, London: Vintage 1994 edition, p. 180). The Rajk/ Rubashov analogy has often been made.

14 L. Varga (ed.) (2001), pp. 22-3; Farkas, pp. 203-4; Kádár testimony to the Kovács committee, 23 April 1956, in L. Varga (ed.) (2001), p. 663; Tibor Hajdu (1992) [a], 'Farkas és Kádár Rajknál' (Farkas and Kádár with Rajk), *Társadalmi Szemle* 1992/4, especially pp. 74-5; Vladimir Farkas, 'Egy koronatanú hozzászolása' (Comments of a chief witness), *Magyar Hírlap*, 18 March 1992, HU-OSA 300-40-5, Box 87; József Köböl, interviewed by Gábor Havas (1986), 1956 OHA (no. 24), pp. 210-11.

15 ÁVH officers Márton Károlyi and Gyula Décsi, in L. Varga (ed.) (2001), p. 18.

16 Shawcross (1974), p. 67; Szász, pp. 146-7.

17 Márton Károlyi, in Gábor Kiszely (2000), *ÁVH*, pp. 159-60.

18 L. Varga (ed.) (2001), p. 60.

19 Hajdu (1992) [b], pp. 30-4; Kiszely (2000), pp. 174-5.

20 Kanyó, pp. 53-4; Gábor Péter confession in Koltay and Bródy (eds.), pp. 26-7; L. Varga (ed.) (2001), p. 59 and n. 239.

21 L. Varga (ed.) (2001), p. 61; Kiszely (2000), p. 190.

22 Kádár letter to the Kovács committee, in L. Varga (ed.), pp. 656-7.

23 Kádár memorandum on the Rajk affair, in Rácz (ed.), p. 48; L. Varga (ed.) (2001), p. 63.

24 Tibor Hajdu (in Rácz (ed.), p. 47) states that, 'According to witnesses, Kádár was taken ill during the execution.' Béla Szász wrote in a letter to the author (4 December 1980), 'As Minister of Interior, Kádár attended Rajk's execution and, according to rumour, was seen vomiting after the hanging.'

25 György Aczél, 1956 OHA interview, in *Rubicon*, 2000/7-8, p. 79.

26 Kádár letter to Kovács committee, in L. Varga (ed.) (2001), p. 657.

27 Mihály Farkas, notes for 1956 speech, in Kanyó, p. 119.

28 Péter Rényi, interview with the author, Budapest, 5 July 1999.

Chapter 5: Full Circle

1 Kádár letter to Rákosi, 21 July 1954, in L. Varga (ed.) (2001), p. 640.
2 Bozóky interview.
3 Kontler, p. 413; Litván (ed.), pp. 19, 25-6.
4 Nigel Swain (1992), *Hungary*, pp. 77-80.
5 Huszár (2001), p. 162.
6 Gyarmati (1999), p. 143; Gyarmati in Rácz (ed.), p. 39; Kádár letter to Rákosi, 21 July 1954, in L. Varga (ed.) (2001), p. 639.
7 L. Varga (ed.) (2001), pp. 65-8; Huszár (2001), pp. 154-6.
8 Kádár rehearing statement, in L. Varga (ed.) (2001), p. 465.
9 Kádár memorandum on the Rajk affair, in Rácz (ed.), p. 48; Kádár letter to Rákosi, 21 July 1954, in L. Varga (ed.) (2001), p. 640.
10 Bozóky interview; Éva Bozóky, *Zord idők nyomában* ... (On the trail of tough times ...), pp. 187-8.
11 Kádár memo to Rákosi, 9 February 1951, in L. Varga (ed.) (2001), pp. 179-81.
12 Kádár first letter (supplement to memo of 9 February), 11 February 1951, and second letter (to Rákosi, Gerő, Farkas and Révai), 11 February 1951, in L. Varga (ed.) (2001), pp. 182, 183-5. Emphasis added.
13 Bozóky, p.196; Bozóky interview.
14 MK4; Farkas, p. 333.
15 András Hegedüs (1986), *Im Schatten einer Idee* (In the Shadow of an Idea), (1986); 'Jelentés Zöld Sándor haláláról' (Report on the death of Sándor Zöld), Ministry of Interior report, 2 March 1962, in L. Varga (ed.), pp. 198-201; Farkas, pp. 333-6.
16 MK3; Kanyó, pp. 57-8.
17 L. Varga (ed.) (2001), p. 69; Rákosi address to PB, 21 April 1951, in L. Varga (ed.) (2001), p. 210.
18 L. Varga (ed.) (2001), p.95; Bozóky interview; Döme interview; MK4.
19 György Szántó confession, 8 June 1954, in L. Varga (ed.) (2001), pp. 272-3.
20 Interrogation of János Kádár, 18 May 1951, in L. Varga (ed.) (2001), pp. 218, 220; Farkas, p. 341. The original document was destroyed when Kádár was in power.
21 Farkas, p. 349.
22 Shawcross (1974), p. 72; Paul Ignotus (1972), *Hungary*, p. 218; Kopácsi, pp. 96, 294.
23 Kádár rehearing statement, in L. Varga (ed.) (2001), p. 464; Gyurkó (1985), p. 75; Kanyó, p. 59.
24 Miklós Szabó, 'A jellem és a szerep' (Character and role), *Rubicon* 2000/6, p. 33; Tibor Zinner, interview with the author, Budapest, 23 September 2004; Farkas, p 351.
25 Szász, p. 216; Béla Szász, letter to the author (4 December 1980); Sándor Gáspár, interviewed by Márton Kozák (1989-90), 1956 OHA (no. 220), in Rácz (ed.), p. 175; György Aczél, 1956 OHA interview, in Rácz (ed.), p. 188.
26 Kádár interrogation, 18 May 1951, in L. Varga (ed.) (2001), pp. 219-20. Expletive deleted in original Hungarian.
27 Kádár interrogation, 18 May 1951, in L. Varga (ed.) (2001), pp. 225-6.
28 L. Varga (ed.) (2001), pp. 102-3; Gábor Péter confession, 16 May 1954, in L. Varga (ed.) (2001), pp. 270-1; Farkas, p. 353.
29 Report of investigating committee, 19 May 1951, in L. Varga (ed.) (2001), p. 241.
30 Farkas, p. 353; György Szántó confession, 8 June 1954, and János Kádár's confession in his own hand, 9 July 1951, in L. Varga (ed.) (2001), pp. 272-3, 257-62.
31 Rákosi address to CC, 22 May 1951, in L. Varga (ed.) (2001), p. 251.
32 Huszár (2001), p. 190.
33 Jenő Széll, 1956 OHA interview, in *Rubicon*, 2000/7-8, p. 79; István Kovács, 1956 OHA interview, p. 297; notes of conversation between Soviet ambassador Kiselev and István Kovács, 9 August 1953, in Magdolna Baráth (ed.) (2002), *Szovjet nagyköveti iratok*

Magyarországról 1953-1956 (Documents from the Soviet ambassadors in Hungary), p. 80; see also Huszár (2001), pp. 189-90.

34 George Paloczi-Horvath, *The Undefeated*, pp. 208-9.

35 György Szántó's confession about Haraszti investigation, 8 June 1954, in L. Varga (ed.) (2001), p. 282.

36 Kádár rehearing statement, in L. Varga (ed.) (2001), p. 466; Gyula Kállai, interviewed in László Vitézy film, *A legvidámabb barakk* (The happiest barracks).

37 Gábor Péter confession, 16 May 1954, in L. Varga (ed.) (2001), pp. 270-1.

38 Kanyó, p. 78.

39 Kádár letter to Rákosi, February 1952, in L. Varga (ed.) (2001), pp. 284-8.

40 Kádár letter to István Kovács, 3 April 1956, in L. Varga (ed.) (2001), p. 658; L. Varga (ed.) (2001), p. 114.

41 Kanyó, p. 79; Kádár letter to István Kovács, 3 April 1956, in L. Varga (ed.) (2001), p. 658.

42 Kopácsi, p. 104; Kádár letter to Rákosi, 21 July 1954, in L. Varga (ed.) (2001), p. 642.

43 Kanyó, p.79; Kádár letter to István Kovács, 3 April 1956, in L. Varga (ed.) (2001), p. 658.

44 Kádár letter to Rákosi, 21 July 1954, and to István Kovács, 3 April 1956, in L. Varga (ed.) (2001), pp. 641-2 and 658.

Chapter 6: The Apparat's Pin-up

1 Notes of the Hungarian-Soviet meetings, 13 and 16 June 1953, in Csaba Békés, Malcolm Byrne and János M. Rainer (eds), *The 1956 Hungarian Revolution: A History in Documents*, pp. 14-23.

2 Johanna Granville, 'Imre Nagy, aka "Volodya" – a dent in the martyr's halo?' Cold War International History Project *Bulletin*, Issue 5 (Spring 1995), pp. 28, 34-7.

3 Litván (ed.), p. 27.

4 Kádár letter to István Kovács, 3 April 1956, in L. Varga (ed.) (2001), p. 658.

5 Gerő conversation with Soviet Ambassador Kiselev, 18 February 1954, in Baráth (ed.) (2002), p.141.

6 Gyurkó (1985), p. 77; MK4; Huszár (2001), p. 202.

7 Report by prosecutor Pál Bakos (10 June 1954) and proposal by chief prosecutor Kálmán Czakó (14 June 1954) in L. Varga (ed.) (2001), pp. 437-9, 440-3; Huszár (2001), p. 207; MK5.

8 Kádár memorandum on the Rajk affair, in Rácz (ed.), pp. 47-8.

9 Kádár letter to Rákosi, 21 July 1954, in L. Varga (ed.) (2001), pp. 636-42.

10 Kádár rehearing statement, in L. Varga (ed.) (2001), pp. 464-5, 539.

11 Árpád Pünkösti (2001), *Rákosi: bukása, száműzetése és halála* (Rákosi: Downfall, exile and death), p. 204; MK5.

12 Szász, p.216; Péter Földés, interviewed by András B. Hegedűs and András Kovács (1983, 1988), 1956 OHA (no. 150), in *Rubicon*, 2000, 7/8, p. 80; Éva Bozóky, 1956 OHA interview, in Rácz (ed.), pp. 174-5; Bozóky interview.

13 Pünkösti, (2001), pp. 203-4.

14 Szász, p. 216; Gyurkó (1985), pp. 84-5; Kanyó, p. 93; Kádár letter to PB, 16 May 1955, in L. Varga (ed.) (2001), p. 652.

15 MK5.

16 Ernő Lakatos, interview with the author, Budapest, 12 December 2002; Huszár (2001), p. 234.

17 Mária letter to Kádár, 4 November 1954, in Huszár (ed.) (2002), p. 688.

18 Kádár letter to Mária, 30 November 1955, in Huszár (ed.) (2002), pp. 702-3.

19 Kádár letters to Mária 4 November 1954 and 2 February 1955, in Huszár (ed.) (2002), pp. 688-90 and 698-9.

20 MK1.

21 Szász, pp. 216-8; MK3.

22 Kádár letter to Rákosi, 11 November 1954, in L. Varga (ed.) (2001), pp. 645-50.

23 Jenő Széll, 1956 OHA interview, in Rácz (ed.), p. 176; Huszár (2001), p. 228.

[24] Miklós Vásárhelyi, 1956 OHA interview, in Rácz (ed.), p. 175.
[25] Rákosi and Hegedüs conversation with Andropov, 29 April 1956, in Éva Gál et al. (eds), *A "Jelcin-Dosszié", Szovjet dokumentumok 1956-ról (The 'Yeltsin Dossier': Soviet Documents about 1956)*, pp. 23-4; Kádár letter to PB, 16 May 1955, in L. Varga (ed.) (2001), pp. 651-2.
[26] György Aczél, 1956 OHA interview, in Rácz (ed.), p. 175; Henrik Vass, interviewed by Márton Kozák (1987-88), 1956 OHA (no. 100), in *Rubicon*, 2000/7-8, p. 80; István Eörsi, *Emlékezés a régi szép időkre* (Memories of the good old days), pp. 18-19.
[27] Kanyó, p. 94.
[28] Kopácsi, p. 103.
[29] János M. Rainer (1999), *Nagy Imre: 1953-1958*, pp. 168, 187; Gyula Háy, *Született 1900-ban (Born 1900)*, p. 398.
[30] Imre Pozsgay, first interview with the author, Budapest, 24 June 2002.
[31] Miklós Vásárhelyi, 1956 OHA interview, in Rácz (ed.), p. 175.
[32] Jenő Széll, 1956 OHA interview, in Rácz (ed.), pp. 175-6.
[33] György Aczél, 1956 OHA interview, in Rácz (ed.), p. 175.
[34] L. Varga (ed.) (2001), pp. 131-2; Huszár (2001), pp. 242-7.
[35] Mátyás Rákosi, *Visszaemlékezések 1944-1956* (Memoirs 1944-1956), volume 2, p. 1000.
[36] Jenő Széll, 1956 OHA interview, in Rácz (ed.), p. 176.
[37] Kádár letter to István Kovács, 3 April 1956, in L. Varga (ed.) (2001), pp. 659-60; Rákosi conversation with Andropov, 18 April 1956, in Baráth (ed.) (2002), p. 276.
[38] Paloczi-Horvath, pp.272-5; Shawcross (1974), pp.77-8.
[39] Hegedüs (1986), p. 104; Kopácsi, p. 261; Jenő Széll, 1956 OHA interview, in Rácz (ed.), p. 175.
[40] Kádár testimony to the Kovács committee, 23 April 1956, in L. Varga (ed.) (2001), pp. 663-4.
[41] L. Varga (ed.) (2001), p. 136; Andropov conversations with Rákosi (6 May 1956), Kovács (7 May 1956) and Gerő (11 May 1956) in Baráth (ed.) (2002), pp. 282-5, 286-91, 295-8.
[42] Rákosi conversation with Andropov, 6 May 1956, in Baráth (2002), p. 284; Rákosi and Hegedüs conversation with Andropov, 29 April 1956 in Gál et al., pp. 23-4.
[43] Suslov report to Moscow, 13 June 1956, in Vyacheslav Sereda and Alexander Stikalin (eds), *Hiányzó lapok 1956 történetéből* (Missing pages from the history of 1956), pp. 21-4; Jenő Széll, 1956 OHA interview in Rácz (ed.), p. 175.
[44] Andropov telegram, 10 July 1956, in Baráth (ed.) (2002), p. 323.
[45] There are differing interpretations as to where and when the decision was taken to remove Rákosi; see, for example, Pünkösti (2001), pp. 399-401, L. Varga (ed.) (2001), p. 143 and Huszár (2001), pp. 265-8.
[46] Andropov report of 13 July meeting, in Sereda and Stikalin (eds), pp. 47-8.
[47] Andropov report of Kádár-Mikoyan meeting, 14 July 1956, in Sereda and Stikalin (eds), pp. 49-56.
[48] Pünkösti (2001), pp. 425-8.
[49] Pünkösti (2001), p. 412.
[50] Andropov conversations with Hegedüs (18 September 1956) and with Kovács (20 September 1956), in Baráth (ed.) (2002), pp. 348-52, 353-9; Andropov conversation with Gerő, 2 September 1956, in Sereda and Stikalin (eds), pp. 77-80; Huszár (2001), pp. 284-7.
[51] András Kovács, interviewed by István Lugossy (1992), 1956 OHA (no. 241), in *Rubicon*, 2000/7-8, p. 82.
[52] Tibor Méray, *Thirteen days that shook the Kremlin*, pp. 54-5.
[53] Kádár letters to Mária, 13, 21 and 27 September 1956, in Huszár (ed.) (2002), pp. 703-4, 707, 709-10.
[54] Szász, p. 235.
[55] Andropov conversation with Gerő and Hegedüs, 23 July 1956, in Baráth (ed.) (2002), p. 327; Hegedüs (1986), p. 210; Litván (ed.), p. 50; Huszár (2001), p. 296.
[56] Ferenc Váli, cited in Shawcross (1974), p. 286.

Chapter 7: Our Glorious Uprising

[1] Paul E. Zinner (1962), *Revolution in Hungary*, p. 244; Hegedüs (1986), p. 217. Much of the chronology in this chapter draws on Békés et al.; Julianna Horváth and Zoltán Ripp (eds), *Ötvenhat és a hatalom (October '56 and the authorities)*; and on the accounts given on the website of the 1956 Institute, www.rev.hu/history_of_56/naviga/index.htm

[2] György Kövér, *Losonczy Géza*, pp. 266-9; Sándor Revész (1999), *Egyetlen élet: Gimes Miklós története (A Singular Life: The Story of Miklós Gimes)*, p. 299.

[3] Kövér, p. 269, n. 24; András B. Hegedűs, 'The Petőfi Circle: The Forum of Reform in 1956' in Terry Cox (ed.), *Hungary 1956 – Forty Years On*, p. 128; László Gyurkó (2001), *A bakancsos forradalom (The foot-soldiers' revolution)*, p. 35.

[4] Zoltán Ripp, 'A pártvezetés végnapjai' (The last days of the party leadership) in Horváth and Ripp (eds), p. 173; Méray, p.71.

[5] Ripp in Horváth and Ripp (eds), p. 180; Kopácsi, pp. 121-3.

[6] Gyurkó (1985), p. 90.

[7] Váli, pp. 268-9; Hegedüs (1986), pp. 219-20.

[8] I am grateful to George Schöpflin for pointing out Nagy's speedy adjustment to me.

[9] Hegedüs (1986), pp. 223-5; Jenő Györkei and Miklós Horváth (cds), *Soviet Military Intervention in Hungary 1956*, pp. 11-13.

[10] Ripp in Horváth and Ripp (eds), pp. 194-5, 204-5; Gyurkó (2001), p. 86; Ágnes Ságvári, *Mert nem hallgathatok* (Because I cannot remain silent), pp. 86-8.

[11] MK6.

[12] Report by Mikoyan and Suslov, 24 October 1956, in Gál et al., pp. 47-9; Méray, pp. 105-6.

[13] Ripp in Horváth and Ripp (eds), p. 213.

[14] László Varga (ed.) (1989), *A forradalom hangja* (Voice of the revolution), pp. 54-5.

[15] Békés et al. (eds), pp. 196-7; Györkei and Horváth (eds), pp. 36-40.

[16] Report by Mikoyan and Suslov, 25 October 1956, in Gál et al., pp. 50-1; Hegedüs (1986), pp. 235-6; Gyurkó (2001), pp. 147-50, summarises the conflicting evidence.

[17] For differing eye-witness accounts, see Hegedüs (1986), pp. 235-6, and György Marosán (1989a), *A tanúk még élnek* (The witnesses still live), pp. 76-7. For differing interpretations, see Ripp in Horváth and Ripp (eds), pp. 22-4 , Gyurkó (2001), pp. 147-50, and Rainer (1999), pp. 259-60.

[18] L. Varga (ed.) (1989), pp. 71-2.

[19] Report by Mikoyan and Suslov, 26 October 1956, in Békés et al. (eds), pp. 237-9.

[20] Donáth (1992), p. 108; Kövér, pp. 274-5; Donáth and Losonczy letter to PB, 26 October 1956, in Horváth and Ripp (eds), p. 140.

[21] Hegedüs (1986), p. 242; Donáth (1992), p. 110.

[22] Report by Mikoyan and Suslov, 26 October 1956, in Békés et al. (eds), pp. 237-9.

[23] CC, 26 October 1956, in Horváth & Ripp (eds), pp. 50-81.

[24] Report by Mikoyan and Suslov, 26 October 1956, in Békés et al. (eds), pp. 237-9.

[25] Report by Mikoyan and Suslov, 26 October 1956, in Békés et al. (eds), p. 238.

[26] Hegedüs (1986), pp. 232-3.

[27] Report by Mikoyan and Suslov, 27 October 1956, in Békés et al. (eds), pp. 251-2..

[28] Report by Mikoyan and Suslov, 27 October 1956, in Békés et al. (eds), p. 252.

[29] Rainer (1999), p. 276 and n. 33; Ripp in Horváth and Ripp (eds), pp. 277-9.

[30] Report by Mikoyan and Suslov, 27 October 1956, in Békés et al. (eds), p. 252.

[31] PB, 28 October 1956, and Soviet Presidium of same day, in Békés et al. (eds), pp. 254, 266.

[32] PB, 28 October 1956, in Békés et al. (eds), pp. 253-61.

[33] Revész (1999), p. 313.

[34] PB, 28 October 1956, in Békés et al. (eds), especially pp. 258-61; Hegedüs (1986), pp. 239-41.

[35] Kovrig, p. 306.

[36] MK6.

[37] Report by Mikoyan and Suslov, 29 October 1956, in Gál et al., pp. 60-1.

[38] Temporary Central Committee meeting, 11 November 1956, in Békés et al. (eds), p. 408.

[39] L. Varga (ed.) (1989), p. 229.

[40] Méray, p. 168; L. Varga (ed.) (1989), p. 280.

[41] Per Olaf Csongovai, interviewed by László Eörsi (1992), 1956 OHA (no. 420), in Rácz (ed.), pp. 176-7.

[42] MK6.

[43] Méray (pp. 163-5) reports this as fact. Warsaw Pact withdrawal was certainly being discussed on 31 October: see Nagy speech outside Parliament (L. Varga (ed.) (1989), pp. 292-3) and inner cabinet meeting that morning (in Békés et al. (eds), pp. 314-5).

[44] Kopácsi, p.179. He gives a date of 30 October, but Mikoyan and Suslov left Budapest on the 31st.

[45] Temporary CC meeting, 11 November 1956, in Békés et al. (eds), p. 410.

[46] Miklós Vásárhelyi 1956 OHA interview, in Rácz (ed.), pp. 177-8; Gyurkó, (2001), p. 378.

[47] Willman cable to Warsaw, 1 November 1956, in Békés et al. (eds), pp. 326-7.

[48] Gyurkó (1985), p. 99.

[49] Jenő Széll, Szilárd Ujhelyi, 1956 OHA interviews, in Rácz (ed.), p. 177.

[50] Jenő Széll, 1956 OHA interview, in Rácz (ed.), p. 177.

[51] CPSU CC Presidium meeting (Kádár and Münnich present), 2 November 1956, in Békés et al. (eds), p. 338.

[52] Miklós Vásárhelyi, 1956 OHA interview, in Rácz (ed.), pp. 177-8.

[53] Péter Földés, 1956 OHA interview, in *Rubicon* 2000/7-8, p. 84.

[54] Shawcross (1974), pp. 83-4.

[55] Soviet Presidium meeting (Kádár and Münnich present), 2 November 1956, in Békés et al. (eds), pp. 338-9; Gyurkó (2001), p. 382.

[56] Cabinet meeting, 1 November 1956; Andropov report, 1 November 1956: in Békés et al. (eds), pp. 328-9, 330-1.

[57] György Heltai interview with an American journalist, 12 December 1956; reproduced in *The Hungarian Quarterly* 37, no. 142 (1996), pp. 42-53. See also György Heltai, interviewed by János Kenedi (1988), 1956 OHA (no. 184), in Rácz (ed.), p. 177.

[58] Andropov report, 1 November 1956, in Békés et al. (eds), p. 331.

[59] L. Varga (ed.) (1989), pp. 370-1.

[60] Gyurkó (2001), pp. 383, 389; Miklós Vásárhelyi, *Beszélgetések Vásárhelyi Miklóssal* (Conversations with Miklós Vásárhelyi) p. 145.

Chapter 8: Whirlwind

[1] Nikita Khrushchev (1970), *Khrushchev Remembers*, p. 418.

[2] Working notes of CPSU CC Presidium meeting, 31 October 1956, in Békés et al. (eds), p. 307.

[3] Working notes of CPSU CC Presidium meeting, 30 October 1956, in Békés et al. (eds), p. 297.

[4] Working notes of CPSU CC Presidium meeting, 31 October 1956, in Békés et al. (eds), p. 308.

[5] Khrushchev (1970), p. 424; Veljko Mićunović, *Moscow Diary*, p. 136; Nyers interview.

[6] Rákosi letter to Khrushchev, 15 December 1956, in Sereda & Stikalin (eds), pp. 196-7.

[7] CPSU CC Presidium meeting, 1 November 1956, in Vyacheslav Sereda & János M. Rainer (eds), *Döntés a Kremlben* (Decision in the Kremlin), pp. 69-74; Mikoyan comments in CPSU CC meeting, 24 June 1957, in Békés et al. (eds), p. 528.

[8] Sándor Herpai, interviewed by László Varga (1988), 1956 OHA (no. 171), and Jenő Széll, 1956 OHA interview, reproduced in Rácz (ed.), p. 178; Gyurkó (2001), pp. 389-90; Huszár (2001), pp. 333-4; Vásárhelyi, p. 145.

[9] Huszár (2001), p. 334, citing an interview with Soviet diplomat Valeri Musatov. György Aczél, 1956 OHA interview, in Rácz (ed.), p.178, mentions a brief Kádár-Andropov discussion without specifying where it took place.

[10] Kádár-Andropov meeting, 3 September 1956, in Baráth (ed.), pp. 343-7.

[11] Huszár (2001), p. 334; there is partial confirmation in Györkei & Horváth (eds), p. 247.

[12] Andropov report to Moscow, 2 November 1956, in Gál et al., pp. 81-2.

[13] Jenő Széll and Péter Földés, 1956 OHA interviews, reproduced in Rácz (ed.), p.178; Vásárhelyi, p. 145; MK 6.

[14] Györkei & Horváth (eds.), pp. 151, 154.

[15] Nikolai Dzhuba, interview in Miklós Kun, 'Birodalmi helytartók' (Imperial Governors), MTV television film 1996. Dzhuba recalled Kádár asking what the comrades would say 'in Szolnok', but Kádár could not have known at this point how he would return to Hungary. See also György Aczél, 1956 OHA interview, in Rácz (ed.), p.178.

[16] János M. Rainer, 'The Road to Budapest, 1956: New Documents on the Kremlin's Decision to Intervene (Part Two)', *The Hungarian Quarterly* 37, no. 143 (1996), pp. 23-4.

[17] CPSU CC Presidium meeting (Kádár and Münnich present), 2 November 1956, in Békés et al. (eds), pp. 336-40.

[18] Mićunović, pp. 132-40. Khrushchev (1970), pp. 420-2.

[19] Kádár speech at CC meeting, 12 April 1989. MOL M f. 4/259 ő.e., in Rácz (ed.), p. 214.

[20] Khrushchev recollections, in Békés et al. (eds), p. 355.

[21] L. Varga (ed.) (1989), pp. 461-3.

[22] Mikoyan comments in CPSU CC meeting, 24 June 1957, in Békés et al. (eds), p. 528.

[23] Khrushchev recollections, in Békés et al. (eds), p. 355.

[24] Working notes (Horváth) of CPSU CC Presidium, 3 November 1956, in Békés et al. (eds), pp. 359-61.

[25] Rákosi letter to Khrushchev, 15 December 1956, in Sereda & Stikalin (eds), pp. 196-7.

[26] Working notes (Malin) of CPSU CC Presidium, 3 November 1956, in Békés et al. (eds), pp. 356-8; Rákosi, Vol. 2, p. 1036; György Aczél, 1956 OHA interview, in Rácz (ed.), p.178; Huszár (2001), p. 341 and p. 401, n. 164; Gyurkó (2001), p. 397.

[27] Working notes (Malin and Horváth) of CPSU CC Presidium, 3 November 1956.

[28] 'New clues about Kádár's whereabouts before 4 November 1956' (Hungarian SR/12, RFE Research, 21 November 1986) (Alfred Reisch), HU-OSA 300/40/5, Box 87; Zinner (1962), p. 337, n. 1; Münnich statement in Paul E. Zinner (ed.) (1956), *National Communism and Popular Revolt in Eastern Europe*, pp. 473-4; Kádár declaration in Gál et al., pp. 89-93.

[29] Györkei and Horváth (eds), pp. 250-52, 259.

[30] L. Varga (ed.) (1989), p. 487.

[31] Rainer (1999), pp. 340-41; Szántó memorandum, in József Kiss, Zoltán Ripp & István Vida (eds), *Top Secret*, p. 228.

[32] Kovács letter to Khrushchev, 10 January 1957, in Gál et al. (eds), p. 158; 'New clues about Kádár's whereabouts before 4 November 1956.'

[33] Marosán (1989a), pp.125-8.

[34] Working notes from CPSU CC Presidium, 4 November 1956, in Békés et al. (eds), pp. 385-6; 6 November pp. 392-4. Notes for meeting of 5 November in Sereda & Rainer (eds), p. 100.

[35] For contradictory accounts of the journey, see Marosán (1989a), pp 128-9, and Gyula Varadi, interviewed by Mrs Miklós Vásárhelyi (1990), 1956 OHA (no. 233), in *Rubicon* 2000/7-8, p. 85.

[36] György Aczél, 1956 OHA interview, in Rácz (ed.), p. 179.

Chapter 9: The Maggots of Counter-Revolution

[1] Sándor Feri ('F.S'), interviewed by Ferenc Kubinyi (1985-86), 1956 OHA (no. 51), in Rácz (ed.), p. 179.

[2] Lakatos interview.

[3] Lakatos interview; MK 7; Andropov telegram to Moscow, 8 November 1956, in Sereda & Stikalin (eds), pp. 143-4; Magdolna Baráth, 'Magyarország a Szovjet diplomáciai iratokban, 1957-1964' (Hungary in Soviet diplomatic documents), in János M. Rainer (ed.) (2003b), *Múlt Századi Hétköznapok* (Daily life in the last century), p. 61.

[4] *Népszabadság*, 12 November 1956. (www.rev.hu/history_of_56/ora5/index.htm)

5 Temporary CC, 11 November 1956 in Karola Némethné Vágyi and Levente Sipos (eds), *A Magyar Szocialista Munkáspárt ideiglenes vezető testületeinek jegyzőkönvei* (Minutes of the temporary leadership bodies of the MSZMP) (volume 1), pp. 25-51. Translation by Csaba Farkas in Békés et al. (eds), pp. 408-17.

6 Serov telegram to Khrushchev, 9 November 1956, in Elena D. Orekhova, Vyacheslav T. Sereda & Alexander S. Stikalin, *Sovietskii Soyuz i vengerskii krizis, 1956 goda: Dokumenty* (The Soviet Union and the Hungarian Crisis in 1956: Documents), pp. 630-32.

7 Ságvári, p. 115.

8 Kádár speech to activists, 13 November 1956, (extracts) in Kiss et al. (eds), pp. 212-21.

9 Andropov telegram to Moscow, 8 November 1956, Gromyko telegram to Kádár via Andropov, 9 November 1956; in Sereda & Stikalin (eds), pp. 143-4, 229-31.

10 Kádár-Soldatić meeting, 16 November 1956, in Kiss et al. (eds), pp. 233-35.

11 Kiss et al. (eds), p. 25, based on communication from György Aczél.

12 Malenkov, Suslov and Aristov telegram, 17 November 1956; in Sereda & Stikalin (eds), p. 236.

13 Temporary Executive Committee (IIB), 23 November 1956 in Vágyi and Sipos (eds), pp. 95-102; Kádár-Vidić meeting, 21 November 1956, in Kiss et al., pp. 269-71.

14 For accounts of the kidnapping, see Judit Ember, *Menedékjog* (Right of asylum).

15 *Népszabadság*, 27 November 1956.

16 Malenkov group report to Moscow. 26 November 1956, in Sereda and Stikalin (eds), p. 181.

17 Levente Sipos, 'A Népszabadság letiltott cikke 1956 novemberében' (*Népszabadság*'s forbidden article in November 1956), *Múltunk*, 1992/1; Rényi interview; Marosán (1989a), p. 151; IIB, 11 December 1956 in Vágyi and Sipos (eds), pp. 249-58.

18 CC, 24 November 1956; in Vágyi and Sipos (eds) pp. 107-17.

19 Report of Hungarian-East German talks, 20 November 1956, RGANI f. 5. opsis 28. delo 395. (Baráth); IIB, 21 November 1956, in Vágyi and Sipos (eds), pp. 71-94.

20 Khrushchev (1970), p. 424.

21 Malenkov group report to Moscow, 26 November 1956, Sereda and Stikalin (eds), p. 181.

22 Malenkov group report to Moscow, 22 November 1956; Sereda and Stikalin (eds), p. 170.

23 IIB, 23 November 1956, in Vágyi and Sipos (eds), pp. 95-106.

24 Note of Malenkov, Suslov and Aristov's talks with Kádár, 1 December 1956, in Orekhova et al. (eds), pp. 711-14; Nikita Khrushchev (1990), *Khrushchev Remembers: The Glasnost Tapes*, pp. 125-6. In his earlier (1970) volume of memoirs, Khrushchev stated that he visited Hungary at around this time, but he was probably confusing this with his visit in January 1957. See János M. Rainer (2003a), *Ötvenhat után* (After '56), p. 40, and n. 5 &6.

25 CC, 2-3 December 1956, in Vágyi and Sipos (eds), pp. 139-236; resolution, pp. 238-46.

26 Baikov telegram to CPSU CC, 28 December 1956, in Békés et al. (eds), pp. 485-86.

27 Czechoslovak minutes of Budapest meeting, 1-4 January 1957, in Békés et al. (eds), pp. 492-93.

28 Rainer (1999),p. 378; Kádár-Zhou meeting in Békés et al. (eds), pp. 496-503.

29 Johanna Granville, *The First Domino: International Decision-making during the Hungarian Crisis of 1956*, pp. 133, 136-7.

30 IIB, 12 February 1957, in Karola Némethné Vágyi and Károly Urbán (eds), *A Magyar Szocialista Munkáspárt ideiglenes vezető testületeinek jegyzőkönvei* (Minutes of the temporary leadership bodies of the MSZMP) (volume 2), pp. 107-36.

31 Temporary CC, 26 February 1957, in Vágyi and Urbán (eds), pp. 157-226.

32 First the first interpretation, see Éva Standeisky, *Az írók és a hatalom* (The writers and the authorities), pp. 254-7; for the second, Melinda Kalmár, *Ennivaló és hozomány: A kora kádárizmus ideológiája* (Food and dowry: the ideology of early Kádárism), pp. 29-37.

33 Kanyó, p. 180.

34 Magdolna Baráth, 'Magyarország és a Szovietunió' (Hungary and the Soviet Union) in János M. Rainer (ed.) (2004), *'Hatvanas Évek' Magyarországon* (Hungary in the '60s), p. 41.

35 IIB, 2 April 1957, in Vágyi and Urbán, pp. 346-65.

[36] Mátyás Szűrös, interviewed by Péter Pál Tóth (1991), 1956 OHA (no. 426), in Rácz (ed.), p. 182.

[37] Ponomarev report to Moscow, 12 March 1957, in Sereda and Stikalin (eds), pp. 260-3.

[38] IIB, 2 April 1957, in Vágyi and Urbán, pp. 346-65.

[39] Békés et al. (eds), p. 369; Gyurkó (1985), p. 107; Peter Unwin, *Voice in the Wilderness: Imre Nagy and the Hungarian Revolution*, p. 7; István Katona, 'A "szentély": Látogatás Kádár János hivatalában' (The 'sanctum': a visit to János Kádár's office') in Rácz (ed.), p. 205.

[40] CC resolution, 5 December 1956, in Vágyi and Sipos (eds), pp. 238-46.

[41] István Huszár second interview with the author, Budapest, 13 December 2002.

[42] PB, 6 August 1957. MOL M-KS 288.f. 5/38 ő.e.

[43] PB, 6 August 1957. MOL M-KS 288.f. 5/38 ő.e.

[44] Iván T. Berend (1990), *The Hungarian economic reforms 1953-1988*, pp. 62-83; William F. Robinson, *The Pattern of Reform in Hungary*, pp. 21-28; Mária Ormos, 'A konszolidáció problémai 1956 és 1958 között' (Problems of consolidation between 1956 and 1958), *Társadalmi Szemle*, 1989/ 8-9, p. 53.

[45] Kádár speech to party conference, 27 June 1957, in János Kádár (1962), *Socialist Construction in Hungary*, p. 78.

[46] Andropov telegram to Khrushchev, 18 December 1956, in Sereda and Stikalin (eds), pp. 185-6; IIB, 17 December 1956 and temporary CC meeting, 28 December 1956, in Vágyi and Sipos (eds), pp. 259-72, 281-300; minutes of Budapest meeting, 1-4 January 1957, in Békés et al. (eds), pp. 489-93.

[47] Temporary CC meeting, 26 February 1957, in Vágyi and Urbán (eds) pp. 157-236; Sándor Kelemen, interviewed by András Körösényi (1988), 1956 OHA (no. 172), in *Rubicon* (2000/7-8), p. 87.

[48] Kalmár, pp. 64-78; Secretariat, 7 September 1957. MOL M-KS 288.f. 7/13 ő.e.

[49] Kádár speech to party conference, 27 June 1957, in Kádár (1962), pp. 89-90.

[50] Expanded CC meeting, 3 July 1957, in Karola Némethné Vágyi et al. (eds), *A Magyar Szocialista Munkáspárt Központi Bizottságának 1957-1958. Évi Jegyzőkönvei*, (Minutes of the Hungarian Socialist Workers' Party Central Committee for the years 1957-1958), p. 32.

[51] Serov telegram to Khrushchev, 9 November 1956, in Orekhova et al. (eds), pp. 630-32.

[52] PB, 10 December 1957. MOL M-KS 288.f.5/54 ő.e.

[53] Sándor M. Kiss, interview with the author, Esztergom, 18 August 2004.

[54] PB, 22 October 1957. MOL M-KS 288.f.5/47 ő.e. For the lack of implementation, see István Bikki, 'A politikai rendőrség újjászervezése és működése' (The reorganisation and workings of the political police), in *Rubicon* 2002/6-7, p. 38.

[55] Ferenc Nezvál, interviewed by Katalin Mérő (1987), 1956 OHA (no. 72), in Rácz (ed.), p.181

[56] PB, 2 July 1957, MOL M-KS 288.f. 5/33 ő.e.; 22 October 1957, MOL M-KS 288.f. 5/47 ő.e.

[57] András Gerő and Iván Pető, *Unfinished Socialism*, p. 15.

[58] Reproduced in Tibor Zinner, *A kádári megtorlás rendszere* (The Kádárist reprisals system), pp. 216-19. For an analysis of the philosophy of the reprisals, see Litván (ed.), pp. 141-8.

[59] IIB, 2 April 1957, in Vágyi and Urbán (eds), pp. 346-65.

[60] Andropov letter to CPSU CC, 26 August 1957, in Békés et al. (eds), pp. 539-40.

[61] Andropov memorandum to CPSU CC, 29 August 1957, in Békés et al. (eds), pp. 541-2.

[62] PB, 16 December 1957. MOL M-KS 288.f. 5/55 ő.e.

[63] CC, 21 December 1957, in Vágyi et al. (eds) pp. 153-68.

[64] PB, 5 February 1958. MOL M-KS 288.f. 5/65 ő.e.

[65] CC, 14 February 1958, in Vágyi et al. (eds) pp. 237-46.

[66] PB, 28 December 1957. MOL M-KS 288.f. 5/59 ő.e. Valeri Musatov, *Predvestniki buri: Politicheskie krizisy v Vostochnoi Evrope* (Harbingers of the storm: political crises in Eastern Europe), p. 97.

[67] CC, 21 December 1957, in Vágyi et al. (eds) pp. 153-68.

[68] See, for example, comments by Géza Revész, Dezső Kiss and Sándor Bórbely; CC, 14 February 1958, in Vágyi et al. (eds) pp. 237-46.

69 See in particular János M. Rainer, 'Hosszu menetelés a csúcsra 1954-1958' (Long road to the top) in Rácz (ed.), pp. 62-8.

70 György Litván in Alajos Dornbach (ed.), *The Secret Trial of Imre Nagy*, p. 167.

71 Rainer (1999), p. 421.

72 PB, 27 May 1958. MOL M-KS 288.f. 5/80 ő.e.

73 Révész (1999), pp. 411-4.

74 Bozóky interview; Sereda and Rainer (eds), pp. 210-11; Békés et al. (eds), p. 394, n. 80.

75 Rainer (1999), pp. 430-1.

76 National Security Council, 19 June 1958; at http://dosfan.lib.uic.edu/ERC/frus/frus58-60x1/03easteur2.html

77 Endre Marton, *The Forbidden Sky*, p. 211; emphasis added.

78 See, among other examples: PB, 2 July 1957. MOL M-KS 288.f. 5/33 ő.e; Nezvál letter to Kádár, 4 September 1957. MOL M-KS 288.f. 47/719 ő.e.

79 PB, 10 December 1957. MOL M-KS 288.f. 5/54 ő.e.

80 Békés et al. (eds), p. 375; Zinner, p. 421; the figure of twenty-six thousand people sentenced is from Zinner interview.

81 Litván (ed.), p. 70.

82 George Konrád (1984), *Antipolitics*, p. 158.

83 Béla Kelen, 1956 OHA interview, in Rácz (ed.), p.183.

84 Kádár-Gorbachev meeting, 25 September 1985, in Baráth and Rainer (eds), p. 50; see also Ormos, p. 56.

85 Tibor Huszár, 'A hatalmi gépezet újjáépítése, a represszió túlsúya, a kiigazítás esélye 1956-1960' (The reconstruction of the machinery of power, the predominance of repression, the prospect of reappraisal), in Tibor Huszár and János Szabó (eds), *Restauráció vagy kiigazítás* (Restoration or reappraisal), p. 139, n. 151; Tibor Huszár (2003), *Kádár 1957-1989*, p. 79.

Chapter 10: Foundations

1 Révész (ed.)/Aczél, p. 111. For Münnich's early role, see Ságvári, p. 108.

2 Révész (ed.)/Aczél, p. 111; Lakatos interview.

3 Ságvári, p. 125; Kopácsi, p. 260; Révész (ed.)/Aczél, pp. 111-12.

4 Baikov report on conversation with Sándor, 23 September 1957, Gál et al. (eds), pp. 204-06; Révész (ed.)/Aczél, p. 111.

5 Rainer (2003a), pp. 39-72; Khruschev (1970), p. 427. For other accounts, see Kanyó, p. 136, and Ságvári, p. 215.

6 *Népszabadság*, 11 April 1958, HU-OSA 300/40/6, Box 16, 'Kádár János – official'.

7 Marjai interview.

8 Gyurkó interview.

9 Baráth in Rainer (ed.) (2003b), p. 61; Kádár to Suslov, 4 November 1958, MOL M-KS 288.f. 47/721 ő.e.; Kádár to Mária, 23 January 1959 in Huszár (ed.) (2002), pp. 719-21.

10 Fedor Burlatsky, *Khrushchev and the first Russian Spring*, p. 86.

11 Musatov interview; Mátyás Szűrös, interview with the author, Budapest, 10 December 2002; Mátyás Szűrös, 'Kádár és a szovjet vezetés' (Kádár and the Soviet leadership), *Rubicon*, 2000/7-8, p. 95.

12 Dmitri Volkogonov, *The Rise and Fall of the Soviet Empire*, p. 354.

13 Baráth in Rainer (ed.) (2003b), p. 66.

14 Mária to Kádár, 31 October 1958, in Huszár (ed.) (2002), pp. 714-16.

15 Ságvári, p. 124.

16 Kertész/Kádár letters, March-July 1958, in Huszár (ed.) (2002), pp. 739-41.

17 Huszár (ed.) (2002), p. 741, n.1 and pp. 742-6; Huszár (2001), p. 12; MK5.

18 Bognár interview; Gyurkó (1985), p. 5.

19 Iván Pető, 'Változások a változatlanságért' (Change for the sake of no change) in Rácz (ed.), p. 116.

20 Rainer (2003a), p. 79.

[21] Pál Romány, 'A "változatlan agrárpolitika" változásai' (Changes in the 'unchanging agrarian policy') in Rácz (ed.), p. 122.

[22] Henrik Vass and Ágnés Ságvári (eds), *A Magyar Szocialista Munkáspárt határozati és dokumentunai 1956-1962* (Resolutions and documents of the Hungarian Socialist Workers Party), pp. 114-38.

[23] Politburo 3 December 1957. MOL M-KS. 288.f. 5/ 53 ő.e.

[24] Iván T. Berend (1983), *Gazdasági útkeresés 1956-1965* (Search for an economic path), pp. 267-9, 308.

[25] Zsuzsanna Varga *Politika, paraszti érdekérvényesítés és szövetkezetek Magyarországon 1956-1967* (Politics, peasant defence of interests and co-operatives in Hungary 1956-1967 (2001), p. 49; Ferenc Donáth (1980), *Reform and Revolution: Transformation of Hungary's Agriculture 1945-1970*, pp. 281-2.

[26] CC, 5-7 December 1958, in Némethné Vágyi et al. (eds), p. 715; Mátyás Szűrös, 1956 OHA interview, in Rácz (ed.), p.182.

[27] Vass and Ságvári (eds), pp. 222-32.

[28] Baráth in Rainer (ed.) (2003b), p. 74.

[29] PB, 28 October 1958. MOL M-KS 288.f. 5/101 ő.e.

[30] Némethné Vágyi et al. (eds), pp. 684-869.

[31] Vass and Ságvári (eds), pp. 326-37.

[32] Tibor Huszár, *Beszélgetések Nyers Rezsővel* (Conversations wih Rezső Nyers), p. 231 (hereafter Huszár/Nyers).

[33] Martha Lampland, *The Object of Labor*, pp. 179, 189-92.

[34] Berend (1983), pp. 257-59; CC, 6 March 1959; in Anna S. Kosztricz et al. (eds), *A Magyar Szocialista Munkáspárt Központi Bizottságának 1959-1960. évi jegyzőkönyvei* (Minutes of the MSZMP Central Committee 1959-1960), p. 22.

[35] Nigel Swain (1985), *Collective Farms which work?*, p. 30.

[36] CC, 6 March 1959; in Kosztricz et al. (eds), p. 73. The translation is that of Tim Wilkinson in Romsics (1999).

[37] Donáth (1980), pp. 274, 290.

[38] Lampland, p. 195; Berend (1983), pp. 273, 276-7.

[39] Donáth (1980), p. 277; Zs. Varga (2001), pp. 28-9, 39-40.

[40] Zs. Varga (2001), pp. 59-60. CC secret session, 12 February 1960, in Kosztricz et al. (eds), pp. 511-12.

[41] Huszár/Nyers, p. 235, though Nyers attributes the plotting to Stikov's predecessor Gromov (see also n. 48); Baráth in Rainer (ed.) (2003b), pp. 61-2, 73.

[42] Stikov report on meeting with Kádár, 15 August 1959. AVPRF f. 077. opsis 40. papka 204. delo 4. (Baráth).

[43] CC, 22 October 1959, in Kosztricz et al. (eds), p. 317.

[44] CC secret session, 12 February 1960, in Kosztricz et al. (eds), pp. 514-5.

[45] Vass and Ságvári (eds), pp.561-72.

[46] Zs. Varga (2001), pp. 64-5

[47] Stikov reports on meetings with Kádár, 12 October 1959 (RGANI f. 5. opsis 49. delo 198) and 5 March 1960 (AVP RF f. 077. opsis 42. papka 212. delo. 5). (Baráth).

[48] János Radványi, *Hungary and the Superpowers*, p. 168, n. 26; Sándor Gáspar in Vitézy, 'The happiest barracks', though Gáspar attributes the incident to Gromov and places it in early 1958.

[49] Révész (1997), p. 85; András Veres, '"Mi általában nem udvarolunk az iróknak". Az irók és a hatalom a hatvanas évek Magyarországon' ('In general we don't pay court to the writers': The writers and the authorities in 'Sixties Hungary), *Rubicon*, 2004/8-9, pp. 71-81.

[50] Veres, p. 72.

[51] Révész (1997), p. 94.

[52] Gyurkó interview.

[53] Révész (ed.)/Aczél, p. 109.

54 Révész (ed.)/Aczél, p. 115.

55 Kádár letter to Kállai, Kiss and Némes, 24 March 1958; MOL M-KS. 288.f. 47/722 ő.e.

56 István Huszár, first interview with the author, Budapest, 7 December 2001.

57 CC, 25 July 1958, in Némethné Vágyi et al. (eds), p. 494.

58 Kádár/ Kodály letters, September-October 1959, in Huszár (ed.) (2002), pp. 141-7 – translation from *The Hungarian Quarterly* 43, no. 168 (2002), pp. 133-41.

59 Tőkés (1996), p. 68.

60 Vass and Ságvári (eds), pp. 238-68, 276-309.

61 Kalmár, pp. 150-52, Révész (1997), pp. 98-100.

62 Béla Háry in Vitézy, 'The happiest barracks'.

63 PB 22 February 1972. MOL M-KS 288.f. 5/575 ő.e.

64 Éva Standeisky, 'Kádár és az értelmiség' (Kádár and the intellectuals) in Rácz (ed.), pp. 136-40.

65 CC, 30 March 1960; in Kosztricz et al., p. 547.

66 Arkady Shevchenko, *Breaking with Moscow*, pp. 95-100; MK9.

67 *Népszabadság*, 4 October 1960, HU-OSA 300/40/6, Box 16, 'Kádár János – official'; Radványi, p. 93.

68 Vass and Ságvári (eds), p. 474.

69 Zs. Varga (2001), pp. 72-6; Donáth (1980), pp. 294-9.

70 Miklós Szabó, 'Az utolsó népi demokratikus egyházüldözes' (The last people's democratic church persecution) in Sándor Révész (ed.) (2000), *Beszélő évek 1957-1968* (Beszélő Years, 1957-1968), pp. 224-7.

71 Sandor Szerényi, CC secret session, 12 February 1960, in Kosztricz et al. (eds), p. 518.

72 Rainer (2003a), p. 98.

Chapter 11: Khrushchev's Apprentice

1 George Schöpflin, *Politics in Eastern Europe*, pp. 129-30.

2 Levente Sipos, 'Hiányos leltár' (Incomplete inventory), part 1, *Társadalmi Szemle*, 11/1994, pp. 72-3.

3 Rainer (2003a), pp. 113-14.

4 CC, 17 November 1961. MOL M-KS 288.f. 4/44 ő.e.

5 *Népszabadság*, 10 December 1961, HU-OSA 300/40/5, Box 81.

6 Sipos, (1994), part 1, p. 74.

7 Report to CC, 14-16 August 1962. MOL M-KS 288.f. 4/53 ő.e.

8 Sipos, (1994), part 2, *Társadalmi Szemle*, 12/1994, pp. 69-77; CC, 14-16 August 1962. MOL M-KS 288.f. 4 /55 ő.e.

9 Magdolna Baráth, 'Csendes elbocsátások, a felelősség kérdése 1962' (Peaceful dismissals: the question of responsibility 1962), *Rubicon* 2002/6-7, p. 43.

10 PB proposition: CC meeting, 11-12 October 1962. MOL M-KS 288.f. 4/59 ő.e.

11 Lakatos interview; Révész (ed.)/Aczél, p. 111.

12 Marosán letter to CC, 1 September 1962; attachment 2 (b), CC meeting 11-12 October 1962. MOL M-KS 288.f. 4/58 ő.e. Levente Sipos, 'Szakítás. Marosán György és Kádár János' (Split: György Marosán and János Kádár), *Rubicon*, 2004/8-9, pp. 50-1.

13 Marosán letter to Kádár, 1 September 1962; attachment to CC meeting 11-12 October 1962. MOL M-KS 288.f. 4/58 ő.e.

14 Kádár to Marosán, 6 September 1962; attachment to 11-12 October CC.

15 Sipos (2004), pp. 53-4; Karola Némethné Vágyi and Levente Sipos, 'A Marosán-ügy 1962-ben' (The 1962 Marosán affair), *Múltunk*, 1-2, 1994; Kádár-Marosán letters attachments to 11-12 October CC.

16 Huszár first interview ; István Huszár, 'Asszisztáltunk a hibás döntésekhez' (We assisted in wrong decisions – interview with Árpád Pünkösti, *Népszabadság*, 1 February 1991), HU-OSA 300/40/5, Box 87.

17 János Berecz, interview with the author, Budapest, 27 June 2002.

[18] Lakatos interview; Pozsgay first interview.

[19] Marosán letter to CC, 1 September 1962; attachment 2 (b), CC meeting 11-12 October 1962. MOL M-KS 288.f. 4/58 ő.e.

[20] Révész (ed.)/Aczél, p. 112.

[21] HU-OSA 300/40/6, Box 16, 'Kádár János – unofficial/ confidential'.

[22] Paul Lendvai (1998), *Blacklisted: A journalist's life in Central Europe*, pp. 157-58.

[23] Burlatsky, pp. 87-88.

[24] 'Hungarians pick over dictator's tasteless legacy' (Lucy Hooker, *The Guardian*, 20 March 1993); 'For those in search of Communist kitch, auction is place to be (Ernest Beck, *The Wall Street Journal Europe*, March 1993); 'Luxury train of Communist leadership goes capitalist' (AP, 27 April 1994): all HU-OSA 300/40/5, Box 87; Gyurkó (1985), p. 17.

[25] Pozsgay first interview.

[26] Comments by Béla Hári, Károly Németh and Frigyes Puja in Vitézy, 'The happiest barracks'. István Katona, 'Egy korszaknak ad nevet' (He named an age), *Népszabadság*, 7 July 1989, HU OSA 300-40-5, Box 87. For corruption being more prevalent at local level, see Patrick H. O'Neil, *Revolution from Within. The Hungarian Socialist Workers' Party and the Collapse of Communism*, p. 81 and n. 27.

[27] Katona in Rácz (ed.), p. 205; HU-OSA 300-40-6, Box 16. 'Kádár János – unofficial/ confidential'.

[28] Katona in Rácz (ed.), pp. 203-7.

[29] János Berecz, 'Milyennek láttam Kádárt?'(How did I view Kádár?) in Rácz (ed.) p. 190; Burlatsky, p. 88.

[30] Piroska Döme, 'János'. PIL 942.f 2 ő.e.

[31] Kádár report to Eighth Congress, in Kádár (1965), pp. 57, 64.

[32] Kádár report to Eighth Congress, in Kádár (1965), p. 91.

[33] Illyés to Kádár (enclosing Kállai letter), 9 July 1961; Kádár to Illyés, 11 July 1961; in Huszár (ed.) (2002), pp. 189-90.

[34] Kádár report to Eighth Congress; in Kádár (1965), p. 69.

[35] Tőkés (1996), pp. 140-6; O'Neil, p. 40; Stephen White, John Gardner and George Schöpflin, *Communist Political Systems: An Introduction*, p. 141.

[36] Romsics (1999), p. 335.

[37] State Department memorandum of conversation with Radványi on 13 January 1964; Foreign Relations of the United States: Johnson administration, Volume XVII: www.state.gov/www/ about_state/history/vol_xvii/m.html

[38] Csaba Békés, 'Hungary and the Warsaw Pact 1954-89', Parallel History Project on NATO and the Warsaw Pact, www.isn.ethz.ch/php/documents/collection_13/texts/intro.htm#2. (hereafter Békés/PHP).

[39] For different views on the significance of Péter, see Radványi, p. 91 and p. 172, n.4, and Békés/PHP.

[40] NSC meeting, 8 November 1956, in Békés et al. (eds), p. 401.

[41] Radványi, pp. 92-93.

[42] Radványi, pp. 92-93, 110-14.

[43] Kádár report to Eighth Congress, in Kádár (1965), pp. 54-5; Radványi, pp. 115-20, 140-50.

[44] Attila Szakolcai, 'Az amnesztia' in Révész (ed.) (2000), pp. 328-30.

[45] Adrienne Molnár (ed.), *A 'Hatvanas Évek' Emlékezete'* (Memories of the 'Sixties), pp. 55-69; Adrienne Molnár and György Litván, 'Szabadulás után. Az ötvenhatos elítéltek visszailleszkedése' (After release: the readjustment of the condemned '56-ers) in *Rubicon*, 2004/8-9, pp. 36-42; Zsuzsanna Kőrösi and Adrienne Molnár, *Carrying a Secret in my Heart … Children of the Victims of the Reprisals after the Hungarian Revolution in 1956. An Oral History*, pp. 63-9.

[46] Bundy to LBJ, 14 April 1964: see n. 37.

[47] Vass and Ságvári (eds), pp. 238-46.

[48] MK9.

49 'Kölcsönösnek éreztem a rokonszenvet' (I felt that the sympathy was mutual), *Népszabadság*, 8 July 1989. HU-OSA 300/40/5, Box 87.

50 PB, 10 June 1958, in Csaba Szabó, 'Magyarország és a Vatikan' (Hungary and the Vatican) in Rainer (ed.) (2004), p. 74.

51 Szabó in Rainer (ed.) (2004), p. 83.

52 Jonathan Luxmoore and Jolanta Babiuch, *The Vatican and the Red Flag*, pp. 113-4.

53 Berend (1990), pp. 116-18.

54 PB, 11 June 1963. MOL M-KS 288.f. 5/304 ő.e.

55 CC, 17 November 1961. MOL M-KS 288.f. 4/44 ő.e; Baráth in Rainer (ed.) (2004), pp. 50-1; HU-OSA 300/40/6, Box 16. 'Kádár János – unofficial/ confidential.'

56 Berend (1990), pp. 89-92, 108-9. László Szamuely, 'The second wave of the mechanism debate and the 1968 economic reform in Hungary', *Acta Oeconomica*, no. 33, 1-2 (1985), p. 44.

57 PB, 6 August 1957. MOL M-KS 288.f. 5/38ő.e.

58 François Fejtő, *A History of the People's Democracies*, pp. 158-60; Baráth in Rainer (ed.) (2003a), pp. 84-5.

59 Berend (1990), pp. 89-90.

60 Rezső Nyers, 'Visszapillantás az 1968-as reformra' (Looking back at the 1968 reform), *Valóság* 31, 8 (1988).

61 Swain (1992), pp. 91-92; György Földes, 'Barátság a felsőfokon. Kádár és Hruscsov' (Friendship at the top. Kádár and Khrushchev) in Rácz (ed.), p. 93.

62 Kádár to Khrushchev, 21 June 1961, in Huszár (ed.) (2002), pp. 188-89.

63 MK9.

64 William F. Taubman, *Khrushchev*, p. 476.

65 Lajos Czinege in Vitézy, 'The happiest barracks'.

66 Földes in Rácz (ed.), p. 93.

67 PB, 22 February 1972. MOL M-KS 288.f. 5/575 ő.e.

68 *Népszabadság*, 4 April 1964; HU-OSA 300/40/5, Box 82.

69 Martin Page and David Berg, *Unpersoned: The Fall of Nikita Sergeyevitch Khruschev*, pp. 142-3; Földes in Rácz (ed.), p. 94.

70 Report by Party and Mass Organisations and Agitation and Propaganda Departments, PB 3 November 1964. MOL M-KS 288.f. 5/344 ő.e.

71 PB, 16 October 1964. MOL M-KS 288.f. 5/346 ő.e.

72 PB, 16 October 1964. MOL M-KS 288.f. 5/346 ő.e.

73 *Népszabadság*, 20 October 1964. HU-OSA 300/40/5, Box 82.

74 HU OSA 300-40-6, Box 16. 'Kádár János – unofficial/ confidential.'

75 Miklós Kun, *Prague Spring – Prague Fall*, pp. 212-13, n.11.

76 Kun, pp. 40, 212-13; Page and Burg, pp. 149-50.

77 PB, 3 November 1964. MOL M-KS 288.f. 5/349 ő.e. Baráth in Rainer (ed.) (2004), p. 53.

78 Csaba Békés, 'Magyar-Szovjet Csúcstalálkozók 1957-1965' (Hungarian-Soviet summit conferences, 1957-1965) in *Évkönyv* (Yearbook) VI, 1956-os Intézet, pp. 147, 165; HU-OSA 300/40/6, Box 16. 'Kádár János – unofficial/ confidential.'

79 Baráth in Rainer (ed.) (2004), pp. 53-5.

80 MK9; Baráth in Rainer (ed.) (2004), p.53.

81 Khrushchev to Kádár, 8 December 1967; Kádár reply and letter to Brezhnev, both 12 January 1968, in Huszár (ed.) (2002), pp. 331-33.

82 Kádár telegram 13 September 1971 and Nina Petrovna reply (undated): MOL M-KS 288.f. 47/750 ő.e.

Chapter 12: Goulash

1 Kádár, speech to Eighth Congress, in Kádár (1965), p. 67. Michael Shafir, 'Eastern Europe' in Martin McCauley (ed.), *Khrushchev and Khrushchevism*, p. 179, n. 13.

2 János Kornai, *Evolution of the Hungarian Economy 1848-1988, Vol. II, Paying the Bill for Goulash-Communism*, pp. 58-61.

3   Henrik Vass (ed.) (1978) [a] *A Magyar Szocialista Munkáspárt határozati és dokumentumai 1963-1966* (Resolutions and documents of the Hungarian Socialist Workers Party), pp. 94-109.

4   Nyers (1988); Nyers interview.

5   Judy Batt (1988), *Economic Reform and Political Change in Eastern Europe*, pp. 130-1; Robinson, p. 85.

6   János Pap, interviewed by Márton Kozák (1987), 1956 OHA (no. 106), in Rácz (ed.), p. 185; Baráth in Rainer (ed.) (2004), p. 55.

7   Robinson, p. 88; Szűrös, 'Kádár and the Soviet leadership.'

8   Musatov interview; Szűrös, 'Kádár and the Soviet leadership.'

9   HU OSA 300-40-6, Box 16, 'Kádár János – unofficial/ confidential'; Genisov report on 24 October 1964 meeting with Kádár, AVP RF f. 077. op. 47. papka 230. gy. 8 (Baráth).

10 György Péteri (2002), 'Purge and patronage: Kádár's counter-revolution and the field of economic research in Hungary, 1957-1958', *Contemporary European History*, Volume 11, Part 1, February 2002.

11 Nyers (1988); Rezső Nyers, 'Kádár és a reformok' (Kádár and the reforms) in Rácz (ed.), pp. 133-5.

12 Huszár first interview.

13 Mátyás Timár, interview with the author, Budapest, 24 October 2003.

14 Iván Pető, 'A gazdaságirányítási mechanizmus és a reform megitélésének változásai a hatvanas évek közepén' (The economic mechanism and changing assessments of reform in the mid-sixties), *Medvetánc* 1986.4 – 1987.1, p. 66; Huszár/Nyers, p. 303.

15 PB, 3 November 1964. MOL M-KS 288.f. 5/349 ő.e.

16 PB, 9 November 1965. MOL M-KS 288.f. 5/379 ő.e.; CC, 25-27 May 1966, MOL M-KS 288.f. 4/80 ő.e.

17 Nyers in Rácz (ed.), p. 135.

18 Nyers (1988).

19 Pető (1986-87), p. 65.

20 PB, 3 May 1966, MOL M-KS 288.f. 5/394 ő.e.

21 Nyers (1988).

22 PB, 29 September 1965. MOL M-KS 288.f. 5/375 ő.e; Nyers (1988).

23 PB, 9 November 1965. MOL M-KS 288.f. 5/379 ő.e.; Csikós-Nagy interview.

24 Nyers interview; CC 18-20 November 1965. MOL M-KS 288.f. 4/76 ő.e; Vass (ed.) (1978) [a], pp. 235-66.

25 HU-OSA 300/40/6, Box 16, 'Kádár János – unofficial/ confidential'.

26 Robinson, p. 82; Tibor Zinner, 'Büntetőjog és hatalom' (Criminal law and power), *Múltunk*, 1998.2, p. 205 n. 91.

27 Miklós Szabó, 'A klasszikus kádárizmus 1960-1968' (Classical Kádárism, 1960-68)', in Rácz (ed.), pp. 80-81.

28 Katona in Rácz (ed.), p. 206.

29 Szabó in Rácz (ed.), p. 81.

30 Révész (1997), pp. 136-43.

31 PB, 3 May 1966. MOL M-KS 288.f. 5/394 ő.e.

32 CC, 25-27 May 1966. MOL M-KS 288.f. 4/80 ő.e.

33 Nyers in Rácz (ed.), p. 135; PB, 10 May 1966. MOL M-KS 288.f. 5/395 ő.e

34 Földes in Rácz (ed.), p. 106.

35 Gyurkó (1985), p. 139; Imre Pozsgay, third interview with the author, Budapest, 18 February 2004.

36 György Földes (2005), 'Kádár János és az erdélyi magyarság' (János Kádár and the Hungarians of Transylvania), especially pp. 71-5.

37 Fejtő, pp. 272-7.

38 Kalmár, p. 250; Romsics (1999), p. 405.

39 Foreign Ministry proposal to PB, 17 January 1967. MOL M-KS 288.f.5/415 ő.e.

Translation by Andreas Bocz. www.isn.ethz.ch/php/documents/collection_13/docs/translations_12.htm

40 Mihály Ruff, 'A magyar-NSZK kapscolatok 1960-1963' (Hungarian-West German relations, 1960-63), *Múltunk*, 1999.3, p.5.

41 Békés/PHP.

42 PB, 13 February 1967. MOL M-KS 288.f.5/ 417ő.e. Translation by Andreas Bocz, at www.isn.ethz.ch/php/documents/collection_13/docs/translations_13.htm

43 Huszár (2003), pp. 207-8.

44 Hillenbrand report to State Department, 30 November 1967. http://www.state.gov/www/about_state/history/vol_xvii/n.html, document 113; Martin J. Hillenbrand, *Fragments of our time: Memoirs of a diplomat*, p. 252. For his subsequent view, see 'Conversation with Ambassador Házi', Airgram A-396 from US Embassy (Budapest) to Secretary of State; 17 May 1968; 'US policy assessment: Hungary', Airgram A-2 from US Embassy (Budapest) to Secretary of State, 10 January 1969; both unheaded folder; Box 2183 Subject-Numeric Files 1967-69, Political and Defense; RG 59 General Records of the Department of State; NARA.

45 PB, 6 June 1967, MOL M-KS 288.f.5/426 ő.e; PB, 12 December 1967, MOL M-KS 288.f5/441 ő.e.

46 László Ballai, interview with the author, Budapest, 6 December 2001; Timár interview.

47 Jenő Fock, 'A hatalmat szolgalatként értelmezte' (He thought of power as service), *Népszabadság*, 8 July 1989. HU-OSA 300/40/5, Box 87; Huszár second interview.

48 PB, 15 November 1966. MOL M-KS 288.f. 5/409 ő.e.

49 Berend (1990), pp. 171-7.

50 Péter Havas, interviewed by Katalin Máté and Katalin E. Koncz (1983), 1956 OHA, (no. V.109), p. 187; Timár interview.

51 CC, 23-24 November 1967. MOL M-KS 288.f. 4/89 ő.e.

52 Romsics (1999), p. 337.

53 Zsuzsanna Varga, 'Illúziók és realitásokaz új gazdasági mechanizmus történetében' (Illusions and realities in the history of the New Economic Mechanism) in Rainer (ed.) (2004), p. 118.

54 Robinson, p. 108; Romsics (1999), pp. 342-3.

55 Timár interview.

56 MOL M-KS 288.f. 5/441 ő.e; Baráth in Rainer (ed.) (2004), pp. 56-7; János Fekete, interview with the author, Budapest, 13 December 2002.

57 CC, 23-24 November 1967. MOL M-KS 288.f. 4/ 89 ő.e.

Chapter 13: 1968: 'But You Know Them, Don't You?'

1 István Vida, 'János Kádár and the Czechoslovak Crisis of 1968', *The Hungarian Quarterly* 35, no. 135 (1994), p. 108; William Shawcross (1990), *Dubček*, p. 118; Dubček letter to Kádár, 18 September 1987, in Huszár (ed.) (2002), pp. 662-6.

2 Kádár report to PB of 23 January on his meeting with Dubček, on 20 January 1968, in Kanyó, pp. 223-9.

3 Alexander Dubček, *Hope Dies Last*, p. 133; 'János Kádár's Report to the HSWP Politburo on His Meetings with Alexander Dubček, January 20, 1968 (Excerpts)' in Jaromír Navrátil et al. (eds), *The Prague Spring '68*, p. 41, n. 12; Kieran Williams, *The Prague Spring and its aftermath*, p. 65, n. 13.

4 Kádár report on 4 February 1968 meeting, in Kanyó, pp. 229-31; Tibor Huszár, *1968: Prága, Budapest, Moszkva* (1998[a]), p. 23.

5 Williams, pp. 63-70; Zdeněk Mlynář, *Night Frost in Prague*, pp. 101-4.

6 Kun, pp. 221-2.

7 V.K. Volkov, 'A szovjet pártokrácia és az 1968-as prágai tavasz' (The Soviet partyocracy and the 1968 Prague Spring), *Társadalmi Szemle*, 1995/1, p. 74.

8 Navrátil et al. (eds), p. 81.

9 Huszár (1998[a]), pp. 26-33; Kun, pp. 223-5; Dubček, p. 133; Révész (ed.)/Aczél, p. 114.

[10] 'Stenographic account of the Dresden meeting, March 23, 1968' (excerpts), in Navrátil et al. (eds), pp. 64-72; Kádár account to PB of meeting, in Kanyó, pp. 231-35; Williams, pp. 71-2; Huszár (1998[a]), pp. 50-9; Vida, pp. 110-12.

[11] 'Minutes of the secret meeting of the 'five' in Moscow, May 8, 1968 (excerpts)', in Navrátil et al. (eds), p. 138.

[12] 'Minutes of the secret meeting of the 'five' in Moscow, May 8, 1968 (excerpts)', in Navrátil et al. (eds), pp. 132-43; Huszár (1998[a]), pp. 84-91, drawing on Kádár account to PB of 14 May 1968.

[13] Huszár (1998[a]), pp. 114-19, 130; Kun, pp. 227-9 and p. 229 n. 74.

[14] Kun, pp. 230-1; Huszár (1998[a]), pp. 144-5.

[15] For different interpretations, see Kun, p. 231, Huszár (1998[a]), p. 145.

[16] Huszár (1998[a]), pp. 152-3.

[17] Révész (ed.)/Aczél, p. 114.

[18] For some indications of Fock's attitude, see Tőkés (1996), p. 52, Williams, p. 110.

[19] 'Feljegyzés Kádár János és J.V. Andropov 1968 december 6-7-i beszélgetésről' (Notes of the December 6-7 1968 conversation between János Kádár and Y.V. Andropov) in *Társadalami Szemle*, 1995/1, p. 89; Williams, pp. 92-6; Vida, pp.114-15; Huszár (1998[a]), pp. 146-57.

[20] Dubček, p. 162; 'Transcript of the Warsaw meeting, July 14-15, 1968 (excerpts)', in Navrátil et al. (eds), pp. 215-7; Kádár report to CC, 7 August 1968, and Fock recollections in Kanyó, pp. 238-40, 246; Huszár (1998[a]), pp. 159-64.

[21] Kádár report to CC, 7 August 1968, in Kanyó, p. 240; Ervin Weit, *At the Red Summit*, pp. 211, 213.

[22] 'Transcript of the Warsaw meeting, July 14-15, 1968 (excerpts), in Navrátil et al. (eds), pp. 212-33; Weit, p. 201.

[23] Shelest diary, in Kun, p.123; Weit, p. 209.

[24] Kádár report to CC, 7 August 1968, in Kanyó, p. 243; 'Notes of Kádár-Andropov conversation', p. 92.

[25] Kanyó, pp. 219-20.

[26] Huszár (1998[a]), pp. 180-2; Kádár report to CC, 7 August 1968, in Kanyó, pp. 240-1.

[27] Kun, pp. 72-3 and n. 13; Huszár (1998[a]), pp. 154-8, 206.

[28] Williams, pp. 120-1, Navrátil et al. (eds), p. 187.

[29] Kun, pp. 71-3, 125-6.

[30] Kun, p. 233; Navrátil et al. (eds), p. 277 n. 103; Vida, p. 118; Huszár (1998[a]), p. 194 n. 50.

[31] Huszár (1998[a]), pp. 203-4; Williams, pp. 120-1; Navrátil et al. (eds), pp. 187-8.

[32] Williams, p. 102.

[33] Mlynář, pp. 155-7.

[34] Kádár report to CC, 7 August 1968, in Kanyó, pp. 237-46; excerpts in Navrátil et al. (eds), pp. 331-2; Huszár (1998[a]), pp. 230-41.

[35] Shelest diary in Kun, p. 127; Navrátil et al. (eds.), pp. 324-5; Huszár (1998[a]), p. 243.

[36] 'János Kádár's report on Soviet-Hungarian talks at Yalta, August 12-15, 1968', in Navrátil et al. (eds), pp. 360-2; Huszár (1998[a]), pp. 251-8.

[37] Kanyó, p. 219.

[38] Summary of Dubček-Kádár meeting, 17 August 1968, in Navrátil et al. (eds), pp. 370-2; Dubcek, p. 173; Huszár (1998[a]), p. 258, n. 113; Mlynář, p. 157.

[39] Volkov, p. 82.

[40] 'Notes of Kádár-Andropov conversation', p. 87, n. 19; 'Minutes of the First Post-Invasion Meeting of the 'Warsaw Five' in Moscow, August 24, 1968, in Navrátil et al. (eds), pp. 474-6; Huszár (1998[a]), pp. 272-4.

[41] Williams, p. 155; 'Stenographic account of the meeting of the 'Warsaw Five' in Moscow, September 27, 1968 (excerpts), in Navrátil et al. (eds), p. 507.

[42] Dubček letter to Kádár, 18 September 1987, and Kádár letter to Mátyás Szűrös and Géza Kótai, 19 October 1987, in Huszár (ed.[a]) (2002), pp. 662-7; Kádár conversation with Gorbachev, 25 September 1985, in Rainer and Baráth (eds), p. 48; Dubček, p.173.

43 'Notes of Kádár-Andropov conversation', pp. 86-94.
44 Dubček, pp. 178-9.
45 Kanyó, p. 221.

Chapter 14: Crisis of Confidence

1 Csikós-Nagy interview.
2 Kádár notes in first two cases, 26 January and 3 February 1971; MOL M-KS 288.f. 47/750 ő.e.; other cases MOL M-KS 288.f. 47/751 ő.e.
3 Kádár to Biszku and Aczél, 10 June 1970. MOL M-KS 288.f.47/748 ő.e.
4 Ignác Romsics (2003), *Volt egyszer egy rendszerváltás* (Once there was a regime change), p. 159.
5 Tőkés (1996), p. 53.
6 Révész (1997), pp.166-69. George Gomori, 'Hungarian and Polish attitudes on Czechoslovakia, 1968' and Rudolf L. Tőkés, 'Hungarian Intellectuals' Reaction to the Invasion of Czechoslovakia', in E.J. Czerwinski and Jaroslaw Piekalkiewicz (eds), *The Soviet Invasion of Czechoslovakia and its effects on Eastern Europe*.
7 Révész (1997), pp. 219-20.
8 Kádár to Sándor and CC Secretaries, 9 June 1970. MOL M-KS 288.f. 47/748 ő.e.; Miklós Vásárhelyi, 1956 OHA interview in Rácz (ed.), p. 186; Bozóky interview.
9 Robinson, p. 231.
10 Huszár/Nyers, p. 310; Tőkés (1996), pp. 259-60.
11 Robinson, pp. 226-7; Attila Urbán, 'Kádár politikai rendőrsége' (Kádár's political police) in *Rubicon*, 2002/6-7, pp. 58-9.
12 Swain (1992), p. 117; Berend (1990), pp. 172-6, 194-200; Nyers (1988).
13 Károly Attila Soós, 'Béralku és "sérelmi politika"' (Wage bargaining and 'grievance politics'), *Medvetánc*, 1984. 2-3.
14 Tőkés (1996), p. 106.
15 Nyers (1988). See also Szamuely, p. 63.
16 Kádár letter to Fock, Apró, Fehér and CC Secretaries, 16 October 1970. MOL M-KS 288.f. 47/748 ő.e.
17 Kádár (1974), p. 270.
18 Mátyás Szűrös, 1956 OHA interview, in Rácz (ed.), p. 183. 'Views of Party First Secretary Kádár on Cardinal Mindszenty', Telegram 665 from US Embassy (Budapest) to Secretary of State; 1 December 1967; folder SOC 12-1 HUNG; Box 3071; Central Foreign Policy Files 1967-69, Social; RG 59 General Records of the Department of State; NARA.
19 Árpád Pünkösti (2001), *Rákosi: Bukása, száműzetése és halála* (Rákosi: Downfall, exile and death), pp. 516-57; Gábor Murányi, 'The Plotter's Field' in *The Hungarian Quarterly* 37, no. 141 (1996), pp. 100-3.
20 Gábor Adriányi, *A Vatikán keleti politikája és Magyarország 1939-1978: A Mindszenty-ügy* (The Vatican's Eastern policy and Hungary 1939-78: The Mindszenty affair), pp. 84-86. 'Hungarian-Vatican relations', Telegram 648 from US Embassy (Budapest) to Secretary of State; 21 April 1971; folder POL 31-1 HUNG-US; Box 2354 Subject-Numeric Files 1970-73, Political and Defense; RG 59 General Records of the Department of State; NARA. György Majtényi and Orsolya Ring (eds), *Közel-Múlt* (The Near Past), pp. 20-35.
21 Memorandum from Comrade Miklós, 7 July 1971. MOL M-KS 288.f. 47/751 ő.e.
22 István Mészáros, *Mindszenty és az 'Ostpolitik'* (Midzenty and Ostpolitik) p. 159.
23 Mészáros, pp. 200-8; József Mindszenty, *Memoirs*, pp. 232-47.
24 Csaba Békés, 'Magyar külpolitika a szovjet szövetségi rendszerben 1968-1989' (Hungarian foreign policy in the Soviet al.liance system), in Ferenc Gazdag and László J. Kiss (eds), *Magyar külpolitika a 20. Században* (Hungarian foreign policy in the twentieth century) pp. 144-7; Békés/PHP.
25 PB 13 July 1971, MOL M-KS 288f. 5/ 559 ő.e.; Nyers interview.
26 Huszár/Nyers, pp. 327, 346; György Földes, 'Kötélhúzás felsőfokon. Kádár és Brezsnyev' (Tug of war at the top. Kádár and Brezhnev) in Rácz (ed.), p. 110; Musatov interview.

[27] András Hegedüs, 'A nagyvállalatok és a szocializmus' (Large companies and socialism), *Közgazdasági Szemle*, January 1984; Erzsébet Szalai, 'A reformfolyamat új szakasza és a nagyvállalatok' (The new reform era and large companies) *Valóság*, May 1982.

[28] Pozsgay third interview; Huszár/Nyers, p. 355.

[29] Pozsgay third interview.

[30] István Katona in Vitézy, 'The happiest barracks'; PB, 16 May 1972. MOL M-KS 288.f. 5/581 ő.e.

[31] PB, 27 July and 7 September 1971. MOL M-KS 288.f. 5/560 ő.e.; MOL M-KS 288.f. 5/563 ő.e.

[32] PB, 16 November 1971. MOL M-KS 288.f. 5/568 ő.e.

[33] György Földes (1995), *Az eladósodás politikatörténete* (The political history of indebtedness), p. 65.

[34] Musatov interview.

[35] Record of Brezhnev call on 7 February 1972. MOL M-KS 288.f. 47/752 ő.e.

[36] Musatov interview; Szűrös, 'Kádár and the Soviet leadership.'

[37] Kádár report (dated 18 February) and PB, 22 February 1972. MOL M-KS 288.f. 5/575 ő.e.

[38] PB, 22 February 1972. MOL M-KS 288.f 5/575 ő.e.

[39] István Horváth, interview with the author, Budapest, 22 October 2003.

[40] PB, 16 May 1972. MOL M-KS 288.f. 5/581 ő.e.

[41] Kádár letter to PB, 10 May 1972; in PB, 18 May 1972. MOL M-KS 288.f. 5/581(1) ő.e.

[42] Huszár (2003), p. 237.

[43] Révész (ed.)/Aczél.

[44] Horváth interview.

[45] PB, 18 May 1972. MOL M-KS 288.f. 5/581 (1); Béla Biszku in Vitézy,'The happiest barracks.'

[46] PB, 22 May 1972. MOL M-KS 288.f. 5/581 (2) ő.e.

[47] CC, 14-15 June 1972. MOL M-KS 288.f. 4/117 ő.e.; PB, 27 June 1972. MOL M-KS 288.f. 5/584 ő.e.; Record of Brezhnev phone call, 18 July 1972. MOL M-KS 288.f. 47/752 ő.e.

[48] PB, 19 May 1972. MOL M-KS 288.f. 5/581 (1) ő.e.

[49] Donáth to Kádár, 25 May, Déry to Kádár 26 May 1972; Kádár replies both dated 14 June 1972. MOL M-KS 288.f. 47/754 ő.e.

[50] Kádár speech, 25 May 1972, reprinted as 'János Kádár: Reflections at sixty', *New Hungarian Quarterly*, No. 48, winter 1972. See also Kádár (1974), pp. 394-404.

[51] Révész (1997), p. 113.

Chapter 15: A Worker's State

[1] Révész (ed.)/Aczél, p. 121; Katona in Rácz (ed.), p. 206.

[2] Kádár talks with Soviet ambassador Pavlov, 6 September, 9 October and 13 November 1972; MOL M-KS 288.f. 47/752 ő.e.; Földes in Rácz (ed.), p. 111.

[3] CC, 14-15 November 1972. MOL M-KS 288.f. 4/119 ő.e.

[4] Földes in Rácz (ed.), p. 111; Note (21 November 1972) of Brezhnev call to Kádár. MOL M-KS 288.f. 47/752 ő.e.

[5] Nyers (1988); Berend (1990), p. 209. Resolution in Henrik Vass (ed.) (1978) [b], *A Magyar Szocialista Munkáspárt határozati és dokumentumai 1971-1975* (Resolutions and documents of the Hungarian Socialist Workers Party), pp. 369-94.

[6] CC, 14-15 November 1972. MOL M-KS 288.f. 4/119 ő.e; Swain (1992), pp.123-8.

[7] Péter Havas, 1956 OHA interview, p. 181; Berend (1990), pp. 214-30.

[8] Révész (1997), pp. 190-2, 202-6; Éva Standeisky, 'Egység és megosztottság a Magyar Szocialista Munkáspártban' (Unity and division in the Hungarian Socialist Workers' Party), *Rubicon* 1998/1, pp. 31-2.

[9] Pozsgay third interview; Révész (ed.)/Aczél, pp. 119-20; Tőkés (1996), p. 244.

[10] Ballai interview.

[11] Tőkés (1996), pp. 172-3.

12 Horváth interview.

13 CC, 19-20 March 1974. MOL M-KS 288.f. 4/125 ő.e.

14 György Konrád, interview with the author, Budapest, 29 November 2004; Révész (1997), pp. 230-1.

15 Memorandum of Kádár-Brezhnev telephone conversation, 7 June 1973. MOL M-KS 288.f. 47/755 ő.e.

16 György Péteri, 'Pirruszi győzelem. A 'MEGÉV-ügy' és a politikai stilus változása a hosszú hatvanas években' (Pyrrhic victory: The MEGÉV affair and the changing political style during the long 'Sixties) in Rainer (ed.) (2004), pp. 318-38. Huszár/Nyers, pp. 324-6.

17 Révész (1997), pp. 219-20.

18 Csikós-Nagy interview; Huszár/Nyers, pp. 366-7.

19 Timár interview.

20 Huszár (2003), p. 250.

21 Pozsgay third interview; Huszár/Nyers, pp. 365-8; Huszár (2003), p. 253; Révész (1997), pp. 220, 223.

22 CC, 19-20 March 1974. MOL M-KS 288.f. 4/125 ő.e; Musatov interview.

23 Huszár/Nyers, p. 368; Fock, 'He thought of power as service'; Kádár letter to Komócsin, 1 April 1974, MOL M-KS 288.f. 47/757 ő.e.

24 CC, 19-20 March 1974. MOL M-KS 288.f. 4/125 ő.e.

25 Horváth interview.

26 Memorandum of Kádár-Brezhnev phone conversation, 9 April 1974, and of Kádár-Brezhnev talks, 3 August 1974; MOL M-KS 288.f. 47/757 ő.e. Gyula Horn, interview with the author, Budapest, 18 August 2004.

27 PB, 28 July 1977. MOL M-KS 288.f. 5/723 ő.e.

28 'Memorandum for Comrade János Kádár: Our economic situation and foreign trade prices', 23 December 1974. MOL M-KS 288.f. 47/757 ő.e. Földes in Rácz (ed.), p. 112.

29 Andor László, István Hetényi and Akos Balassa, interviews in Rita Bozzai and Zoltán Farkas (eds), Hitelválság (Credit crunch), pp. 19-21, 95-6, 151-3.

30 Andor László interview in Bozzai and Farkas (eds), pp. 15, 17; Földes (1995), pp. 70-6; Fock, 'He thought of power as service.'

31 'Memorandum for Comrade János Kádár'; Fock, 'He thought of power as service.' István Hetényi interview in Bozzai and Farkas (eds), pp. 96-7.

32 Berend (1990), pp. 218, 220.

33 CC, 19-20 March 1974; MOL M-KS 288.f. 4/125 ő.e.

34 'Speech at Political Academy, 2 September 1974. Kádár on external and domestic policies' (Hungary/13, RFE Research, 24 October 1974). HU-OSA 300/40/5, Box 87.

35 Brezhnev to Kádár 3, February 1975, and Kádár reply, 24 February 1975, in Huszár (ed.) (2002), pp. 463-67; Földes in Rácz (ed.), pp. 112-13; Kádár letter to Brezhnev, 17 July 1978. MOL M-KS 288.f. 47/762 ő.e.; Report to PB on conference of socialist leaders, 24 March 1975. MOL M-KS 288.f. 47/759 ő.e.

36 Huszár/Nyers, p. 410.

37 CC, 15 May 1975, MOL M-KS 288.f. 4/138 ő.e; Nyers (1988).

38 Nigel Swain, 'The evolution of Hungary's agricultural system since 1967' in Paul Hare, Hugo Radice and Nigel Swain (eds), Hungary: A Decade of Economic Reform, pp. 245-46; Berend (1990), pp. 216-17.

39 Földes (1995), pp. 91-101; Ákos Balassa, interview in Bozzai and Farkas (eds), pp. 153-4; Lendvai (1988), p. 74.

Chapter 16: Mitteleuropa Man

1 Helmut Schmidt, Die Deutschen und ihre Nachbarn (The Germans and their neighbours), p. 519.

2 Kádár (1985), pp. 379-82.

3 Békés in Gazdag and Kiss (eds), p. 155.

4 Henry Kissinger, Years of Renewal, p. 644.

[5] CC, 19-20 April 1978. MOL M-KS 288.f. 4/156 ő.e.

[6] Marjai interview.

[7] Telegram 2574 from US Embassy Budapest to Secretary of State, 9 August 1975 (FOIA).

[8] Memorandum on Kádár-Brezhnev meeting, 27 July 1977. MOL M-KS 288.f. 47/761 ő.e.

[9] Lendvai (1988), p. 64. Berecz in Rácz (ed.), p. 192.

[10] Lendvai (1988), p. 65; Philip M. Kaiser, *Journeying Far and Wide*, p. 294.

[11] Kádár (1985), pp. 382-94, 425-30; 'Kádár's visit to Italy and Papal audiences' (Hungarian SR/21, RFE Research, 15 June 1977), 'Kádár's visit to Vienna' (Hungarian SR/46, RFE Research, 14 December 1976). HU-OSA 300/40/5, Box 87.

[12] Berecz, pp. 255-6; François Mitterrand, *L'abeille et l'architecte: Chronique* (The Bee and the Architect: Diaries), Flammarion Paris, 1978, pp. 345-7. HU-OSA 300/40/5, Box 84.

[13] Schmidt, pp. 540-1; 'Kádár visit to FRG ends satisfactorily' (Hungarian SR/24, RFE Research, 14 July 1977); HU-OSA 300/40/5, Box 87.

[14] 'Brandt to Hungary as Kádár's guest: the dialogue continues' (Hungarian SR/8, RFE Research, 4 April 1978); HU OSA 300/40/5, Box 87. Berecz, pp. 266-8.

[15] 'Brandt to Hungary ...'; Berecz, pp. 242, 246, 266-68; Horn interview; Kádár to Brandt, 31 July 1978, in Huszár (ed.) (2002), pp. 512-14. – translation from Tibor Hajdu, 'Yours Sincerely, János Kádár', *The Hungarian Quarterly* 43, no. 168 (2002), p. 128.

[16] Musatov, p. 78.

[17] 'The Wind and the Willow Tree' (RAD Background Report/201 (Hungary), RFE Research, 7 October 1977 (William F. Robinson). HU-OSA 300/40/5, Box 87.

[18] Pozsgay first interview; József Füleki, interview with the author, Budapest, 3 July 1999.

[19] Huszár first interview.

[20] Tőkés (1996), p. 66; Révész (ed.)/Aczél, P. 117.

[21] Huszár first interview; Mátyás Szűrös, 1956 OHA interview, in Rácz (ed.), p. 187.

[22] Huszár first interview; Fejti interview.

[23] Lakatos interview; Lakatos in Rácz (ed.), pp. 198-9.

[24] Berecz interview; Berecz, p. 362.

[25] Zinner interview; the 'prolet-Victorian' phrase I owe to Professor Rudolf Tőkés.

[26] István Hetényi and Ákos Balassa, interviews in Bozzai and Farkas (eds), pp. 97-8, 156.

[27] István Huszár, 'We assisted in wrong decisions'; Földes (1995), pp. 108-10; Marjai interview.

[28] PB, 12 July 1977, MOL M-KS 288.f. 5/722 ő.e; Földes (1995), pp. 112-15.

[29] Földes (1995), p. 115; Memo on Kádár-Brezhnev meeting, 26 July 1977, MOL M-KS 288.f. 47/761 ő.e.; Ferenc Havasi, interview in Bozzai and Farkas (eds), pp. 35-6.

[30] Message of Pope Paul VI to Kádár, 9 June 1977, MOL M-KS 288.f. 47/761 ő.e., reproduced in Huszár (ed.) (2002), pp. 494-5; 'Kádár's visit to Italy and Papal audiences' (Hungarian SR/21, RFE Research, 15 June 1977), HU-OSA 300/40/5, Box 87; Peter Hebblethwaite, *Paul VI: The First Modern Pope*, pp. 686-7.

[31] CC, 19-20 April 1978. MOL M-KS 288.f. 4/156 ő.e; 'Kádár sizes up the national and international situation' (Hungarian SR/15, RFE Research, 14 June 1978), HU-OSA 300/40/5, Box 87; Mészáros, pp. 209-10; Margit Balogh, 'Egyház és egyházpolitika a Kádár-korszakban' (Church and church policy in the Kádár era), *Eszmélet* (34) (1997).

[32] Daniel C. Thomas, *The Helsinki Effect*, pp. 183-6; Christopher Long, interview with the author, Oxford, 15 October 2002, and follow-up e-mail, 21 October 2002.

[33] PB, 11 July 1972. MOL M-KS 288.f. 5/585 ő.e. (including report by Péter and note by Aczél, both dated 6 July).

[34] Puhan memorandum on Rogers-Kádár meeting of 7 July 1972, Department of State telegram 133194 from Secretary of State to US Embassy (Budapest), 22 July 1972; folder ORG 7 S, 7-20-72; Box 176 Subject-Numeric Files 1970-73, Administration; RG 59 General Records of the Department of State; NARA.

[35] Tibor Glant, *A szent korona amerikai kalandja* (The Holy Crown's American adventure), especially pp. 43-9, 58-9. 'The Crown of St. Stephen: Should we return it?', NSC

memorandum (29149), Sonnenfeld to Kissinger, 5 June 1971; folder Hungary (Volume 1); Box 693; NSC Country Files (Europe); Nixon Presidential Materials Staff, NARA.

36 Glant, pp. 75-6; Kaiser, p. 287.

37 Glant, pp. 85, 97-8; Telegram 4421 from US Embassy Budapest to Secretary of State, 22 December 1977; State Department telegram 305669 from Secretary of State to US Embassy Budapest, 23 December 1977 (FOIA).

38 Kaiser, pp. 292-3; Memorandum, Robert King to Zbigniew Brzezinski, 9 January 1978, folder 'Hungary, 1/78 to 1/81', Box 27, National Security Adviser files – country series, JCPL; 'Kádár, a canny but ageing politician' (Henry Brandon, *New York Times*, 27 May 1978) HU-OSA 300/40/5, Box 84.

39 Kaiser, p. 288.

40 Rényi note of meeting, 19 December 1978; MOL M-KS 288.f. 47/762 ő.e.

41 Memorandum, Bob King to David Aaron, 12 May 1978, folder 'Hungary, 1/78 to 1/81', Box 27, National Security Adviser files – country series, JCPL.

42 Horn interview.

43 Szűrös, 'Kádár and the Soviet leadership'; Révész (ed.)/Aczél, pp. 118-19; Marjai interview.

44 Berecz, p. 358; Berecz interview.

45 Földes (2005), pp. 86-91.

46 Vass (ed.) (1978) [b], pp. 830-49.

47 Földes (2005), p. 90.

48 Konrád (1984), p. 156. György Litván, 'A Kádár-kép metamorfózosiai' (Metamorphoses in the Kádár image) in Rácz (ed.), pp. 14-15.

49 George Schöpflin, 'Hungary: an Uneasy Stability', in Archie Brown and Jack Gray (eds), *Political Culture and Political Change in Communist States*, pp. 139-41, 154; Rudolf L. Tokes (1997), 'Murmur and Whispers. Public Opinion and Legitimacy Crisis in Hungary, 1972-1989' (*The Carl Beck Papers in Russian & East European Studies*, Number 1206, Center for Russian and East European Studies, University of Pittsburgh, April 1997), pp. 52-7.

50 Ferenc Havasi, István Hetényi and Ákos Balassa, interviews in Bozzai and Farkas (eds), pp. 34, 36, 98, 156-8.

51 PB, 6 April 1977. MOL M-KS 288.f. 5/715 ő.e.; CC, 20 October 1977. MOL M-KS 288.f. 4/151 ő.e.; Berend (1990), pp. 240-2.

52 CC, 1 December 1977. MOL M-KS 288.f. 4/153 ő.e.; Ferenc Havasi, Ede Bakó and Imre Tarafás, interviews in Bozzai and Farkas (eds), pp. 38, 223, 234-6; Tőkés (1996), p. 461, n. 84; Földes (1995), pp. 121, 127-8.

53 CC, 19-20 April 1978, MOL M-KS 288.f. 4/156 ő.e.

54 András Nyírő et al. (eds), *Segédkönyv a Politkai Bizottság tanulmányozásához* (Handbook for the study of the Politburo), p. 265; Tőkés (1996), p. 460, n. 81; Emil Kimmel, *Végjáték a Fehér Házban* (Endgame in the White House), p. 132.

Chapter 17: Credit Crunch

1 Berend (1990), p. 243; Havasi interview in *Figyelő*, 28 December 1977, in Gábor Koltay and Péter Bródy (1989) *'Erdemei elismerése mellett ...' Beszélgetések Havasi Ferencel* ('With recognition of his merits ...' Conversations with Ferenc Havasi), pp. 119-26; István Horváth and István Németh, *... És a falak leomlanak: Magyarország és a német egység 1945-1990* (... And the walls fell down: Hungary and German unity 1945-90), p. 164.

2 Ferenc Havasi, interview in Bozzai and Farkas (eds), pp. 39-40; Földes (1995), p. 130.

3 Földes (1995), pp. 129-33.

4 Kádár letter to Brezhnev, 17 July 1978; MOL M-KS 288.f. 47/ 762 ő.e.

5 Memorandum of Kádár-Brezhnev meeting, 28 July 1978; MOL M-KS 288.f.47/ 762 ő.e.

6 Földes (1995), pp. 135-7, 143.

7 PB, 20 March 1979. MOL M-KS 288.f. 5/768 ő.e; Földes (1995), pp. 150-2; Tőkés (1996), p. 256; Révész (ed.)/Aczél, p. 118.

8 Tőkés (1996), p. 234; Kaiser, pp. 295-6.

[9] PB, 20 March 1979. MOL M-KS 288.f. 5/768 ő.e.

[10] István Simon and Károly Szerencsés (eds), *Azok a kádári 'szép' napok: Dokumentumok a hetvenes évek történetéből* (Those 'nice' days of Kádárism: documents from the history of the seventies), pp. 277-8, 292-4; Tőkés (1997), pp. 40-2.

[11] János Fekete, interview in Bozzai and Farkas (eds), p. 259.

[12] Huszár first interview; István Huszár, 'We assisted in wrong decisions.'

[13] Memorandum of Kádár-Kirilenko meeting, 22 October 1979. MOL M-KS 288.f. 47/763 ő.e.

[14] Message from Pavlov to Kádár, 5 September 1979. MOL M-KS 288.f. 47/763 ő.e.

[15] Confidential interview.

[16] Békés in Gazdag and Kiss (eds), pp. 156-62. Kádár letters to Brandt and Schmidt, 6 February 1980 in Huszár (ed.) (2002), pp. 548-53.

[17] Memorandum of talks between Gyula Horn and Soviet official Vadim Zaglagin, 16 July 1980. MOL M-KS 288.f. 47/764 ő.e.; Békés in Gazdag and Kiss (eds), pp. 162-3; Horváth and Németh, pp. 167-69.

[18] Berend (1990), pp. 259-63; Timár interview.

[19] PB, 19 February 1980, MOL M-KS 288.f. 5/793 ő.e; Berend (1990), pp. 266-74, 278-82; Tőkés (1996), pp. 112-14.

[20] Timár interview; PB, 19 February 1980. MOL M-KS 288.f. 5/ 793 ő.e; Kádár (1985), p. 456.

[21] Berend (1990), pp. 272-76; Paul Marer, 'Hungary's balance of payments crisis and response 1978-84' (Joint Economic Committee, US Congress), p. 312; Ákos Balassa, interview in Bozzai and Farkas (eds), p. 161.

[22] Földes (1995), pp. 173-6.

[23] Excerpt from Kádár-Husák conversation, 12 November 1980, in Oldřich Tůma, 'The Czechoslovak Communist Regime and the Polish Crisis 1980-1981', *Cold War International History Project Bulletin 11*,   p. 66.

[24] Pozsgay third interview.

[25] János Tischler, 'Kádár and the Polish crisis 1980-1981', *The Hungarian Quarterly* 39, no. 151 (1998), pp. 106, 115 n.4.

[26] Mark Kramer, 'Soviet policy during the Polish crisis', *Cold War International History Project Bulletin 5*; Mark Kramer (translation and introduction), 'The Warsaw Pact and the Polish Crisis of 1980-81: Honecker's Call for Military Intervention', *Cold War International History Project Bulletin 5*; Vojtech Mastny, 'The Soviet Non-Invasion of Poland in 1980-81 and the End of the Cold War', *Cold War International History Project Working Paper 23*.

[27] PB, 9 December 1980. MOL M-KS 288.f. 5/815 ő.e.

[28] Huszár (2003), pp. 278-9.

[29] Tischler, p. 112.

[30] PB, 9 December 1980. MOL M-KS 288.f. 5/815 ő.e.

[31] Miklós Haraszti, 'A civil kurázsitól a civil társadalomig. Magyar szamizdattörténet' (From civil courage to civil society: a history of Hungarian samizdat), *Rubicon* 2004/ 5-6, pp. 22-9; László Rajk, interview with the author, 25 June 2002; Konrád interview.

[32] PB, 2 and 30 March 1982. MOL M-KS 288.f. 5/848 and 850 ő.e.

[33] Földes (1995), pp. 268-9; Marer, p. 301.

[34] Telegram 6664 from US Embassy Budapest to Secretary of State, 23 November 1981 (FOIA). Padraic Fallon and David Shirreff, 'The Betrayal of East Europe' (*Euromoney*, September 1982, pp. 22, 25).

[35] Brezhnev-Kádár letters, 4 and 5 November 1980. MOL M-KS 288.f. 47/764 ő.e.

[36] Memorandum of Kádár-Brezhnev meeting, 27 July 1981; memorandum of Kádár-Brezhnev exchange of letters, 2 September 1981. MOL M-KS 288.f. 47/765 ő.e.

[37] PB, 15 September 1981. MOL M-KS 288.f. 5/836 ő.e.; János Fekete, interview with the author, Budapest, 13 December 2002.

[38] Lázár to Tikhonov, 2 November 1981, MOL M-KS 288.f. 47/765 ő.e.

[39] Fekete interview.

40 Telegrams 5819 and 6414 from US Embassy Budapest to Secretary of State, 8 October and 7 November 1981 (FOIA).

41 Révész (ed.)/Aczél, p. 118; Telegram 6414 from US Embassy Budapest to Secretary of State, 7 November 1981 (FOIA); confidential interview.

42 Ede Bakó, interview in Bozzai and Farkas (eds), p. 227; Timár interview; Musatov interview.

43 PB, 15 September 1981. MOL M-KS 288.f. 5/836 ő.e.; CC letter, 18 September 1981, document 3 in János Tischler, 'The Hungarian party Leadership and the Polish Crisis of 1980-81', *Cold War International History Project Bulletin 11*.

44 PB, 22 December 1981 and 5 January 1982. MOL M-KS 288.f. 5/843 and 844 ő.e; Berecz, pp. 327-30; Révész (ed.)/Aczél, p. 122.

45 Marer, pp. 303-6; Fallon and Shirreff, pp. 19-30; Földes (1995), p. 186.

46 Földes (1995), p. 188; PB, 29 April 1982. MOL M-KS 288.f. 5/852 ő.e.; Telegram 9625 from US Embassy Bonn to Secretary of State, 4 May 1982 (FOIA).

47 Schmidt to Kádár, 18 December 1981, in Huszár (ed.) (2002), p. 564; Horváth and Németh, pp. 174-6.

48 Schmidt, p. 537; Schmidt-Kádár correspondence in Huszár (ed.) (2002), pp. 584-6, 676-7; Horn interview; Horváth and Németh, p. 176.

49 János Kádár (1985), *A békéért, népünk boldogulásáért: Beszédek és cikkek, 1981-1985* (For peace and the people's prosperity: Speeches and articles, 1981-1985), pp. 50-1; Huszár (2003), p. 277.

50 Telegram 115188 from Secretary of State to US Embassy Budapest, 29 April 1982 (FOIA).

Chapter 18: Limits

1 János Kis, 'Thoughts on the Near Future', *Beszélő*, No. 3, May 1982, cited in Rudolf L. Tőkés (1984), 'Hungarian Reform Imperatives', *Problems of Communism* 33, 4 (1984), p. 8.

2 Horváth interview; Pozsgay third interview; László Lengyel, 'A kádárizmus alkonya' (Twilight of Kádárism), in Rácz (ed.), pp. 160-1.

3 Huszár (2003), p. 280; Csikós-Nagy interview; Imre Pozsgay, 'Késő Kádár-korszak és az MSZMP' (The late Kádár era and the MSZMP), in *Rubicon*, 2004/ 5-6, pp. 78-9.

4 PB, 9 November 1982. MOL M-KS 288.f. 5/866 ő.e; Földes (1995), pp. 196-200.

5 Tőkés (1984), p. 11.

6 István Bodzabán and Antal Szalay (eds), *A puha diktatúrától a kemény demokráciáig* (From soft dictatorship to tough democracy), p. 48; Révész (ed.)/Aczél, pp. 121-2.

7 George P. Shultz, *Turmoil and Triumph*, p. 126.

8 '*Beszélő* describes censorship and reviews biography of Kádár' (Hungarian SR/6, RFE Research, 22 April 1983) (Judith Pataki), HU-OSA 300/40/5, Box 87; Rajk interview.

9 'Az egység, az összeforrottság társadalmunk fő ereje' (Unity, togetherness is the main strength of our society), *Magyar Nemzet*, 30 April 1983, HU-OSA 300/40/5, Box 85; 'Domestic politics: What Kádár did not say on television' (Hungarian SR/8, RFE Research, 30 May 1983) (Alfred Reisch), HU-OSA 300/40/5, Box 87; Földes, pp. 203-6; Swain (1992), p.135.

10 Kádár to Andropov, 18 April 1983, and Andropov reply, 20 May 1983, in Huszár (ed.) (2002), pp. 599-600.

11 'Kádár policies get seal of approval from new Soviet leadership?' (RAD Background Report/195 (Hungary), RFE Research, 11 August 1983) (Alfred Reisch), HU-OSA 300/40/5, Box 87.

12 Horn interview.

13 István Horváth (former ambassador to Bonn), interview, 'Pushing back the curtain', BBC Radio; Horváth and Németh, pp. 165-6, 182-4; István Szokai (CC International Affairs Department) interview in Bodzabán and Szalay (eds), p. 99.

14 Shultz, p. 693.

15 Andropov to Kádár, 28 October 1983, and Kádár reply, 1 November 1983, in Koltay and Bródy (eds) (1990), pp. 106-10; Szűrös interview; Gati, pp. 203-4; István Szokai (CC International Affairs Department) interview in Bodzabán and Szalai (eds), p. 99.

[16] Margaret Thatcher, *The Downing Street Years*, pp. 454-6; 'Memorandum to the President', Telegram 382878 from Secretary of State to US Delegation, 17 December 1985 (FOIA).

[17] Horn interview.

[18] United Nations Economic Commission for Europe, *Economic Survey of Europe in 1989-1990*, tables on pp. 387, 391, 409-10, 414-15; Marer, pp. 313-14; Fallon and Shirreff, p. 28; Éva Kerpel and David G. Young, *Hungary to 1993: Risks and rewards of reform*, EIU Economic Prospects Series Special Report No. 1153, pp. 62-3, 66-7.

[19] Tőkés (1984), pp. 12-13 (the study cited was by János Kornai); László Csaba, 'The Recent Past and the Future of the Hungarian Reform: An Overview and Assessment', p. 21, and Katalin Botos, 'Foreign Economic Relations: Hungary and International Capital Markets', p. 50, both in Roger A. Clarke (ed.), *Hungary: The Second Decade of Economic Reform*.

[20] Kornai, pp. 38-47; Berend (1990), pp. 278-90; Kerpel and Young, pp. 49-53.

[21] Elemér Hankiss, *East European Alternatives*, pp. 46-8; Rudolf Andorka, Tamás Kolosi, Richard Rose and György Vukovitch (eds.), *A Society Transformed: Hungary in Time-Space Perspective*, pp. 53-5, 58-60; Jacques Rupnik, *The Other Europe*, pp. 169-70, 175-76.

[22] O'Neil, p. 51; Romsics (1999), pp. 412-13.

[23] PB, 26 April 1983. MOL M KS 288.f. 5/881 ő.e.

[24] Révesz (1997), pp. 303-4.

[25] Révész (1997), p. 327.

[26] Tőkés (1984), p. 11; Révész (1997), pp. 331-3; Földes (1995), p. 213.

[27] Földes (1995), pp. 207-9; Timár interview.

[28] Koltay and Bródy (1989), p. 71; Timár interview.

[29] Miklós Pullai (Planning Office) interview in Bodzabán and Szalai (eds), p. 70; Swain (1992), pp. 138-42.

[30] Ákos Balassa, interview in Bozzai and Farkas (eds), pp. 164-5; Földes (1995), pp. 211-13; Tőkés (1996), p. 273.

[31] Földes (1995), pp. 213-16; Koltay and Bródy (1989), p.72.

[32] Mikhail Gorbachev, 'Kádár János', translated from his memoirs by Erna Páll, in Rácz (ed.), pp. 166-7; Katona in Rácz (ed.), p.205; Bodzabán and Szalay (eds), pp. 48-50.

[33] Hedrick Smith, *The Power Game*, pp. 371-2. Telegram 058494 from Secretary of State to US Embassy Lisbon (attention Michael Deaver), 27 February 1985; Telegram 060557 from Secretary of State to US Embassy Budapest, 28 February 1985; Telegram 2230 from US Embassy Budapest to Secretary of State, 21 March 1985 (FOIA).

[34] Révész (1997), pp. 335-9.

[35] Révész (1997), p. 221; Tőkés (1996), pp. 106, 233; Berecz, pp. 180-6.

[36] For an in-depth account of the careers of Grósz, Berecz and Pozsgay, see Tőkés (1996), pp. 217-49.

[37] Pozsgay third interview; Elizabeth Windsor, *Financial Times*, 26 September 1974, HU-OSA 300/40/6, Box 16, 'Kádár János – official'; Telegram 10177 from US Embassy Budapest to Secretary of State, 4 December 1985 (FOIA).

[38] Földes (1995), pp. 268-9; Ákos Balassa and János Fekete interviews in Bozzai and Farkas (eds), pp. 170-1, 262.

[39] Földes (1995), pp. 228-30; Miklós Pulai, interview in Bodzabán and Szalay (eds), pp. 70-1.

[40] Földes (1995), p. 232; Bodzabán and Szalay (eds), p. 51.

[41] Földes (1995), p. 234; Koltay and Bródy (1989), p. 69.

[42] Huszár first interview.

Chapter 19: 'The Brutuses Showed Up'

[1] Bodzabán and Szalay (eds), p. 51.

[2] Geoffrey Hosking, *A History of the Soviet Union 1917-1991*, pp. 456-7; Jacques Lévesque, *The Enigma of 1989. The USSR and the Liberation of Eastern Europe*, pp. 52-59.

[3] Kádár-Gorbachev meeting, 25 September 1985, in Baráth and Rainer (eds), pp. 43-77.

4 Musatov interview; Imre Pozsgay, second interview with the author, Budapest, 10 December 2002.

5 Tőkés (1996), pp. 263-8; Romsics (1999), p. 421; O'Neil, pp. 88-90.

6 Pozsgay first interview; Tőkés (1996), pp. 236-40.

7 Timothy Garton Ash (1989), 'A Hungarian Lesson', in *The Uses of Adversity*, p. 136; Kádár-Gorbachev meeting, 25 September 1985, in Baráth and Rainer (eds), p. 62.

8 János Vargha interview, 'Pushing Back the Curtain'; Romsics (2003), pp. 31, 48; Révész (1997), p. 338.

9 Berecz interview.

10 Garton Ash (1989), pp. 136-41; 'Crackdown in Hungary' (Per Waestberg et al.), *New York Review of Books*, 29 May 1986; Révész (1997), pp. 358-9; Romsics (2003), pp. 48-9.

11 Romsics (2003), p. 48; Rajk interview.

12 Rezső Nyers interview, in Bodzabán and Szalay (eds), p. 67.

13 Bodzabán and Szalay (eds), pp. 52-3; Gorbachev in Rácz (ed.), pp. 168-9; 'Kádár óvatossága átragadt a vezetésre: Beszélgetés Grósz Károllyal múltról, jelenről, jövőről' (Kádár's caution infected the leadership: a conversation with Károly Grósz about the past, present and future) (1) (Ferenc Kőszegi, Jenő István Szatmári) (*Pesti Hirlap*, 4 April 1991), HU-OSA 300/40/5, Box 87; Gyula Thurmer, interview, 'Pushing Back The Curtain.'

14 Peter Unwin, interview with the author, London, 11 April 2000; Unwin, pp. 7-8; Sir Malcolm Rifkind, interview with the author, London, 15 October 2003.

15 Tőkés (1996), p. 274; Huszár (2003), p. 28; Sir Bryan Cartledge, interview with the author, Oxford, 15 October 2002; Lakatos interview; Zoltán Farkas interview, in 'Pushing Back the Curtain.'

16 Letter from de Larosière to Kádár, 27 November 1985, and Kádár's reply, 18 December 1985, in Huszár (ed.) (2002), pp. 633-5.

17 Dr. Horst Teltschik, interview with the author, Berlin, 20 January 2005; Horváth and Németh, pp. 181-6, 213-21; István Horváth interview, 'Pushing Back the Curtain.'

18 Révész (1997), pp. 362-6; Berecz, pp. 454-5.

19 Valeri Musatov, interview in Bodzabán and Szalay (eds), pp. 97-8; Lakatos interview.

20 Ákos Balassa, György Zdeborsky and Ede Bakó, interviews in Bozzai and Farkas (eds), pp. 172, 178-9, 224; Földes (1995), pp. 268-9.

21 'Central Committee meets: no party leadership changes yet' (Hungarian SR/13, RFE Research, 23 December 1986) (Alfred Reisch), HU-OSA 300/40/5, Box 87; Károly Grósz interview in Bodzabán and Szalay (eds), p. 103. Földes (1995), pp. 252-6.

22 'The Kádár question: to go or not to go?' (Hungarian SR/13, RFE Research, 23 December 1986) (Alfred Reisch), HU-OSA 300/40/5, Box 87; Lengyel in Rácz (ed.), p. 162.

23 O'Neil, pp. 46-8; Romsics (1999), pp. 412-13.

24 Miklós Németh interview, 'Pushing Back the Curtain.'

25 Tőkés (1996), pp. 233, 245; Lendvai (1988), p. 135-37.

26 Lendvai (1988), pp. 132-3, 136-7; Tőkés (1996), pp. 243-4, 248; 'Hungarian high politics on the eve of the party conference' (RFE Research, RAD Background Report/70 (Hungary), 22 April 1988) (Richard Kemeny), HU-OSA 300/40/5, Box 87.

27 Károly Grósz interview in Bodzabán and Szalay (eds), p. 104; Lendvai (1988), pp. 137-9; Horváth and Németh, pp. 271-80; István Horváth interview in 'Pushing Back the Curtain.'

28 Tőkés (1996), pp. 276-7; Fock, 'He looked on power as service.'

29 RFE Hungarian Monitoring, 16 September 1987, HU-OSA 300/40/5, Box 86; Tőkés (1996), pp. 277-8; Lendvai (1988), pp. 139-40.

30 Révész (1997), pp. 355-8; László Lengyel interview in Bodzabán and Szalay (eds), p. 92.

31 László Lengyel, interview in Bodzabán and Szalay (eds), pp. 92-3; Huszár (2003), pp. 298-301; László Lengyel, 'Kádár utolsó beszéde' (Kádár's Last Speech) in Rácz (ed), pp. 209-10.

32 'Kádár returns to China to seal restoration of party relations' (Hungarian SR/12, RFE Research, 30 October 1987) (Alfred Reisch), HU-OSA 300/40/5, Box 87; MK 10; Fejti interview.

33 'Hungarian high politics on the eve of the party conference' (RFE Research, RAD Background Report/70 (Hungary), 22 April 1988) (Richard Kemeny), HU OSA 300/40/5, Box 87; report on Kádár visit to Moscow, 31 October – 8 November 1987, in Baráth and Rainer (eds), pp. 120-1.

34 Pozsgay second interview ; Romsics, (2003), pp. 73-5.

35 Lakatos interview; Tőkés (1996), pp. 279-80; memorandum from Vadim Medvedev to Mikhail Gorbachev, March 1988, in Baráth and Rainer (eds), pp. 207-8.

36 Medvedev memorandum; Tőkés (1996), p. 282; Romsics (2003), p. 74; O'Neil, p. 64 n. 99.

37 Károly Grósz interview in Bodzabán and Szalay (eds), p. 104; Medvedev memorandum.

38 Rezső Nyers interview in Bodzabán and Szalay (eds), pp. 89-92; Révész (1997), p. 385; Nyers interview; George Schöpflin, Rudolf L. Tőkés and Iván Volgyes, 'Leadership Change and Crisis in Hungary', *Problems of Communism* 37 (1988), p. 35.

39 Tőkés (1996), p. 279; 'Hungary: Revolt' (Eastern Europe, 4 May 1988), HU-OSA 300/40/5, Box 86; Berecz interview.

40 Zoltán Farkas interview, 'Pushing Back the Curtain.'

41 Gyula Thurmer interview, 'Pushing Back the Curtain'; Romsics (2003), p. 74; Medvedev memorandum.

42 Romsics (2003), pp. 74-75; 'Hungary: Revolt'; O'Neil, p. 63.

43 Károly Grósz interview in Bodzabán and Szalay (eds), pp. 103-5; Koltay and Bródy (1989), p. 23.

44 Lendvai (1988), pp. 146-47; 'Hungary: Revolt'; Miklós Németh interview, 'Pushing Back the Curtain.'

45 Schöpflin et al., passim; Tőkés (1996), pp. 283-4; Koltay and Bródy (1989), p. 22; Rezső Nyers interview in Bodzabán and Szalay (eds), pp. 101-3; Gorbachev in Rácz (ed.), p. 170.

46 Kádár-Gorbachev telephone conversation, 19 May 1988, in Baráth and Rainer (eds), pp. 122-5.

47 Kádár-Gorbachev telephone conversation.

48 RFE Hungarian Monitoring, 20 May 1988, HU-OSA 300/40/5, Box 86; 'Kádár's speech at the National Congress' (Hungarian SR/7, Radio Free Europe Research, 3 June 1988) (Alfred Reisch), HU-OSA 300/40/5, Box 87; Romsics (2003), p. 76.

49 'Grósz, new Hungarian PC chief, surrounded by reformers' (Sylvie Kauffmann, *Le Monde*, 24 May 1988); 'Hungarian Communist party meets' (Paula Butturini, B-Wire/ *Chicago Tribune*, 21 May 1988); 'Hungary sweeps out Kádár in major reform shake-up' (Reuter, 22 May 1988): all HU-OSA 300/40/5, Box 86.

50 Pozsgay second interview; Gyurkó interview.

51 *Népszabadság*, 23 May 1988 (edited version of speech); 'Kádár calls for national unity in closing speech' (AP, 22 May 1988); 'Hungary ends Kádár's rule after 31 years' (Kay Withers, B-Wire, 23 May 1988): all HU-OSA 300/40/5, Box 86.

52 'Grósz, new Hungarian PC chief …'; 'Hungary ends Kádár's rule …'; 'Agencies early morning' (Reuter, 23 May 1988): all HU OSA 300/40/5, Box 86.

53 Koltay and Bródy (1989), pp. 26-8; Mátyás Szürös interview in Bodzabán and Szalay (eds), p. 103.

54 Tőkés (1996), pp. 284-5; Pozsgay second interview; Lendvai (1988), pp. 149-50; O'Neil, pp. 65-6 and n. 102.

55 'Hungary ends Kádár's rule …'; 'AP and Reuter on Kádár out as party boss' (22 May 1988); 'Hungary sweeps out Kádár in major reform shake-up' (Reuter, 22 May 1988); 'Agencies early morning from Budapest' (B-Wire, AP) (23 May 1988): all HU-OSA 300/40/5, Box 86.

56 Katona in Rácz (ed.), p. 206.

Chapter 20: Ghosts

1 'Nem akart főtitkár lenni: Beszélgetés Grósz Károllyal múltról, jelenről, jövőről' (He did not want to be General Secretary: Károly Grósz talks about the past, present and future) (2) (Ferenc Kőszegi, Jenő István Szatmári) (*Pesti Hírlap*, 5 April 1991), HU-OSA 300/40/5, Box 87; Kimmel, p. 132.

2 Lévesque, p. 86.

3 Fejti interview; 'A pártelnökség tagjainak nyilatkozata' (Statements by members of the party leadership, *Népszabadság*, 7 July 1989), HU-OSA 300/40/5, Box 87; 'Kádár interview with Finnish TV reported' (Hungarian TV/B, 13 June 1988), HU-OSA 300/40/5, Box 86.

4 'A Hungarian looks back' (B-Wire, Flora Lewis article *New York Times*, 9 October), HU-OSA 300/40/5, Box 86.

5 Berecz interview.

6 Dornbach, pp. 11-13; Rainer (2003a), pp. 206-15.

7 Tőkés (1997), p. 59.

8 Romsics (2003), p. 159; Huszár (2003), pp. 308-9; MK 10; Kimmel, p. 119.

9 Kádár speech to CC, 12 April 1989, MOL M-KS 288.f. 4/259 ő.e., in Rácz (ed.), p. 216; Kimmel, pp. 46, 102.

10 Tőkés (1996), pp. 298-303; Romsics (2003), pp. 129-31;Lévesque, pp. 86-90, 93-109, 128-42.

11 'Kádár's departure discussed' (168 Hours/ MTI in English, 13 May 1989), HU-OSA 300/40/5, Box 86; Mátyás Szűrös, 1956 OHA interview, in Rácz (ed.), p. 188.

12 István Tamás, 'Mit mond Kádár János?' (What does János Kádár say?), *Élet és Irodalom*, 3 February 1989, HU-OSA 300/40/5, Box 86; 'Kádár publicly criticised' (Hungarian SR/3, Radio Free Europe Research, 24 February 1989) (Judith Pataki), HU-OSA 300/40/5, Box 87; Romsics (2003), p. 150.

13 Kimmel, p. 67; Kádár remarks at CC of 20-21 February 1989, in Kanyó, p. 267.

14 Huszár (2003), pp. 309-12; Kimmel, p. 106; Kanyó, pp. 15-18, 122-5.

15 Kanyó, p.137.

16 Kanyó, pp. 269-71; Huszár (2003), pp. 312-13.

17 Kimmel, pp. 102, 119; Huszár (2003), p. 313.

18 Pozsgay second interview; Lengyel in Rácz (ed.), pp. 211-12; Huszár (2003), pp. 313-18; Romsics (2003), p. 159.

19 Kádár speech to CC, 12 April 1989, MOL M-KS 288.f. 4/259 ő.e., reproduced in Rácz (ed.), pp. 213-16. Text with exegesis: Mihály Kornis, 'Kádár' in *Sóhajok hídja* (Bridge of Sighs), pp. 91-169.

20 'Kádár's departure discussed' (168 Hours/ MTI in English, 13 May 1989), HU-OSA 300/40/5, Box 86; Kimmel, pp. 101-2; Pozsgay second interview.

21 Huszár first interview.

22 I am grateful to Professor Sándor M. Kiss for this suggestion.

23 Berecz interview; Kimmel, p. 128.

24 Nyers interview; Huszár (2003), p. 318; Kimmel, p. 129.

25 Dornbach, pp. 13-14; Romsics (2003), p. 151.

26 'Dubcek interview on Budapest television' (NCA/B, 18 April 1989), HU-OSA 300/40/5, Box 86; 'Kádár stripped of last remaining party functions' (Hungarian SR/8, Radio Free Europe Research, 30 May 1989) (Judith Pataki & Alfred Reisch), HU-OSA 300/40/5, Box 87; Farkas statement in Kanyó, pp. 115-21.

27 CC to Kádár and his reply, 8 and 10 May 1989, in Huszár (ed.) (2002), pp. 678-80.

28 Kanyó, p. 272; Révész (ed.)/Aczél, p. 124; MK10; Tőkés (1996), p. 324.

29 Aczél letters to Mária Kádár, 27 April 1989, and to János Kádár, 24 May 1989, in Huszár (ed.) (2002), p. 783.

30 Révész (ed.)/Aczél, p. 125; Kimmel, p. 131.

31 'Aged leader retired from party posts' (B-Wire/ Washington Post, 9 May 1989, Imre Karacs), HU-OSA 300/40/5, Box 86; Kimmel, p. 131; Jaruzelski letter to Kádár, 10 April 1989, in Huszár (ed.) (2002), pp. 677-8; Musatov, p. 82; Kanyó, p. 270.

[32] Romsics (2003), p. 152; Rainer (2003a), pp. 212-13.

[33] Kádár letter to CC, 26 May 1989, in Huszár (ed.) (2002), p. 680.

[34] Romsics (2003), pp. 150-58; Timothy Garton Ash (1990), *We The People*, pp. 49-53; Unwin, pp. 14-19.

[35] Timothy Garton Ash, 'Revolution in Hungary and Poland', *New York Review of Books*, 17 August 1989; see also Garton Ash (1990), p. 53.

[36] Garton Ash (1990), p. 53; Kimmel, pp. 130, 132.

[37] MK10; Gábor L. Kelemen, 'Kádár János utolsó napjai' (The Last Days of János Kádár), *Magyar Hírlap*, 12 September 1990; Berecz in Rácz (ed.), p. 195.

[38] Fock, 'He saw power as service.'

[39] Musatov interview.

[40] Swain (1992), pp. 185-224.

[41] Rezső Nyers, Károly Grósz, Miklós Németh and Imre Pozsgay, 'Búcsú' (Farewell) (*Népszabadság*, 7 July 1989). HU-OSA 300/40/5, Box 87.

[42] Tőkés (1996), p. 423.

[43] Timothy Garton Ash, 'Hungary's Revolution: Forty Years On', *New York Review of Books*, 14 November 1996.

[44] Schöpflin, pp. 127-31, 151-2.

[45] László Lengyel, 'Kádár és kora' (Kádár and his era) (*Népszabadság*, 6 July 1994). I am grateful to Sándor Révész for emphasising how Kádár's prosaic objectives suited the times.

[46] CC, 23-24 November 1967. MOL M-KS 288.f.4/ 89 ő.e.; 'Notes of Kádár-Andropov conversation.'

[47] Huszár/Nyers, p. 324.

[48] Tőkés (1996), p. 269 and p. 483, n. 40, referring also to the work of László Lengyel; Konrád (1984), p. 159; for related issues, see Schöpflin in Brown and Gray (eds), pp. 131-58.

[49] Kiss interview.

[50] Miklós Haraszti, *The Velvet Prison: Artists under State Socialism*; Elemér Hankiss, *East European Alternatives*, pp. 35-36.

[51] Miklós Szabó, 'Kádár's Pied Piper', *The Hungarian Quarterly* 38, no. 147 (1997), pp. 91-103.

[52] O'Neil, pp. 41-52; White, Gardner and Schöpflin, p. 141; Tőkés (1996), pp. 143-60.

[53] László Lengyel, 'Magyar Ellenzékek' (Hungarian Oppositions) in *Rubicon* 2004/5-6, pp. 86-95.

[54] Andorka, Kolosi, Rose and Vukovich (eds), pp. 195-202; Jan Delhey and Verena Tobsch, 'Satisfaction with democracy and its sources: the cases of East Germany and Hungary', in Detlef Pollack, Jörg Jacobs, Olaf Müller and Gert Pickel (eds), *Political Culture in Post-Communist Europe: Attitudes in new democracies*, pp. 115-31.

[55] Mária Vásárhelyi, 'Csalóka emlékezet' (Deceptive memory), *Élet és irodalom*, year 47, issue 24. For the 1999 poll, see Introduction, n. 1.

[56] Lengyel in Rácz (ed.), p. 209; Révész (ed.)/Aczél, pp. 124-5.

[57] Eric Hobsbawm, *The Age of Extremes. The Short Twentieth Century, 1914-1991* (London: Abacus, 1995).

[58] 'The Last Days of János Kádár'; RFE Hungarian monitoring, 3 July 1989, HU-OSA 300/40/5, Box 8; Romsics (2003), p. 160.

[59] RFE Hungarian reports, 4 July 1989; 'Kádár's condition reported worsening', A-Wire, 5 July 1989; 'Doctors say Kádár's condition has not improved', A-Wire, 5 July 1989: all HU-OSA 300/40/5, Box 87.

[60] 'The Last Days of János Kádár'; RFE Hungarian monitoring, 6 July 1989, and 'Elhunyt Kádár János' (János Kádár is dead), *Népszabadság*, 7 July 1989: both HU-OSA 300/40/5, Box 87.

[61] Romsics (1999), p. 433.

[62] 'Politikája az országot szolgálta' (His policy served the country) *Népszabadság*, 7 July 1989, HU-OSA 300/40/5, Box 87.

[63] 'Interview with Hungarian journalists', 6 July 1989: http://bushlibrary.tamu/edu/research / papers/1989/89070605.html

[64] 'The death and burial of János Kádár' (Hungarian SR/12, Radio Free Europe Research, 27 July 1989, Alfred Reisch), HU-OSA 300/40/5, Box 87; Romsics (2003), p. 161; Kimmel, p. 133.

[65] Romsics (2003), p. 162.

[66] Tőkés (1997), p. 49; Romsics (2003), pp. 163-4; various articles in *Népszabadság*, 15 July 1989, HU-OSA 300/40/5, Box 87.

BIBLIOGRAPHY

Books by János Kádár

Over a dozen different editions of Kádár's speeches, articles and interviews were published during his thirty-year leadership of Hungary. Most of their contents are reproduced in the English translations listed below. Where I have taken quotations directly from a Hungarian edition, this is identified in full in the notes.

Socialist Construction in Hungary: Selected Speeches and Articles, 1957-1961 (Budapest: Corvina, 1962)

On the Road to Socialism: Selected Speeches and Interviews, 1960-1964 (Budapest: Corvina, 1965)

For a Socialist Hungary: Speeches, Articles, Interviews 1968-1972 (Budapest: Corvina, 1972)

Socialism and Democracy in Hungary: Speeches, Articles, Interviews 1957-1982 (Budapest: Corvina, 1984)

Selected Speeches and Interviews (Oxford: Pergamon Press, 1985) [with an 'Introductory Biography' by László Gyurkó – see 'Books and articles in books' below]

The Renewal of Socialism in Hungary: Selected Speeches and Interviews 1957-1986 (Budapest: Corvina, 1987)

Collections of primary documents

Magdolna Baráth (ed.), *Szovjet nagyköveti iratok Magyarországról 1953-1956: Kiszeljov és Andropov titkos jelentései* (Documents from the Soviet Ambassadors in Hungary 1953-1956: Kiselev and Andropov's Secret Reports) (Budapest: Napvilág, 2002)

Magdolna Baráth and István Feitl (eds), *A Magyar Szocialista Munkáspárt ideiglenes vezető testuleteinek jegyzőkönvei. III. kötet: 1957. április 5 – 1957. május 17.* (Minutes of the

temporary leadership bodies of the MSZMP: Volume 3, 5 April 1957 – 17 May
1957) (Budapest: Interart, 1993)
Magdolna Baráth and János M. Rainer (eds), *Gorbacsov tárgyalásai magyar vezetôkke:
Dokumentumok az egykori SZKP és MSZMP archívumaiból 1985-1991* (Gorbachev's
talks with Hungarian leaders: Documents from the former CPSU and MSZMP
archives 1985-1991) (Budapest: 1956-os Intézet, 2000)
Magdolna Baráth and Zoltán Ripp (eds), *A Magyar Szocialista Munkáspárt ideiglenes vezető
testuleteinek jegyzőkönvei. IV. kötet: 1957. május 21 – 1957. június 24.* (Minutes of the
temporary leadership bodies of the MSZMP: Volume 4, 21 May 1957 – 24 June
1957) (Budapest: Interart, 1994)
Csaba Békés, Malcolm Byrne and János M. Rainer (eds), *The 1956 Hungarian Revolution:
A History in Documents* (Budapest: CEU Press, 2002)
Gergő Bendegúz Cseh, Melinda Kalmár and Edit Pór (eds), *Zárt, Bizalmas, Számozott:
Tájékoztatáspolitika és cenzúra 1956-1963* (Restricted, Confidential, Numbered:
Information Policy and Censorship 1956-1963) (Budapest: Osiris, 1999)
Alajos Dornbach (ed.), *The Secret Trial of Imre Nagy* (Westport, CT: Praeger, 1994)
István Feitl (ed.), *A Magyar Szocialista Munkáspárt Központi Bizottsága Titkárságának
jegyzőkönyvei: 1957. július 1. – December 31.* (Minutes of the Secretariat of the CC of
the MSZMP) (Budapest: Napvilág, 2000)
Éva Gál, András B. Hegedűs, György Litván and János M. Rainer (eds), *A 'Jelcin-
Dosszié': Szovjet dokumentumok 1956-ról* (The 'Yeltsin dossier': Soviet documents
from 1956) (Budapest: Századvég/ 1956-os Intézet, 1993)
Tibor Huszár (ed.), *Kedves, jó Kádár Elvtárs! Válogatás Kádár János Levelezéséből 1954-1989*
(Dear Comrade Kádár: A Selection from János Kádár's Correspondence, 1954-
1989) (Budapest: Osiris, 2002)
Lajos Iszák and Miklós Kun (eds), *'Moszkvának jelentjük ...' Titkos dokumentumok 1944-
1948* ('Reporting to Moscow ...': Secret Documents 1944-1948) (Budapest:
Századvég, 1994)
András Kanyó, *Kádár János – Végakarat* (János Kádár: Last Will and Testament)
(Budapest: Hírlapkiadó, 1989)
József Kiss, Zoltán Ripp & István Vida (eds), *Top Secret: Magyar-Yugoszláv Kapcsolatok
1956. Dokumentumok.* (Top Secret: Hungarian-Yugoslav Relations, 1956:
Documents) (Budapest: MTA Jelenkor-kutató Bizottság, 1995)
Gábor Koltay & Péter Bródy (eds), *El nem égetett dokumentumok* (Unburned
Documents) (Budapest: Szabad Tér, 1990)
Anna S. Kosztricz et al (eds), *A Magyar Szocialista Munkáspárt Központi Bizottságának
1959-1960. évi jegyzőkönyvei* (Minutes of the MSZMP Central Committee 1959-
1960) (Budapest: Magyar Országos Leveltár, 1999)
Magyar Szocialista Munkáspárt Központi Bizottsága, *VII./ VIII./ IX./ X./ XI./
XII./ XIII. Kongresszusának jegyzőkönyvei* (Minutes of the Seventh – Thirteenth
Congresses of the MSZMP) (Budapest: Kossuth, 1960-1985)
—. *A Magyar Szocialista Munkáspárt Országos Értekezletének jegyzőkönyvei, 1957. június 27-
29* (Minutes of the National Conference of the MSZMP, 27-29 June 1957)
(Budapest: Kossuth, 1957)

—. *A Magyar Szocialista Munkáspárt Országos Értekezletének jegyzőkönyvei, 1988. május 20-22* (Minutes of the National Conference of the MSZMP, 20-22 May 1988) (Budapest: Kossuth, 1988)

György Majtényi & Orsolya Ring (eds), *Közel-Múlt: Húsz történet a 20. századból* (The Near Past: Twenty Histories from the Twentieth Century) (Budapest: Magyar Országos Levéltár, 2002)

Jaromír Navrátil et al (eds), *The Prague Spring 1968: A National Security Archive Documents Reader* (Budapest: CEU Press, 1998)

Elena D. Orekhova, Vyacheslav T. Sereda & Aleksandr S. Stykhalin (eds), *Sovietskii Soyuz i vengerskii krizis, 1956 goda: Dokumenty* (The Soviet Union and the Hungarian Crisis in 1956: Documents) (ROSSPEN, Moscow, 1998)

Zoltán Ripp and Julianna Horváth (eds), *Ötvenhat októbere és a hatalom: A Magyar Dolgozók Pártja vezető testületeinek dokumentumai 1956. október 24- október 28.* (October '56 and the Authorities: Documents of the Leading Bodies of the Hungarian Workers' Party, 24-28 October 1956) (Budapest: Napvilág, 1997)

Vyacheslav Sereda and János M. Rainer (eds), *Döntés a Kremlben, 1956: A szovjet pártelnökség vitái Magyarországról (Decision in the Kremlin, 1956: The Soviet Party Presidium's Debates about Hungary)* (Budapest: 1956-os Intézet, 1996)

Vyacheslav Sereda & Alexander Stikalin (eds), *Hiányzó lapok 1956 történetéből: Dokumentumok a volt SZKP KB levéltárából* (Missing Pages from the History of 1956: Documents from the Archives of the Former CPSU CC) (Budapest: Móra Ferenc Könyvkiadó, 1993)

István Simon and Károly Szerencsés (eds), *Azok a kádári 'szép' napok: Dokumentumok a hetvenes évek történetéből* (Those 'Nice' Kádár Years: Documents from the History of the Seventies) (Budapest: Kairosz, 2004)

Karola Némethné Vágyi et al (eds), *A Magyar Szocialista Munkáspárt Központi Bizottságának 1957-1958. évi jegyzőkönvei* (Minutes of the Hungarian Socialist Workers' Party Central Committee for the years 1957-1958) (Budapest: Magyar Országos Leveltár, 1997)

Karola Némethné Vágyi and Levente Sipos (eds.), *A Magyar Szocialista Munkáspárt ideiglenes vezető testületeinek jegyzőkönvei. I. kötet. 1956. november 11 – 1957. január 14.* (Minutes of the temporary leadership bodies of the MSZMP: Volume 1, 11 November 1956 – 14 January 1957) (Budapest: Interart, 1993)

Karola Némethné Vágyi and Károly Urbán (eds), *A Magyar Szocialista Munkáspárt ideiglenes vezető testületeinek jegyzőkönvei. II. kötet: 1957. január 25 – 1957. április 2.* (Minutes of the temporary leadership bodies of the MSZMP: Volume 2, 25 January 1957 – 2 April 1957) (Budapest: Interart, 1993)

László Varga (ed.), *A forradalom hangja: Magyarországi rádióadások, 1956. október 23 – november 9.* (Voice of the Revolution: Hungarian radio broadcasts, 23 October – 9 November 1956) (Budapest: Századvég/ Nyilvánosság Klub, 1989)

—. (ed.), *Kádár János bírái előtt: Egyszer fent, egyszer lent 1949-1956* (János Kádár Before his Judges: Ups and Downs, 1949-1956) (Budapest: Osiris, 2001)

Henrik Vass (ed.), *A Magyar Szocialista Munkáspárt határozati és dokumentunai 1956-1962* (Resolutions and documents of the MSZMP, 1956-1962) (Agnés Ságvári co-editor) (Budapest: Kossuth, 3rd edition, 1979)

—. *A Magyar Szocialista Munkáspárt határozati és dokumentunai 1963-1966* (Resolutions and documents of the MSZMP, 1963-1966) (Budapest: Kossuth, 2nd edition, 1978 [a])

—. *A Magyar Szocialista Munkáspárt határozati és dokumentunai 1967-1970* (Resolutions and documents of the MSZMP, 1967-1970) (Budapest: Kossuth, 1974)

—. *A Magyar Szocialista Munkáspárt határozati és dokumentunai 1971-1975* (Resolutions and documents of the MSZMP, 1971-1975) (Budapest: Kossuth, 1978 [b])

—. *A Magyar Szocialista Munkáspárt határozati és dokumentunai 1975-1980* (Resolutions and documents of the MSZMP, 1975-1980) (Budapest: Kossuth, 1983)

—. *A Magyar Szocialista Munkáspárt határozati és dokumentunai 1980-1985* (Resolutions and documents of the MSZMP, 1980-1985) (Budapest: Kossuth, 1988)

—. *A Magyar Szocialista Munkáspárt határozati és dokumentunai 1985-1989* (Resolutions and documents of the MSZMP, 1985-1989) (Budapest: Interart, 1994)

Paul E. Zinner (ed.), *National Communism and Popular Revolt in Eastern Europe: A Selection of Documents on Events in Poland and Hungary, February – November, 1956* (New York: Columbia University Press, 1956)

Books and articles in books

Jan Adam, *Economic Reforms in the Soviet Union and Eastern Europe since the 1960s* (New York: St. Martin's Press, 1989)

Gábor Adriányi, *A Vatikán keleti politikája és Magyarország 1939-1978: A Mindszenty-ügy* (The Vatican's Eastern Policy and Hungary, 1939-1978: The Mindszenty Affair) (Budapest: Kairosz, 2004)

Rudolf Andorka, Tamás Kolosi, Richard Rose, György Vukovich (eds), *A Society Transformed: Hungary in Time-Space Perspective* (Budapest: CEU Press, 1999)

Neal Ascherson, *The Polish August* (London: Penguin, 1981)

Magdolna Baráth, 'A Belügyminisztérium "megtisztítása" a volt ÁVH-soktól, 1956-1962' (The 'cleansing' of the Interior Ministry of former ÁVH staff, 1956-1962) in *Évkönyv* (Yearbook) VII, edited by Éva Standeisky and János M. Rainer (Budapest: 1956-os Intézet, 1999)

'Az Állambiztonsági irátok selejtezése, megsemmisítése' (The weeding out and destruction of State Security documents) in *Trezor* 3, edited by György Gyarmati (Budapest: Állambiztonsági Szolgálatok Történeti Levéltára, 2004)

Judy Batt, *Economic Reform and Political Change in Eastern Europe: A Comparison of the Czechoslovak and Hungarian Experiences* (London: Macmillan, 1998)

—. *East Central Europe from Reform to Transformation* (London: Pinter/ Royal Institute of International Affairs, 1991)

Trevor Beeson, *Discretion and Valour: Religious Conditions in Russia and Eastern Europe* (London: Fontana, 1974)

Csaba Békés, 'Magyar-Szovjet Csúcstalálkozók 1957-1965' (Hungarian-Soviet summit conferences, 1957-1965) in *Évkönyv* (Yearbook) VI, edited by András B. Hegedűs et al (Budapest: 1956-os Intézet, 1998)

—. 'Magyarország és az Európai Biztonsági Értekezlet előkészítése 1965-1970' (Hungary and the preparation of the European Security Conference 1965-1970) in

Évkönyv (Yearbook) XII, edited by János M. Rainer and Éva Standeisky (Budapest: 1956-os Intézet, 2004)

—. *Európából Európába: Magyarország konfliktusok kereszttüzében, 1945-1990* (From Europe to Europe: Hungary in the Crossfire of Conflicts, 1945-1990) (Budapest: Gondolat, 2004)

János Berecz, *Vállalom* (My Undertaking) (Budapest: Budapest-Print, 2003)

Iván T. Berend, *Gazdasági útkeresés, 1956-1965* (Search for an economic path, 1956-1965) (Budapest: Magvető, 1983)

—. *The Hungarian Economic Reforms 1953-1988* (Cambridge: Cambridge University Press, 1990)

Michael R. Beschloss & Strobe Talbott, *At the Highest Levels: The Inside Story of the End of the Cold War* (Boston: Little, Brown, 1993)

Nicholas Bethell, *Gomulka: His Poland and His Communism* (London: Longman, 1969)

István Bodzabán & Antal Szalay (eds), *A puha diktatúrától a kemény demokráciáig* (From Soft Dictatorship to Tough Democracy) (Budapest: Pelikán, 1994)

Éva Bozóky, *Zord idők nyomában ...* (On the trail of tough times ...) (Pécs: Pannónia, 1998)

Rita Bozzai & Zoltán Farkas (eds), *Hitelválság: Adósságaink története* (Credit Crunch: The Story of Our Indebtedness) (Budapest: Codex, 1991)

Willy Brandt, *Erinnerungen* (Memoirs) (Berlin: Ullstein, 1994)

Adam Bromke & Philip E. Uren (eds), *The Communist States and the West* (New York: Praeger, 1967)

Fedor Burlatsky, *Khrushchev and the First Russian Spring.* Translated by Daphne Skillen (London: Weidenfeld and Nicolson, 1991)

Agostino Casaroli, *Il martirio della pazienza: La Santa Sede e i paesi comunisti (1963-89)* (The Martyrdom of Patience: The Holy See and the Communist Countries, 1963-1989) (Turin: Einaudi, 2000)

Michael Charlton, *The Eagle and the Small Birds: Crisis in the Soviet Empire: from Yalta to Solidarity* (BBC, 1984)

Roger A. Clarke (ed.), *Hungary: The Second Decade of Economic Reform* (London: Longman, 1989)

Robert Conquest, *The Great Terror: A Reassessment* (London: Pimlico, 1992)

Terry Cox (ed.), *Hungary 1956 – Forty Years On* (London: Frank Cass, 1997)

E.J. Czerwinski and Jaroslaw Piekalkiewicz (eds), *The Soviet Invasion of Czechoslovkia: Its Effects on Eastern Europe* (New York: Praeger, 1972)

Ferenc Donáth, *Reform and Revolution: Transformation of Hungary's Agriculture, 1945-1970.* Translated by Gizela Vizmathy-Susits, translation revised by Timothy Wilkinson (Budapest: Corvina Books, 1980)

—. *A Márciusi Fronttól Monorig: Tanulmányok, vázlatok, emlékezések* (From the March Front to Monor: Studies, Drafts, Recollections) (Budapest: MTA Közgazdaságtudományi Intézet/ Századvég, 1992)

Alexander Dubček, *Hope Dies Last: The Autobiography of Alexander Dubček.* Edited and translated by Jiři Hochman (New York: Kodansha International, 1993)

William Echikson, *Lighting the Night: Revolution in Eastern Europe* (London: Pan, 1991)

Judit Ember, *Menedékjog-1956: A Nagy Imre-csoport elrablása* (Right of Asylum, 1956: The Kidnapping of the Imre Nagy Group) (Budapest: Szabad Tér, 1990)

István Eörsi, *Emlékezés a régi szép időkre* (Memories of the Good Old Days) (Budapest: Napra-Forgó, 1988)

Vladimir Farkas, *Nincs Mentség: Az AVH alezredese voltam* (No Excuses: I Was an ÁVH Lieutenant-Colonel) (Budapest: Interart, 1990)

François Fejtő, *A History of the People's Democracies: Eastern Europe since Stalin*. Translated by Daniel Weissbort (London: Penguin, 1974)

Andrew Felkay, *Hungary and the USSR 1956-1988: Kádár's Political Leadership* (New York: Greenwood Press, 1989)

György Földes, *Az eladósodás politikatörténete 1957-1986* (The political history of indebtedness 1957-1986) (Budapest: Maecenas, 1995)

——. 'Kádár János és az erdélyi magyarság' (János Kádár and the Hungarians of Transylvania) in György Földes and Zsolt Gálfalvi (eds.), *Nemzetiség-felelősség: Írások Gáll Ernő emlékére* (Nationality and responsibility: writings in memory of Ernő Gáll) (Budapest: Napvilag, 2005)

Timothy Garton Ash, *The Uses of Adversity: Essays on the Fate of Central Europe* (Cambridge: Granta, 1989)

——. *We The People: The Revolution of '89 Witnessed in Warsaw, Budapest, Berlin and Prague* (Cambridge: Granta, 1990)

——. *The Polish Revolution: Solidarity*. Revised edition. (London: Granta/ Penguin, 1991)

Charles Gati, *Hungary and the Soviet Bloc* (Durham, NC: Duke University Press, 1986)

Ferenc Gazdag & László J. Kiss (eds), *Magyar külpolitika a 20. Században: Tanulmányok* (Hungarian Foreign Policy in the Twentieth Century: Studies) (Budapest: Zrínyi, 2004)

András Gerő & Iván Pető, *Unfinished Socialism: Pictures from the Kádár Era*. Translated by James Patterson (Budapest: CEU Press, 1999)

Tibor Glant, *A Szent Korona amerikai kalandja 1945-1978* (The Holy Crown's American Adventure, 1945-1978) (Debrecen: Kossuth Egyetemi Kiadó, 1997)

Misha Glenny, *The Rebirth of History: Eastern Europe in the Age of Democracy* (London: Penguin, 1990)

Johanna Granville, *The First Domino: International Decision-Making During the Hungarian Crisis of 1956* (College Station, TX: Texas A&M University Press, 2004)

György Gyarmati, 'Kádár János és a Belügyminiszterium Államvédelmi Hatósága' (János Kádár and the Interior Ministry's State Security Authority): *Trezor* 1, edited by György Gyarmati (Budapest: Történeti Hivatal, 1999)

László Gyurkó, 'Introductory Biography' translated by György Bánlaki and Mária Végh, in János Kádár, *Selected Speeches and Interviews* (Oxford: Pergamon Press, 1985)

——. *A bakancsos forradalom* (The Foot-Soldiers' Revolution) (Budapest: Kossuth, revised edition, 2001)

Elemér Hankiss, *East European Alternatives* (Oxford: Clarendon Press, 1990)

C.M. Hann, *Market Economy and Civil Society in Hungary* (London: Frank Cass, 1990)

Miklós Haraszti, *A Worker in a Worker's State: Piece-Rates in Hungary*. Translated by Michael Wright. (London: Penguin, 1977)

302 BIBLIOGRAPHY

—. *The Velvet Prison: Artists under State Socialism.* Translated by Katalin and Stephen Landesmann. (London: Penguin, 1989)

Paul Hare, Hugo Radice and Nigel Swain (eds), *Hungary: A Decade of Economic Reform* (London: George Allen and Unwin, 1981)

Gyula Háy, *Született 1900-ban. Emlékezések* (Born 1900: Recollections) (Budapest: Interart, 1990)

Peter Hebblethwaite, *Paul VI: The First Modern Pope* (New York: Paulist Press, 1993)

András Hegedüs, *Im Schatten einer Idee* (In the Shadow of an Idea) (Zürich: Ammann, 1986)

—. *A történelem és a hatalom igézetében: Életrajzi elemzések* (Under the Spell of History and Power: Biographical Analyses) (Budapest: Kossuth, 1988)

Martin J. Hillenbrand, *Fragments of our Time: Memoirs of a Diplomat* (Athens, GA: University of Georgia Press, 1998)

Jörg K. Hoensch, *A History of Modern Hungary, 1867-1986.* Translated by Kim Traynor (London: Longman, 1988)

Leslie Holmes, *Politics in the Communist World* (Oxford: Clarendon Press, 1986)

István Horváth & István Németh, *...és a falak leomlanak: Magyarország és a Német Egység (1945-1990)* (... And the Walls Fell Down: Hungary and German Unity (1945-1990) (Budapest: Magvető, 1999)

Miklós Horváth, *Maléter Pál* (Budapest: H&J Kiadó, revised edition, 2002)

Geoffrey Hosking, *A History of the Soviet Union 1917-1991* (London: Fontana, final edition, 1992)

Tibor Huszár, *1968: Prága, Budapest, Moszkva: Kádár János és a csehszlovákiai intervenció* (1968: Prague, Budapest, Moscow: János Kádár and the intervention in Czechoslovakia) (Budapest: Szabad Tér, 1998[a])

—. *A Politikai Gépezet 1951 Tavaszán Magyarországon: Sántha Kálmán ügye (Esettanulmány)* (The Political Machinery in Hungary in Spring 1951: The Kálmán Sántha affair (Case Study)) (Budapest: Corvina, 1998[b])

—. *Kádár János: Politikai Életrajza.* (János Kádár: A Political Biography) (2 volumes, Budapest: Szabad Tér/ Kossuth, 2001, 2003)

—. *Beszélgetések Nyers Rezsővel* (Conversations with Rezső Nyers) (Budapest: Kossuth, 2004)

Tibor Huszár & János Szabó (eds), *Restauráció vagy kiigazítás: A kádári represszió intézményesülése, 1956-1962* (Restoration or Reappraisal. The Institutionalisation of Kádárist Repression, 1956-1962) (Budapest: Zrínyi, 1999)

Paul Ignotus, *Political Prisoner* (London: Routledge & Kegan Paul, 1959)

—. 'János Kádár – Hungary's Quisling Redeemed' in Rodger Swearingen (ed.), *Leaders of the Communist World* (New York: Free Press, 1971)

—. *Hungary* (London: Ernest Benn, 1972)

Frigyes Kahler, *III/III-as történelmi olvasókönyv* (III/III: A Historical Reader) (2 volumes) (Budapest: Kairosz, 2001-2002)

Frigyes Kahler and Sándor M. Kiss, *'Mától kezdve lövünk': Tíz év után a sortüzekről* ('Starting From Today, We Shoot': About the Shootings, Ten Years On) (Budapest: Kairosz, 2003)

Philip M. Kaiser, *Journeying Far and Wide* (New York: Scribner's, 1992)

Melinda Kalmár, *Ennivaló és hozomány: A kora Kádárizmus ideológiája* (Food and Dowry: The Ideology of Early Kádárism) (Budapest: Magvető, 1998)

Paul Kecskemeti, *The Unexpected Revolution: Social Forces in the Hungarian Uprising* (Stanford, CA: Stanford University Press, 1961)

János Kenedi, *Do It Yourself: Hungary's Hidden Economy* (London: Pluto Press, 1981)

Éva Kerpel and David G. Young, *Hungary to 1993: Risks and Rewards of Reform* (London: *Economist* Intelligence Unit, 1988)

Nikita Khrushchev, *Khrushchev Remembers*. Translated & edited by Strobe Talbott (Boston: Little, Brown, 1970)

—. *Khrushchev Remembers: The Last Testament*. Translated & edited by Strobe Talbott (Boston: Little, Brown, 1974)

—. *Khrushchev Remembers: The Glasnost Tapes*. Translated & edited by Jerrold L. Schecter with Vyacheslav V. Luchkov (Boston: Little, Brown, 1990)

Emil Kimmel, *Végjáték a Fehér Házban: A Helyettes Szóvivő Titkai* (Endgame in the White House: The Deputy Spokesman's Secrets) (Budapest: Téka, 1990)

Henry Kissinger, *Years of Renewal* (London: Phoenix Press paperback edition, 2000)

Gábor Kiszely, *ÁVH: Egy terrorszervezet története* (ÁVH: History of a Terror Organisation) (Budapest: Korona, 2000)

—   *Állambiztonság: 1956-1990*. (State Security: 1956-1990) (Budapest: Korona, 2001)

Gábor Koltay & Péter Bródy, *'Érdemei elismerése mellett …' Beszélgetések Havasi Ferenccel* ('With recognition of his merits …': Conversations with Ferenc Havasi) (Budapest: Szabad Tér, 1989)

George Konrád, *Antipolitics: An Essay*. Translated by Richard E. Allen. (London: Quartet Books, 1984)

László Kontler, *Millennium in Central Europe: A History of Hungary* (Budapest: Atlantisz, 1999)

Sándor Kopácsi, *In the Name of the Working Class*. Translated by Daniel and Judy Stoffman (London: Fontana/ Collins, 1986)

Sándor Kopátsy, *Kádár és kora* (Kádár and his Era) (Budapest: C.E.T Belvárosi Kiadó, no date)

Janos Kornai, The *Evolution of the Hungarian Economy, 1848-1988: Volume II. Paying the Bill for Goulash-Communism* (Highland Lakes, NJ: Atlantic Research and Publications, 2000)

Mihály Kornis, 'Kádár' in *Sóhajok hídja* (Bridge of Sighs) (Budapest: Magvető, 1997)

Zsuzsanna Kőrösi and Adrienne Molnár, *Carrying a Secret in My Heart …: Children of the Victims of the Reprisals after the 1956 Revolution in 1956. An Oral History*. Translated by Rachel Hideg and János Hideg (Budapest: CEU Press, 2003)

György Kövér, *Losonczy Geza: 1917-1957* (Budapest: 1956-os Intézet, 1998)

Bennett Kovrig, *Communism in Hungary: From Kun to Kadar* (Stanford, CA: Hoover Institution Press, 1979)

Miklós Kun, *Prague Spring – Prague Fall: Blank Spots of 1968*. Translated by Hajnal Csatorday. (Budapest: Akadémiai Kiadó, 1999)

Martha Lampland, *The Object of Labor: Commodification in Socialist Hungary* (Chicago, IL: University of Chicago Press, 1995)

Paul Lendvai, *Hungary: The Art of Survival.* Translated by Noel Clark with the author. (London: I.B. Tauris, 1988)

—. *Blacklisted: A Journalist's Life in Central Europe.* Translated by Jean Steinberg with the author. (London: I.B. Tauris, 1998)

—. *The Hungarians: 1000 years of victory in defeat.* Translated by Ann Major. (London: Hurst, 2003)

Jacques Lévesque, *The Enigma of 1989. The USSR and the Liberation of Eastern Europe.* Translated by Keith Martin. (Berkeley, CA: University of California Press, 1997)

Bill Lomax, *Hungary 1956* (London: Allison & Busby, 1976)

John Lukacs, *Budapest 1900: A Historical Portrait of a City and its Culture* (New York: Weidenfeld and Nicolson, 1988)

Jonathan Luxmoore and Jolanta Babiuch, *The Vatican and the Red Flag: The Struggle for the Soul of Eastern Europe* (London: Geoffrey Chapman, 1999)

Paul Marer, 'Hungary's balance of payments crisis and response 1978-84'; and 'Economic Reform in Hungary: from Central Planning to Regulated Market'; both in Joint Economic Committee, US Congress, *East European Economies: Slow Growth in the 1980s (Volume 3: Country Studies on Eastern Europe and Yugoslavia)* (Washington DC: USGPO, 1986)

György Marosán, *A tanúk még élnek* (The Witnesses Still Live) (Budapest: Hírlapkiadó, 1989[a])

—. *Fel kellett állnom* (I Had to Resign) (Budapest: Hírlapkiadó, 1989[b])

Endre Marton, *The Forbidden Sky: Inside the Hungarian Revolution* (Boston: Little, Brown, 1971)

Martin McCaulay (ed.), *Khrushchev and Khrushchevism* (London: Macmillan, 1987)

Tibor Méray, *Thirteen Days That Shook the Kremlin.* Translated by Howard L. Katzander. (London, 1959)

István Mészáros, *Mindszenty és az 'Ostpolitik'* (Mindszenty and 'Ostpolitik') (Budapest: Kairosz, 2001)

Veljko Mićunović, *Moscow Diary.* Translated by David Floyd. (New York: Doubleday, 1980)

József Cardinal Mindszenty, *Memoirs.* (Translated by Richard and Clara Winston) (New York: Macmillan, 1974)

Zdeněk Mlynář, *Night Frost in Prague: The End of Humane Socialism.* Translated by Paul Wilson. (London: Hurst, 1980)

Adrienne Molnár (comp.), *A 'Hatvanas Évek' Emlékezete: Az Oral History Archívum gyűjteményéből* (Memories of the Sixties: From the Collection of the Oral History Archives) (Budapest: 1956-os Intézet, 2004)

Miklós Molnár, *Budapest 1956: A History of the Hungarian Revolution.* Translated by Jennetta Ford. (London: George Allen & Unwin, 1971)

—. *From Bela Kun to Janos Kadar; Seventy Years of Hungarian Communism.* Translated by Arnold J. Pomerans. (Oxford: Berg, 1990)

Valeri Musatov, *Predvestniki buri: Politicheskie krizisy v Vostochnoi Evrope* (Harbingers of the Storm: Political Crises in Eastern Europe) (Moscow: Nauchnaya Kniga, 1996)

Martin Myant, *The Czechoslovak economy 1948-1988: The battle for economic reform* (Cambridge: Cambridge University Press, 1989)

Ferenc Nagy, *The Struggle Behind the Iron Curtain*. Translated by Stephen K. Swift (New York: Macmillan, 1948)

Imre Nagy, *On Communism: In Defense of the New Course* (New York: Praeger, 1957)

András Nyírő et al (eds), *Segédkönyv a Politikai Bizottság tanulmányozásához* (Handbook for the Study of the Politburo) (Budapest: Interart, 1989)

Patrick H. O'Neil, *Revolution from Within: The Hungarian Socialist Workers' Party and the Collapse of Communism* (Cheltenham: Edward Elgar, 1998)

Martin Page and David Burg, *Unpersoned: The Fall of Nikita Sergeyevitch Khrushchev* (London: Chapman and Hall, 1966)

George Pálóczi-Horváth, *The Undefeated* (London: Eland, paperback edition, 1993)

György Péteri, *Academia and State Socialism: Essays on the Political History of Academic Life in Post-1945 Hungary and Eastern Europe* (Highland Lakes, NJ: Atlantic Research and Publications, 1998)

Andrea Pető, *Rajk Júlia* (Budapest: Balassi Kiadó, 2001)

Detlef Pollack, Jörg Jacobs, Olaf Müller, Gert Pickel (eds), *Political Culture in Post-Communist Europe: Attitudes in New Democracies* (Aldershot: Ashgate, 2003)

Kazimierz Z. Poznanski, *Poland's Protracted Transition: Institutional Change and Economic Growth, 1970-1994* (Cambridge: Cambridge University Press, 1996)

Alex Pravda (ed.), *The End of the Outer Empire: Soviet-East European Relations in Transition, 1985-90* (London: Sage/ Royal Institute for International Affairs, 1992)

David Pryce-Jones, *The War That Never Was: The Fall of the Soviet Empire 1985-1991* (London: Weidenfeld and Nicolson, 1995)

Alfred Puhan, *The Cardinal in the Chancery and Other Recollections* (New York: Vantage Press, 1990)

Árpád Pünkösti, *Rákosi: A Hatalomért (1945-1948), A csúcson (1948-1953), Bukása, Száműzetése és halála (1953-71)* (Rákosi: Fighting for Power (1945-1948), At the Summit (1948-1953), Downfall, Exile and Death (1953-1971) (3 volumes, Budapest: Európa, 1992, 1996, 2001)

——. *Rákosi, Sztálin legjobb tanitványa* (Rákosi, Stalin's best disciple) (Budapest: Európa, 2004)

Árpád Rácz (ed.), *Ki volt Kádár? Harag és részrehajlas nélkül a Kádár-életútról* (Who was Kádár? On Kádár's life course, without anger or bias) (Budapest: Rubicon-Aquila, 2001)

János Radványi, *Hungary and the Superpowers: The 1956 Revolution and Realpolitik* (Stanford, CA: Hoover Institution Press, 1972)

János M. Rainer, *Nagy Imre: Politikai életrajz* (Imre Nagy: A Political Biography) (2 volumes, Budapest: 1956-os Intézet, 1996 and 1999)

——. *Ötvenhat után* (After '56) (Budapest: 1956-os Intézet, 2003[a])

——. (ed.), *Múlt századi hétköznapok: Tanulmányok a Kádár-rendser kialakulásának* (Daily Life in the Last Century: Studies of the Formation of the Kádár System) (Budapest: 1956-os Intézet, 2003[b])

——. (ed.), *'Hatvanas Évek' Magyarországon: Tanulmányok* (Hungary in the Sixties: Studies) (Budapest: 1956-os Intézet, 2004)

Mátyás Rákosi, *Visszaemlékezések 1944-1956* (Memoirs, 1944-1956) (2 volumes) (Budapest: Napvilág, 1997)

Sándor Révész, *Aczél és Korunk* (Aczél and Our Age) (Budapest: Sík, 1997)

—. *Egyetlen élet: Gimes Miklós története* (A Singular Life: The Story of Miklós Gimes) (Budapest: Sík/ 1956-os Intézet, 1999)

—. (ed.) *Beszélő évek: A Kádár-korszak története. I. Rész. 1957-1968* (*Beszélő* Years: History of the Kádár Era, Part 1: 1957-1968) (Budapest: Stencil Kulturális Alapítvány, 2000)

Zoltán Ripp, *A pártvezetés végnapjai 1956. október 23-31.* (The Last Days of the Party Leadership, 23-31 October 1956): in Ripp and Horváth (eds) [see 'Collections of primary documents' above]

William F. Robinson, *The Pattern of Reform in Hungary: A Political, Economic and Cultural Analysis* (New York: Praeger, 1973)

Ignács Romsics, *Hungary in the Twentieth Century* (Budapest: Corvina/ Osiris, 1999)

—. *Volt egyszer egy rendszerváltás* (Once There Was a Regime Change) (Budapest: Rubicon-Könyvek, 2003)

Jacques Rupnik, *The Other Europe.* Revised edition. (London: Weidenfeld and Nicolson, 1989)

Ágnes Ságvári, *Mert nem hallgathatok: Egy jó házból való pártmunkás emlékei* (Because I Cannot Remain Silent: Memories of a Party Worker from a Good Family) (Budapest: Magyar Hírlap Könyvek, 1989)

Helmut Schmidt, *Die Deutschen und ihre Nachbarn* (The Germans and their Neighbours) (Berlin: Siedler, 1990)

George Schöpflin, 'Hungary: An Uneasy Stability' in Archie Brown and Jack Gray (eds.), *Political Culture and Political Change in Communist States* (London: Macmillan, 1977)

—. *Politics in Eastern Europe: 1945-1992* (Oxford: Blackwell, 1993)

William Shawcross, *Crime and Compromise: János Kádár and the Politics of Hungary since Revolution* (London: Weidenfeld and Nicolson, 1974)

—. *Dubcek* (London: The Hogarth Press, 1990)

Arkady N. Shevchenko, *Breaking with Moscow* (New York: Alfred A. Knopf, 1985)

George P. Shultz, *Turmoil and Triumph: My Years as Secretary of State* (New York: Scribner's, 1993)

Hedrick Smith, *The Power Game: How Washington Works* (New York: Ballantine Books, 1988)

Éva Standeisky, *Az Írók és a Hatalom 1956-1963* (The Writers and the Authorities 1956-1963) (Budapest: 1956-os Intézet, revised edition, 1996)

Péter F. Sugar et al (eds), *A History of Hungary* (Bloomington and Indianapolis, IN: Indiana University Press, 1990)

Nigel Swain, *Collective Farms Which Work?* (Cambridge: Cambridge University Press, 1985)

—. *Hungary: The Rise and Fall of Feasible Socialism* (London, Verso, 1992)

Sándor Szakács and Tibor Zinner, *A háború 'megváltozott természete': Adatok és adalékok, tények és összefüggések 1944-1948* (The 'Changed Nature' of War: Data and Contributions, Facts and Connections, 1944-1948) (Budapest: Batthyány Társaság, 1997)

Szonja Szelényi, *Equality by Design: The Grand Experiment in Destratification in Socialist Hungary* (Stanford, CA: Stanford University Press, 1998)

György Szoboszlai (ed.), *Democracy and Political Transformation: Theories and East-Central European Realities* (Budapest: Hungarian Political Science Association, 1991)

William Taubman, *Khrushchev: The Man and His Era* (London: Free Press, 2003)

Margaret Thatcher, *The Downing Street Years* (London: HarperCollins, 1993)

Daniel C. Thomas, *The Helsinki Effect: International Norms, Human Rights and the Demise of Communism* (Princeton, NJ: Princeton University Press, 2001)

Rudolf L. Tőkés, *Hungary's Negotiated Revolution: Economic Reform, Social Change and Political Succession, 1957-1990* (Cambridge: Cambridge University Press, 1996)

William J. Tompson, *Khrushchev, A Political Life* (London: Macmillan, 1995)

Krisztián Ungváry, *Battle for Budapest: 100 Days in World War II*. Translated by Ladislaus Löb. (London: I.B. Tauris, 2005 edition)

United Nations Economic Commission for Europe, *Economic Survey of Europe in 1989-90* (New York: United Nations, 1990)

Peter Unwin, *Voice in the Wilderness: Imre Nagy and the Hungarian Revolution* (London: Macdonald, 1991)

George Urban, *The Nineteen Days: A Broadcaster's Account of the Hungarian Revolution* (London: Heinemann, 1957)

Ferenc A. Váli, *Rift and Revolt in Hungary: Nationalism versus Communism* (London: Oxford University Press, 1961)

Peter van Ness (ed.), *Market Reforms in Socialist Societies: Comparing China and Hungary* (Boulder, CO: Lynne Rienner publishers, 1989)

Zsuzsanna Varga, *Politika, paraszti érdekérvéyesítés és szövetkezetek Magyarországon 1956-1967* (Politics, peasant defence of interests and co-operatives in Hungary 1956-1967) (Budapest: Napvilág, 2001)

Zoltan Vas, *Betiltott Könyvem* (My Banned Book) (Budapest: Szabad Tér, 1990)

Miklós Vásárhelyi, *Beszélgetések Vásárhelyi Miklóssal* (Conversations with Miklós Vásárhelyi). Translated from Italian by János Betlen and Imre Barna. (Budapest: Magyar Könyvklub, 2000)

Dmitri Volkogonov, *The Rise and Fall of the Soviet Empire: Political Leaders from Lenin to Gorbachev*. Edited and translated by Harold Shukman. (London: HarperCollins, 1998)

Karl-Eugen Wädekin, *Agrarian Policies in Communist Europe: A Critical Introduction* (The Hague: Allanheld, Osmun, 1982)

Erwin Weit, *At the Red Summit: Interpreter Behind the Iron Curtain*. Translated by Mary Schofield. (New York: Macmillan, 1973)

Stephen White, John Gardner and George Schöpflin, *Communist Political Systems: An Introduction* (London: Macmillan, 1982)

Kieran Williams, *The Prague Spring and its Aftermath: Czechoslovak Politics 1968-1970* (Cambridge: Cambridge University Press, 1997)

Paul E. Zinner, *Revolution in Hungary* (New York: Columbia University Press, 1962)

Tibor Zinner, *A kádári megtorlás rendszere* (The Kádárist Reprisals System) (Budapest: Hamvas Intézet, 2001)

Articles, monographs and magazine editions

Margit Balogh, 'Egyház és egyházpolitika a Kádár-korszakban' (Church and church policy in the Kádár era): *Eszmélet* 34 (1997)

Padraic Fallon and David Shirreff, 'The Betrayal of East Europe': *Euromoney*, September 1982

István Feitl and Karola Némethné Vágyi, '"… csetlunk-botlunk ezekkel a dolgokkal …"': A Rákosi-ügy – 1960-ban' ('We blunder about with these things': The Rákosi affair in 1960): *Társadalmi Szemle* 49, no. 6 (1994)

Johanna Granville, 'Imre Nagy, aka 'Volodya' – a dent in the martyr's halo?' *Cold War International History Project Bulletin*, Issue 5 (Spring 1995)

Tibor Hajdu, 'Farkas és Kádár Rajknál' (Farkas and Kádár with Rajk): *Társadalmi Szemle* 47, no. 4 (1992) [a]

—. 'A Rajk-per háttere és fázisai' (The background to and phases of the Rajk trial): *Társadalmi Szemle* 47, no. 11 (1992) [b]

—. 'The Party Did Everything for You. Preparing the Show Trial: Farkas and Kádár Visit Rajk': *The Hungarian Quarterly* 37, no. 141 (1996)

—. 'Yours Sincerely, János Kádár'(Review of Huszár (ed.), *Kedves, jó Kádár elvtars!*): *The Hungarian Quarterly* 43, no. 168 (2002)

András Hegedüs, 'A nagyvállalatok és a szocializmus'(Large companies and socialism): *Közgazdasági Szemle*, January 1984

Gyorgy Heltai, 'Reform to Revolution' (Interview given to an American journalist, 12 December 1956): *The Hungarian Quarterly* 37, no. 142 (1996)

Peter Kenez, 'The Hungarian Communist Party and the Catholic Church 1945-1948': *The Journal of Modern History* 75, no. 4 (2003)

Mark Kramer, 'Soviet policy during the Polish crisis' and 'The Warsaw Pact and the Polish Crisis of 1980-81: Honecker's Call for Military Intervention': *Cold War International History Project Bulletin*, Issue 5 (Spring 1995)

György Litván, '1957 – The Year After': *The Hungarian Quarterly* 37, no. 143 (1996)

Vojtech Mastny, 'The Soviet Non-Invasion of Poland in 1980-81 and the End of the Cold War': *Cold War International History Project* Working Paper 23

Gábor Murányi, 'The Plotter's Field': *The Hungarian Quarterly* 37, no. 141 (1996)

Rezső Nyers, 'Visszapillantás az 1968-as reformra' (A look back at the 1968 reform): *Valóság* 31, no. 8 (1998)

Mária Ormos, 'A konszolidáció problémai 1956 és 1958 között' (Problems of consolidation between 1956 and 1958): *Társadalmi Szemle* 44, no. 8-9 (1989)

Vera Pécsi. 'The Standard Electric Trial': *The Hungarian Quarterly* 42, no. 162 (2001)

György Péteri, 'Purge and patronage: Kádár's counter-revolution and the field of economic research in Hungary, 1957-1958': *Contemporary European History* 11, part 1 (2002)

Iván Pető, 'A gazdaságirányítási mechanizmus és a reform megítélésének változásai a hatvanas évek középen' (The economic mechanism and changing assessments of reform in the mid-sixties): *Medvetánc*, 1986.4 – 1987.1

Attila Pók, 'Ungarische Motive der Eröffnung auf die Ostpolitik und ihre Bedeutung für die ungarisch-deutschen Beziehungen in den 1970er Jahren' (Hungarian motives for opening to *Ostpolitik* and their significance for Hungarian-German relations in the 1970s): Unpublished conference paper, January 2005

János M. Rainer, 'The Road to Budapest, 1956: New Documentation on the Kremlin's Decision to Intervene': (in two parts): *The Hungarian Quarterly* 37, nos. 142 and 143 (1996)

Rubicon:

—. 1998/1, *Kádár-korszak* (The Kádár era)

—. 2000/6, *Ki volt Kádár?* (Who was Kádár?)

—. 2000/7-8, *Kádár-életút* (Kádár's life course)

—. 2001/3, *Történelmi kitérő 1945-1990* (Historical detour 1945-1990)

—. 2002/6-7, *ÁVO=ÁVH-III/III*

—. 2004/5-6, *Út a rendszerváltás felé* (Road to regime change)

—. 2004/8-9, *A hosszú '60-as évek* (The long '60s)

Mihály Ruff, 'A Magyar-NSZK kapcsolatok 1960-1963' (Hungarian-West German relations, 1960-1963): *Múltunk*, 1999, no. 3

George Schöpflin, Rudolf L. Tőkés & Ivan Volgyes, 'Leadership Change and Crisis in Hungary': *Problems of Communism* 37, no. 5 (1988)

Levente Sipos, 'A *Népszabadság* letiltott cikke 1956 novemberében' (*Népszabadság*'s forbidden article in November 1956): *Múltunk*, 1992, no. 1

—. 'MSZMP dokumentum az ellenzékről, 1980-ból' (An MSZMP document on the opposition from 1980): *Társadalmi Szemle* 47, no. 5 (1992)

—. 'Hiányos leltár' (Incomplete inventory): *Társadalmi Szemle* 47, nos. 11 and 12 (1994)

Károly Attila Soós, 'Béralku és 'sérelmi politika'' (Wage bargaining and 'grievance politics'): *Medvetánc*, 1984.2-3

Lajos Srágli, 'American Capital and the Hungarian Oil Industry': *The Hungarian Quarterly* 42, no. 162 (2001)

Miklós Szabó, 'Kádár's Pied Piper' (Review of Révész, *Aczel és korunk*): *The Hungarian Quarterly* 38, no. 147 (1997)

Erzsébet Szalai, 'A reformfolyamat új szakasza és a nagyvállalatok' (The large companies and the new phase in the reform process): *Valóság*, May 1982

László Szamuely, 'The second wave of the mechanism debate and the 1968 reform of the economic mechanism in Hungary': *Acta Oeconomica*, 33, no. 1-2 (1985)

János Tischler, 'Interconnections: Poland's October and the 1956 Hungarian Revolution': *The Hungarian Quarterly* 38, no. 145 (1997)

—. 'The Hungarian party Leadership and the Polish Crisis of 1980-81': *Cold War International History Project Bulletin*, Issue11 (Winter 1998)

—. 'Kádár and the Polish Crisis 1980-81': *The Hungarian Quarterly* 39, no. 151 (1998)

Rudolf L. Tőkés, 'Hungarian Reform Imperatives': *Problems of Communism* 33, no. 7 (1984)

—. 'Murmur and Whispers. Public Opinion and Legitimacy Crisis in Hungary, 1972-1989': *The Carl Beck Papers in Russian & East European Studies*, Number 1206, Center for Russian and East European Studies, University of Pittsburgh, April 1997

Oldřich Tůma, 'The Czechoslovak Communist Regime and the Polish Crisis 1980-1981': *Cold War International History Project Bulletin*, Number 11 (Winter 1998)

Karola Némethné Vágyi and Levente Sipos, 'A Marosán-ügy 1962-ben' (The 1962 Marosán affair): *Múltunk*, 1994, no. 1-2

Karola Némethné Vágyi and Károly Urbán, 'Az MSZMP és a többpártrendszer 1957-ben: A Varga-féle reformbizottság és a pártvezetés' (The MSZMP and the multi-party system in 1957: The Varga reform committee and the party leadership): *Társadalmi Szemle* 48, no. 8-9 (1993)

György T. Varga & István Szakadát, 'Imé, a nómenklatúrák! Az MDP és a volt MSZMP hatásköri listái' (Behold the nomenklatura! The lists of the MDP and former MSZMP's area of authority): *Társadalmi Szemle* 47, no. 3 (1992)

Zsuzsanna Varga, 'Mezőgazdasági reformmunkalatok 1961-1964' (Agricultural reform tasks 1961-1964): *Múltunk*, 2000, no. 2

—. 'Hatalom, büntetőjog és termelőszövetkezetek Magyarországon az 1970-es években' (Power, criminal law and co-operatives in Hungary in the 1970s): *Jogtörténeti Szemle*, 2003, no. 4

Mária Vásárhelyi, 'Csalóka emlékezet' (Deceptive memory): *Élet és irodalom* 47, issue 24 (2003)

István Vida, ' "… nem egy első díjas műalkotás …": Feljegyzés Kádár János és J.V. Andropov 1968 decemberi találkozójáról' ('… not a prize-winning work of art': Notes of the December 6-7 1968 conversation between János Kádár and Y.V. Andropov): *Tarsadalmi Szemle* 50 no. 1 (1995)

—. 'Janos Kádár and the Czechoslovak Crisis of 1968': *The Hungarian Quarterly* 35, no. 135 (1994)

V.K. Volkov, 'A szovjet pártokrácia és az 1968-as prágai tavasz' (The Soviet partyocracy and the 1968 Prague Spring): *Társadalmi Szemle* 50, no. 1 (1995)

Tibor Zinner, 'Büntetőjog és hatalom' (Criminal law and power): *Múltunk*, 1998, no.2

Broadcasts

'Birodalmi helytartók' (Imperial Governors), television film by Miklós Kun, Magyar Televízió (MTV), 1996

'Kádár János nyugdíjba megy' (János Kádár Goes into Retirement), film directed by Zsuzsa Méry, 1956 Institute, 2002

'A legvidámabb barakk' (The happiest barracks), television series by László Vitézy, MTV, 1991

'Pushing Back the Curtain', presented by Misha Glenny, BBC Radio, 1999

'Titoktartók' (Keepers of Secrets), film by Anna Geréb, Forum Film Alapítvány, 1996

Internet resources

1956 Institute: www.rev.hu

Cold War International History Project: http://wilsoncenter.org/

Hungarian Quarterly: www.hungarianquarterly.com

Parallel History Project of NATO and the Warsaw Pact: www.isn.ethz.ch/php/
US   Department   of   State,   *Foreign   Relations   of   the   United   States*:
    www.state.gov/r/pa/ho/frus/

INDEX